CASE CLOSED

VOLUME 25

Gosho Aoyama

Case Briefing:

Subject:
Occupation:
Special Skills:
Equipment:

Jimmy Kudo, a.k.a. Conan Edogawa
High School Student/Detective
Analytical thinking and deductive reasoning, Soccer
Bow Tie Voice Transmitter, Super Sneakers,
Homing Glasses, Stretchy Suspenders

The subject is hot on the trail of a pair of suspicious men in black when he is attacked from behind and administered a strange substance which physically transforms him into a first grader. When the subject confides in the eccentric inventor Dr. Agasa, they decide to keep the subject's true identity a secret for the safety of everyone around him. Assuming the new identity of first-grader Conan Edogawa, the subject continues to assist the police force on their most baffling cases. The only problem is that most crime-solving professionals won't take a little kid's advice!

Table of Contents

CONFIDEN

CASE CLOSED

Volume 25
Shonen Sunday Edition

Story and Art by GOSHO AOYAMA

MEITANTEI CONAN Vol. 25
by Gosho AOYAMA
© 1994 Gosho AOYAMA
All rights reserved.
Original Japanese edition published by SHOGAKUKAN.
English translation rights in the United States of America, Canada,
the United Kingdom, Ireland, Australia and New Zealand arranged with SHOGAKUKAN.

Translation
Tetsuichiro Miyaki

Touch-up & Lettering
Freeman Wong

Cover & Graphic Design
Andrea Rice

Editor
Shaenon K. Garrity

Printed in the U.S.A.

Published by VIZ Media, LLC
P.O. Box 77010
San Francisco, CA 94107

10 9 8 7 6 5 4 3 2
First printing, September 2008
Second printing, May 2019

VIZ MEDIA
viz.com

FILE 1: ODD ONE OUT?

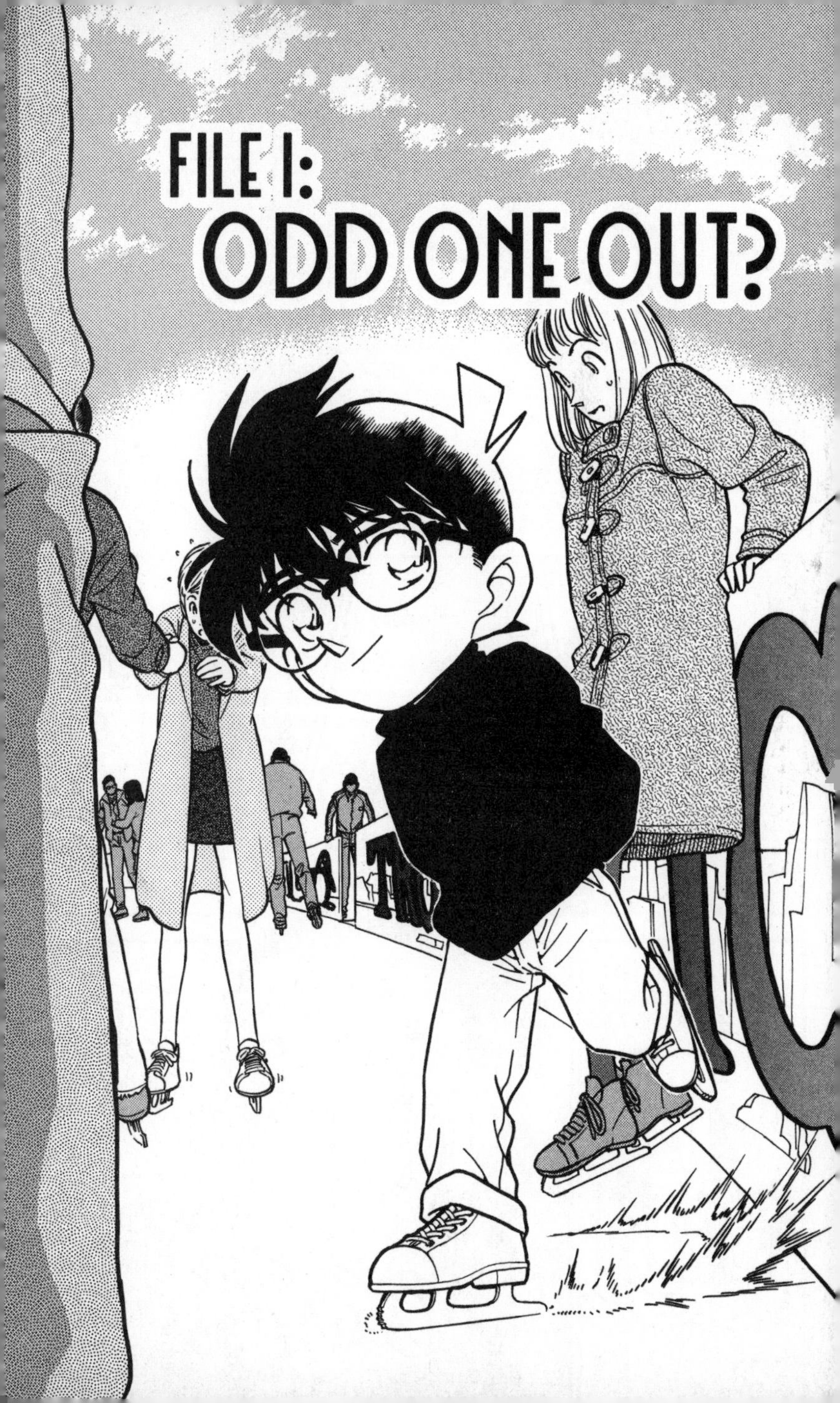

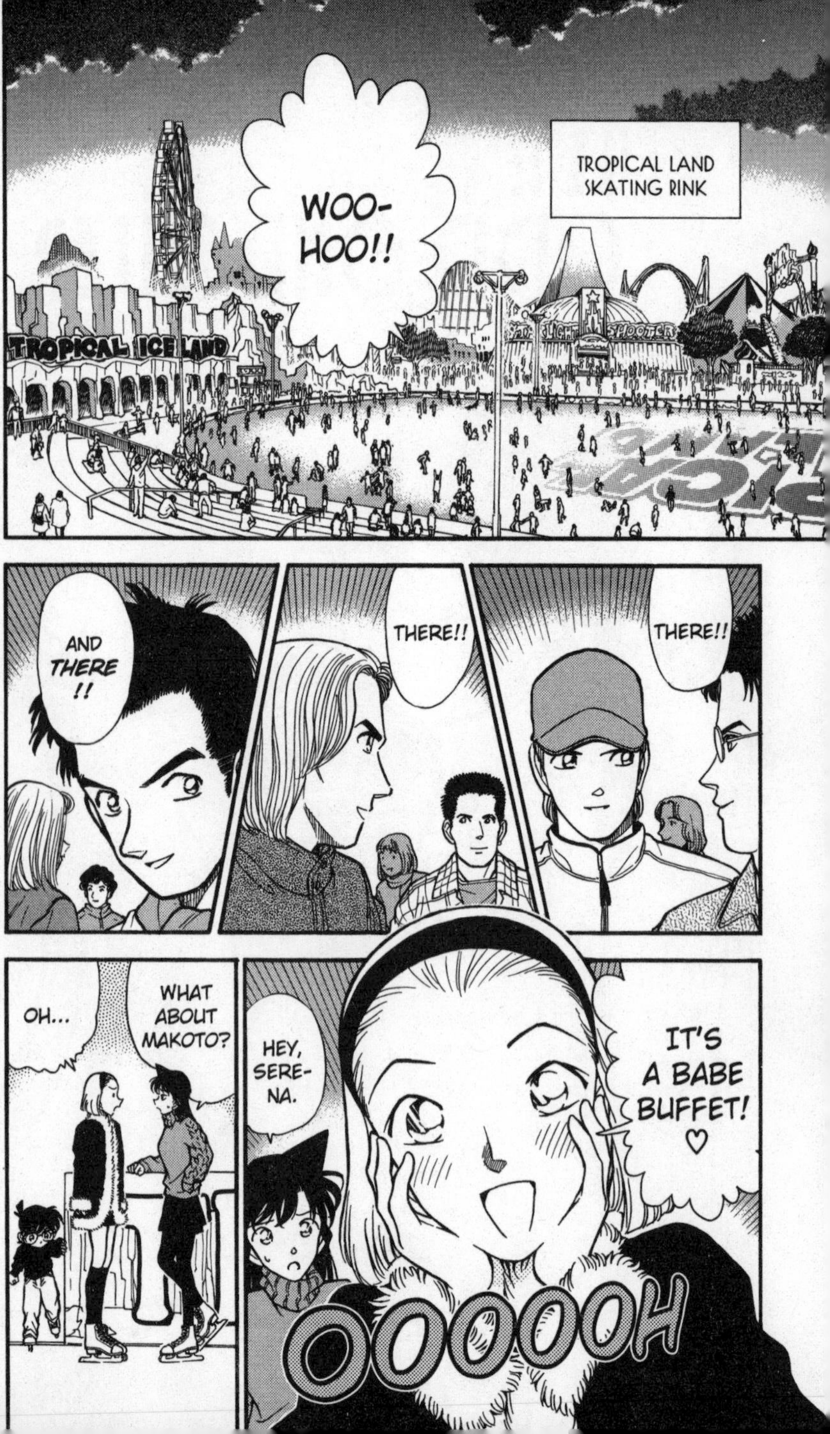
TROPICAL LAND SKATING RINK
WOO-HOO!!
TROPICAL ICE LAND
THERE!!
THERE!!
AND *THERE* !!
IT'S A BABE BUFFET! ♡
HEY, SERE-NA.
OOOOOOH
WHAT ABOUT MAKOTO?
OH...

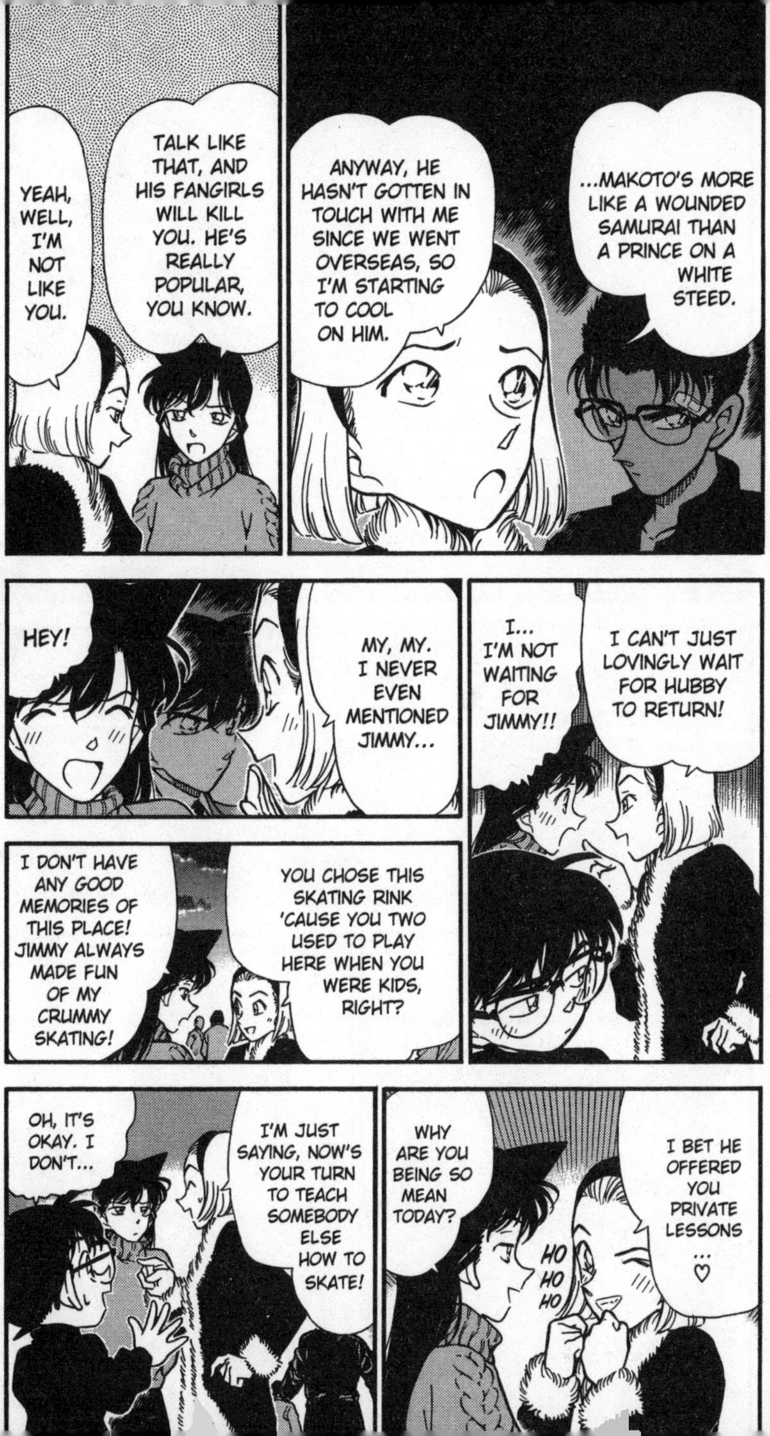
...MAKOTO'S MORE LIKE A WOUNDED SAMURAI THAN A PRINCE ON A WHITE STEED.
ANYWAY, HE HASN'T GOTTEN IN TOUCH WITH ME SINCE WE WENT OVERSEAS, SO I'M STARTING TO COOL ON HIM.
TALK LIKE THAT, AND HIS FANGIRLS WILL KILL YOU. HE'S REALLY POPULAR, YOU KNOW.
YEAH, WELL, I'M NOT LIKE YOU.
I CAN'T JUST LOVINGLY WAIT FOR HUBBY TO RETURN!
I... I'M NOT WAITING FOR JIMMY!!
MY, MY. I NEVER EVEN MENTIONED JIMMY...
HEY!
YOU CHOSE THIS SKATING RINK 'CAUSE YOU TWO USED TO PLAY HERE WHEN YOU WERE KIDS, RIGHT?
I DON'T HAVE ANY GOOD MEMORIES OF THIS PLACE! JIMMY ALWAYS MADE FUN OF MY CRUMMY SKATING!
I BET HE OFFERED YOU PRIVATE LESSONS ...♡
HO HO HO
WHY ARE YOU BEING SO MEAN TODAY?
I'M JUST SAYING, NOW'S YOUR TURN TO TEACH SOMEBODY ELSE HOW TO SKATE!
OH, IT'S OKAY. I DON'T...

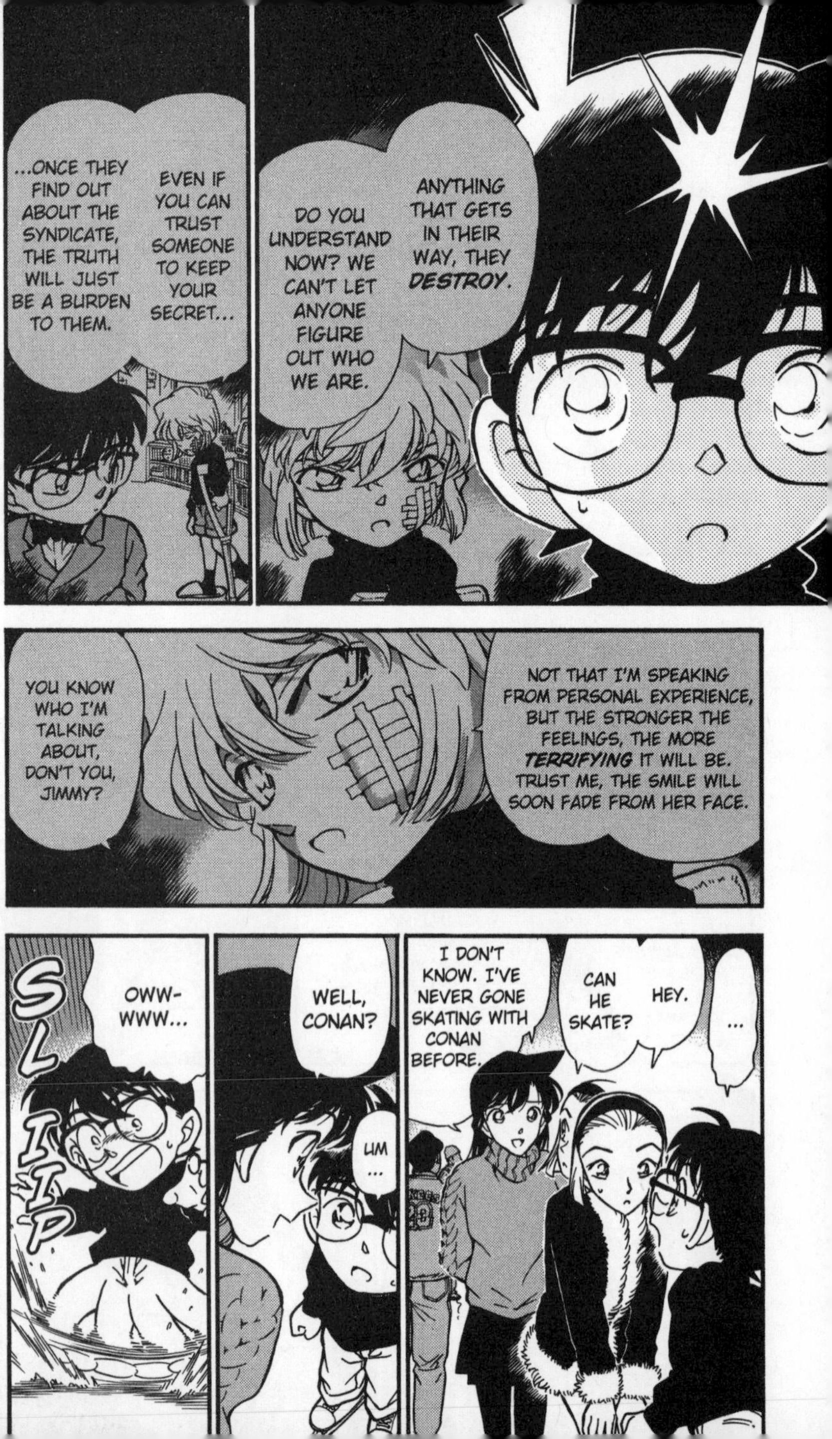
ANYTHING THAT GETS IN THEIR WAY, THEY *DESTROY*.
DO YOU UNDERSTAND NOW? WE CAN'T LET ANYONE FIGURE OUT WHO WE ARE.
EVEN IF YOU CAN TRUST SOMEONE TO KEEP YOUR SECRET...
...ONCE THEY FIND OUT ABOUT THE SYNDICATE, THE TRUTH WILL JUST BE A BURDEN TO THEM.
NOT THAT I'M SPEAKING FROM PERSONAL EXPERIENCE, BUT THE STRONGER THE FEELINGS, THE MORE *TERRIFYING* IT WILL BE. TRUST ME, THE SMILE WILL SOON FADE FROM HER FACE.
YOU KNOW WHO I'M TALKING ABOUT, DON'T YOU, JIMMY?
...
HEY.
CAN HE SKATE?
I DON'T KNOW. I'VE NEVER GONE SKATING WITH CONAN BEFORE.
WELL, CONAN?
UM ...
OWW-WWW...
SLIIIP

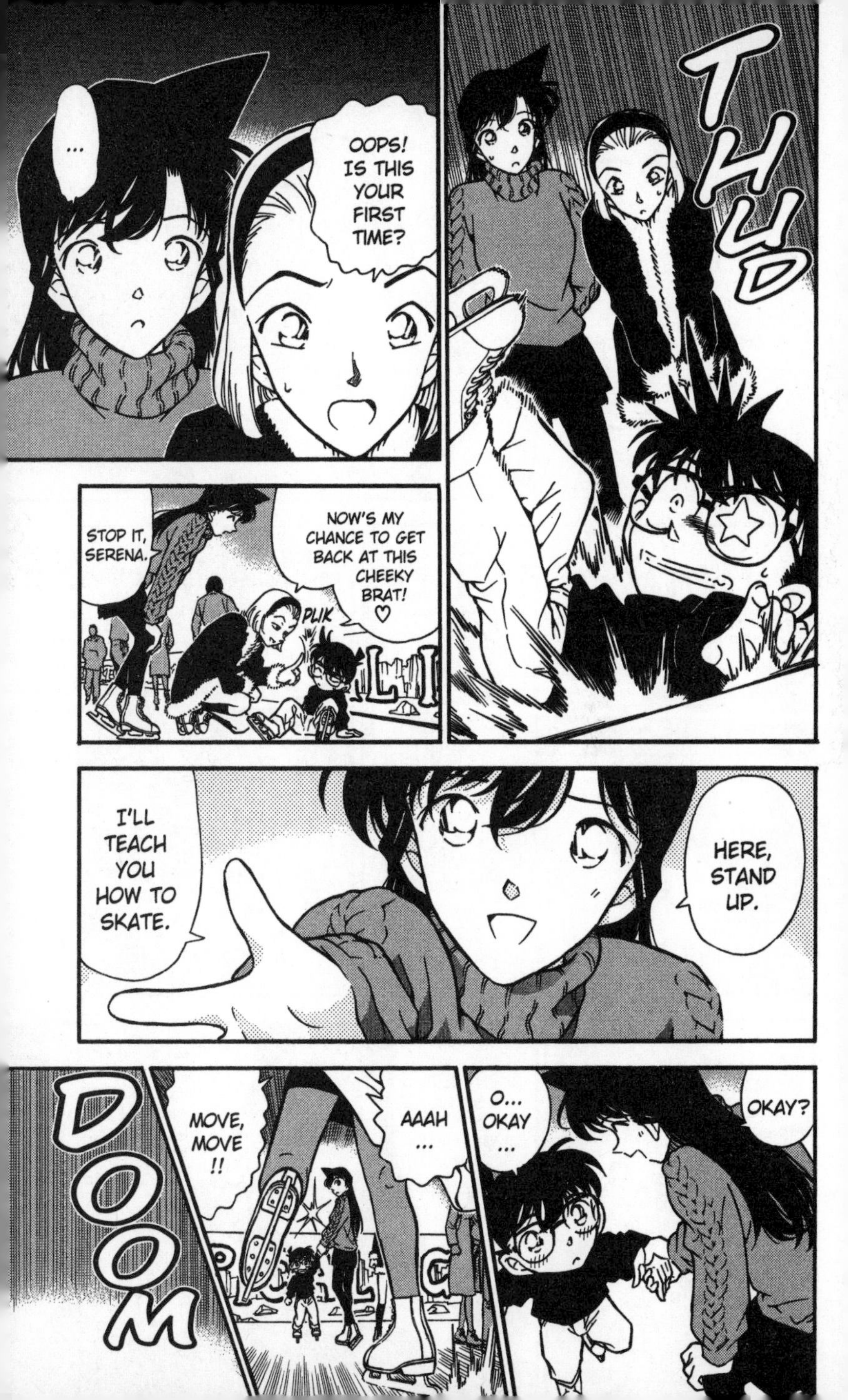
THUD
OOPS! IS THIS YOUR FIRST TIME?
...
NOW'S MY CHANCE TO GET BACK AT THIS CHEEKY BRAT! ♡
PLIK
STOP IT, SERENA.
HERE, STAND UP.
I'LL TEACH YOU HOW TO SKATE.
OKAY?
O... OKAY ...
AAAH ...
MOVE, MOVE !!
DOOM

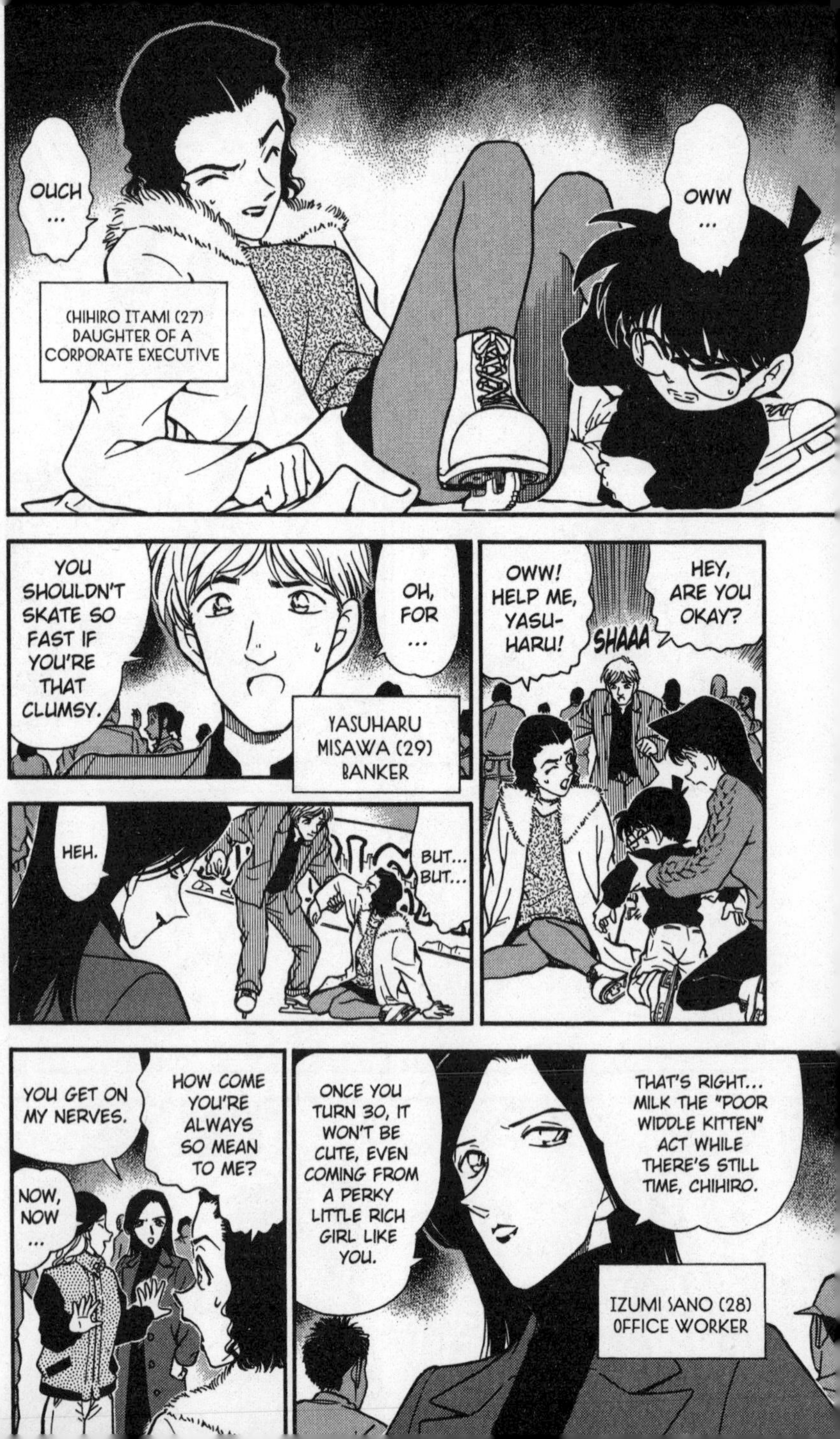
OWW ...
OUCH ...
CHIHIRO ITAMI (27) DAUGHTER OF A CORPORATE EXECUTIVE
HEY, ARE YOU OKAY?
SHAAA
OWW! HELP ME, YASUHARU!
OH, FOR ...
YOU SHOULDN'T SKATE SO FAST IF YOU'RE THAT CLUMSY.
YASUHARU MISAWA (29) BANKER
BUT... BUT...
HEH.
THAT'S RIGHT... MILK THE "POOR WIDDLE KITTEN" ACT WHILE THERE'S STILL TIME, CHIHIRO.
ONCE YOU TURN 30, IT WON'T BE CUTE, EVEN COMING FROM A PERKY LITTLE RICH GIRL LIKE YOU.
IZUMI SANO (28) OFFICE WORKER
HOW COME YOU'RE ALWAYS SO MEAN TO ME?
YOU GET ON MY NERVES.
NOW, NOW ...

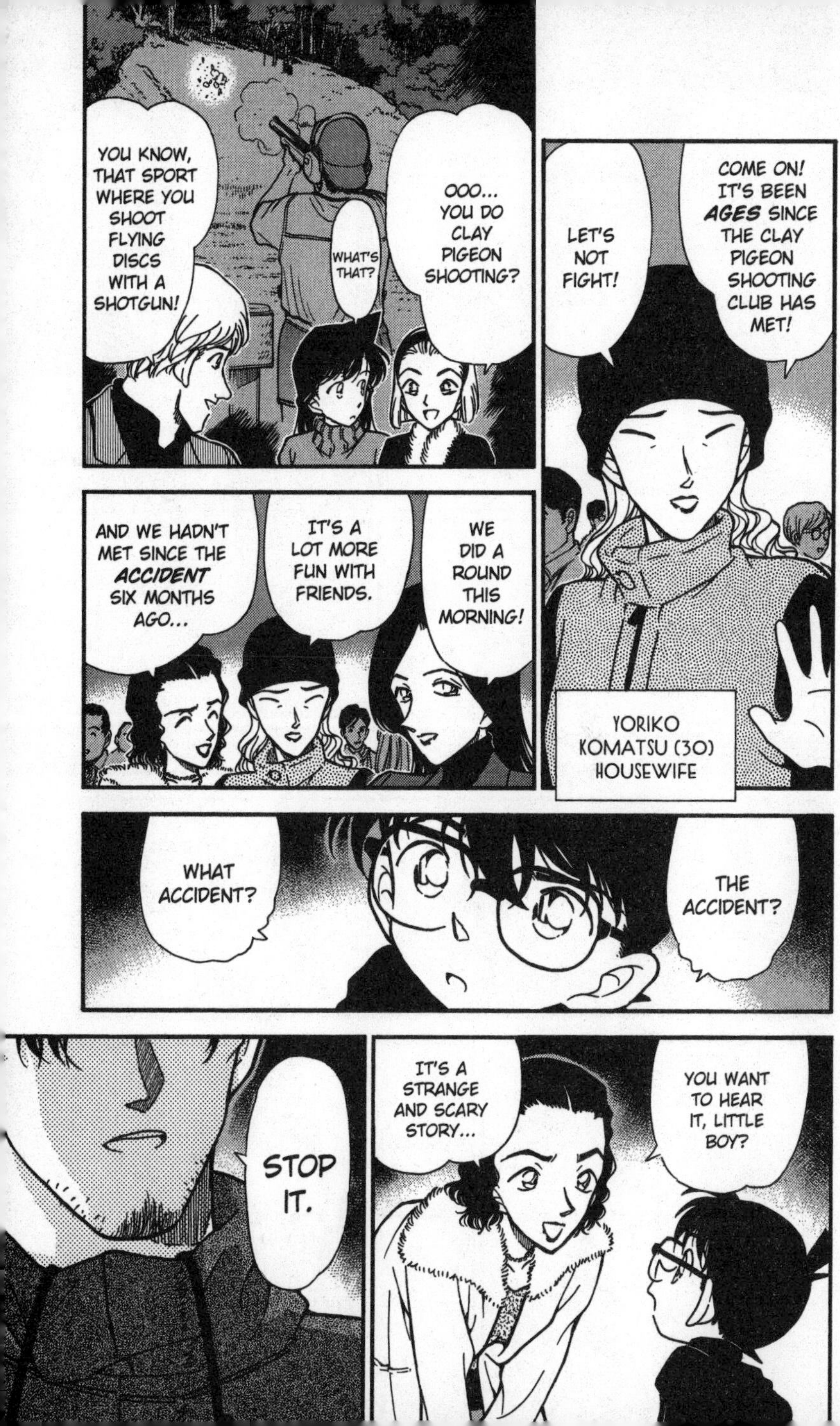
OOO... YOU DO CLAY PIGEON SHOOTING?
WHAT'S THAT?
YOU KNOW, THAT SPORT WHERE YOU SHOOT FLYING DISCS WITH A SHOTGUN!
COME ON! IT'S BEEN AGES SINCE THE CLAY PIGEON SHOOTING CLUB HAS MET!
LET'S NOT FIGHT!
YORIKO KOMATSU (30) HOUSEWIFE
WE DID A ROUND THIS MORNING!
IT'S A LOT MORE FUN WITH FRIENDS.
AND WE HADN'T MET SINCE THE ACCIDENT SIX MONTHS AGO...
THE ACCIDENT?
WHAT ACCIDENT?
YOU WANT TO HEAR IT, LITTLE BOY?
IT'S A STRANGE AND SCARY STORY...
STOP IT.

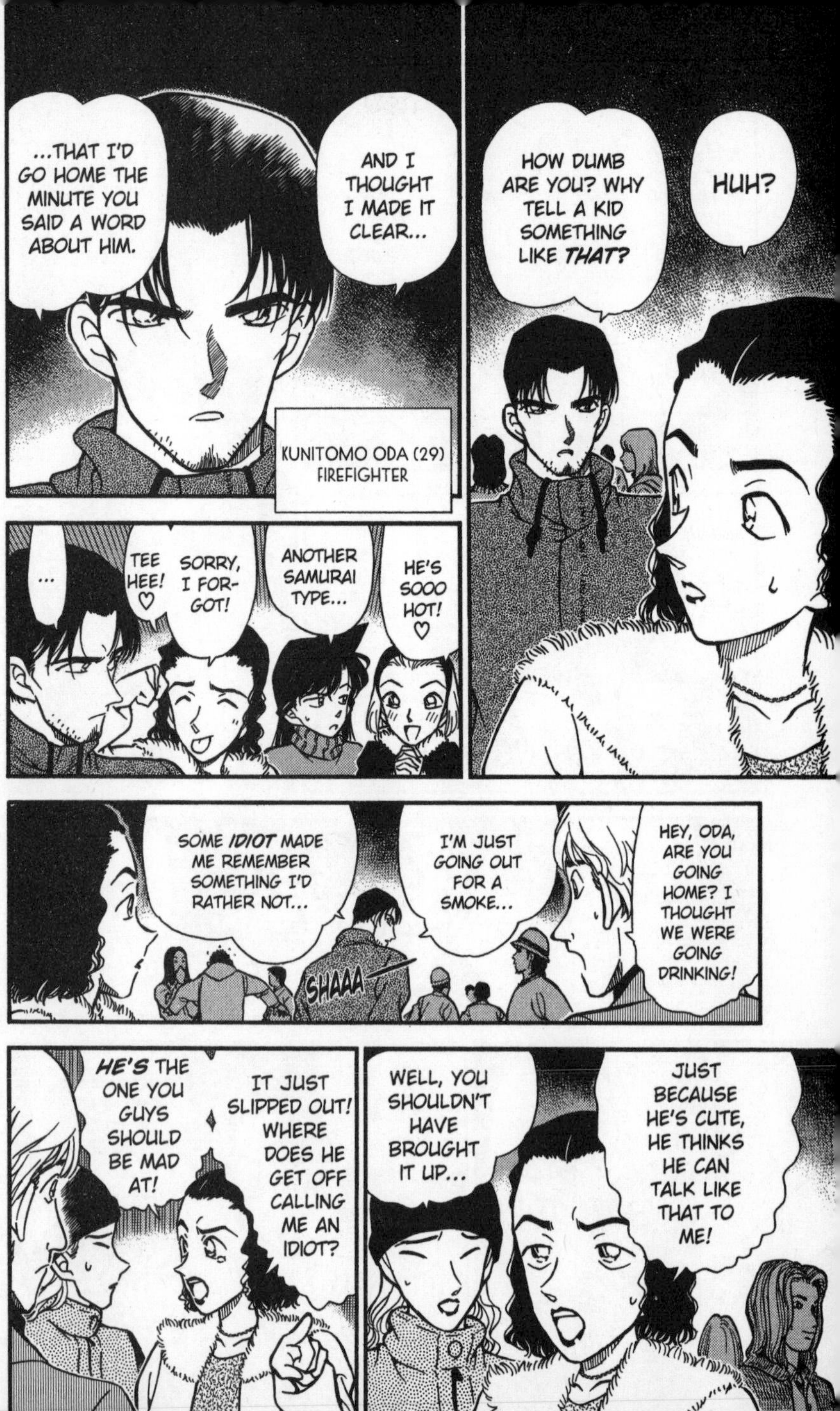
HUH?
HOW DUMB ARE YOU? WHY TELL A KID SOMETHING LIKE *THAT*?
AND I THOUGHT I MADE IT CLEAR...
...THAT I'D GO HOME THE MINUTE YOU SAID A WORD ABOUT HIM.
KUNITOMO ODA (29) FIREFIGHTER
HE'S SOOO HOT! ♡
ANOTHER SAMURAI TYPE...
SORRY, I FOR-GOT!
TEE HEE! ♡
...
HEY, ODA, ARE YOU GOING HOME? I THOUGHT WE WERE GOING DRINKING!
I'M JUST GOING OUT FOR A SMOKE...
SOME *IDIOT* MADE ME REMEMBER SOMETHING I'D RATHER NOT...
SHAAA
JUST BECAUSE HE'S CUTE, HE THINKS HE CAN TALK LIKE THAT TO ME!
WELL, YOU SHOULDN'T HAVE BROUGHT IT UP...
IT JUST SLIPPED OUT! WHERE DOES HE GET OFF CALLING ME AN IDIOT?
HE'S THE ONE YOU GUYS SHOULD BE MAD AT!

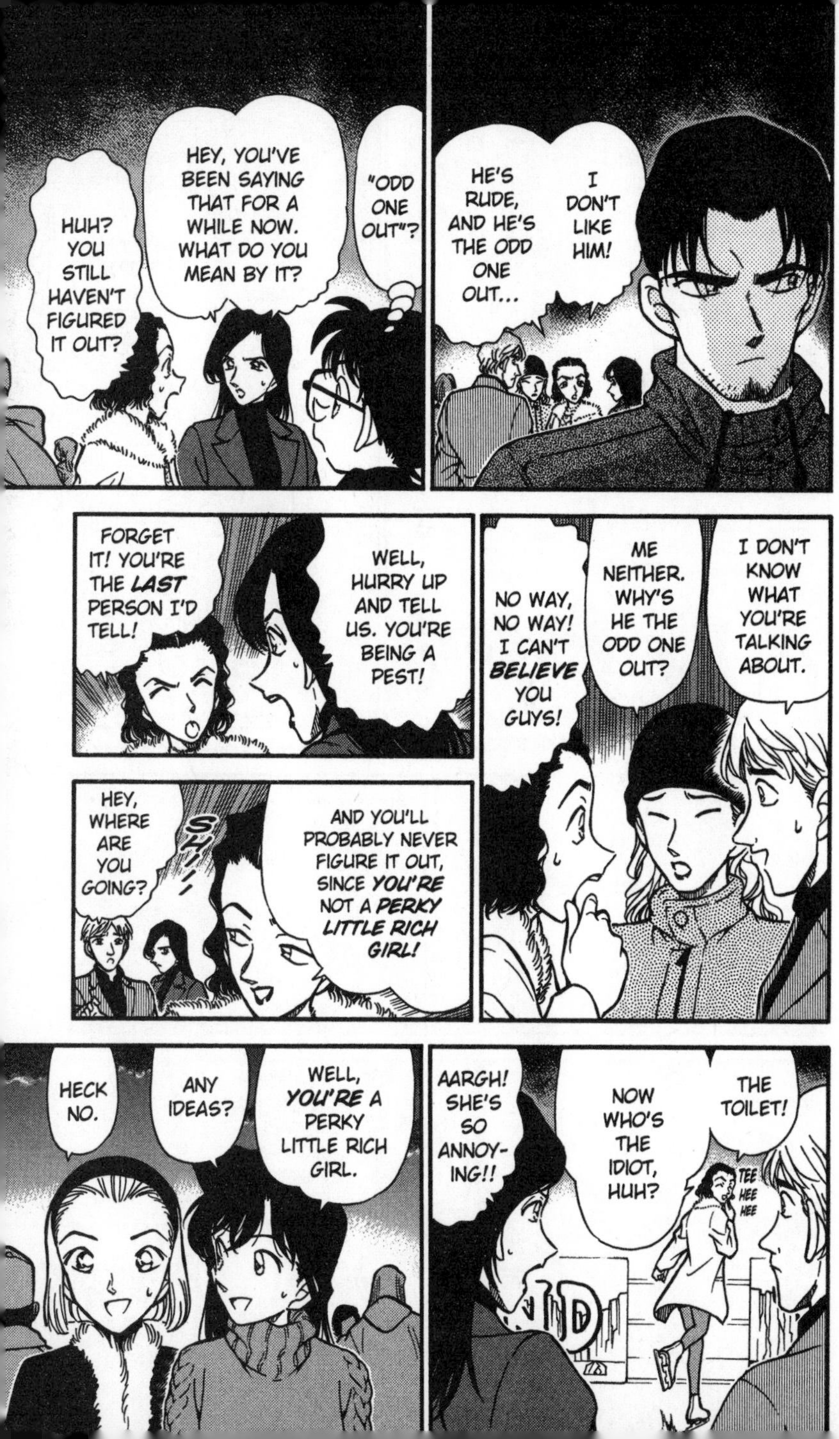
I DON'T LIKE HIM!
HE'S RUDE, AND HE'S THE ODD ONE OUT...
"ODD ONE OUT"?
HEY, YOU'VE BEEN SAYING THAT FOR A WHILE NOW. WHAT DO YOU MEAN BY IT?
HUH? YOU STILL HAVEN'T FIGURED IT OUT?
I DON'T KNOW WHAT YOU'RE TALKING ABOUT.
ME NEITHER. WHY'S HE THE ODD ONE OUT?
NO WAY, NO WAY! I CAN'T ***BELIEVE*** YOU GUYS!
WELL, HURRY UP AND TELL US. YOU'RE BEING A PEST!
FORGET IT! YOU'RE THE ***LAST*** PERSON I'D TELL!
AND YOU'LL PROBABLY NEVER FIGURE IT OUT, SINCE ***YOU'RE*** NOT A ***PERKY LITTLE RICH GIRL!***
SH
HEY, WHERE ARE YOU GOING?
THE TOILET!
NOW WHO'S THE IDIOT, HUH?
TEE HEE HEE
AARGH! SHE'S SO ANNOY-ING!!
WELL, ***YOU'RE*** A PERKY LITTLE RICH GIRL.
ANY IDEAS?
HECK NO.

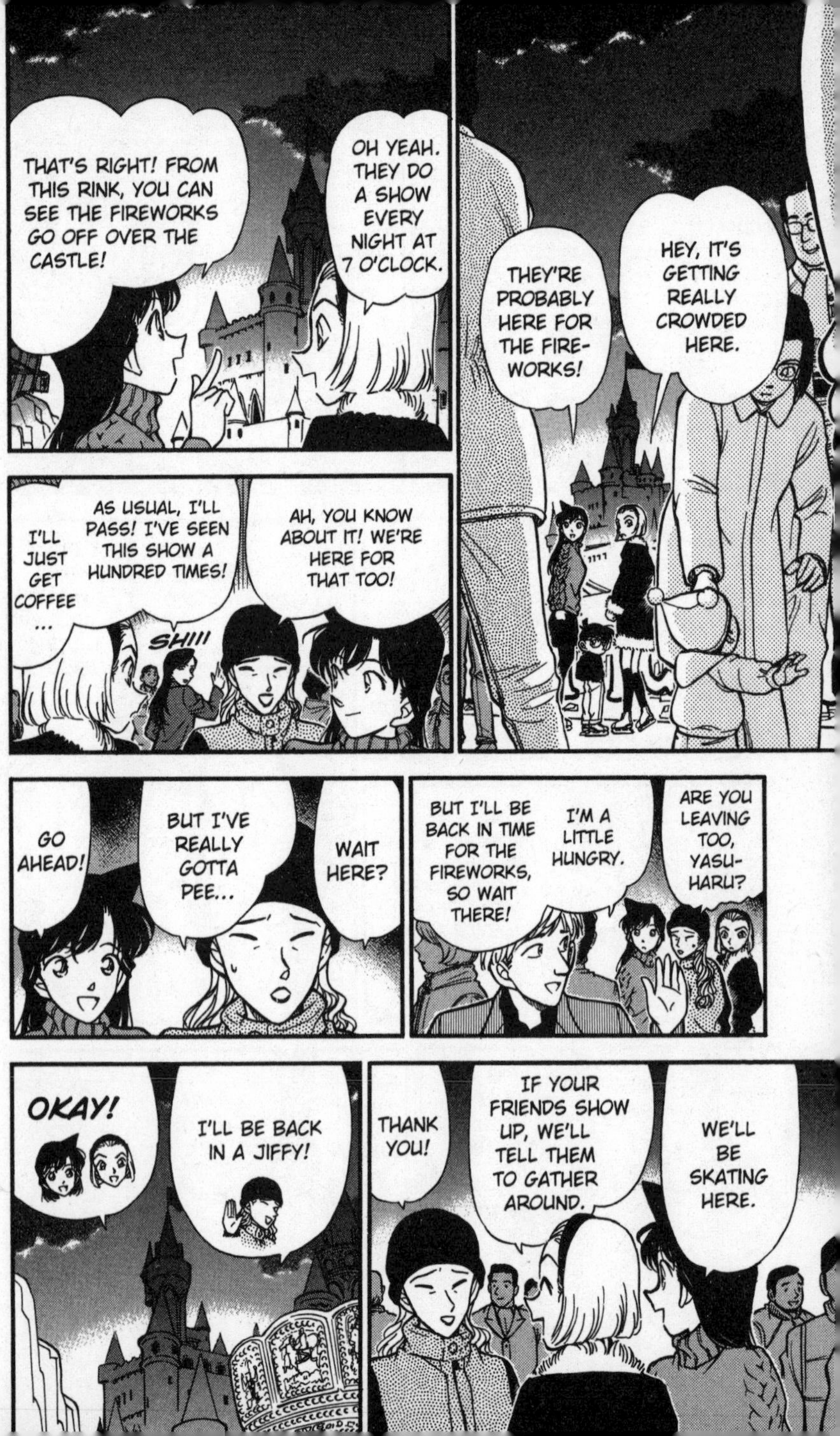
HEY, IT'S GETTING REALLY CROWDED HERE.
THEY'RE PROBABLY HERE FOR THE FIRE-WORKS!
OH YEAH. THEY DO A SHOW EVERY NIGHT AT 7 O'CLOCK.
THAT'S RIGHT! FROM THIS RINK, YOU CAN SEE THE FIREWORKS GO OFF OVER THE CASTLE!
AH, YOU KNOW ABOUT IT! WE'RE HERE FOR THAT TOO!
AS USUAL, I'LL PASS! I'VE SEEN THIS SHOW A HUNDRED TIMES!
SHI!!!
I'LL JUST GET COFFEE...
ARE YOU LEAVING TOO, YASU-HARU?
I'M A LITTLE HUNGRY.
BUT I'LL BE BACK IN TIME FOR THE FIREWORKS, SO WAIT THERE!
WAIT HERE?
BUT I'VE REALLY GOTTA PEE...
GO AHEAD!
WE'LL BE SKATING HERE.
IF YOUR FRIENDS SHOW UP, WE'LL TELL THEM TO GATHER AROUND.
THANK YOU!
I'LL BE BACK IN A JIFFY!
OKAY!

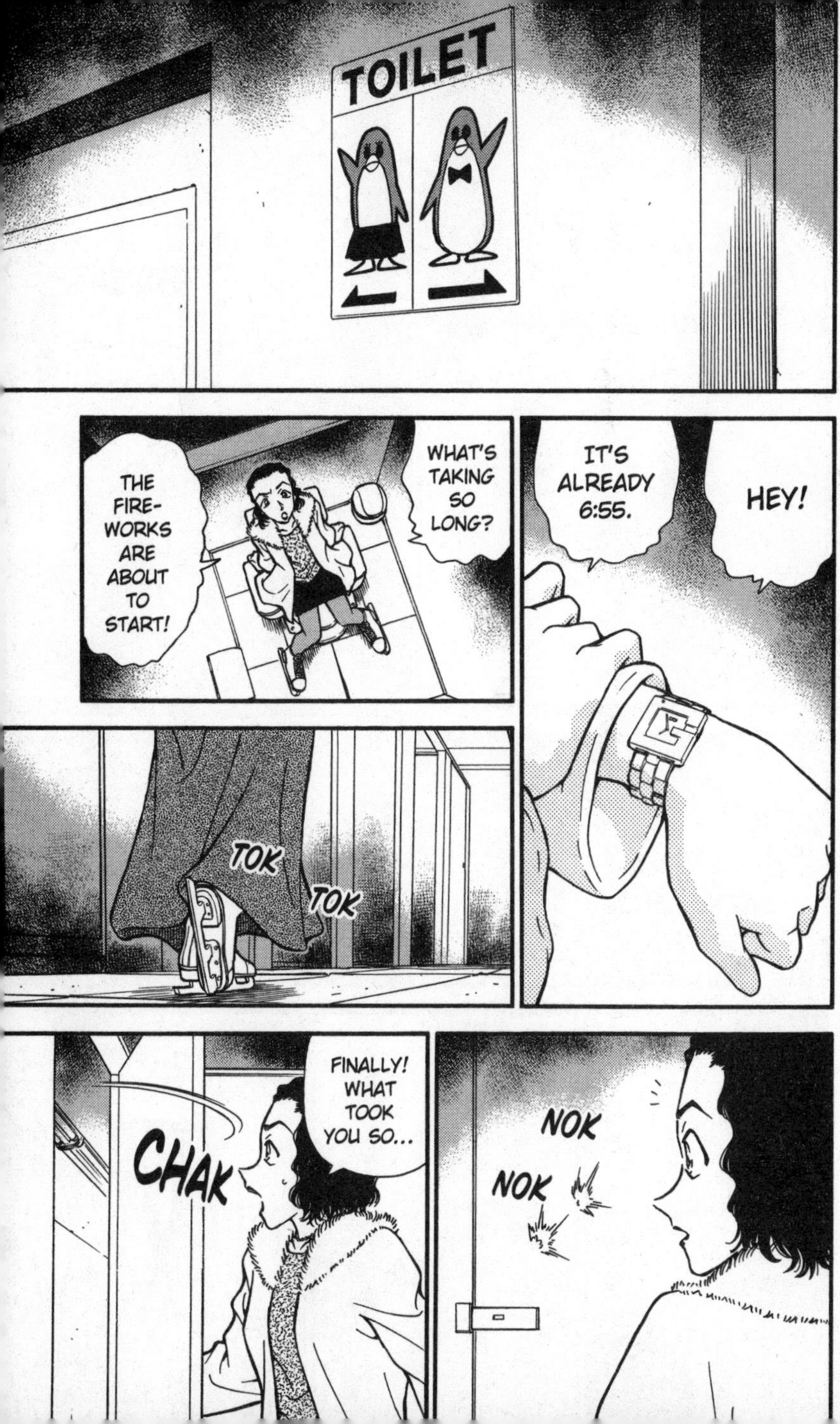
TOILET
HEY!
IT'S ALREADY 6:55.
WHAT'S TAKING SO LONG?
THE FIRE-WORKS ARE ABOUT TO START!
TOK
TOK
NOK
NOK
FINALLY! WHAT TOOK YOU SO...
CHAK

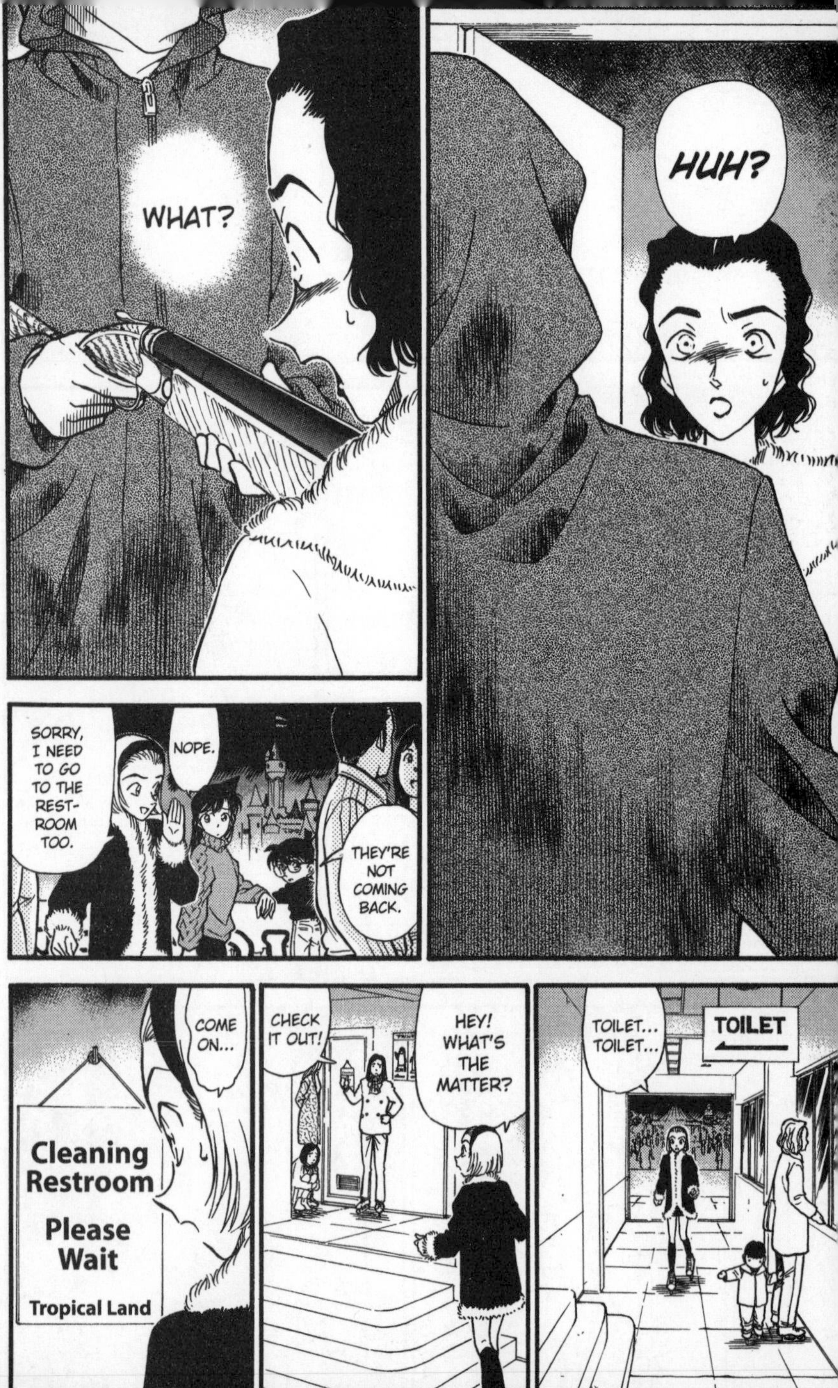
HUH?
WHAT?
THEY'RE NOT COMING BACK.
NOPE.
SORRY, I NEED TO GO TO THE REST-ROOM TOO.
TOILET
TOILET... TOILET...
HEY! WHAT'S THE MATTER?
CHECK IT OUT!
COME ON...
Cleaning Restroom
Please Wait
Tropical Land

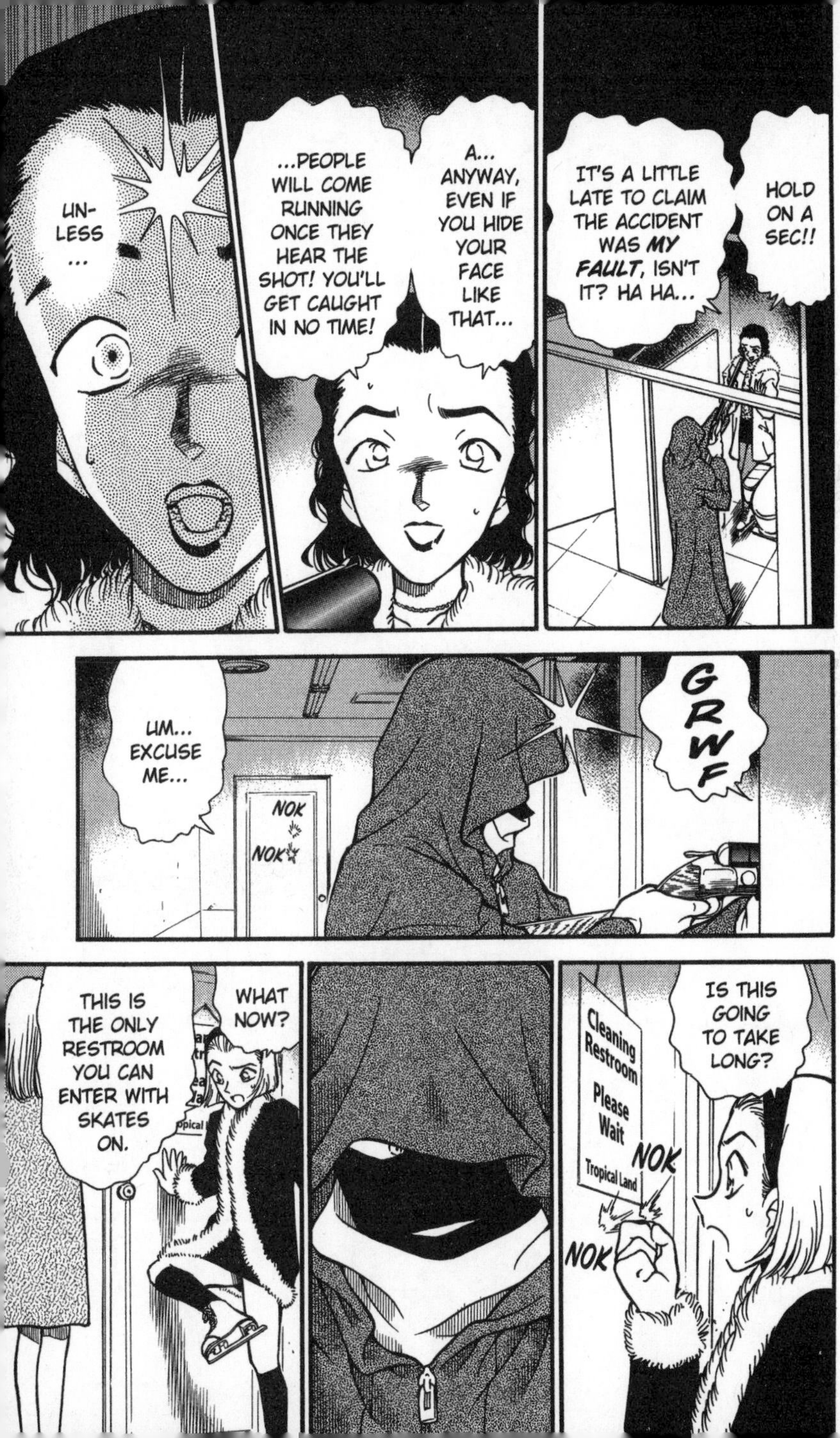
HOLD ON A SEC!!
IT'S A LITTLE LATE TO CLAIM THE ACCIDENT WAS *MY FAULT*, ISN'T IT? HA HA...
A... ANYWAY, EVEN IF YOU HIDE YOUR FACE LIKE THAT...
...PEOPLE WILL COME RUNNING ONCE THEY HEAR THE SHOT! YOU'LL GET CAUGHT IN NO TIME!
UN-LESS...
GRWF
UM... EXCUSE ME...
NOK
NOK
IS THIS GOING TO TAKE LONG?
Cleaning Restroom
Please Wait
Tropical Land
NOK
NOK
WHAT NOW?
THIS IS THE ONLY RESTROOM YOU CAN ENTER WITH SKATES ON.

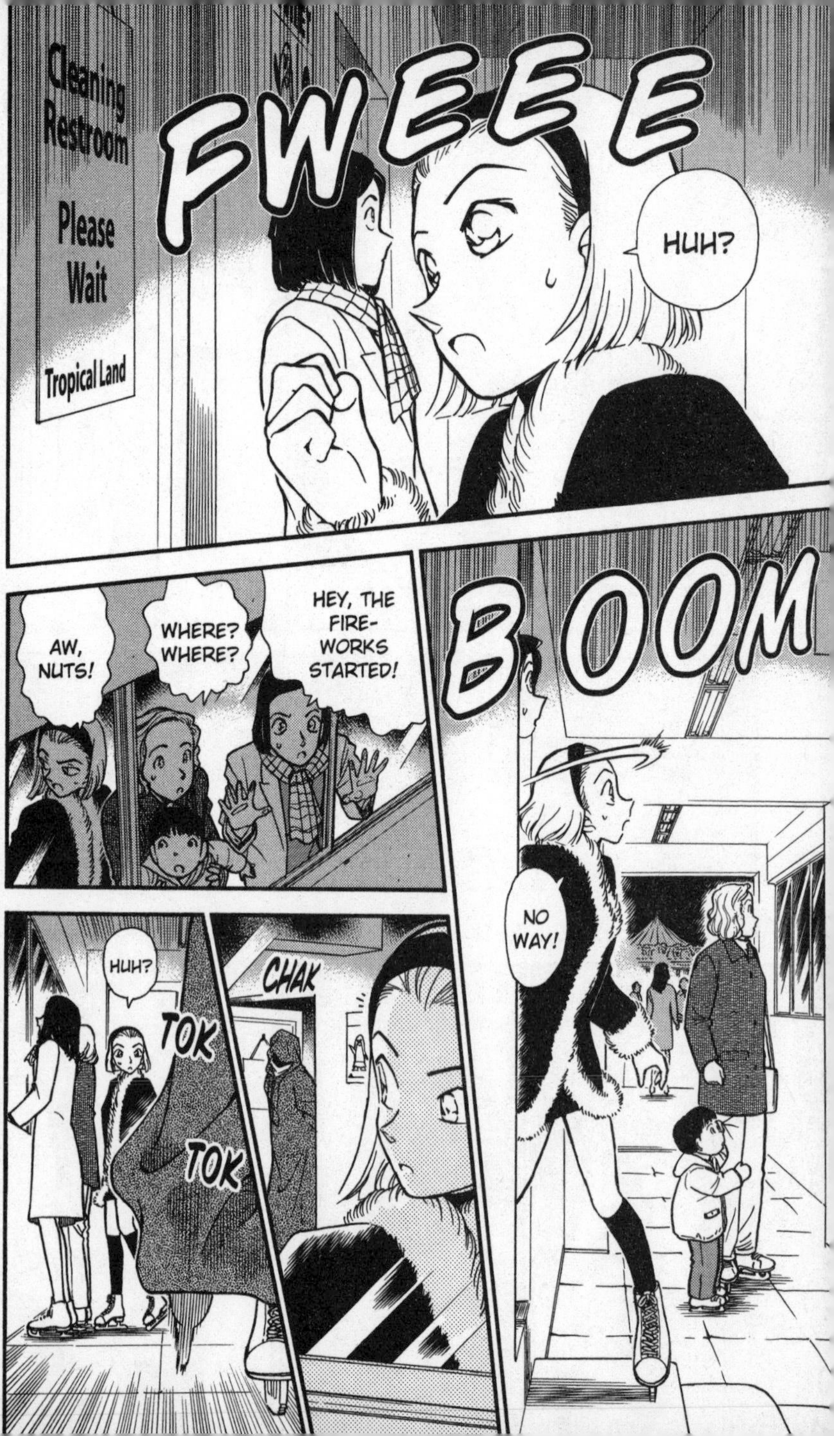
FWEEE
HUH?
Cleaning Restroom
Please Wait
Tropical Land
BOOM
NO WAY!
HEY, THE FIRE-WORKS STARTED!
WHERE? WHERE?
AW, NUTS!
CHAK
HUH?
TOK
TOK

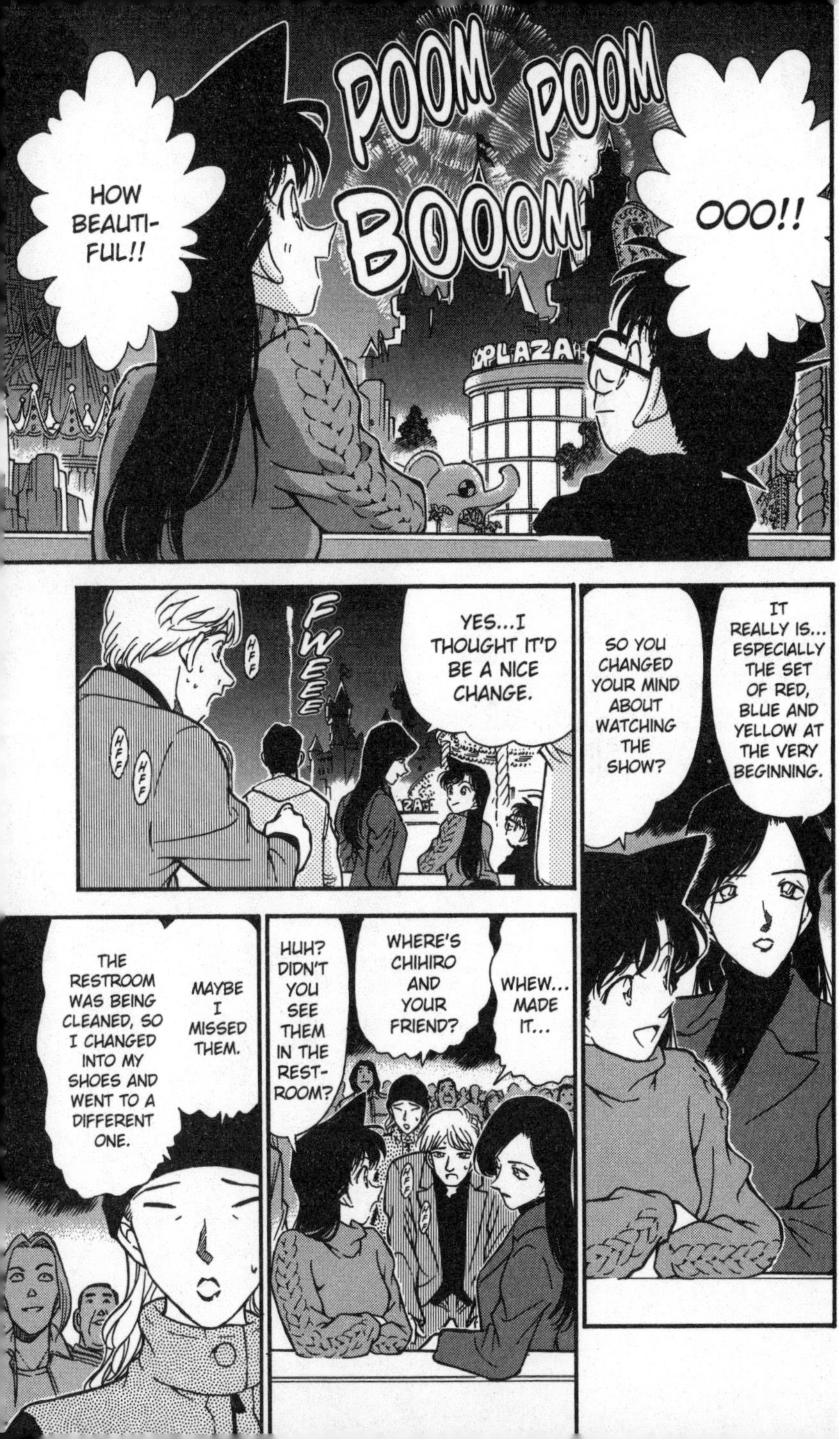
OOO!!
POOM POOM
BOOOM
HOW BEAUTI-FUL!!
IT REALLY IS... ESPECIALLY THE SET OF RED, BLUE AND YELLOW AT THE VERY BEGINNING.
SO YOU CHANGED YOUR MIND ABOUT WATCHING THE SHOW?
YES...I THOUGHT IT'D BE A NICE CHANGE.
FWEEE
HFF
HFF
HFF
WHEW... MADE IT...
WHERE'S CHIHIRO AND YOUR FRIEND?
HUH? DIDN'T YOU SEE THEM IN THE REST-ROOM?
HFF
MAYBE I MISSED THEM.
THE RESTROOM WAS BEING CLEANED, SO I CHANGED INTO MY SHOES AND WENT TO A DIFFERENT ONE.

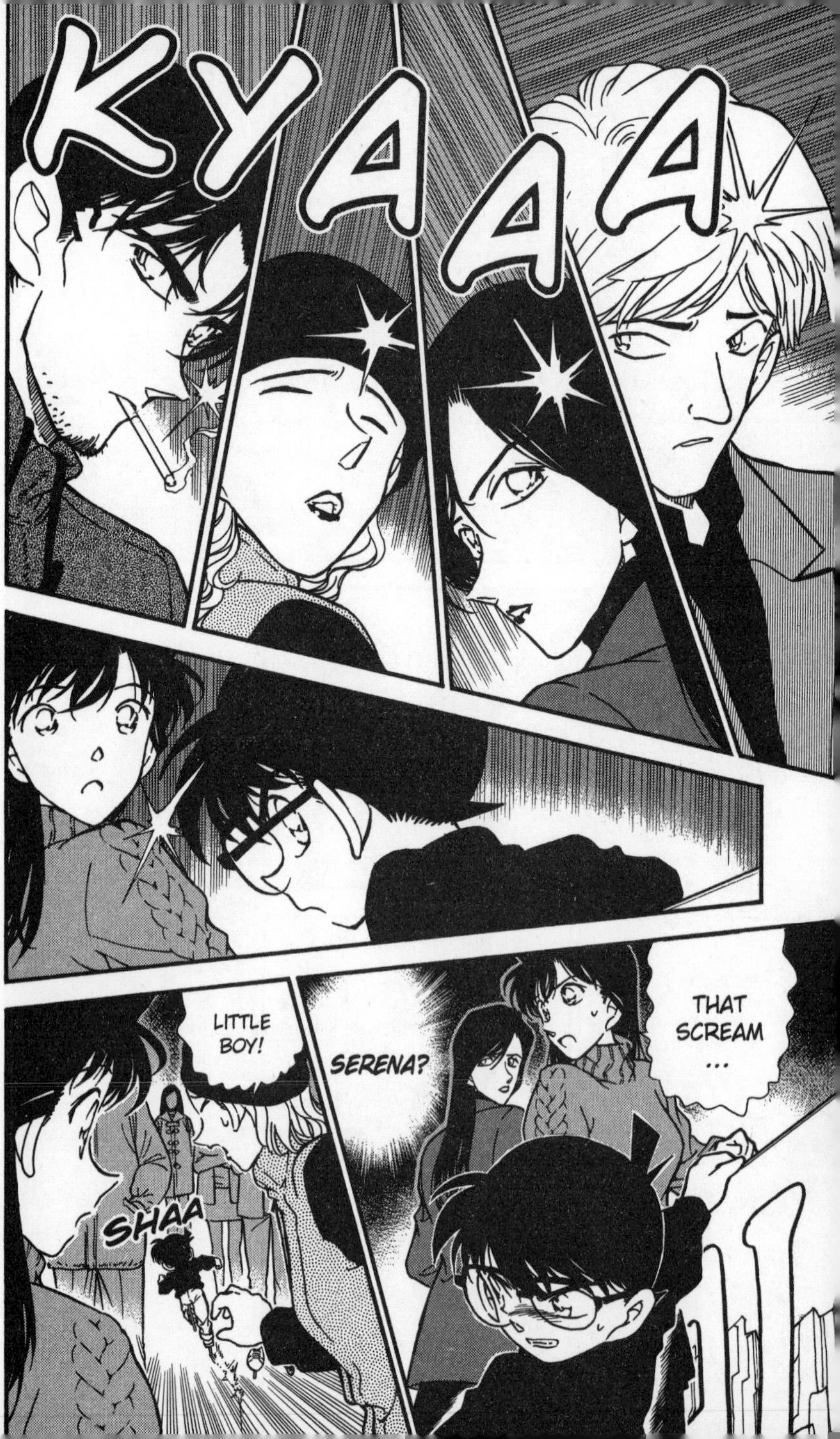
KYAAA
THAT SCREAM ...
SERENA?
LITTLE BOY!
SHAA

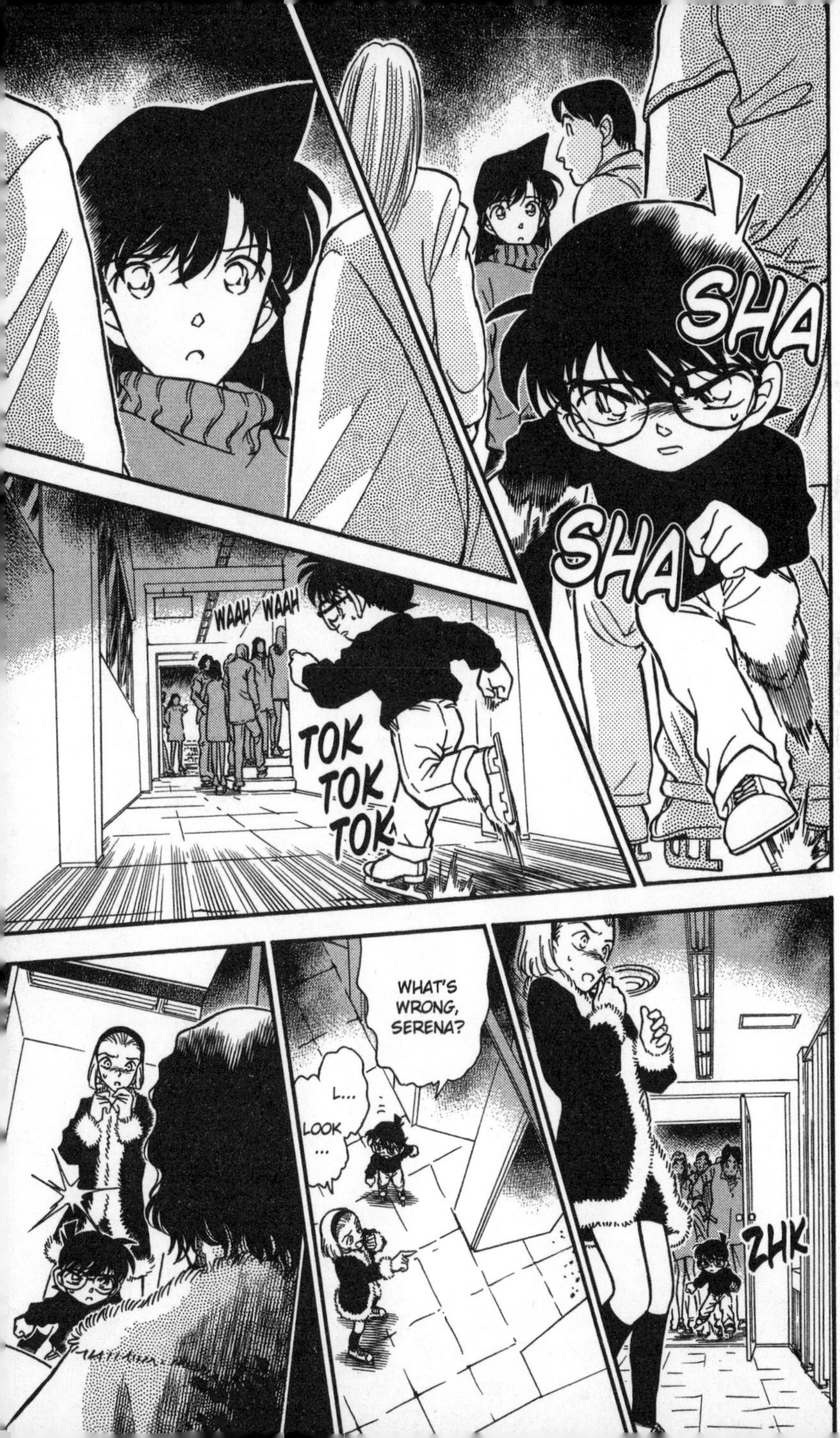
SHA
SHA
WAAH WAAH
TOK TOK TOK
ZHK
WHAT'S WRONG, SERENA?
L...
LOOK ...

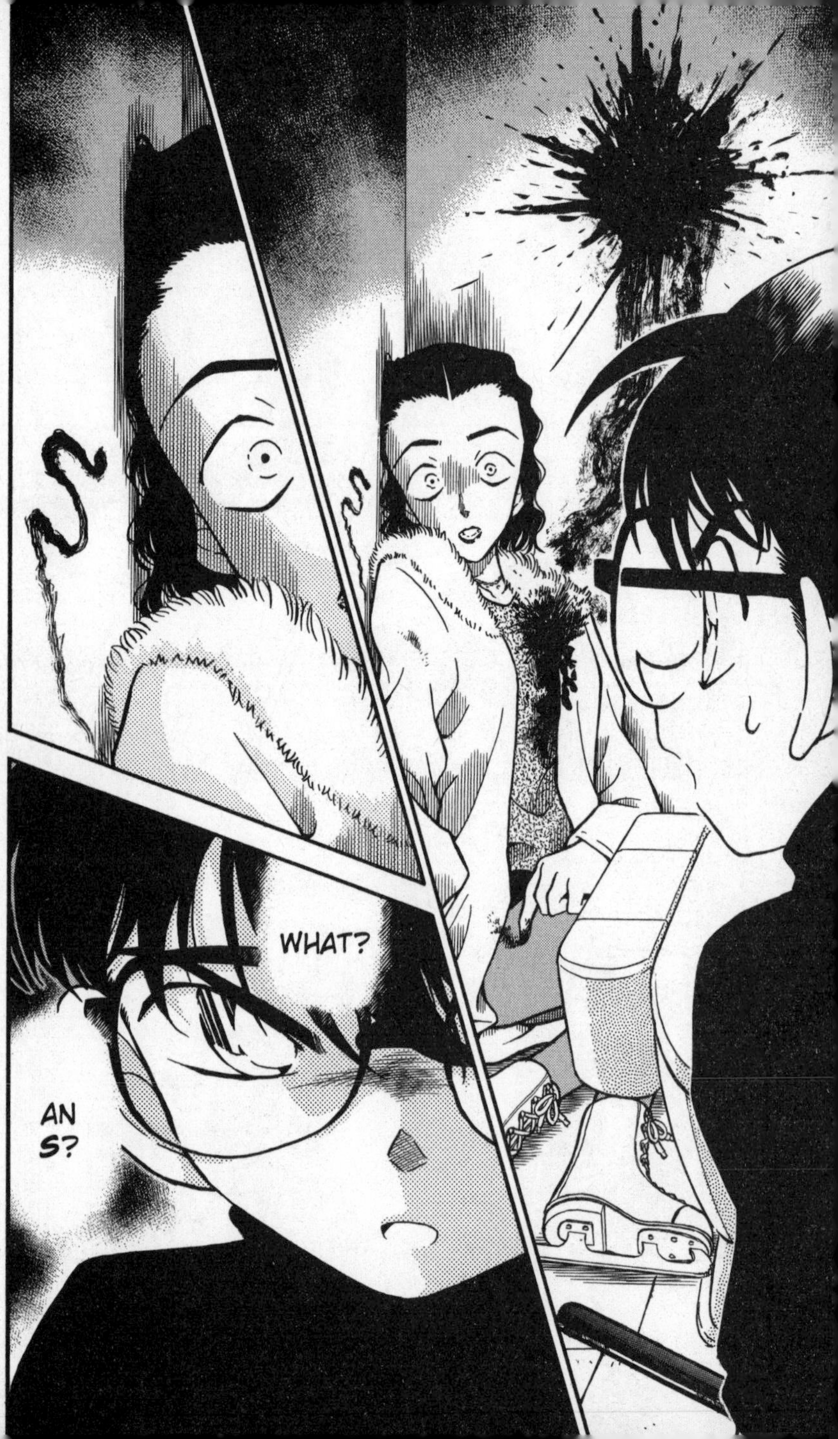
WHAT?
AN S?

THE DEAD DON'T SPEAK

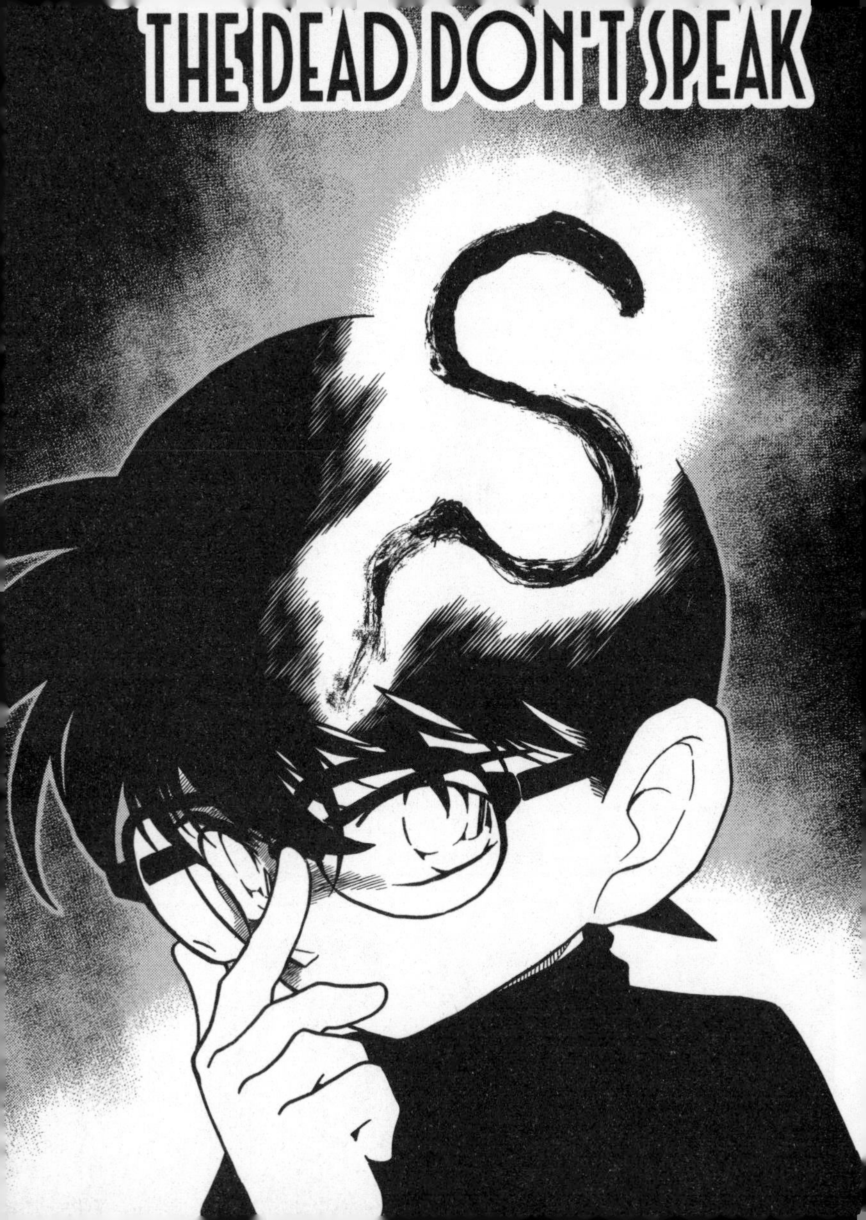

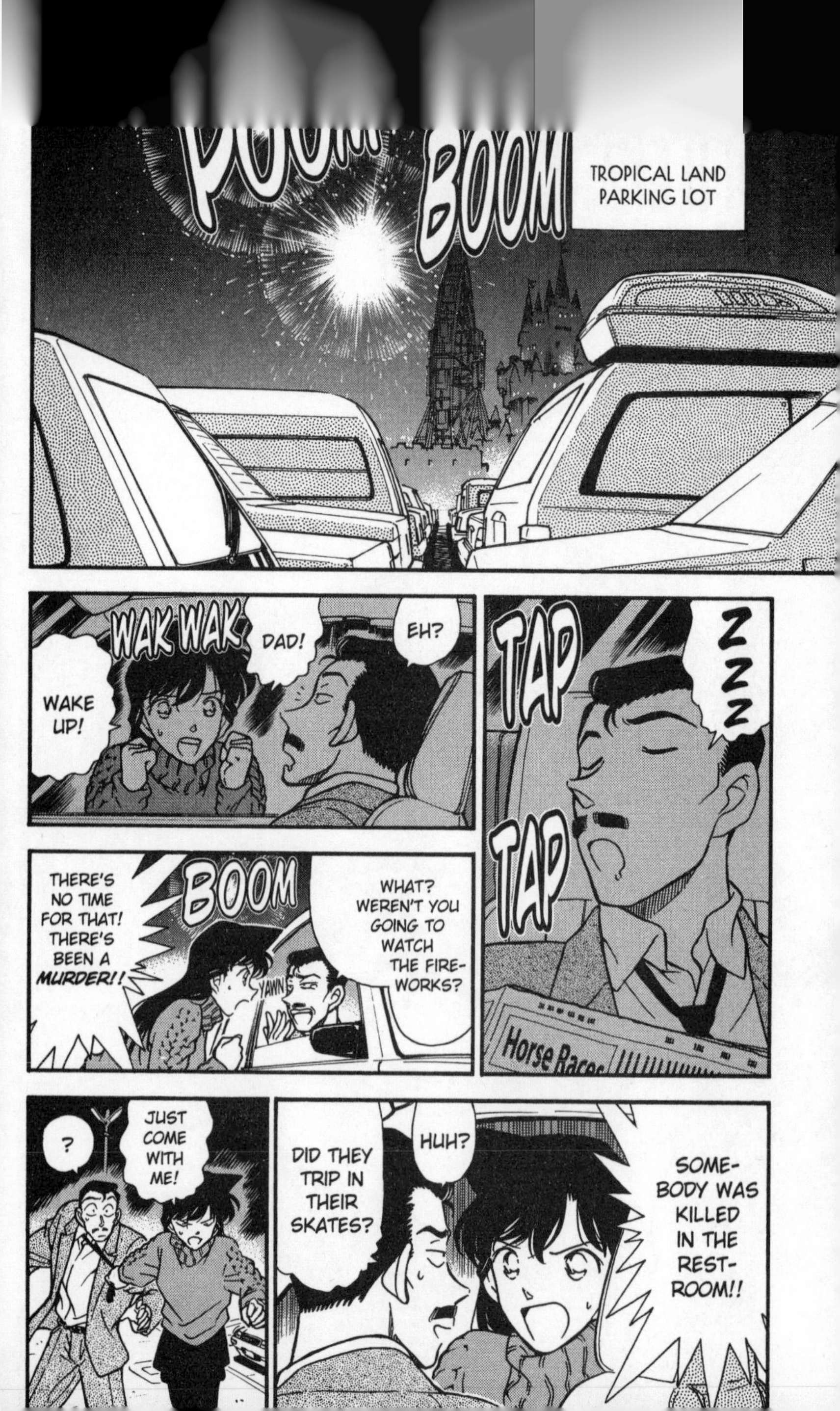

TROPICAL LAND PARKING LOT
BOOM
ZZZ
TAP
TAP
Horse Races
EH?
DAD!
WAK WAK
WAKE UP!
WHAT? WEREN'T YOU GOING TO WATCH THE FIRE-WORKS?
YAWN
BOOM
THERE'S NO TIME FOR THAT! THERE'S BEEN A MURDER!!
SOME-BODY WAS KILLED IN THE REST-ROOM!!
HUH?
DID THEY TRIP IN THEIR SKATES?
JUST COME WITH ME!
?

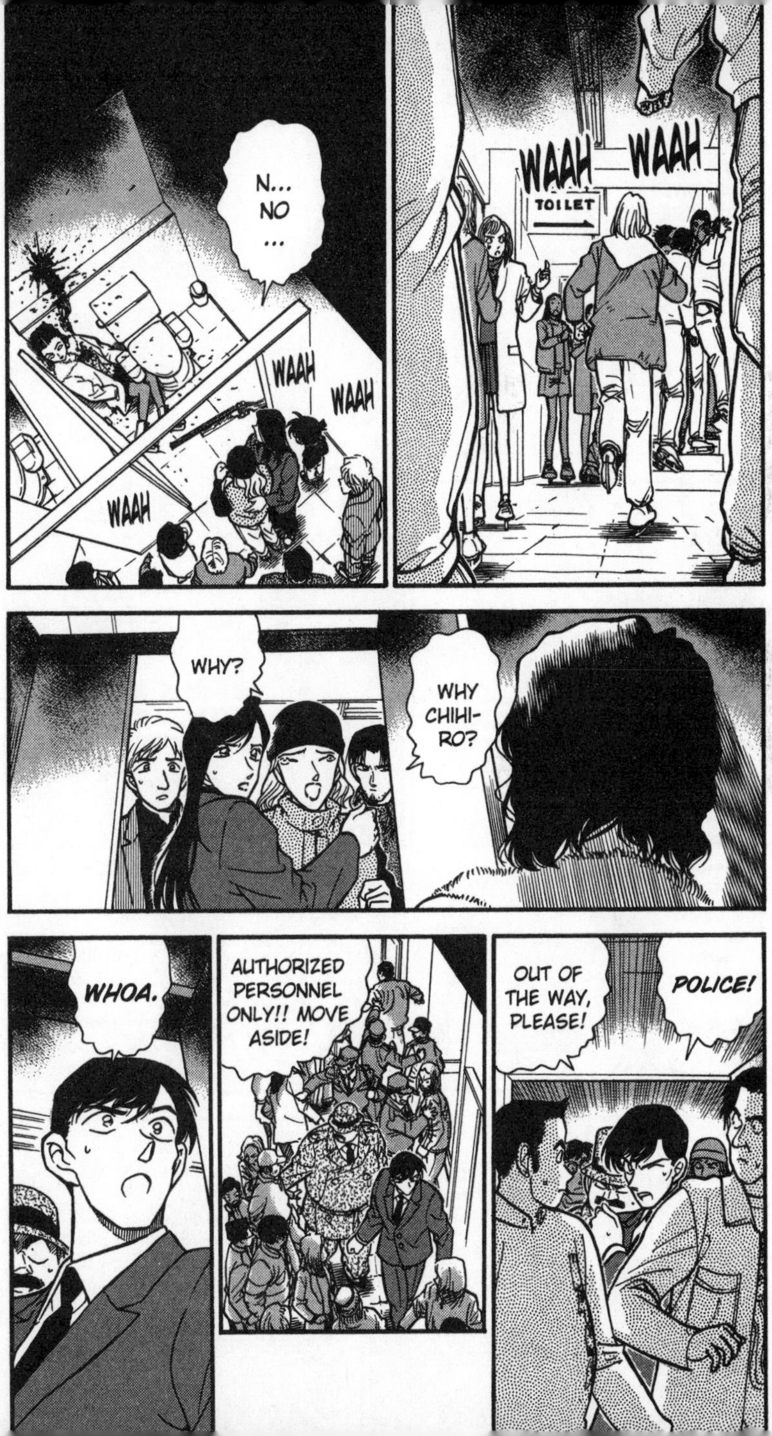
WAAH WAAH
TOILET
N... NO ...
WAAH
WAAH
WAAH
WHY CHIHIRO?
WHY?
POLICE!
OUT OF THE WAY, PLEASE!
AUTHORIZED PERSONNEL ONLY!! MOVE ASIDE!
WHOA.

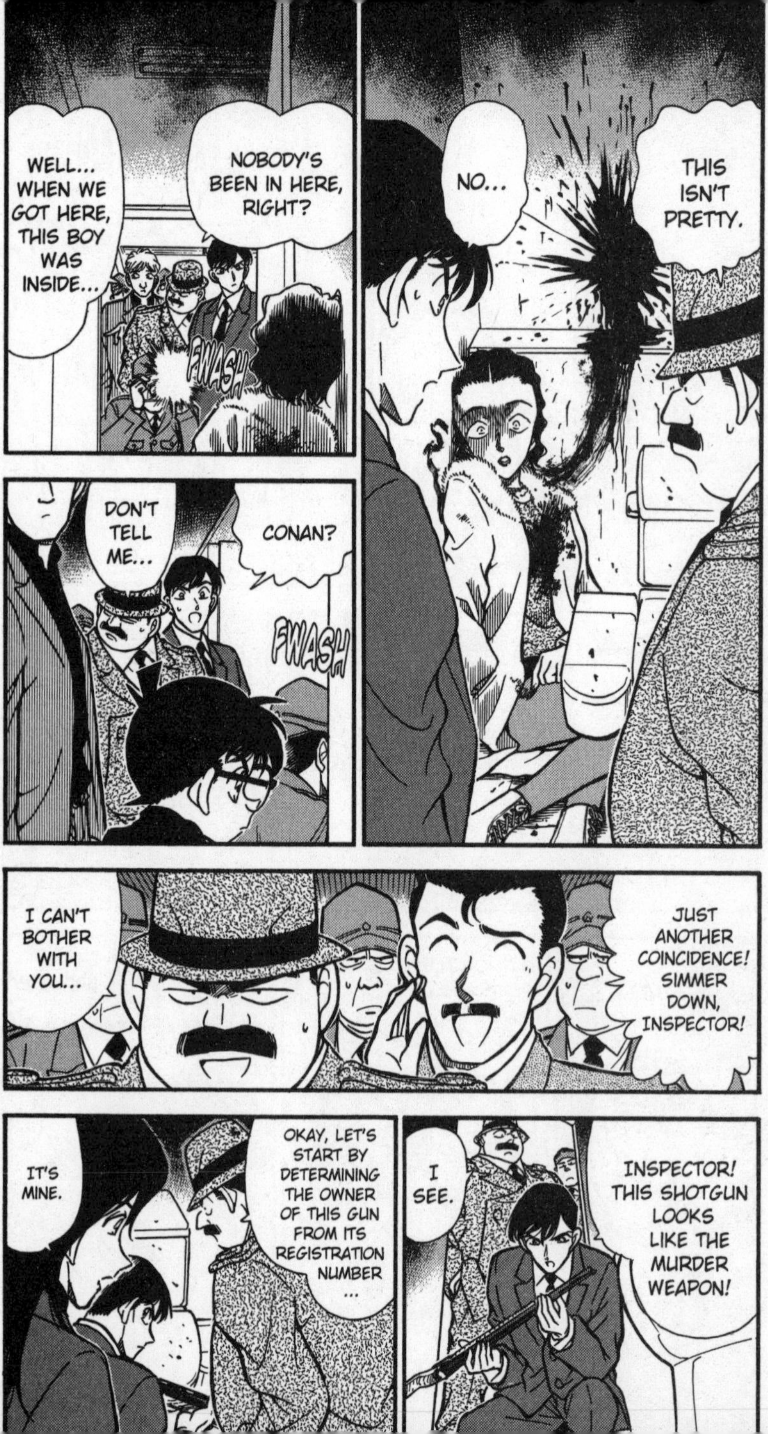
THIS ISN'T PRETTY.
NO...
NOBODY'S BEEN IN HERE, RIGHT?
WELL... WHEN WE GOT HERE, THIS BOY WAS INSIDE...
FWASH
CONAN?
DON'T TELL ME...
FWASH
JUST ANOTHER COINCIDENCE! SIMMER DOWN, INSPECTOR!
I CAN'T BOTHER WITH YOU...
INSPECTOR! THIS SHOTGUN LOOKS LIKE THE MURDER WEAPON!
I SEE.
OKAY, LET'S START BY DETERMINING THE OWNER OF THIS GUN FROM ITS REGISTRATION NUMBER ...
IT'S MINE.

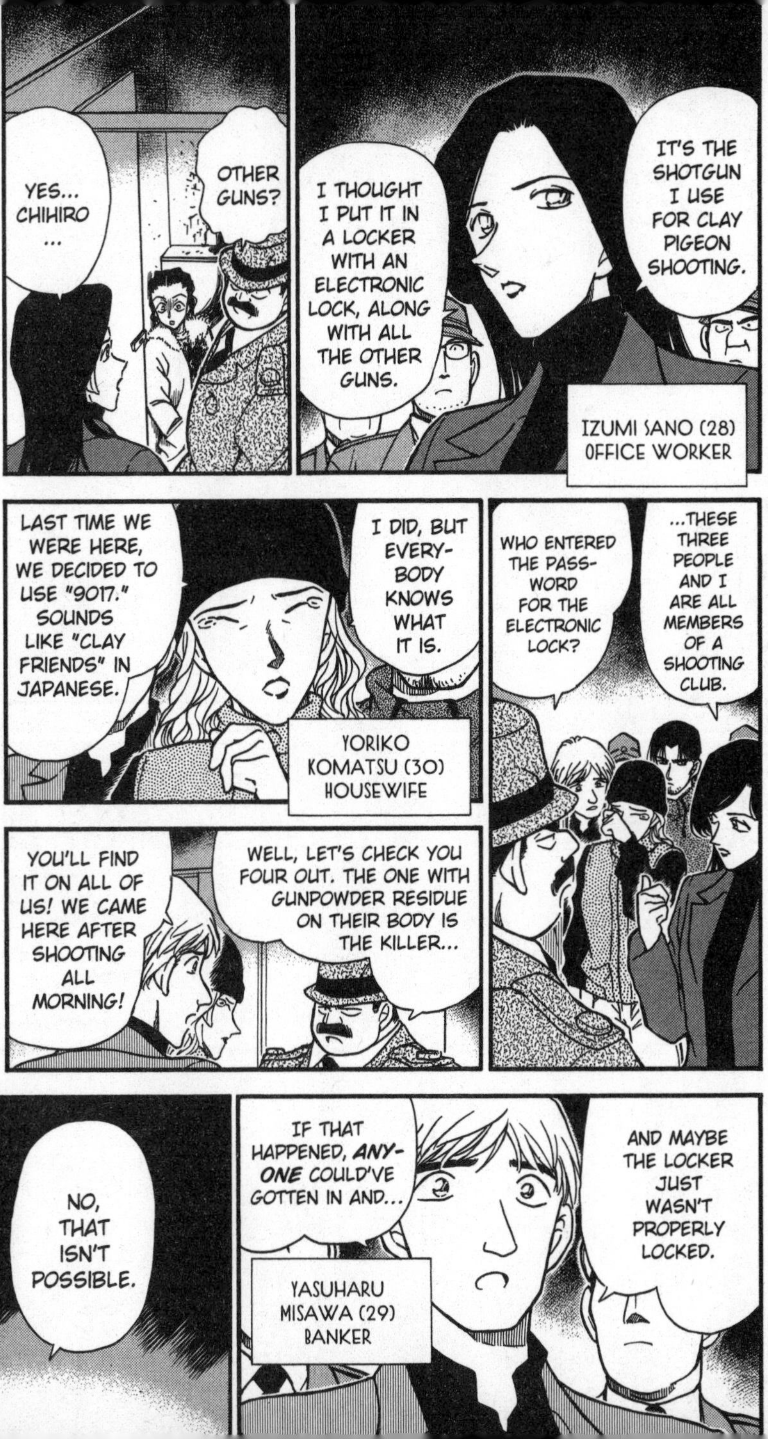
IT'S THE SHOTGUN I USE FOR CLAY PIGEON SHOOTING.
I THOUGHT I PUT IT IN A LOCKER WITH AN ELECTRONIC LOCK, ALONG WITH ALL THE OTHER GUNS.
IZUMI SANO (28) OFFICE WORKER
OTHER GUNS?
YES... CHIHIRO ...
...THESE THREE PEOPLE AND I ARE ALL MEMBERS OF A SHOOTING CLUB.
WHO ENTERED THE PASSWORD FOR THE ELECTRONIC LOCK?
I DID, BUT EVERYBODY KNOWS WHAT IT IS.
LAST TIME WE WERE HERE, WE DECIDED TO USE "9017." SOUNDS LIKE "CLAY FRIENDS" IN JAPANESE.
YORIKO KOMATSU (30) HOUSEWIFE
WELL, LET'S CHECK YOU FOUR OUT. THE ONE WITH GUNPOWDER RESIDUE ON THEIR BODY IS THE KILLER...
YOU'LL FIND IT ON ALL OF US! WE CAME HERE AFTER SHOOTING ALL MORNING!
AND MAYBE THE LOCKER JUST WASN'T PROPERLY LOCKED.
IF THAT HAPPENED, ANYONE COULD'VE GOTTEN IN AND...
YASUHARU MISAWA (29) BANKER
NO, THAT ISN'T POSSIBLE.

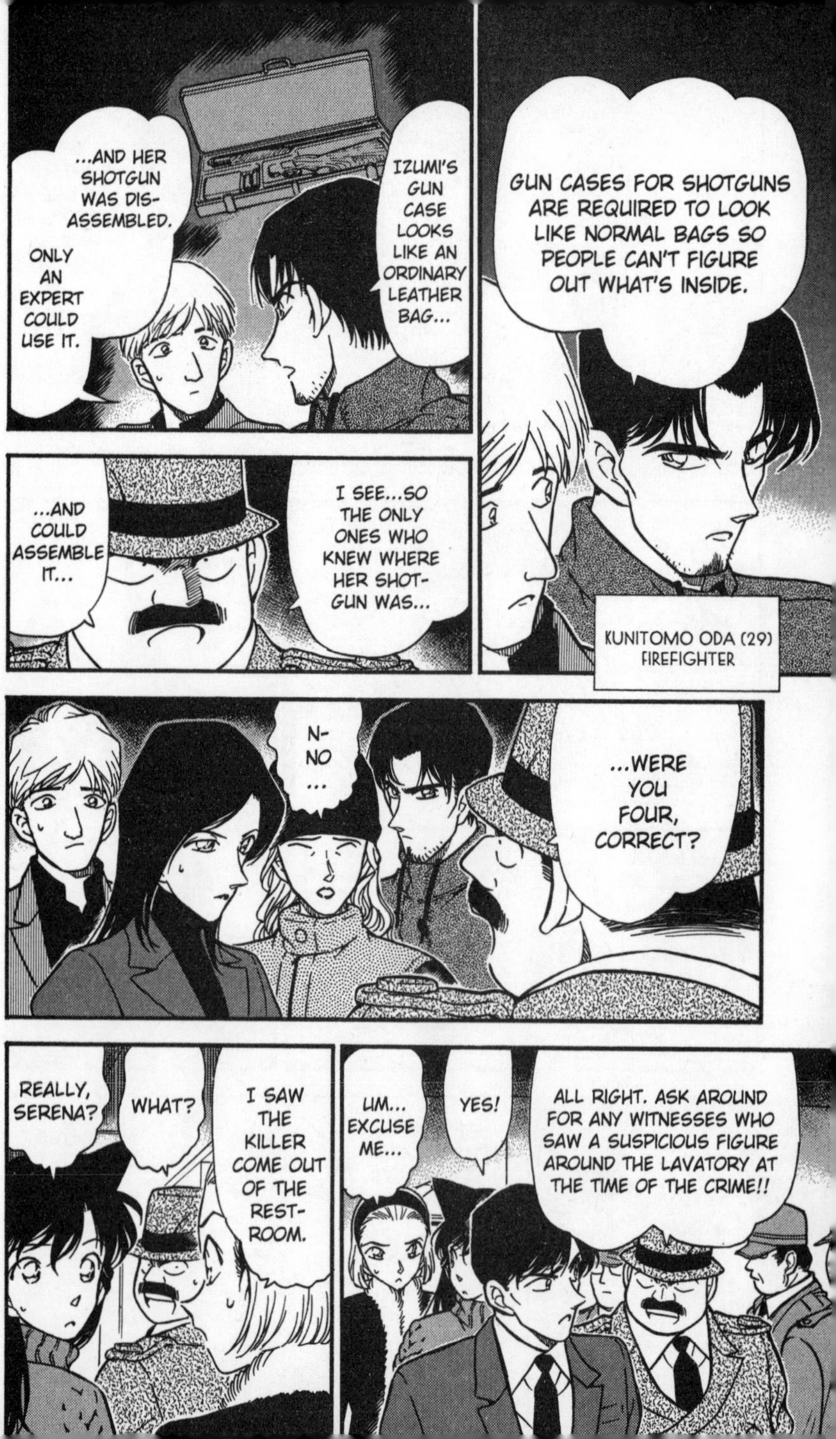
GUN CASES FOR SHOTGUNS ARE REQUIRED TO LOOK LIKE NORMAL BAGS SO PEOPLE CAN'T FIGURE OUT WHAT'S INSIDE.
KUNITOMO ODA (29) FIREFIGHTER
IZUMI'S GUN CASE LOOKS LIKE AN ORDINARY LEATHER BAG...
...AND HER SHOTGUN WAS DIS-ASSEMBLED.
ONLY AN EXPERT COULD USE IT.
I SEE...SO THE ONLY ONES WHO KNEW WHERE HER SHOT-GUN WAS...
...AND COULD ASSEMBLE IT...
...WERE YOU FOUR, CORRECT?
N-NO...
ALL RIGHT. ASK AROUND FOR ANY WITNESSES WHO SAW A SUSPICIOUS FIGURE AROUND THE LAVATORY AT THE TIME OF THE CRIME!!
YES!
UM... EXCUSE ME...
I SAW THE KILLER COME OUT OF THE REST-ROOM.
WHAT?
REALLY, SERENA?

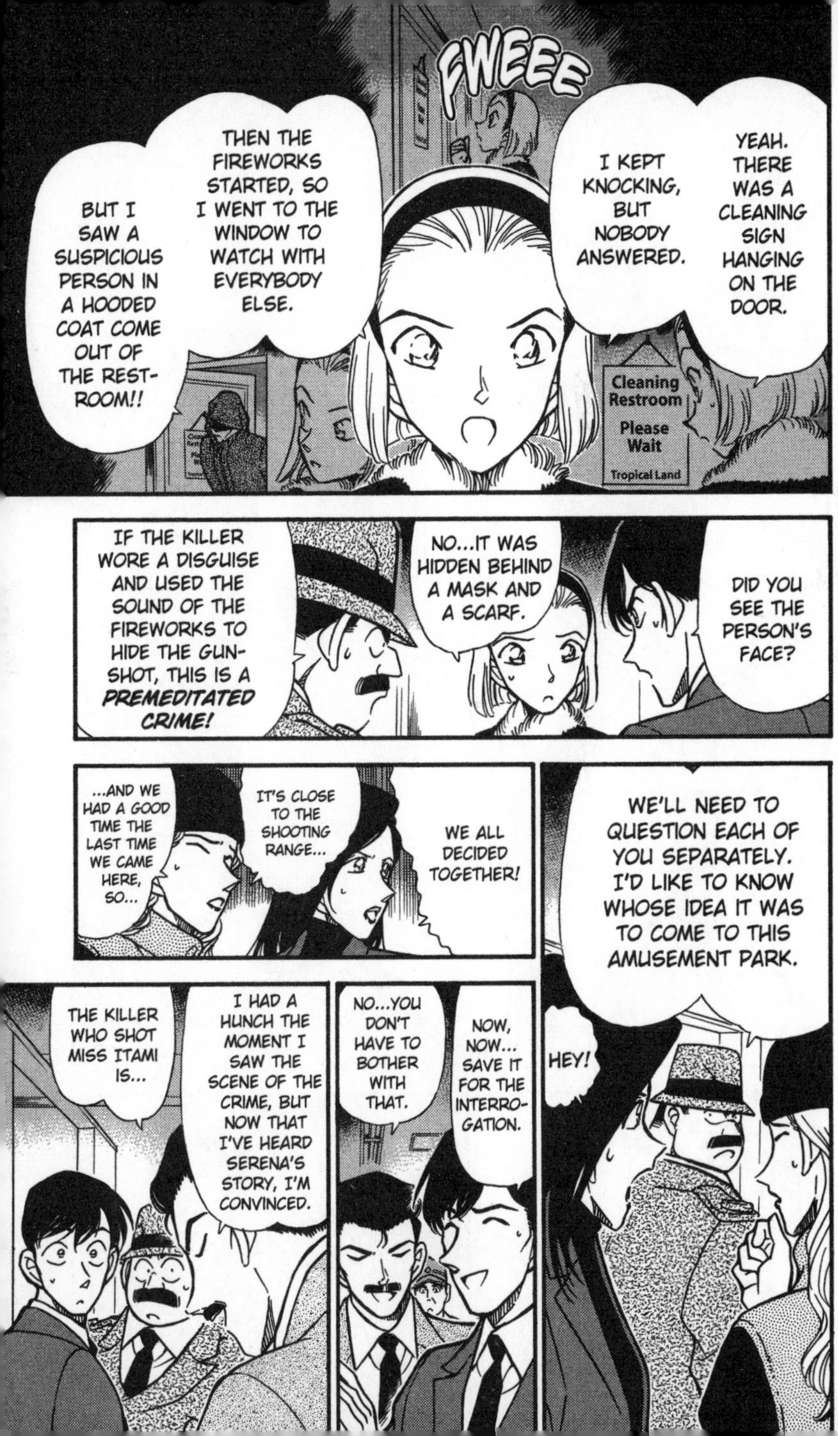
FWEEE
YEAH. THERE WAS A CLEANING SIGN HANGING ON THE DOOR.
I KEPT KNOCKING, BUT NOBODY ANSWERED.
Cleaning Restroom Please Wait Tropical Land
THEN THE FIREWORKS STARTED, SO I WENT TO THE WINDOW TO WATCH WITH EVERYBODY ELSE.
BUT I SAW A SUSPICIOUS PERSON IN A HOODED COAT COME OUT OF THE REST-ROOM!!
DID YOU SEE THE PERSON'S FACE?
NO...IT WAS HIDDEN BEHIND A MASK AND A SCARF.
IF THE KILLER WORE A DISGUISE AND USED THE SOUND OF THE FIREWORKS TO HIDE THE GUN-SHOT, THIS IS A PREMEDITATED CRIME!
WE'LL NEED TO QUESTION EACH OF YOU SEPARATELY. I'D LIKE TO KNOW WHOSE IDEA IT WAS TO COME TO THIS AMUSEMENT PARK.
HEY!
WE ALL DECIDED TOGETHER!
IT'S CLOSE TO THE SHOOTING RANGE...
...AND WE HAD A GOOD TIME THE LAST TIME WE CAME HERE, SO...
NOW, NOW... SAVE IT FOR THE INTERRO-GATION.
NO...YOU DON'T HAVE TO BOTHER WITH THAT.
I HAD A HUNCH THE MOMENT I SAW THE SCENE OF THE CRIME, BUT NOW THAT I'VE HEARD SERENA'S STORY, I'M CONVINCED.
THE KILLER WHO SHOT MISS ITAMI IS...

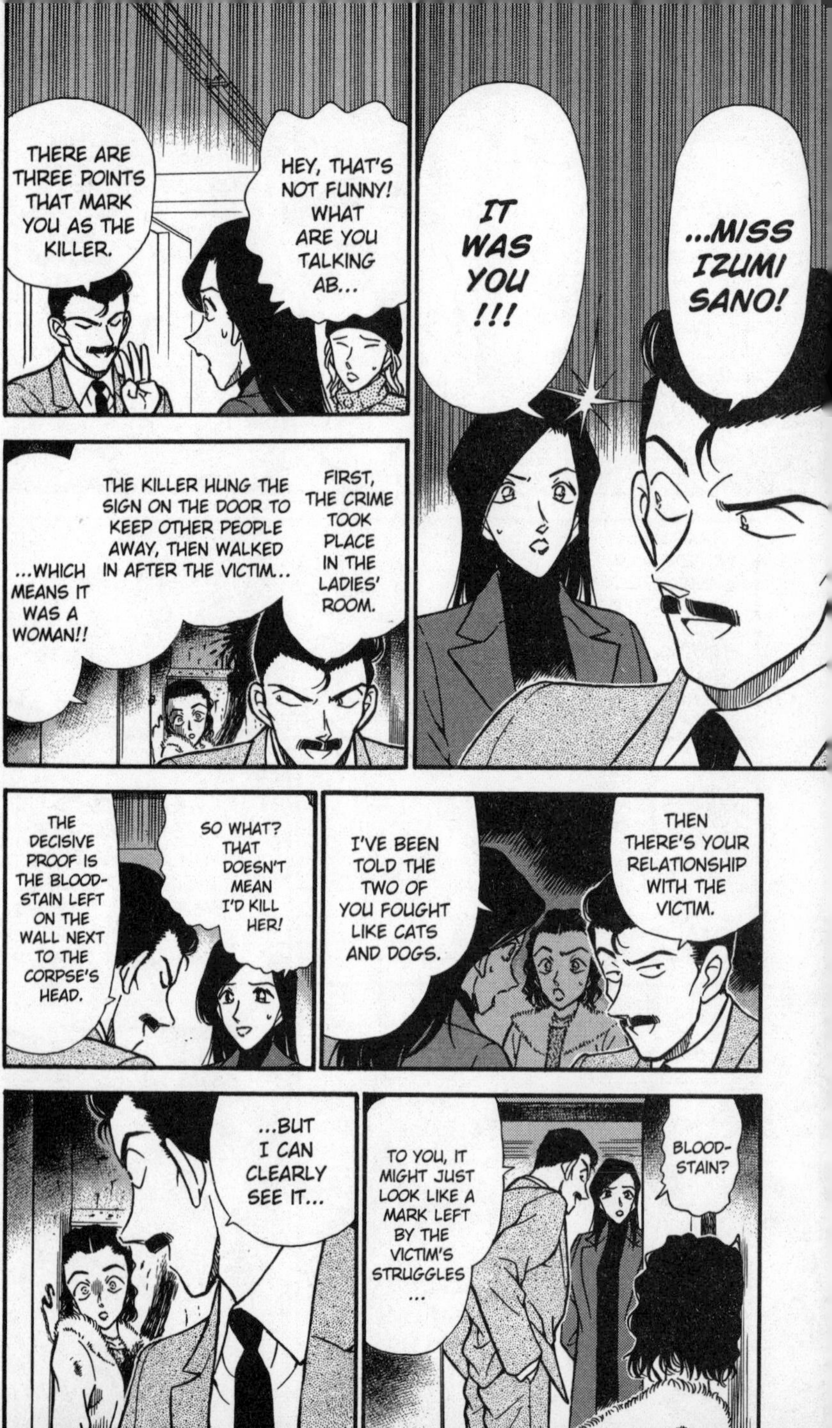
...MISS IZUMI SANO!
IT WAS YOU!!!
HEY, THAT'S NOT FUNNY! WHAT ARE YOU TALKING AB...
THERE ARE THREE POINTS THAT MARK YOU AS THE KILLER.
FIRST, THE CRIME TOOK PLACE IN THE LADIES' ROOM.
THE KILLER HUNG THE SIGN ON THE DOOR TO KEEP OTHER PEOPLE AWAY, THEN WALKED IN AFTER THE VICTIM...
...WHICH MEANS IT WAS A WOMAN!!
THEN THERE'S YOUR RELATIONSHIP WITH THE VICTIM.
I'VE BEEN TOLD THE TWO OF YOU FOUGHT LIKE CATS AND DOGS.
SO WHAT? THAT DOESN'T MEAN I'D KILL HER!
THE DECISIVE PROOF IS THE BLOOD-STAIN LEFT ON THE WALL NEXT TO THE CORPSE'S HEAD.
BLOOD-STAIN?
TO YOU, IT MIGHT JUST LOOK LIKE A MARK LEFT BY THE VICTIM'S STRUGGLES ...
...BUT I CAN CLEARLY SEE IT...

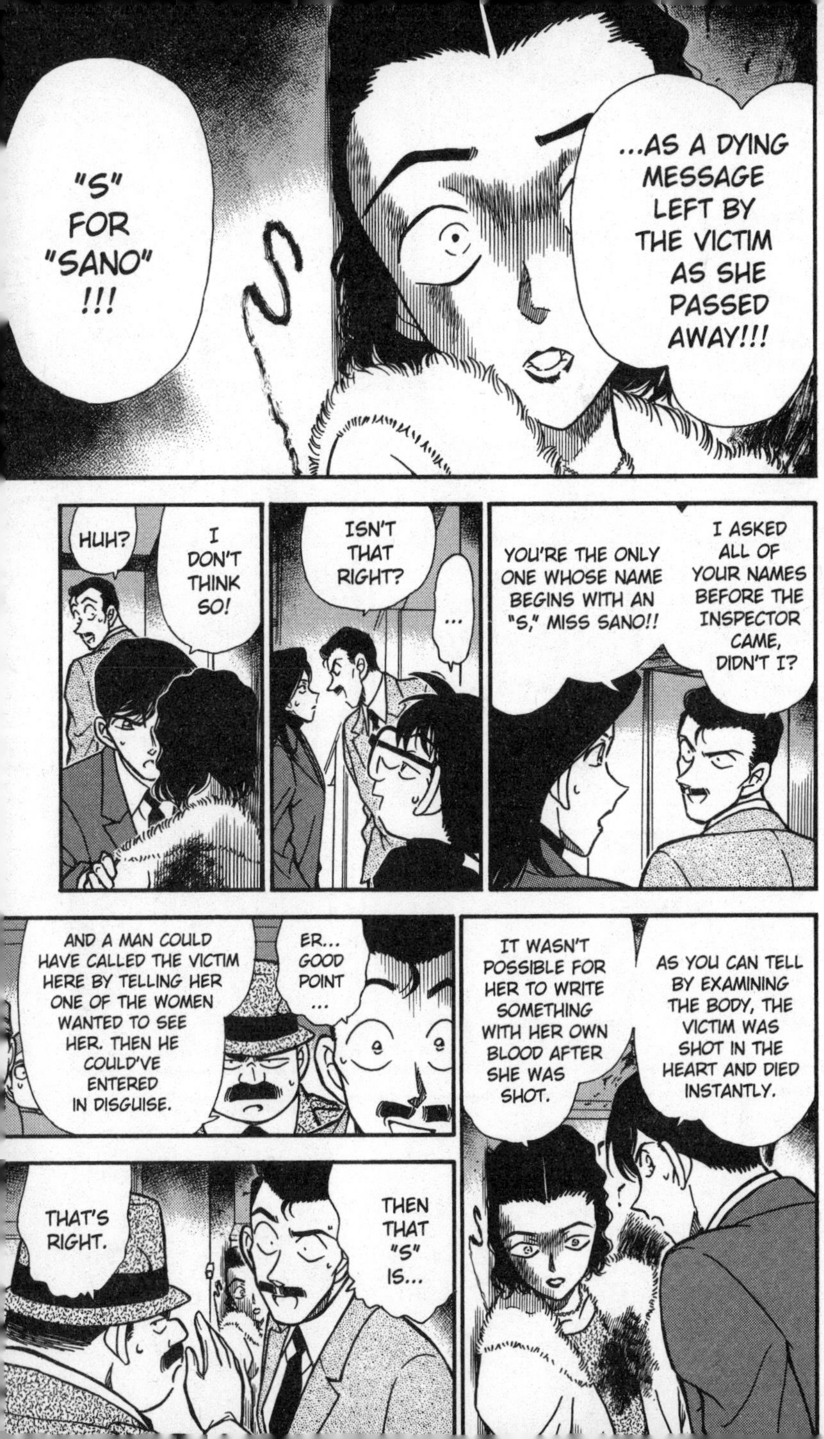
...AS A DYING MESSAGE LEFT BY THE VICTIM AS SHE PASSED AWAY!!!
"S" FOR "SANO" !!!
I ASKED ALL OF YOUR NAMES BEFORE THE INSPECTOR CAME, DIDN'T I?
YOU'RE THE ONLY ONE WHOSE NAME BEGINS WITH AN "S," MISS SANO!!
ISN'T THAT RIGHT?
...
I DON'T THINK SO!
HUH?
AS YOU CAN TELL BY EXAMINING THE BODY, THE VICTIM WAS SHOT IN THE HEART AND DIED INSTANTLY.
IT WASN'T POSSIBLE FOR HER TO WRITE SOMETHING WITH HER OWN BLOOD AFTER SHE WAS SHOT.
ER... GOOD POINT ...
AND A MAN COULD HAVE CALLED THE VICTIM HERE BY TELLING HER ONE OF THE WOMEN WANTED TO SEE HER. THEN HE COULD'VE ENTERED IN DISGUISE.
THEN THAT "S" IS...
THAT'S RIGHT.

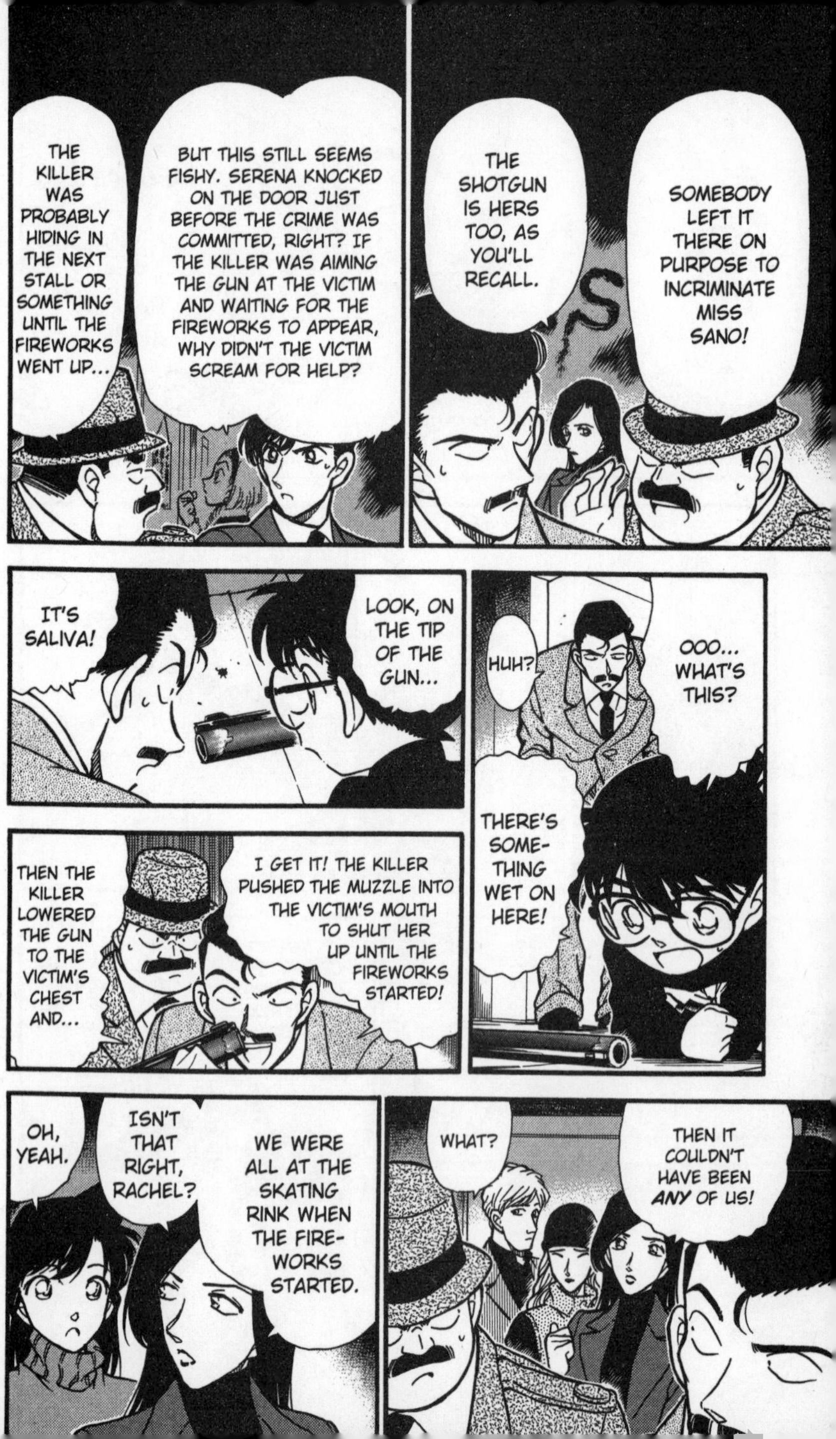
SOMEBODY LEFT IT THERE ON PURPOSE TO INCRIMINATE MISS SANO!
THE SHOTGUN IS HERS TOO, AS YOU'LL RECALL.
BUT THIS STILL SEEMS FISHY. SERENA KNOCKED ON THE DOOR JUST BEFORE THE CRIME WAS COMMITTED, RIGHT? IF THE KILLER WAS AIMING THE GUN AT THE VICTIM AND WAITING FOR THE FIREWORKS TO APPEAR, WHY DIDN'T THE VICTIM SCREAM FOR HELP?
THE KILLER WAS PROBABLY HIDING IN THE NEXT STALL OR SOMETHING UNTIL THE FIREWORKS WENT UP...
OOO... WHAT'S THIS?
HUH?
THERE'S SOME-THING WET ON HERE!
LOOK, ON THE TIP OF THE GUN...
IT'S SALIVA!
I GET IT! THE KILLER PUSHED THE MUZZLE INTO THE VICTIM'S MOUTH TO SHUT HER UP UNTIL THE FIREWORKS STARTED!
THEN THE KILLER LOWERED THE GUN TO THE VICTIM'S CHEST AND...
THEN IT COULDN'T HAVE BEEN *ANY* OF US!
WHAT?
WE WERE ALL AT THE SKATING RINK WHEN THE FIRE-WORKS STARTED.
ISN'T THAT RIGHT, RACHEL?
OH, YEAH.

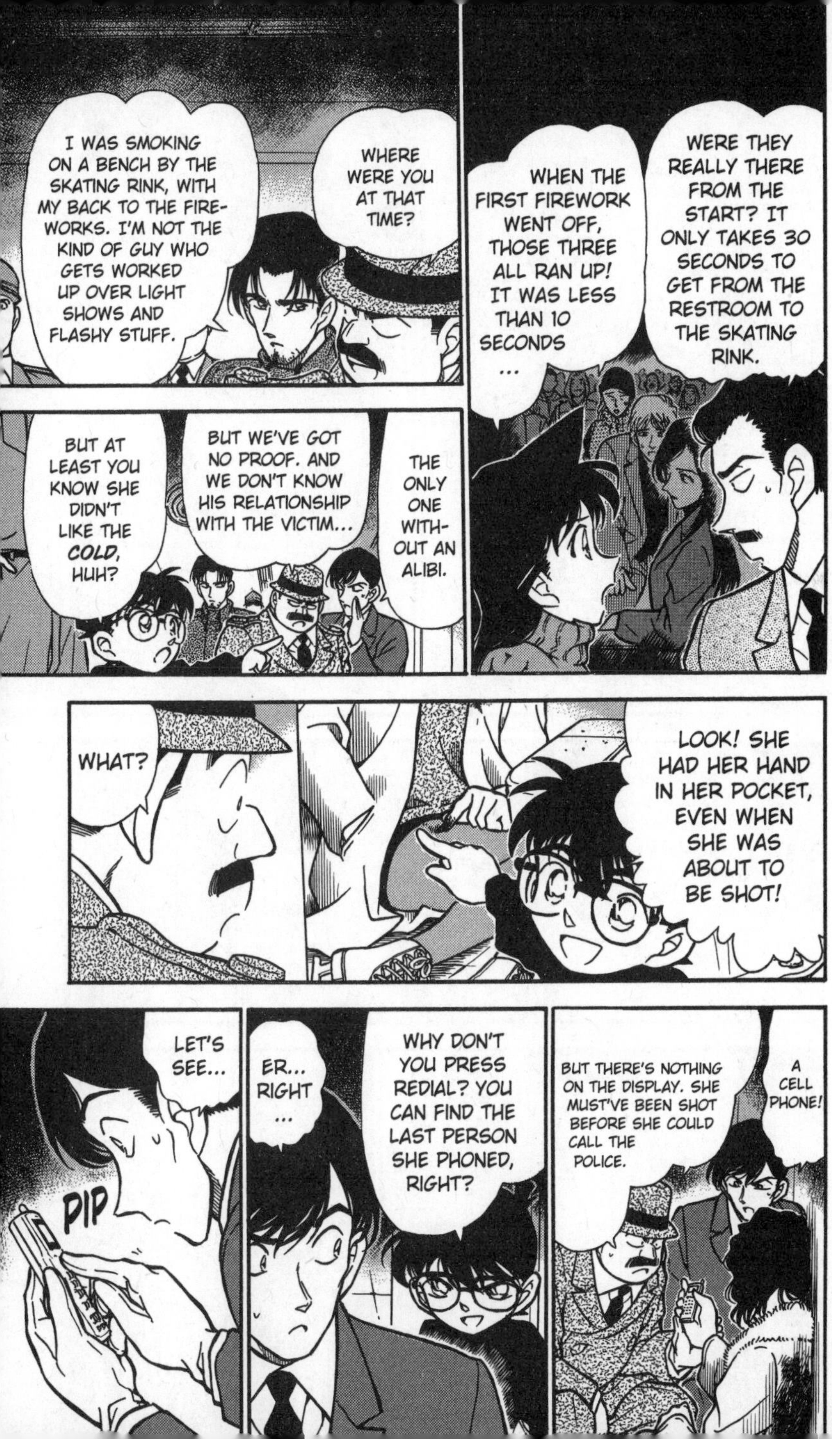
WERE THEY REALLY THERE FROM THE START? IT ONLY TAKES 30 SECONDS TO GET FROM THE RESTROOM TO THE SKATING RINK.
WHEN THE FIRST FIREWORK WENT OFF, THOSE THREE ALL RAN UP! IT WAS LESS THAN 10 SECONDS ...
WHERE WERE YOU AT THAT TIME?
I WAS SMOKING ON A BENCH BY THE SKATING RINK, WITH MY BACK TO THE FIRE-WORKS. I'M NOT THE KIND OF GUY WHO GETS WORKED UP OVER LIGHT SHOWS AND FLASHY STUFF.
THE ONLY ONE WITH-OUT AN ALIBI.
BUT WE'VE GOT NO PROOF. AND WE DON'T KNOW HIS RELATIONSHIP WITH THE VICTIM...
BUT AT LEAST YOU KNOW SHE DIDN'T LIKE THE *COLD*, HUH?
LOOK! SHE HAD HER HAND IN HER POCKET, EVEN WHEN SHE WAS ABOUT TO BE SHOT!
WHAT?
A CELL PHONE!
BUT THERE'S NOTHING ON THE DISPLAY. SHE MUST'VE BEEN SHOT BEFORE SHE COULD CALL THE POLICE.
WHY DON'T YOU PRESS REDIAL? YOU CAN FIND THE LAST PERSON SHE PHONED, RIGHT?
ER... RIGHT ...
LET'S SEE...
PIP

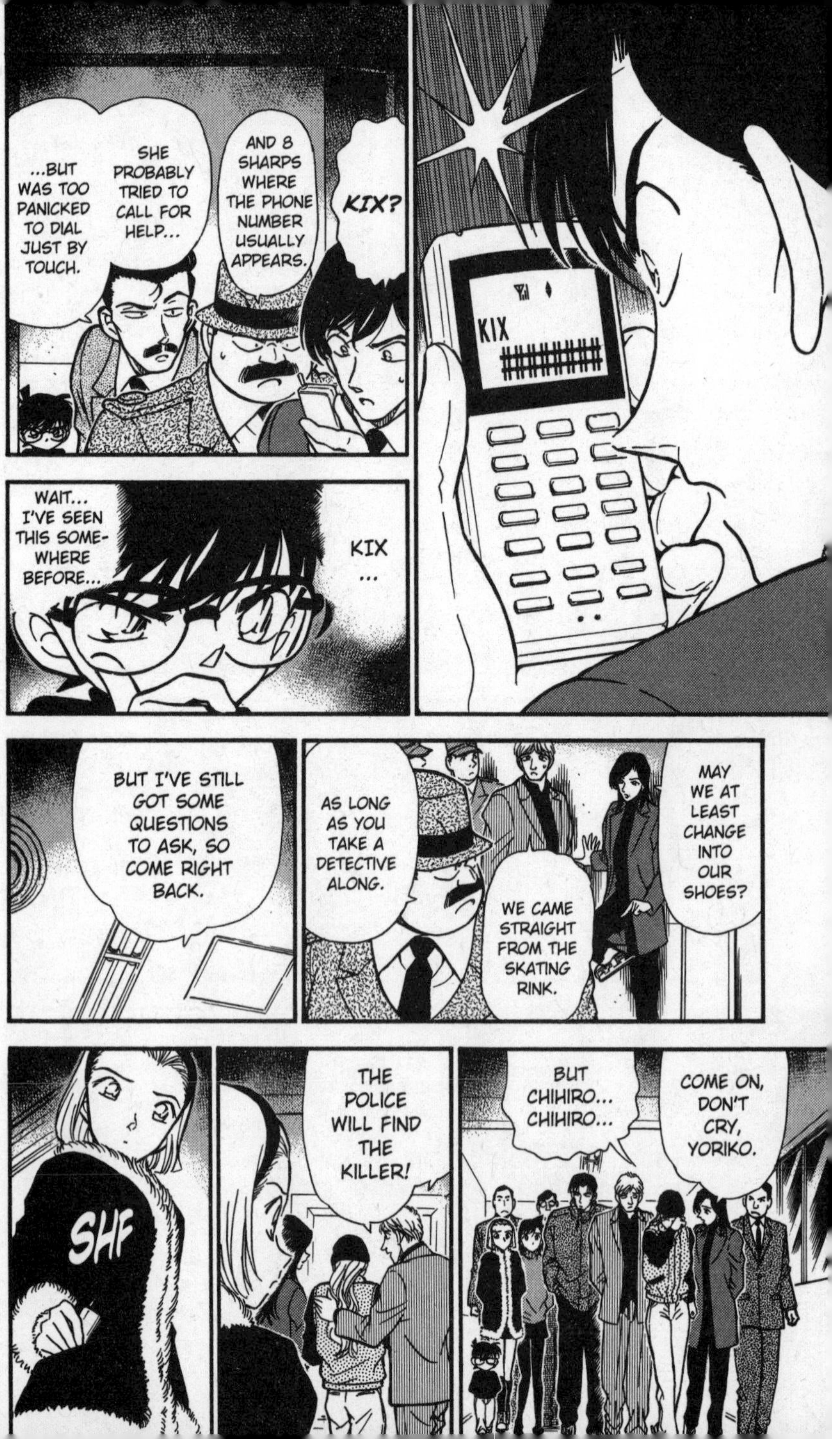
KIX
########
KIX?
AND 8 SHARPS WHERE THE PHONE NUMBER USUALLY APPEARS.
SHE PROBABLY TRIED TO CALL FOR HELP...
...BUT WAS TOO PANICKED TO DIAL JUST BY TOUCH.
KIX ...
WAIT... I'VE SEEN THIS SOME-WHERE BEFORE...
MAY WE AT LEAST CHANGE INTO OUR SHOES?
AS LONG AS YOU TAKE A DETECTIVE ALONG.
WE CAME STRAIGHT FROM THE SKATING RINK.
BUT I'VE STILL GOT SOME QUESTIONS TO ASK, SO COME RIGHT BACK.
COME ON, DON'T CRY, YORIKO.
BUT CHIHIRO... CHIHIRO...
THE POLICE WILL FIND THE KILLER!
SHF

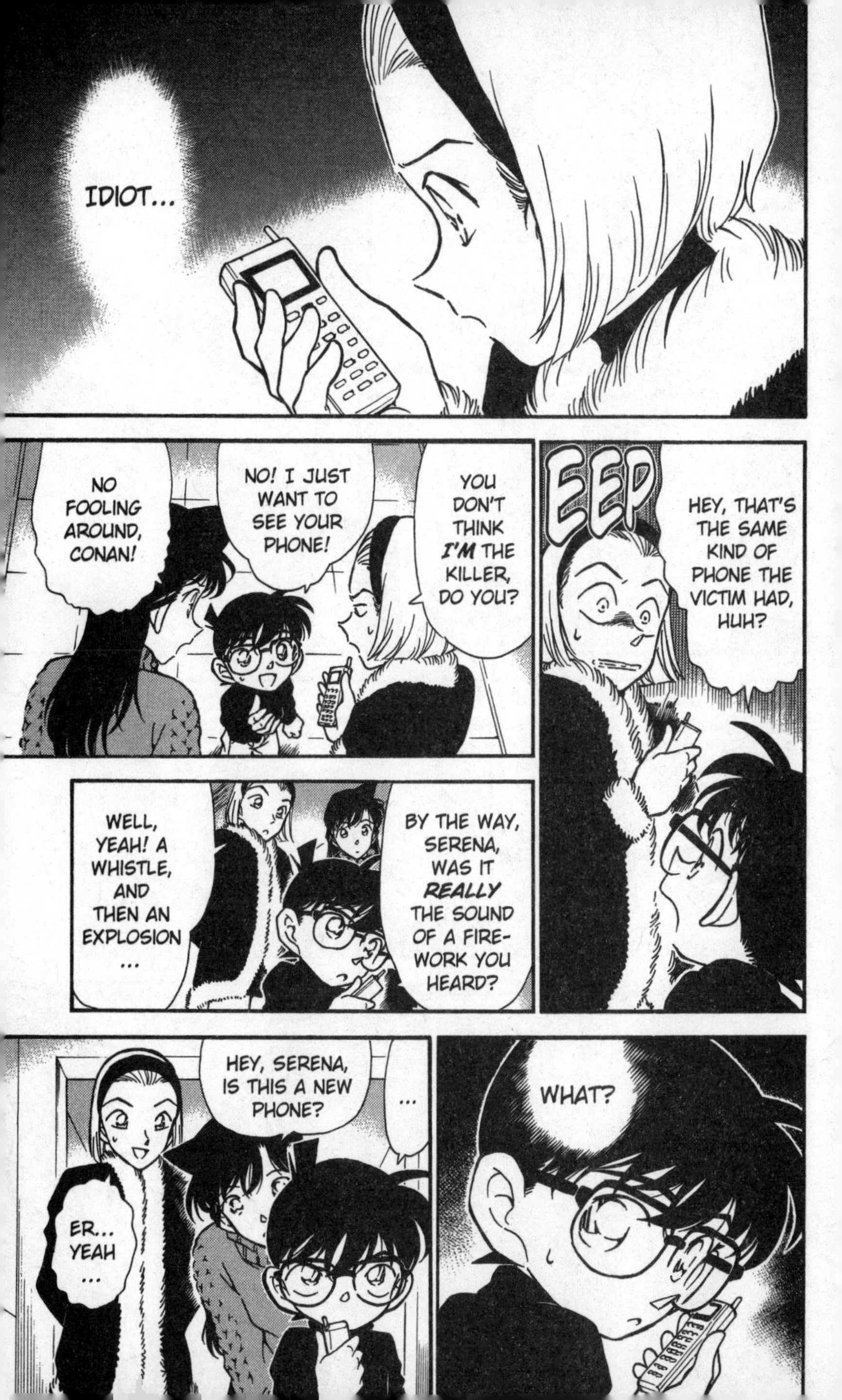
IDIOT...
EEP
HEY, THAT'S THE SAME KIND OF PHONE THE VICTIM HAD, HUH?
YOU DON'T THINK *I'M* THE KILLER, DO YOU?
NO! I JUST WANT TO SEE YOUR PHONE!
NO FOOLING AROUND, CONAN!
BY THE WAY, SERENA, WAS IT *REALLY* THE SOUND OF A FIRE-WORK YOU HEARD?
WELL, YEAH! A WHISTLE, AND THEN AN EXPLOSION ...
WHAT?
...
HEY, SERENA, IS THIS A NEW PHONE?
ER... YEAH ...

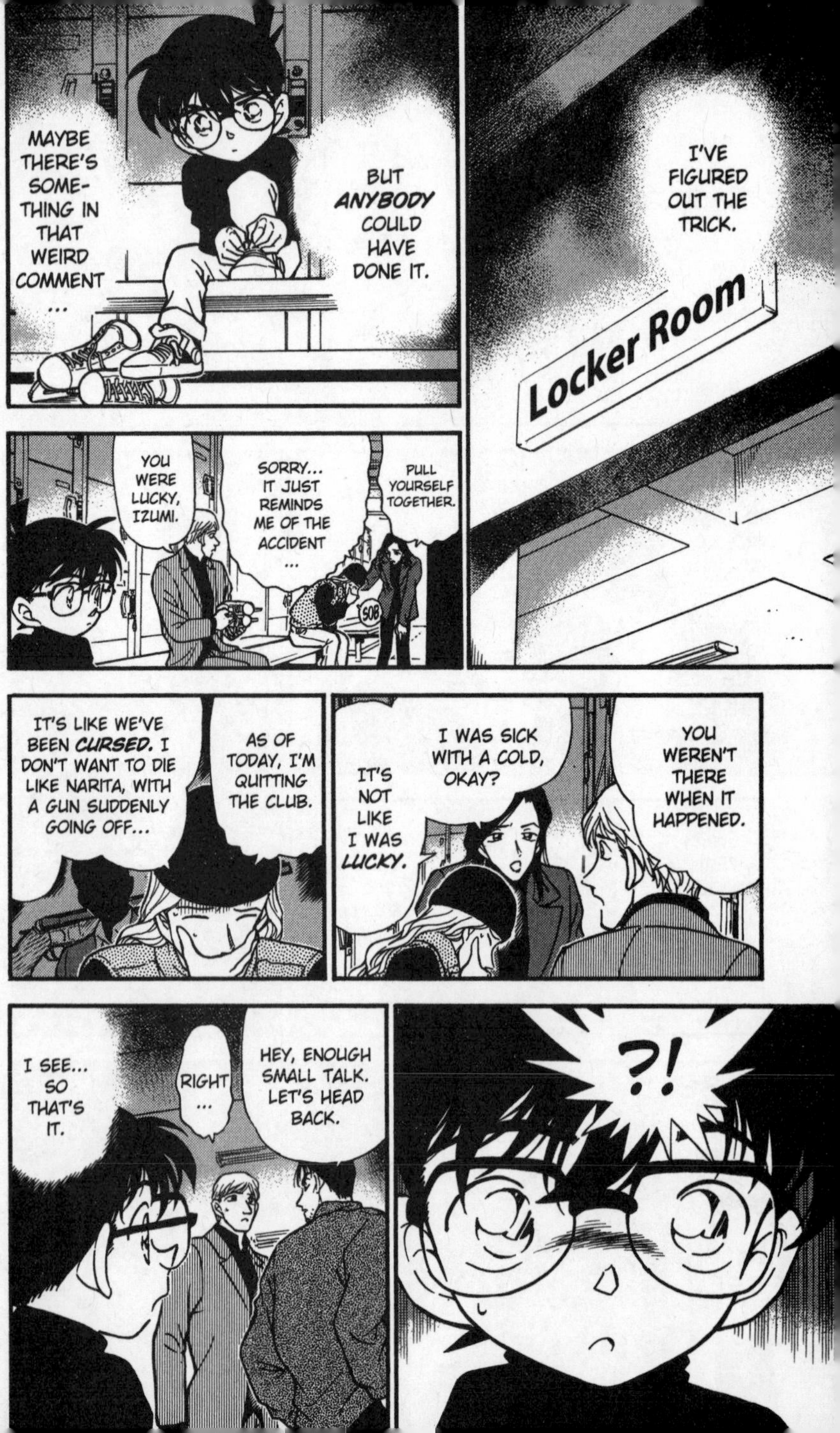
I'VE FIGURED OUT THE TRICK.
Locker Room
...
BUT ANYBODY COULD HAVE DONE IT.
MAYBE THERE'S SOME-THING IN THAT WEIRD COMMENT ...
PULL YOURSELF TOGETHER.
SORRY... IT JUST REMINDS ME OF THE ACCIDENT ...
SOB
YOU WERE LUCKY, IZUMI.
YOU WEREN'T THERE WHEN IT HAPPENED.
I WAS SICK WITH A COLD, OKAY?
IT'S NOT LIKE I WAS LUCKY.
AS OF TODAY, I'M QUITTING THE CLUB.
IT'S LIKE WE'VE BEEN CURSED. I DON'T WANT TO DIE LIKE NARITA, WITH A GUN SUDDENLY GOING OFF...
?!
HEY, ENOUGH SMALL TALK. LET'S HEAD BACK.
RIGHT ...
I SEE... SO THAT'S IT.

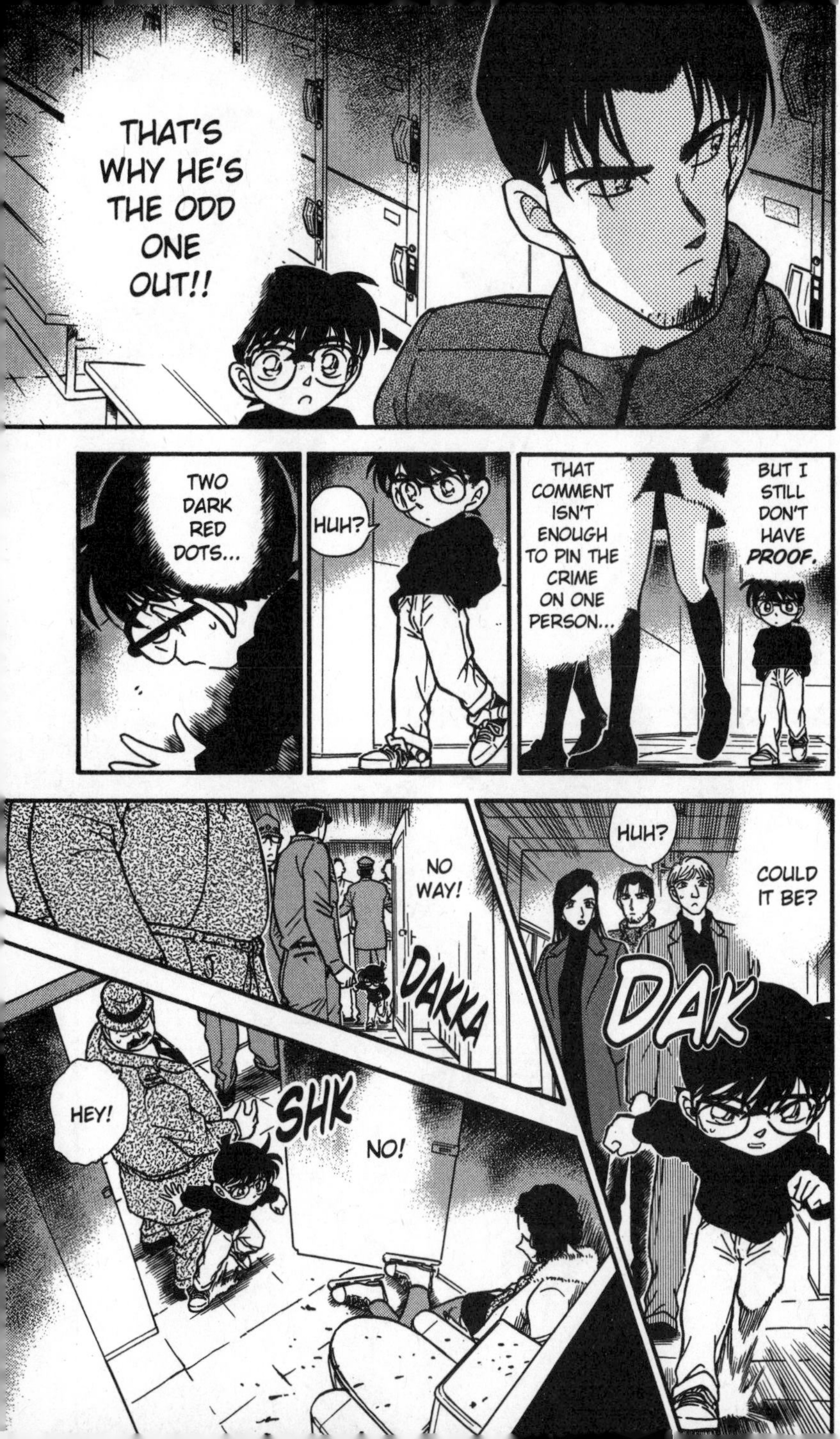
THAT'S WHY HE'S THE ODD ONE OUT!!
BUT I STILL DON'T HAVE PROOF.
THAT COMMENT ISN'T ENOUGH TO PIN THE CRIME ON ONE PERSON...
HUH?
TWO DARK RED DOTS...
HUH?
COULD IT BE?
DAK
NO WAY!
DAKKA
SHK
NO!
HEY!

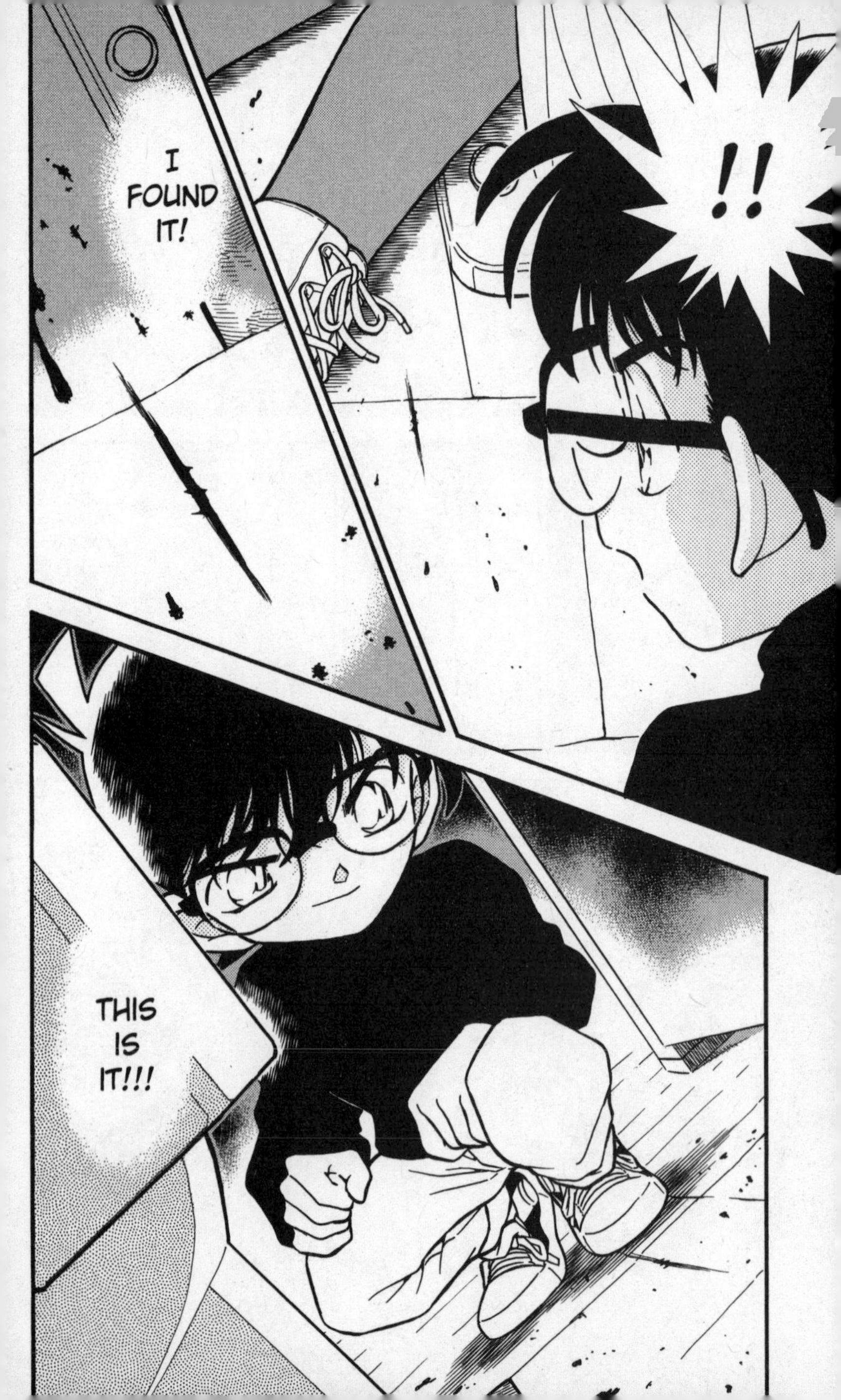
!!
I FOUND IT!
THIS IS IT!!!

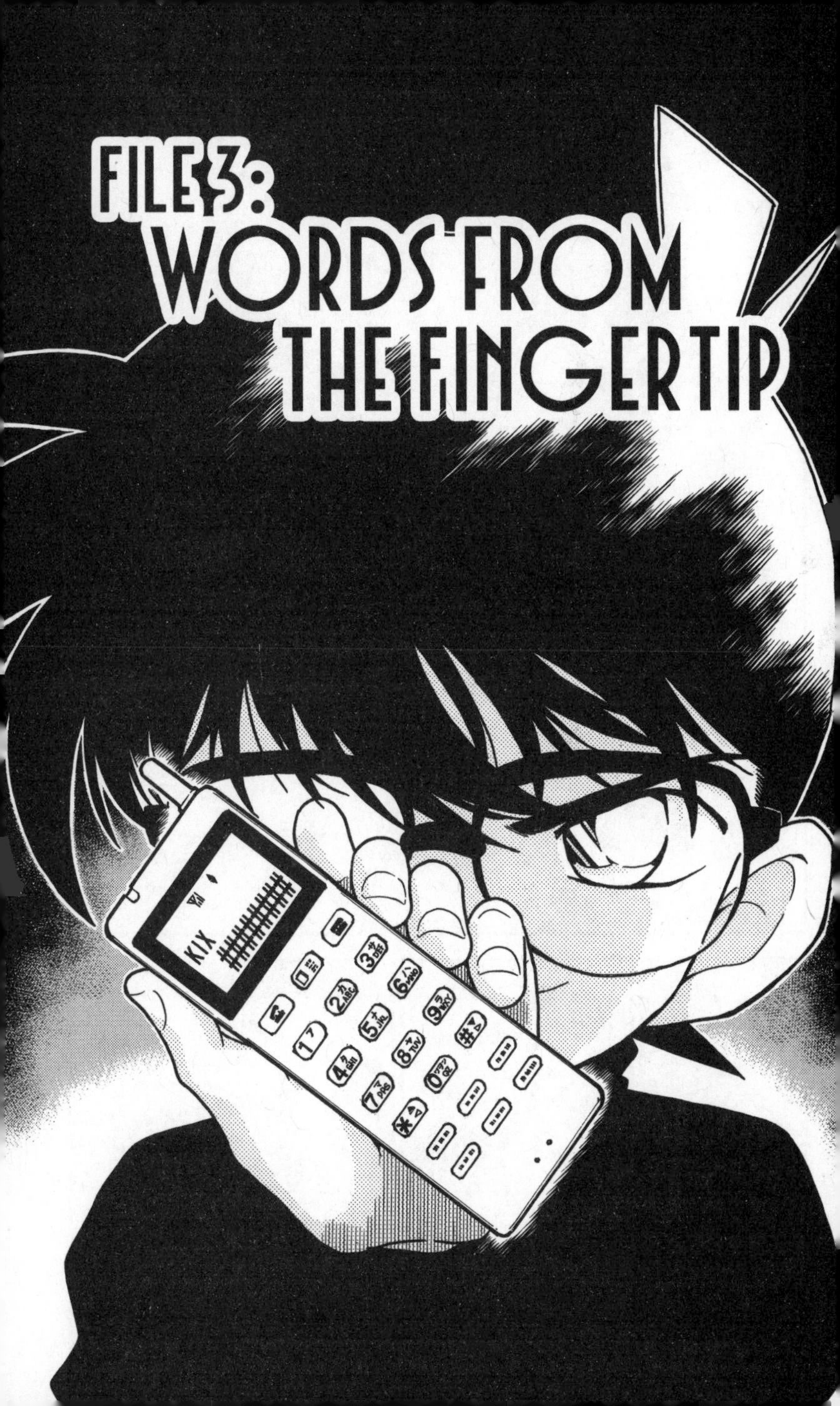
FILE 3:
WORDS FROM THE FINGERTIP
KIX

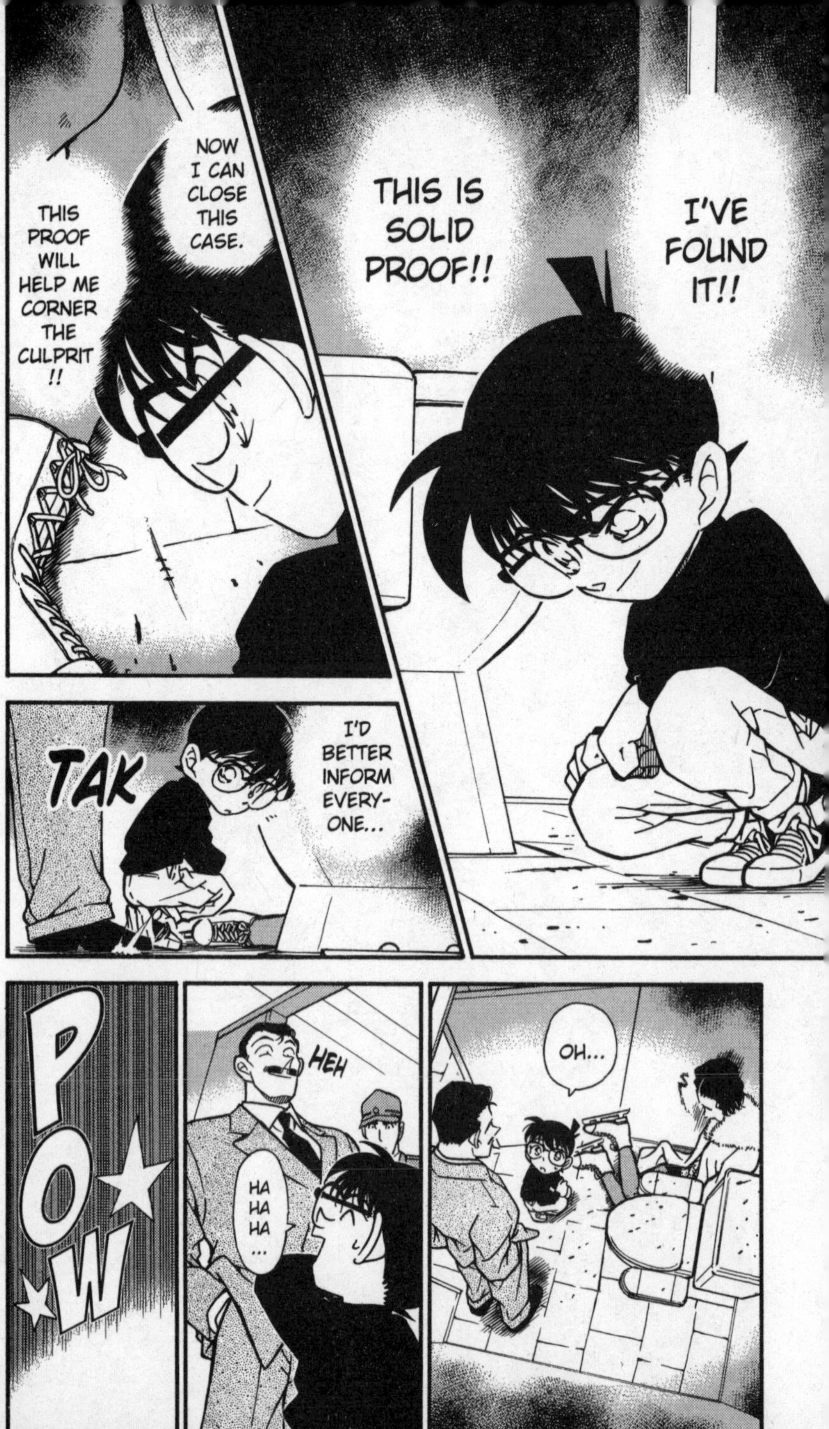
I'VE FOUND IT!!
THIS IS SOLID PROOF!!
NOW I CAN CLOSE THIS CASE.
THIS PROOF WILL HELP ME CORNER THE CULPRIT!!
I'D BETTER INFORM EVERY-ONE...
TAK
OH...
HEH
HA HA HA ...
POW

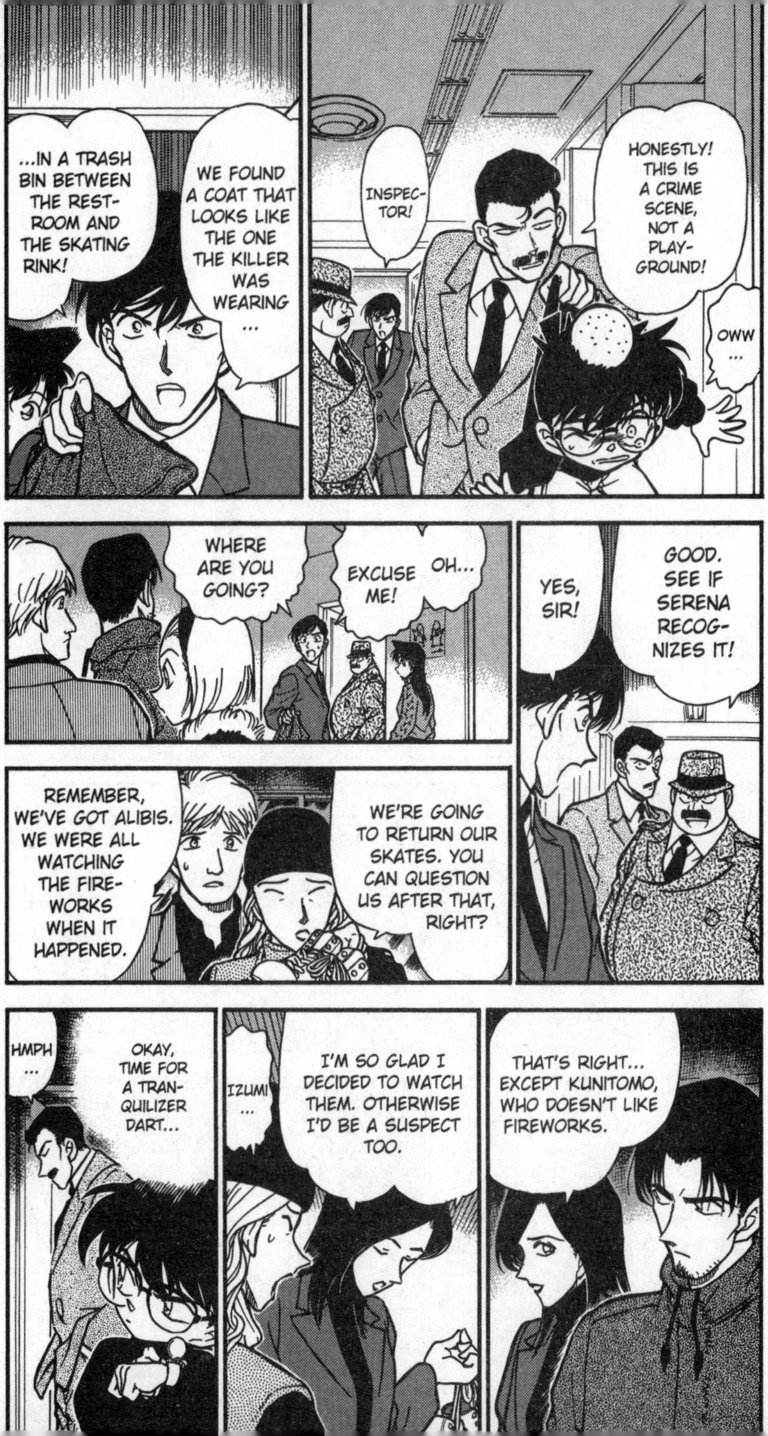
HONESTLY! THIS IS A CRIME SCENE, NOT A PLAYGROUND!
OWW ...
INSPECTOR!
WE FOUND A COAT THAT LOOKS LIKE THE ONE THE KILLER WAS WEARING ...
...IN A TRASH BIN BETWEEN THE RESTROOM AND THE SKATING RINK!
GOOD. SEE IF SERENA RECOGNIZES IT!
YES, SIR!
OH...
EXCUSE ME!
WHERE ARE YOU GOING?
WE'RE GOING TO RETURN OUR SKATES. YOU CAN QUESTION US AFTER THAT, RIGHT?
REMEMBER, WE'VE GOT ALIBIS. WE WERE ALL WATCHING THE FIREWORKS WHEN IT HAPPENED.
THAT'S RIGHT... EXCEPT KUNITOMO, WHO DOESN'T LIKE FIREWORKS.
I'M SO GLAD I DECIDED TO WATCH THEM. OTHERWISE I'D BE A SUSPECT TOO.
IZUMI ...
OKAY, TIME FOR A TRANQUILIZER DART...
HMPH ...

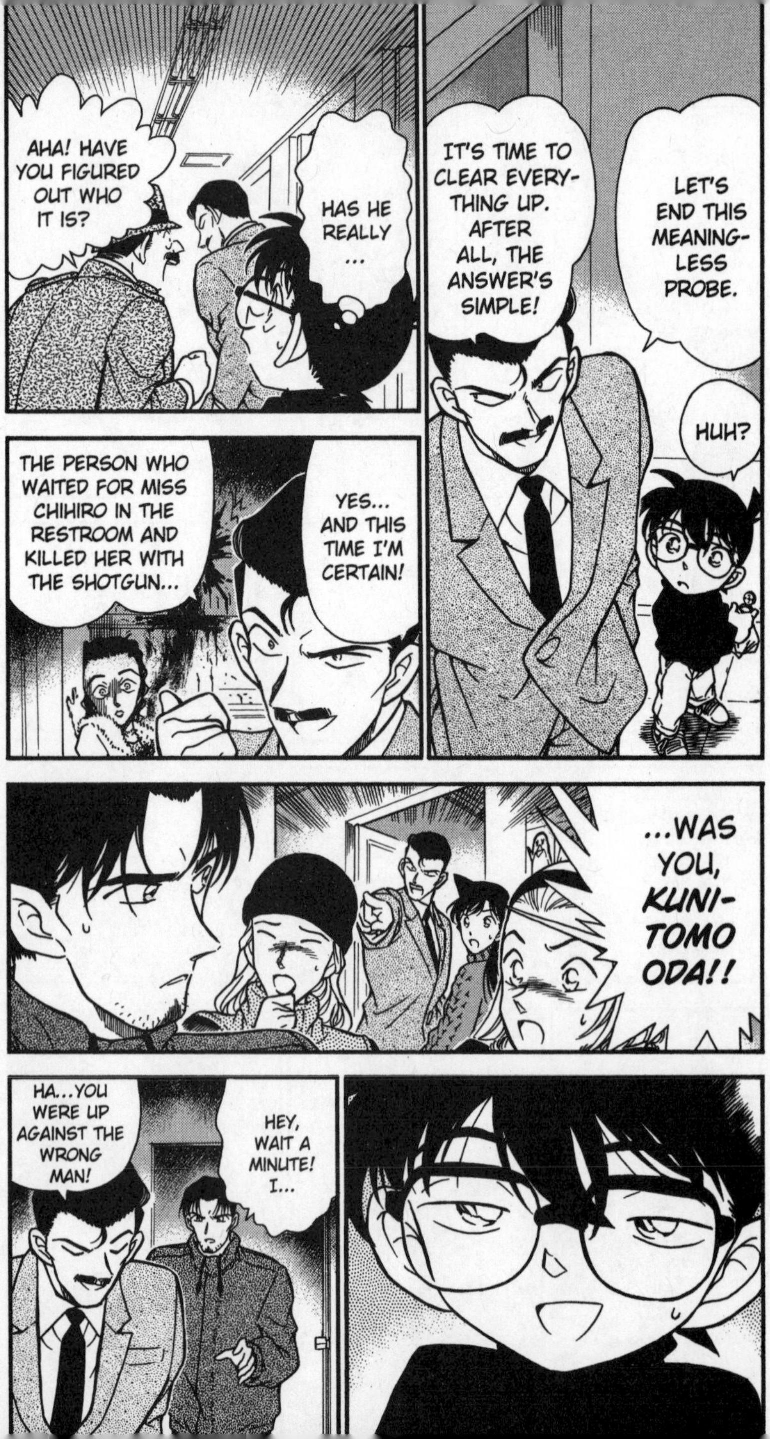
LET'S END THIS MEANING-LESS PROBE.
IT'S TIME TO CLEAR EVERY-THING UP. AFTER ALL, THE ANSWER'S SIMPLE!
HUH?
HAS HE REALLY ...
AHA! HAVE YOU FIGURED OUT WHO IT IS?
YES... AND THIS TIME I'M CERTAIN!
THE PERSON WHO WAITED FOR MISS CHIHIRO IN THE RESTROOM AND KILLED HER WITH THE SHOTGUN...
...WAS YOU, KUNI-TOMO ODA!!
HEY, WAIT A MINUTE! I...
HA...YOU WERE UP AGAINST THE WRONG MAN!

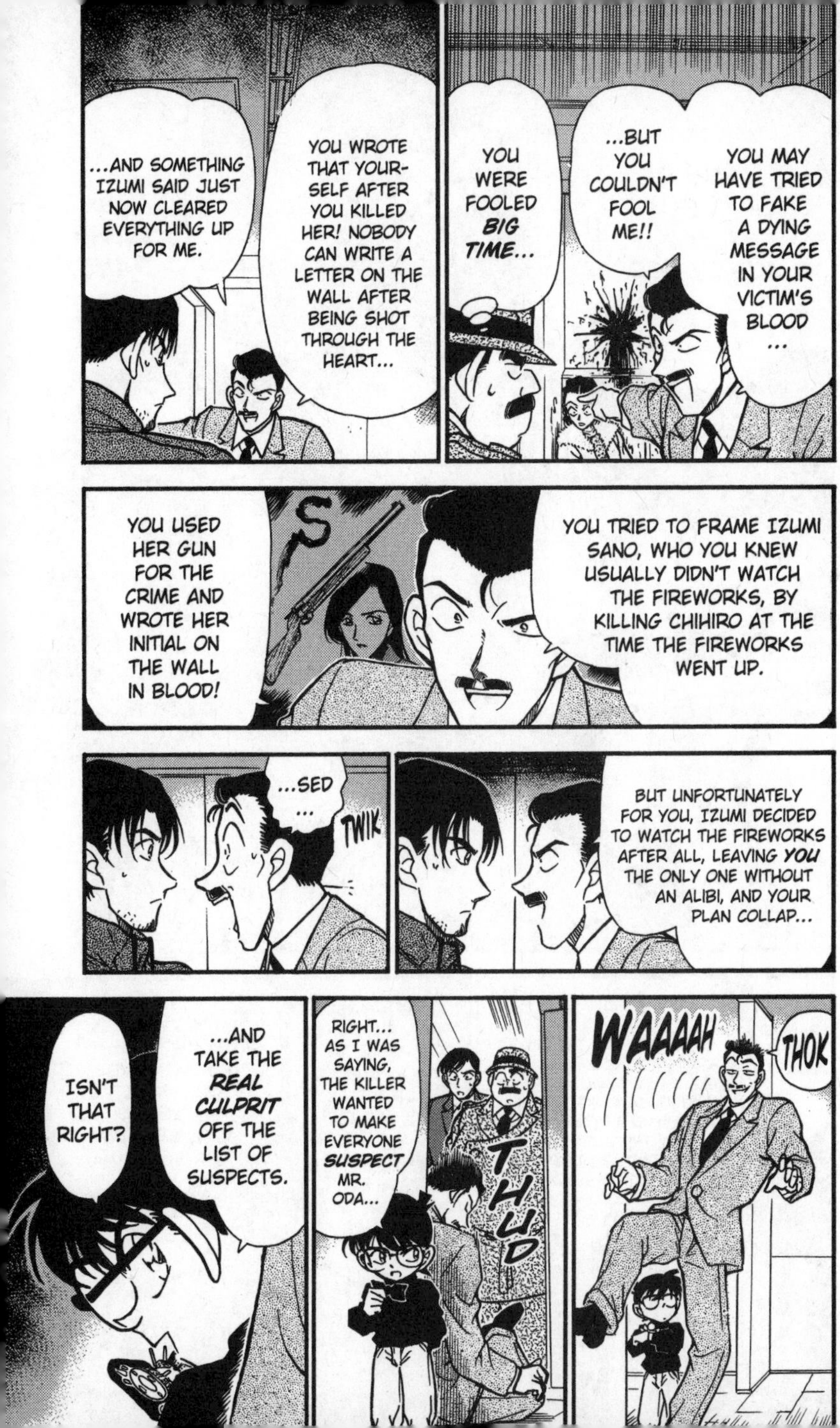
YOU MAY HAVE TRIED TO FAKE A DYING MESSAGE IN YOUR VICTIM'S BLOOD ...
...BUT YOU COULDN'T FOOL ME!!
YOU WERE FOOLED BIG TIME...
YOU WROTE THAT YOURSELF AFTER YOU KILLED HER! NOBODY CAN WRITE A LETTER ON THE WALL AFTER BEING SHOT THROUGH THE HEART...
...AND SOMETHING IZUMI SAID JUST NOW CLEARED EVERYTHING UP FOR ME.
YOU TRIED TO FRAME IZUMI SANO, WHO YOU KNEW USUALLY DIDN'T WATCH THE FIREWORKS, BY KILLING CHIHIRO AT THE TIME THE FIREWORKS WENT UP.
YOU USED HER GUN FOR THE CRIME AND WROTE HER INITIAL ON THE WALL IN BLOOD!
BUT UNFORTUNATELY FOR YOU, IZUMI DECIDED TO WATCH THE FIREWORKS AFTER ALL, LEAVING YOU THE ONLY ONE WITHOUT AN ALIBI, AND YOUR PLAN COLLAP...
...SED ...
TWIK
THOK
WAAAAH
RIGHT... AS I WAS SAYING, THE KILLER WANTED TO MAKE EVERYONE SUSPECT MR. ODA...
THUD
...AND TAKE THE REAL CULPRIT OFF THE LIST OF SUSPECTS.
ISN'T THAT RIGHT?

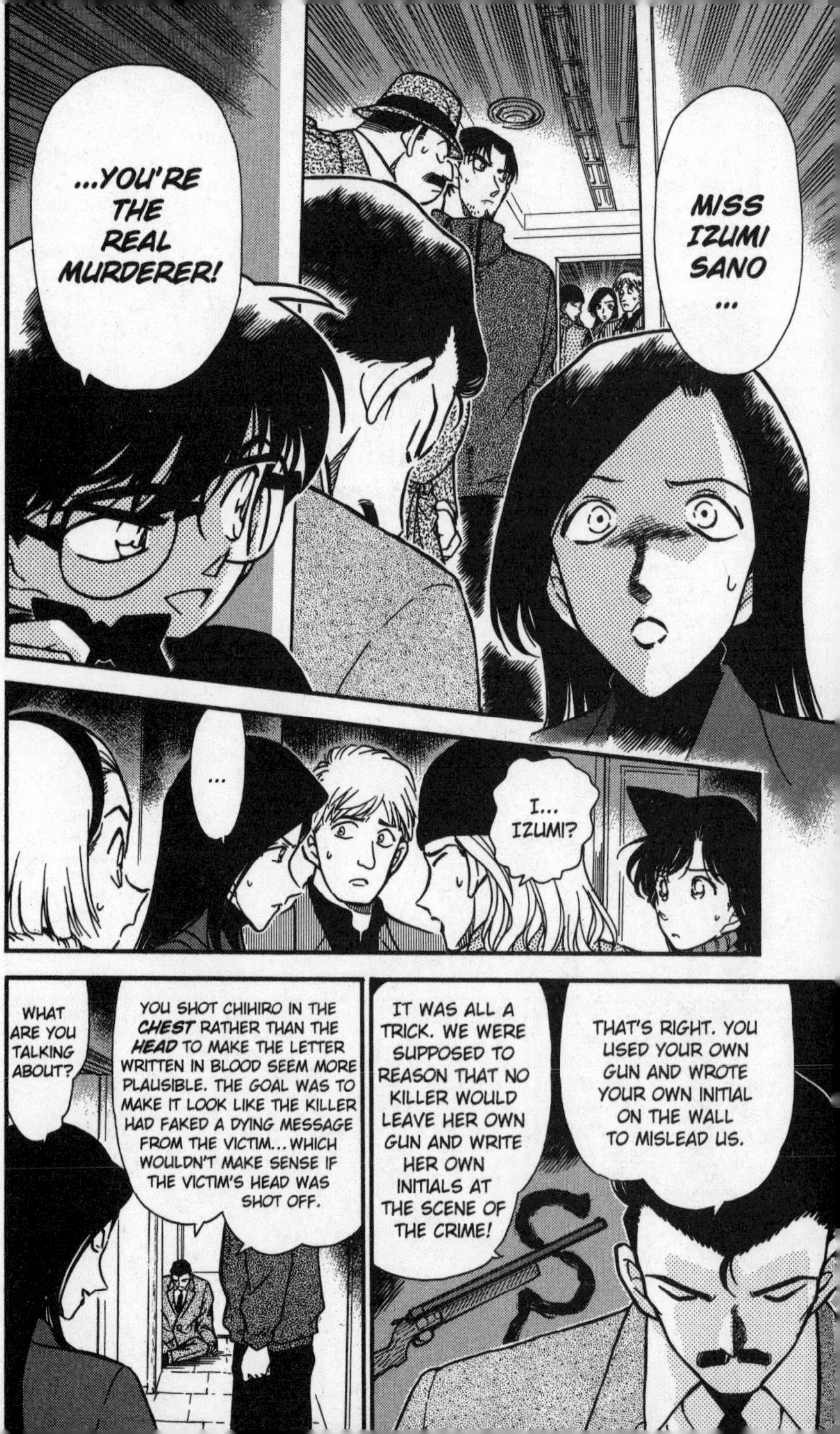
MISS IZUMI SANO ...
...YOU'RE THE REAL MURDERER!
I... IZUMI?
...
THAT'S RIGHT. YOU USED YOUR OWN GUN AND WROTE YOUR OWN INITIAL ON THE WALL TO MISLEAD US.
IT WAS ALL A TRICK. WE WERE SUPPOSED TO REASON THAT NO KILLER WOULD LEAVE HER OWN GUN AND WRITE HER OWN INITIALS AT THE SCENE OF THE CRIME!
YOU SHOT CHIHIRO IN THE CHEST RATHER THAN THE HEAD TO MAKE THE LETTER WRITTEN IN BLOOD SEEM MORE PLAUSIBLE. THE GOAL WAS TO MAKE IT LOOK LIKE THE KILLER HAD FAKED A DYING MESSAGE FROM THE VICTIM... WHICH WOULDN'T MAKE SENSE IF THE VICTIM'S HEAD WAS SHOT OFF.
WHAT ARE YOU TALKING ABOUT?

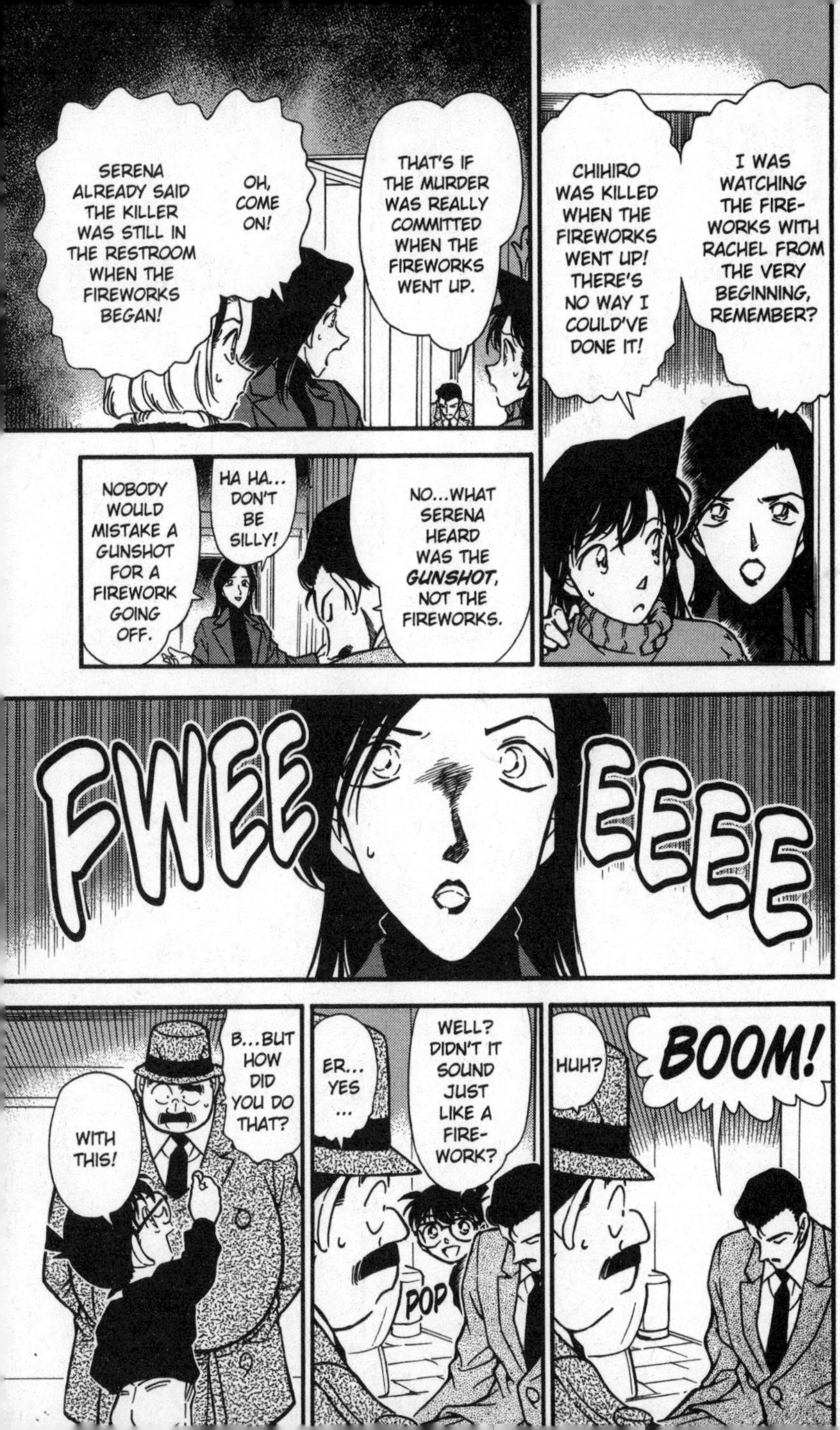
I WAS WATCHING THE FIRE-WORKS WITH RACHEL FROM THE VERY BEGINNING, REMEMBER?
CHIHIRO WAS KILLED WHEN THE FIREWORKS WENT UP! THERE'S NO WAY I COULD'VE DONE IT!
THAT'S IF THE MURDER WAS REALLY COMMITTED WHEN THE FIREWORKS WENT UP.
OH, COME ON!
SERENA ALREADY SAID THE KILLER WAS STILL IN THE RESTROOM WHEN THE FIREWORKS BEGAN!
NO...WHAT SERENA HEARD WAS THE *GUNSHOT*, NOT THE FIREWORKS.
HA HA... DON'T BE SILLY!
NOBODY WOULD MISTAKE A GUNSHOT FOR A FIREWORK GOING OFF.
FWEE EEEE
BOOM!
HUH?
WELL? DIDN'T IT SOUND JUST LIKE A FIRE-WORK?
ER... YES...
POP
B...BUT HOW DID YOU DO THAT?
WITH THIS!

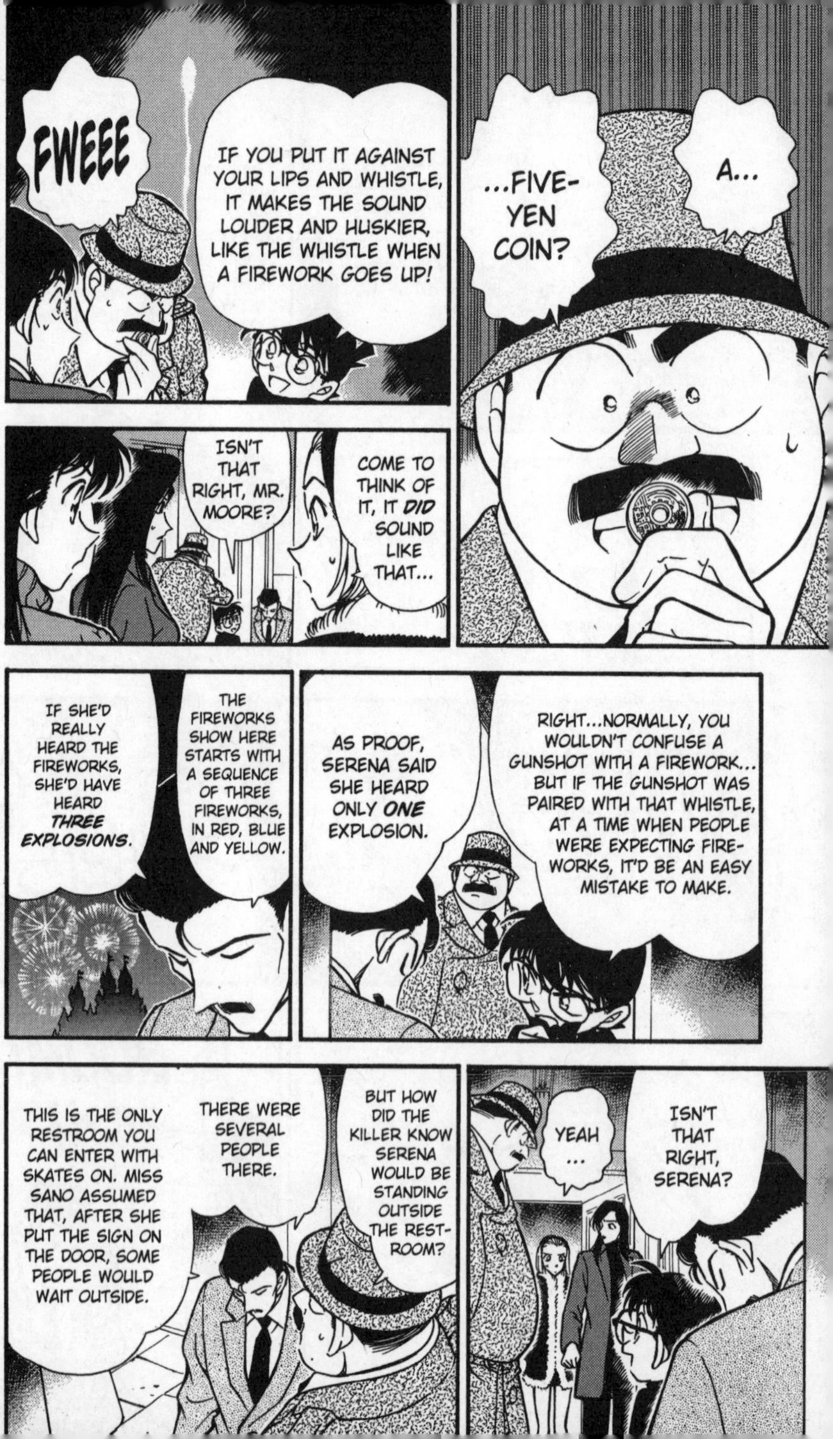
A...
...FIVE-YEN COIN?
IF YOU PUT IT AGAINST YOUR LIPS AND WHISTLE, IT MAKES THE SOUND LOUDER AND HUSKIER, LIKE THE WHISTLE WHEN A FIREWORK GOES UP!
FWEEE
COME TO THINK OF IT, IT *DID* SOUND LIKE THAT...
ISN'T THAT RIGHT, MR. MOORE?
RIGHT...NORMALLY, YOU WOULDN'T CONFUSE A GUNSHOT WITH A FIREWORK... BUT IF THE GUNSHOT WAS PAIRED WITH THAT WHISTLE, AT A TIME WHEN PEOPLE WERE EXPECTING FIREWORKS, IT'D BE AN EASY MISTAKE TO MAKE.
AS PROOF, SERENA SAID SHE HEARD ONLY ***ONE*** EXPLOSION.
THE FIREWORKS SHOW HERE STARTS WITH A SEQUENCE OF THREE FIREWORKS, IN RED, BLUE AND YELLOW.
IF SHE'D REALLY HEARD THE FIREWORKS, SHE'D HAVE HEARD ***THREE EXPLOSIONS***.
ISN'T THAT RIGHT, SERENA?
YEAH ...
BUT HOW DID THE KILLER KNOW SERENA WOULD BE STANDING OUTSIDE THE RESTROOM?
THERE WERE SEVERAL PEOPLE THERE.
THIS IS THE ONLY RESTROOM YOU CAN ENTER WITH SKATES ON. MISS SANO ASSUMED THAT, AFTER SHE PUT THE SIGN ON THE DOOR, SOME PEOPLE WOULD WAIT OUTSIDE.

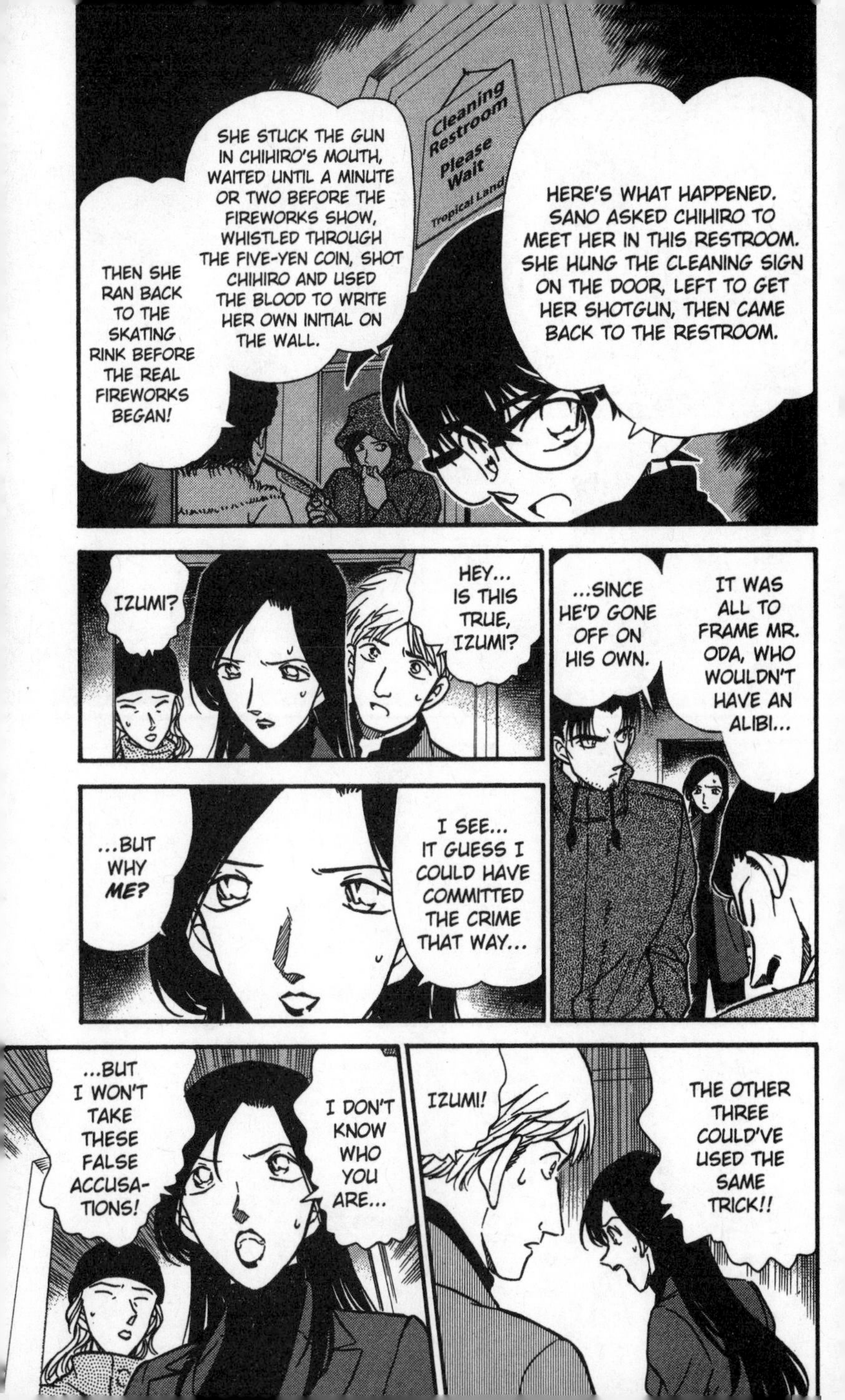
HERE'S WHAT HAPPENED. SANO ASKED CHIHIRO TO MEET HER IN THIS RESTROOM. SHE HUNG THE CLEANING SIGN ON THE DOOR, LEFT TO GET HER SHOTGUN, THEN CAME BACK TO THE RESTROOM.
Cleaning Restroom Please Wait Tropical Land
SHE STUCK THE GUN IN CHIHIRO'S MOUTH, WAITED UNTIL A MINUTE OR TWO BEFORE THE FIREWORKS SHOW, WHISTLED THROUGH THE FIVE-YEN COIN, SHOT CHIHIRO AND USED THE BLOOD TO WRITE HER OWN INITIAL ON THE WALL.
THEN SHE RAN BACK TO THE SKATING RINK BEFORE THE REAL FIREWORKS BEGAN!
IT WAS ALL TO FRAME MR. ODA, WHO WOULDN'T HAVE AN ALIBI...
...SINCE HE'D GONE OFF ON HIS OWN.
HEY... IS THIS TRUE, IZUMI?
IZUMI?
I SEE... IT GUESS I COULD HAVE COMMITTED THE CRIME THAT WAY...
...BUT WHY *ME?*
THE OTHER THREE COULD'VE USED THE SAME TRICK!!
IZUMI!
I DON'T KNOW WHO YOU ARE...
...BUT I WON'T TAKE THESE FALSE ACCUSA-TIONS!

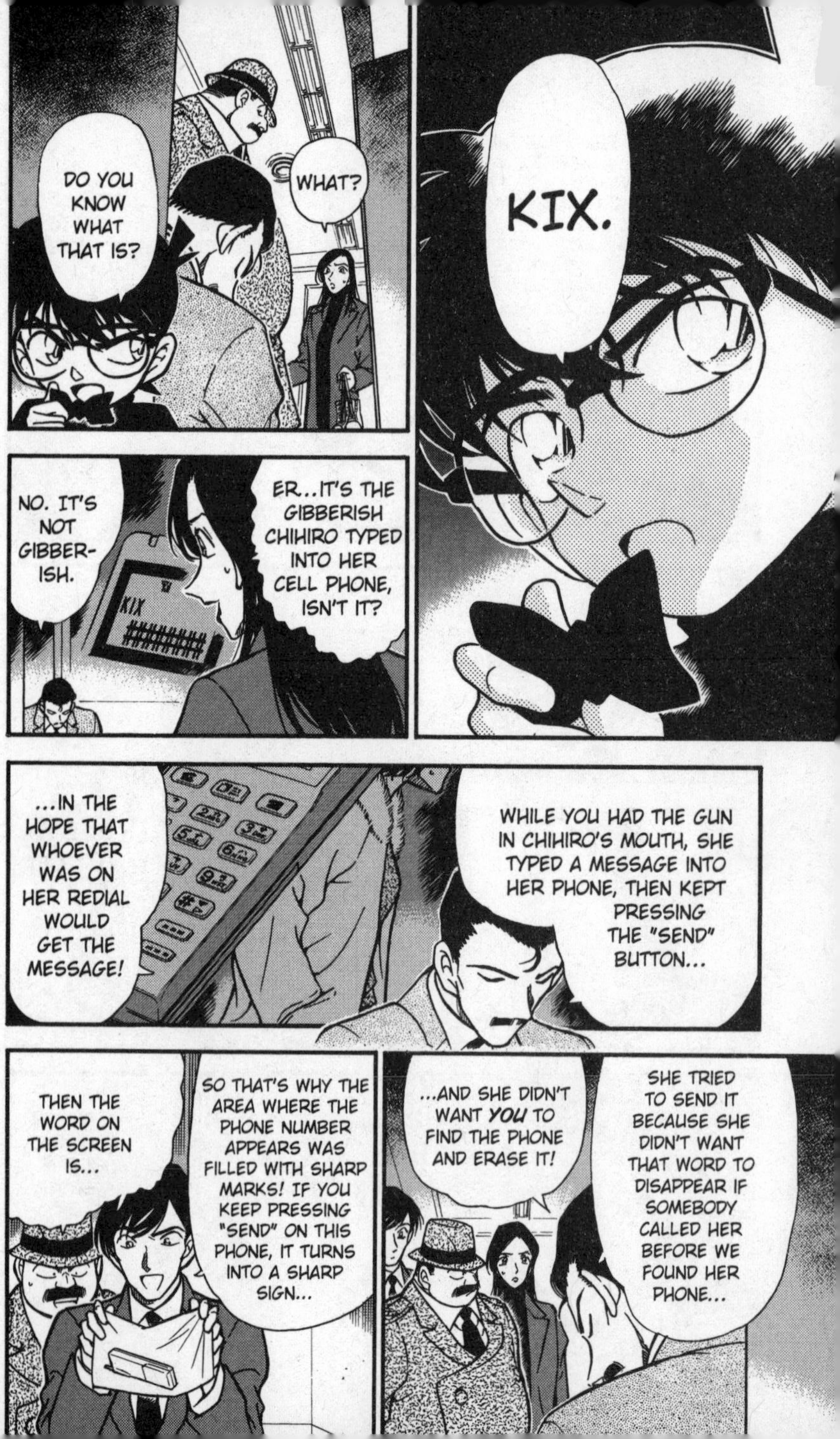
KIX.
WHAT?
DO YOU KNOW WHAT THAT IS?
ER...IT'S THE GIBBERISH CHIHIRO TYPED INTO HER CELL PHONE, ISN'T IT?
NO. IT'S NOT GIBBER-ISH.
KIX
WHILE YOU HAD THE GUN IN CHIHIRO'S MOUTH, SHE TYPED A MESSAGE INTO HER PHONE, THEN KEPT PRESSING THE "SEND" BUTTON...
...IN THE HOPE THAT WHOEVER WAS ON HER REDIAL WOULD GET THE MESSAGE!
SHE TRIED TO SEND IT BECAUSE SHE DIDN'T WANT THAT WORD TO DISAPPEAR IF SOMEBODY CALLED HER BEFORE WE FOUND HER PHONE...
...AND SHE DIDN'T WANT *YOU* TO FIND THE PHONE AND ERASE IT!
SO THAT'S WHY THE AREA WHERE THE PHONE NUMBER APPEARS WAS FILLED WITH SHARP MARKS! IF YOU KEEP PRESSING "SEND" ON THIS PHONE, IT TURNS INTO A SHARP SIGN...
THEN THE WORD ON THE SCREEN IS...

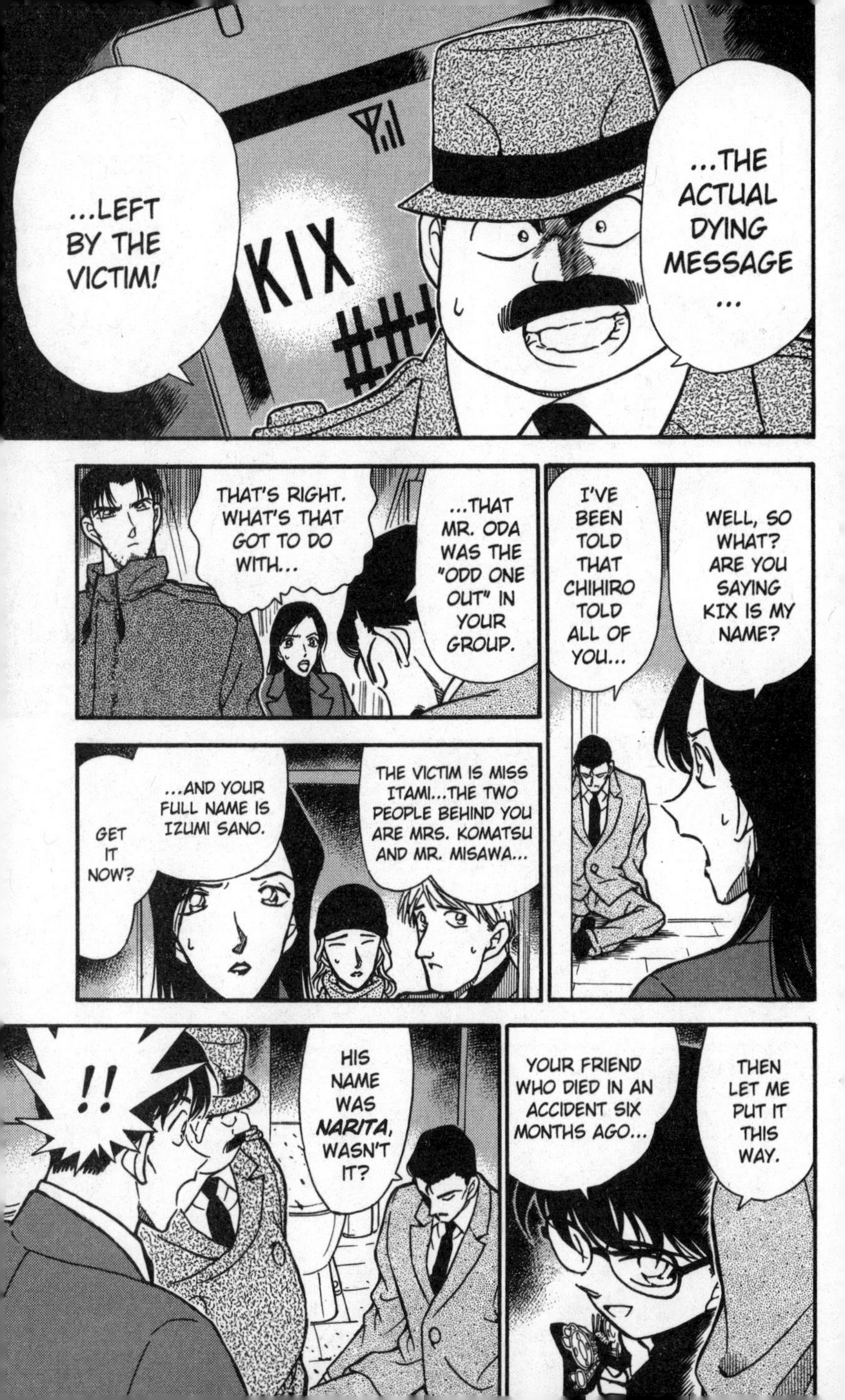
...THE ACTUAL DYING MESSAGE ...
KIX
...LEFT BY THE VICTIM!
WELL, SO WHAT? ARE YOU SAYING KIX IS MY NAME?
I'VE BEEN TOLD THAT CHIHIRO TOLD ALL OF YOU...
...THAT MR. ODA WAS THE "ODD ONE OUT" IN YOUR GROUP.
THAT'S RIGHT. WHAT'S THAT GOT TO DO WITH...
THE VICTIM IS MISS ITAMI...THE TWO PEOPLE BEHIND YOU ARE MRS. KOMATSU AND MR. MISAWA...
...AND YOUR FULL NAME IS IZUMI SANO.
GET IT NOW?
THEN LET ME PUT IT THIS WAY.
YOUR FRIEND WHO DIED IN AN ACCIDENT SIX MONTHS AGO...
HIS NAME WAS *NARITA*, WASN'T IT?
!!

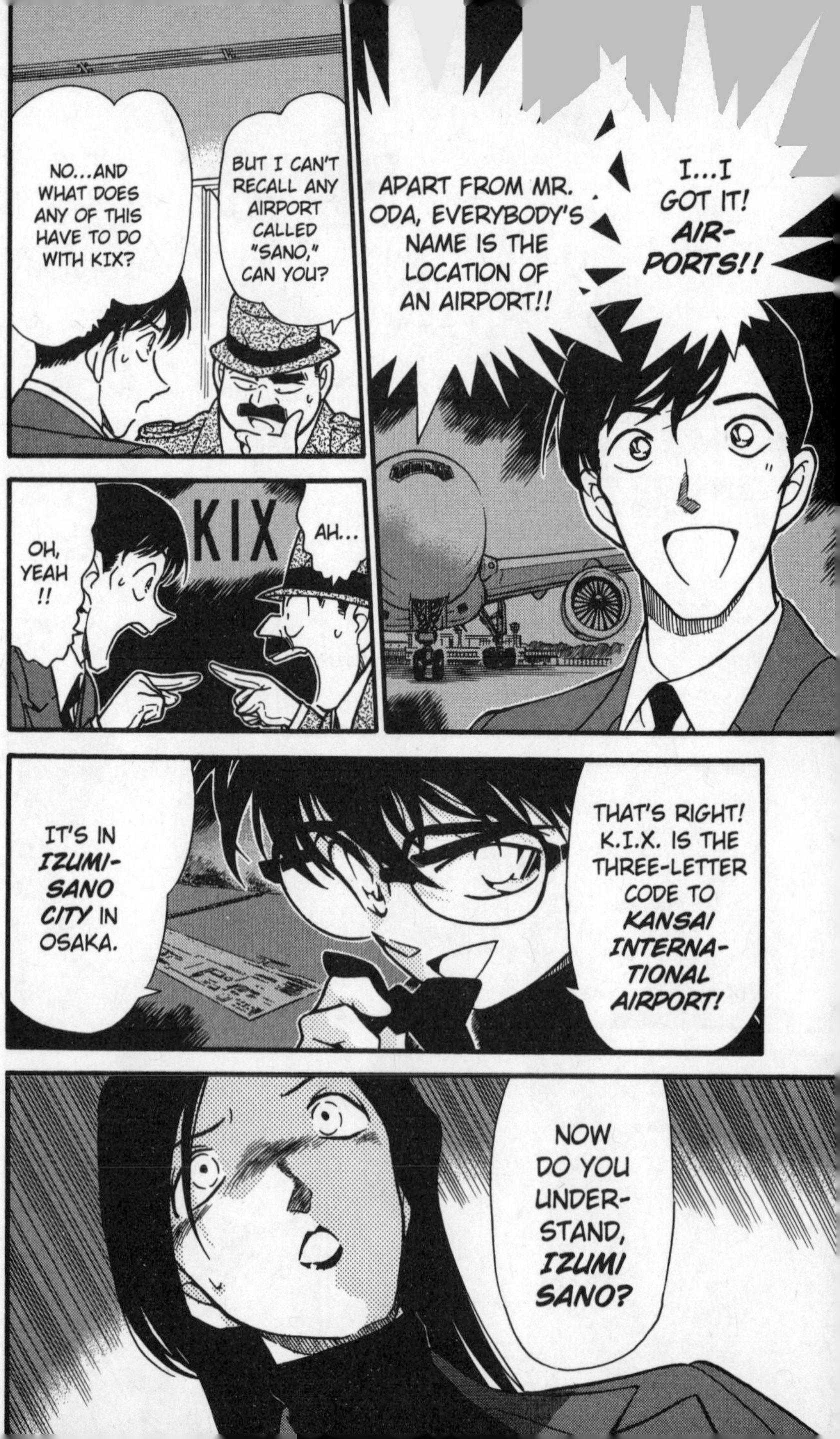
I...I GOT IT! AIR-PORTS!!
APART FROM MR. ODA, EVERYBODY'S NAME IS THE LOCATION OF AN AIRPORT!!
BUT I CAN'T RECALL ANY AIRPORT CALLED "SANO," CAN YOU?
NO...AND WHAT DOES ANY OF THIS HAVE TO DO WITH KIX?
KIX
AH...
OH, YEAH !!
THAT'S RIGHT! K.I.X. IS THE THREE-LETTER CODE TO KANSAI INTERNA-TIONAL AIRPORT!
IT'S IN IZUMI-SANO CITY IN OSAKA.
NOW DO YOU UNDER-STAND, IZUMI SANO?

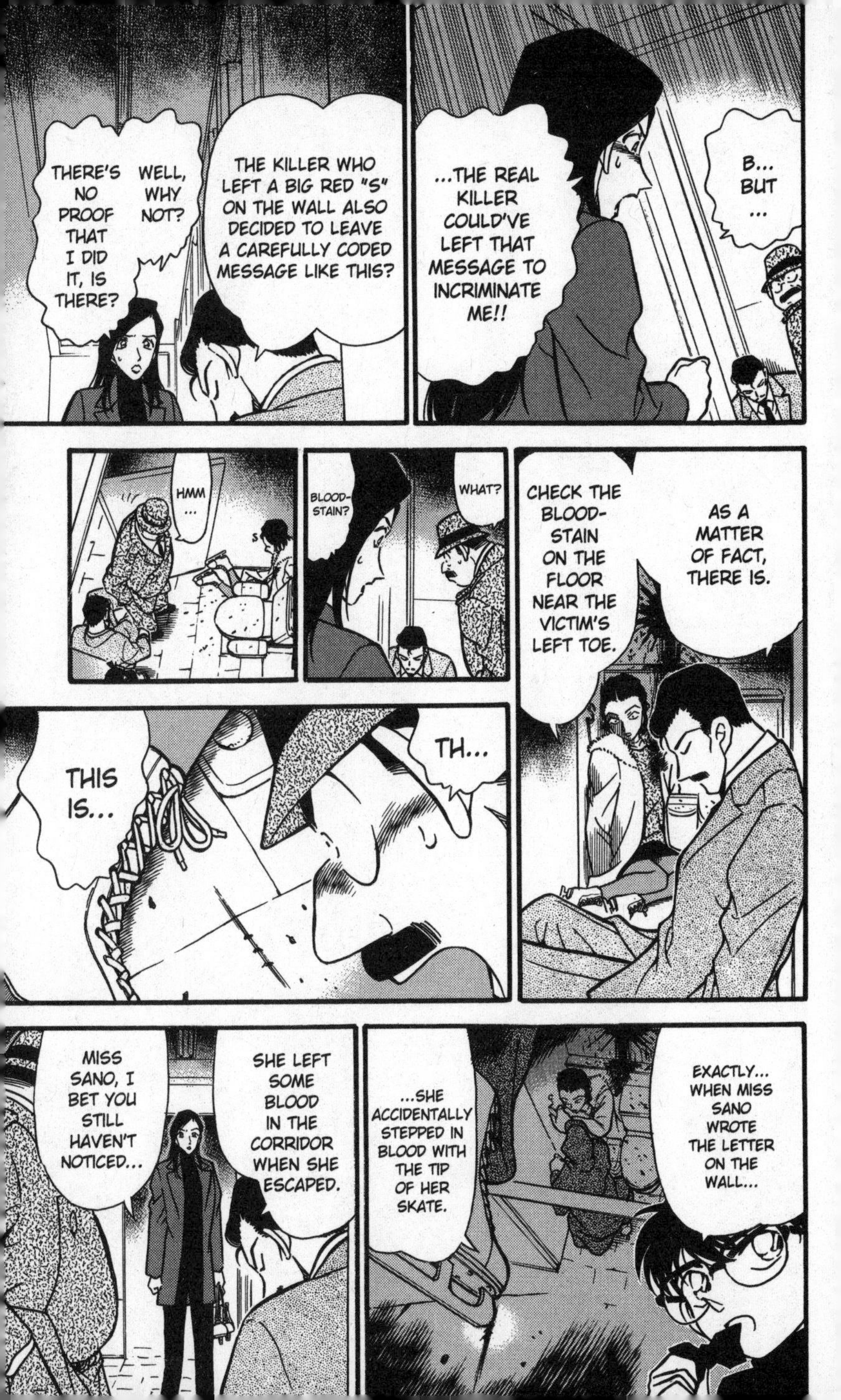
B... BUT ...
...THE REAL KILLER COULD'VE LEFT THAT MESSAGE TO INCRIMINATE ME!!
THE KILLER WHO LEFT A BIG RED "S" ON THE WALL ALSO DECIDED TO LEAVE A CAREFULLY CODED MESSAGE LIKE THIS?
WELL, WHY NOT?
THERE'S NO PROOF THAT I DID IT, IS THERE?
AS A MATTER OF FACT, THERE IS.
CHECK THE BLOOD-STAIN ON THE FLOOR NEAR THE VICTIM'S LEFT TOE.
WHAT?
BLOOD-STAIN?
HMM ...
TH...
THIS IS...
EXACTLY... WHEN MISS SANO WROTE THE LETTER ON THE WALL...
...SHE ACCIDENTALLY STEPPED IN BLOOD WITH THE TIP OF HER SKATE.
SHE LEFT SOME BLOOD IN THE CORRIDOR WHEN SHE ESCAPED.
MISS SANO, I BET YOU STILL HAVEN'T NOTICED...

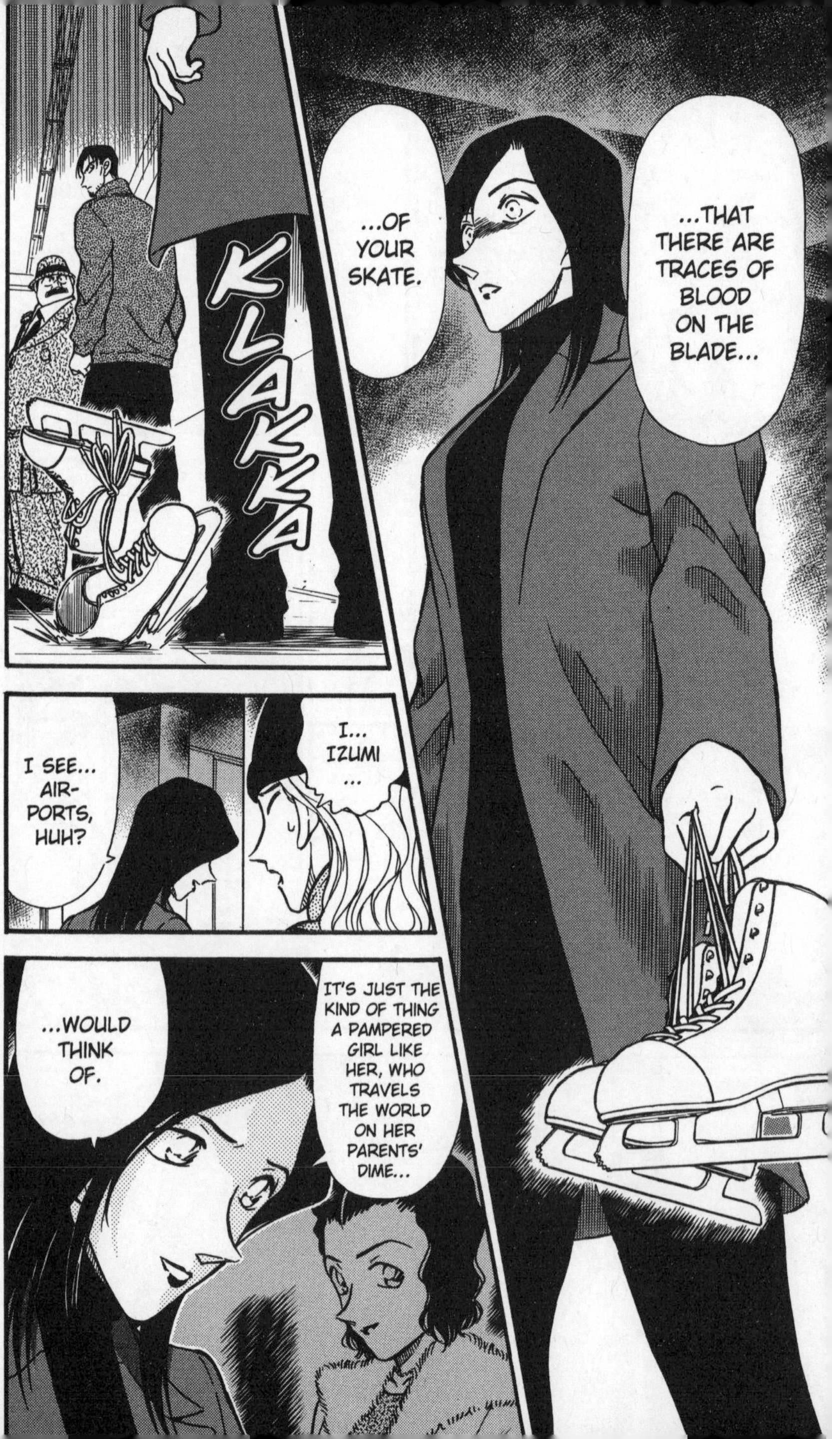
...THAT THERE ARE TRACES OF BLOOD ON THE BLADE...
...OF YOUR SKATE.
KLAKKA
I... IZUMI ...
I SEE... AIR-PORTS, HUH?
IT'S JUST THE KIND OF THING A PAMPERED GIRL LIKE HER, WHO TRAVELS THE WORLD ON HER PARENTS' DIME...
...WOULD THINK OF.

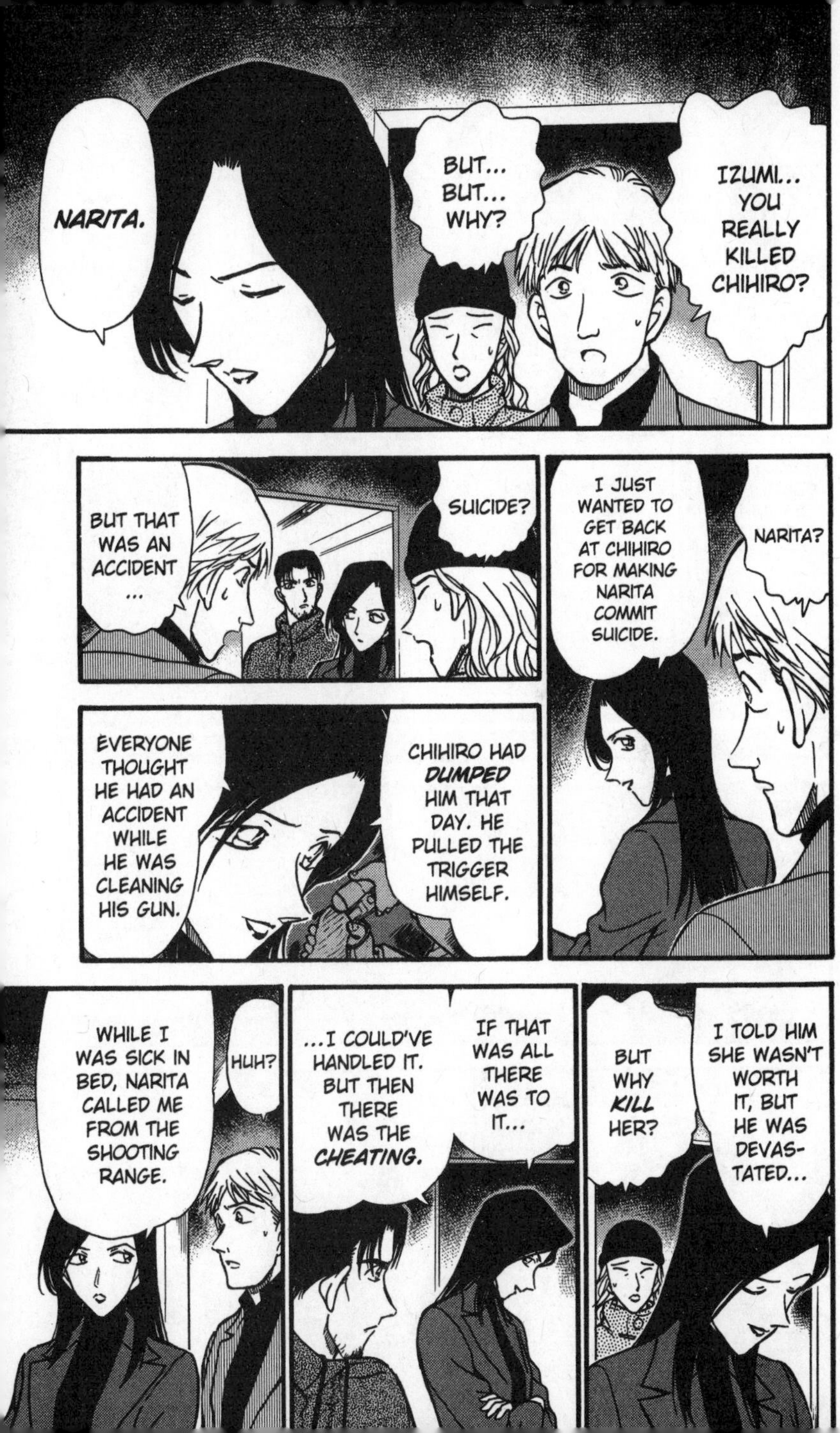
IZUMI... YOU REALLY KILLED CHIHIRO?
BUT... BUT... WHY?
NARITA.
NARITA?
I JUST WANTED TO GET BACK AT CHIHIRO FOR MAKING NARITA COMMIT SUICIDE.
SUICIDE?
BUT THAT WAS AN ACCIDENT ...
CHIHIRO HAD DUMPED HIM THAT DAY. HE PULLED THE TRIGGER HIMSELF.
EVERYONE THOUGHT HE HAD AN ACCIDENT WHILE HE WAS CLEANING HIS GUN.
I TOLD HIM SHE WASN'T WORTH IT, BUT HE WAS DEVAS-TATED...
BUT WHY KILL HER?
IF THAT WAS ALL THERE WAS TO IT...
...I COULD'VE HANDLED IT. BUT THEN THERE WAS THE CHEATING.
HUH?
WHILE I WAS SICK IN BED, NARITA CALLED ME FROM THE SHOOTING RANGE.

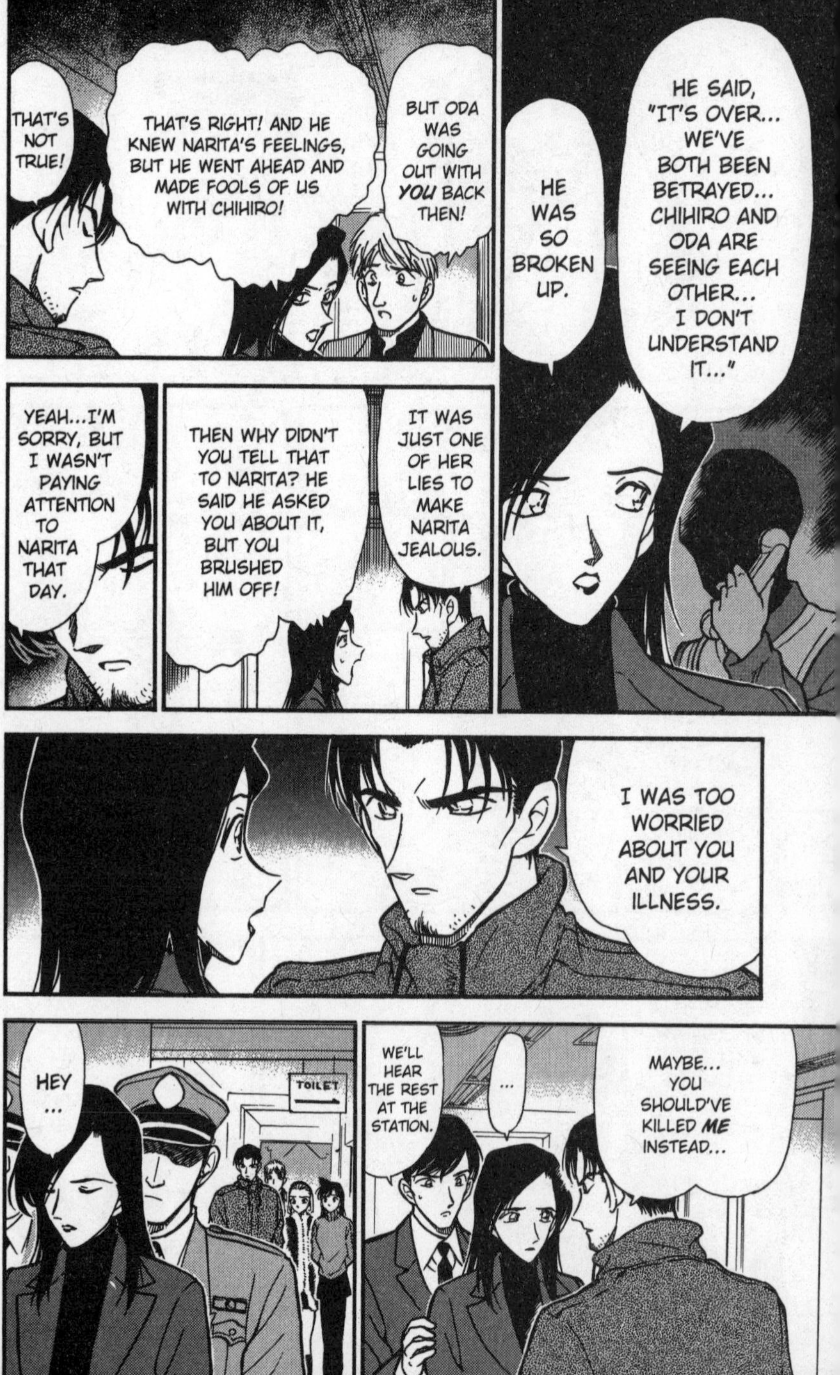

HE SAID, "IT'S OVER... WE'VE BOTH BEEN BETRAYED... CHIHIRO AND ODA ARE SEEING EACH OTHER... I DON'T UNDERSTAND IT..."
HE WAS SO BROKEN UP.
BUT ODA WAS GOING OUT WITH *YOU* BACK THEN!
THAT'S RIGHT! AND HE KNEW NARITA'S FEELINGS, BUT HE WENT AHEAD AND MADE FOOLS OF US WITH CHIHIRO!
THAT'S NOT TRUE!
IT WAS JUST ONE OF HER LIES TO MAKE NARITA JEALOUS.
THEN WHY DIDN'T YOU TELL THAT TO NARITA? HE SAID HE ASKED YOU ABOUT IT, BUT YOU BRUSHED HIM OFF!
YEAH...I'M SORRY, BUT I WASN'T PAYING ATTENTION TO NARITA THAT DAY.
I WAS TOO WORRIED ABOUT YOU AND YOUR ILLNESS.
MAYBE... YOU SHOULD'VE KILLED *ME* INSTEAD...
...
WE'LL HEAR THE REST AT THE STATION.
TOILET
HEY ...

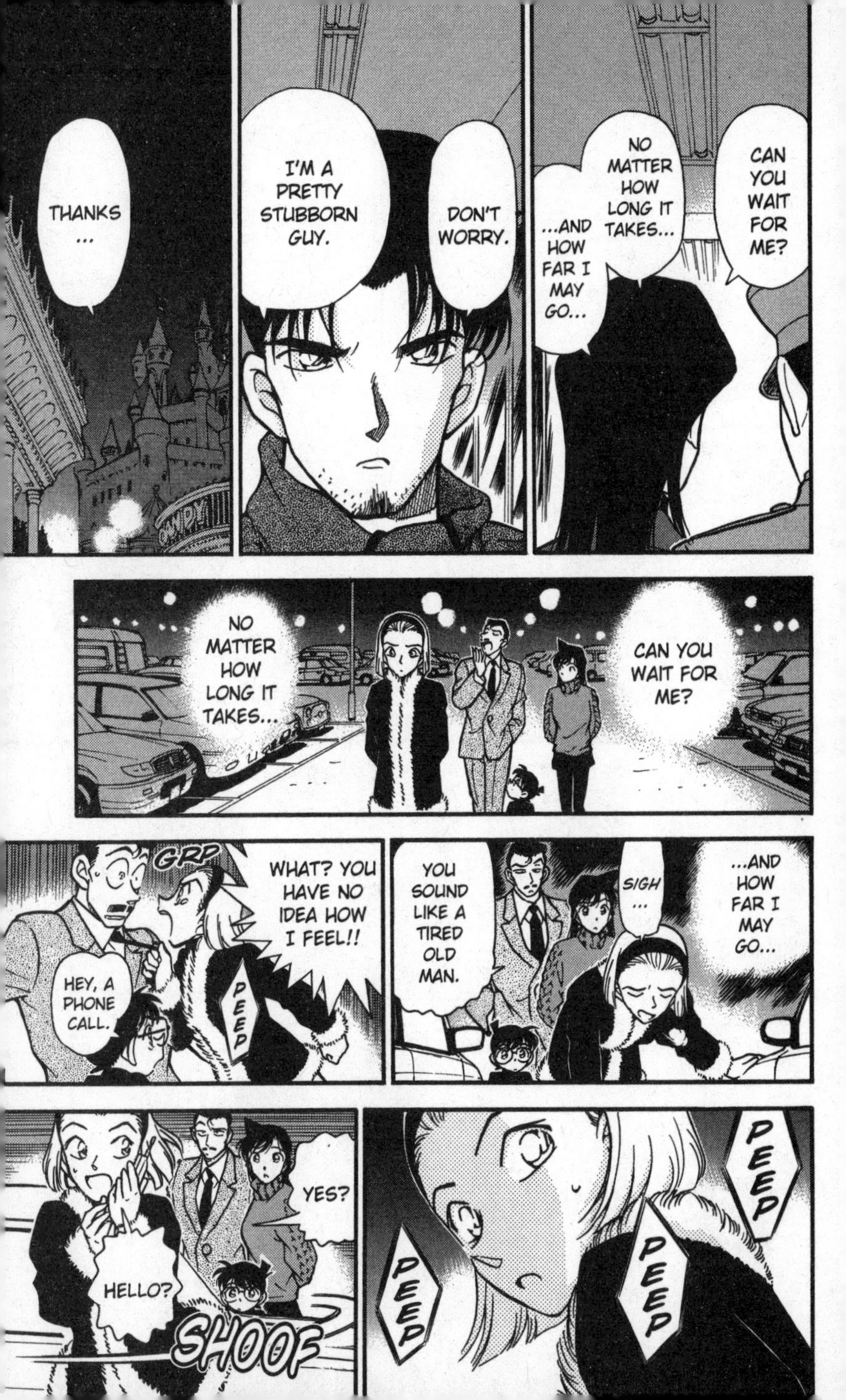
CAN YOU WAIT FOR ME?
NO MATTER HOW LONG IT TAKES...
...AND HOW FAR I MAY GO...
DON'T WORRY.
I'M A PRETTY STUBBORN GUY.
THANKS ...
CAN YOU WAIT FOR ME?
NO MATTER HOW LONG IT TAKES...
...AND HOW FAR I MAY GO...
SIGH ...
YOU SOUND LIKE A TIRED OLD MAN.
WHAT? YOU HAVE NO IDEA HOW I FEEL!!
GRP
PEEP
HEY, A PHONE CALL.
PEEP
PEEP
PEEP
YES?
HELLO?
SHOOF

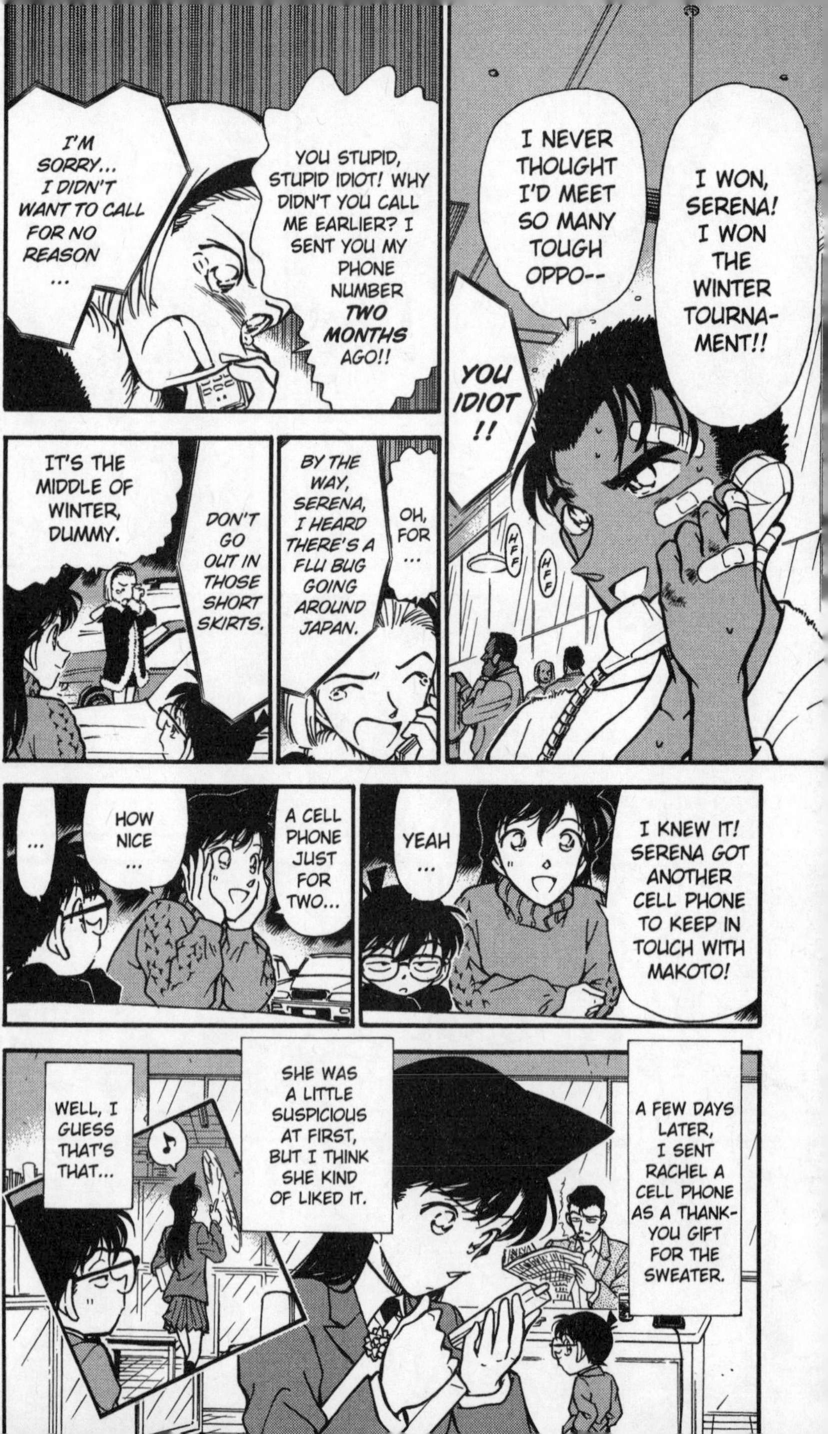
I WON, SERENA! I WON THE WINTER TOURNAMENT!!
I NEVER THOUGHT I'D MEET SO MANY TOUGH OPPO--
YOU IDIOT!!
HFF
HFF
YOU STUPID, STUPID IDIOT! WHY DIDN'T YOU CALL ME EARLIER? I SENT YOU MY PHONE NUMBER TWO MONTHS AGO!!
I'M SORRY... I DIDN'T WANT TO CALL FOR NO REASON...
OH, FOR ...
BY THE WAY, SERENA, I HEARD THERE'S A FLU BUG GOING AROUND JAPAN.
DON'T GO OUT IN THOSE SHORT SKIRTS.
IT'S THE MIDDLE OF WINTER, DUMMY.
I KNEW IT! SERENA GOT ANOTHER CELL PHONE TO KEEP IN TOUCH WITH MAKOTO!
YEAH ...
A CELL PHONE JUST FOR TWO...
HOW NICE ...
...
A FEW DAYS LATER, I SENT RACHEL A CELL PHONE AS A THANK-YOU GIFT FOR THE SWEATER.
SHE WAS A LITTLE SUSPICIOUS AT FIRST, BUT I THINK SHE KIND OF LIKED IT.
WELL, I GUESS THAT'S THAT...

FILE 4: THE SPIDER HOUSE

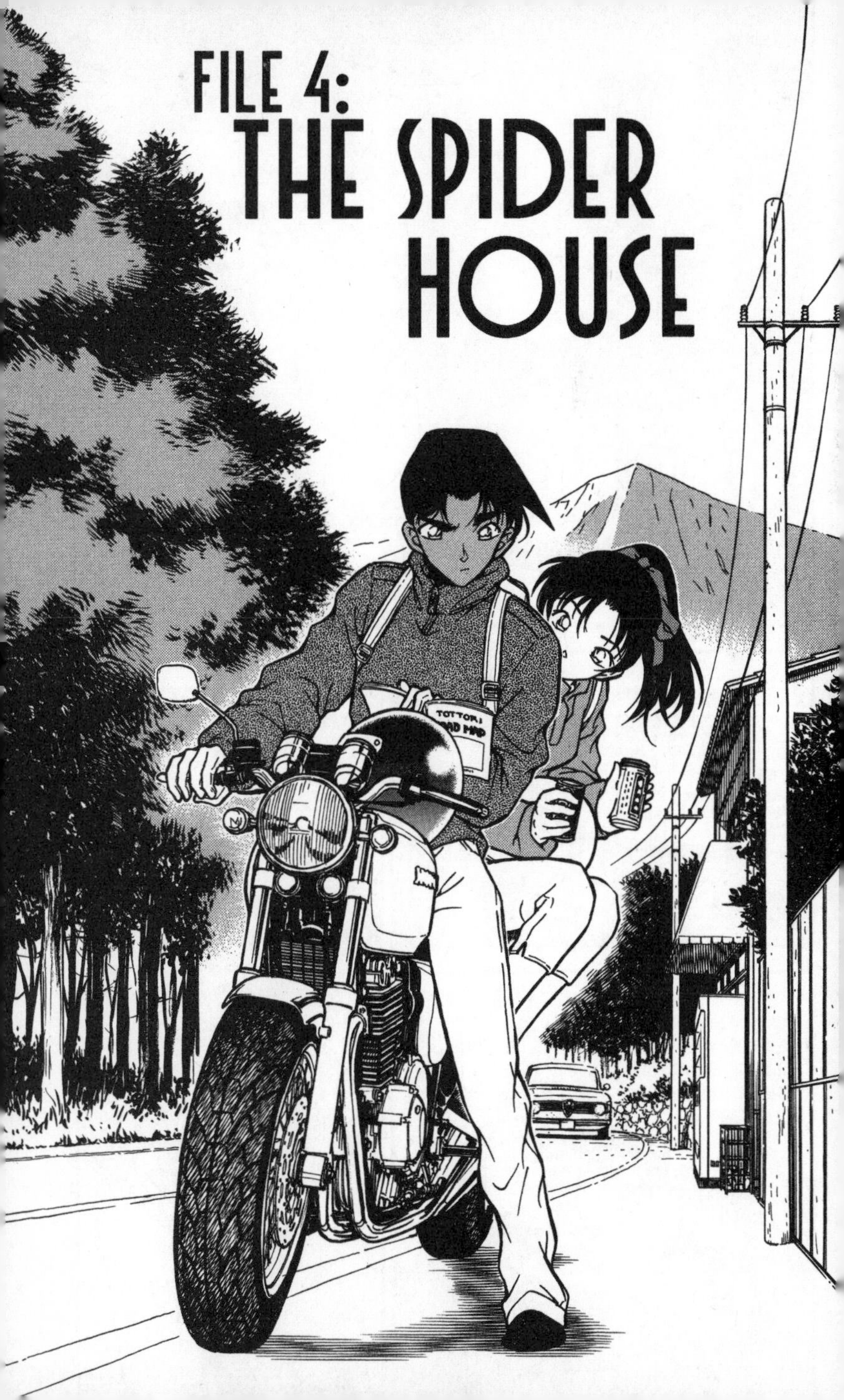
TOTTORI

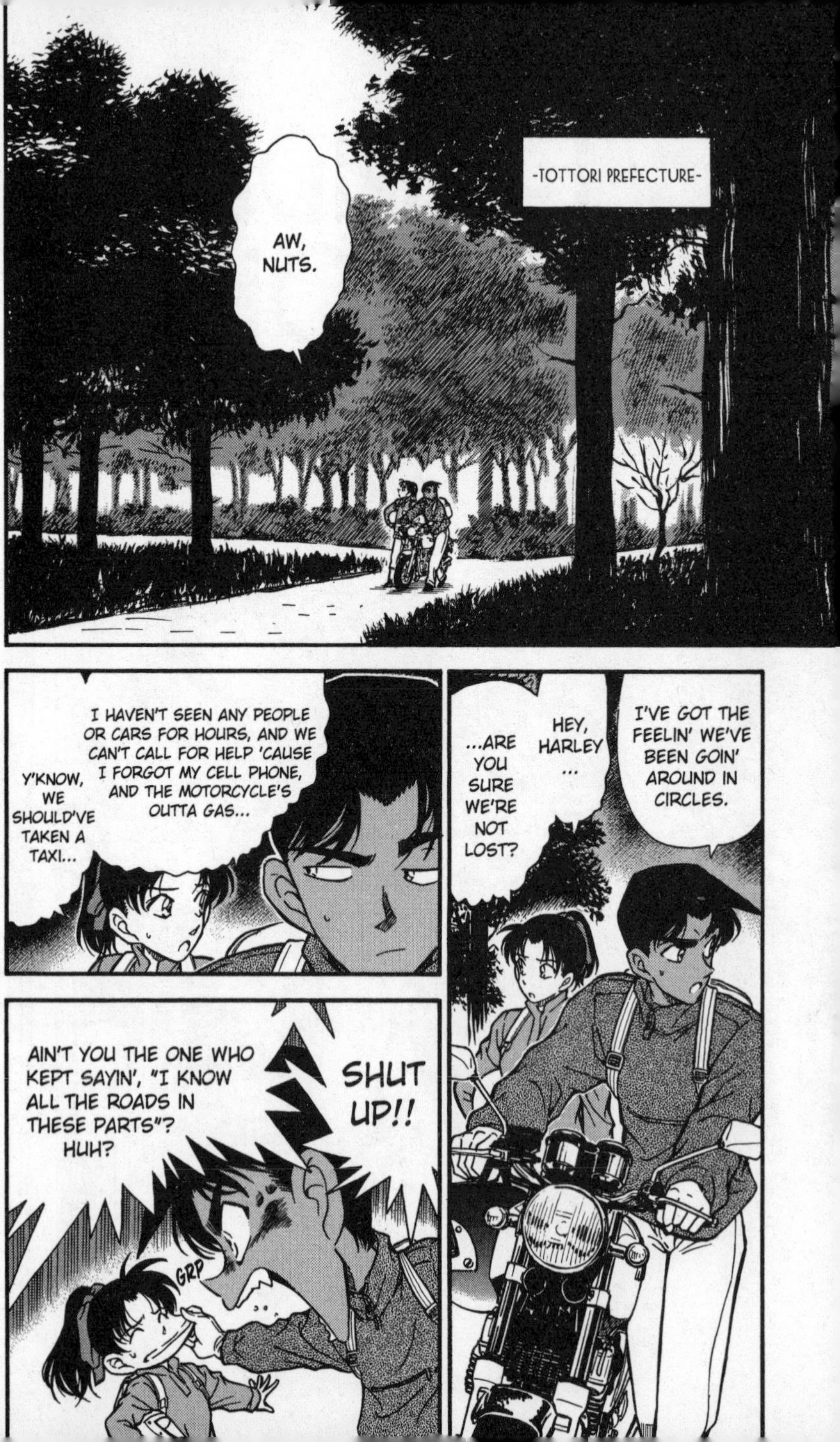
-TOTTORI PREFECTURE-
AW, NUTS.
I'VE GOT THE FEELIN' WE'VE BEEN GOIN' AROUND IN CIRCLES.
HEY, HARLEY ...
...ARE YOU SURE WE'RE NOT LOST?
I HAVEN'T SEEN ANY PEOPLE OR CARS FOR HOURS, AND WE CAN'T CALL FOR HELP 'CAUSE I FORGOT MY CELL PHONE, AND THE MOTORCYCLE'S OUTTA GAS...
Y'KNOW, WE SHOULD'VE TAKEN A TAXI...
SHUT UP!!
AIN'T YOU THE ONE WHO KEPT SAYIN', "I KNOW ALL THE ROADS IN THESE PARTS"? HUH?
GRP

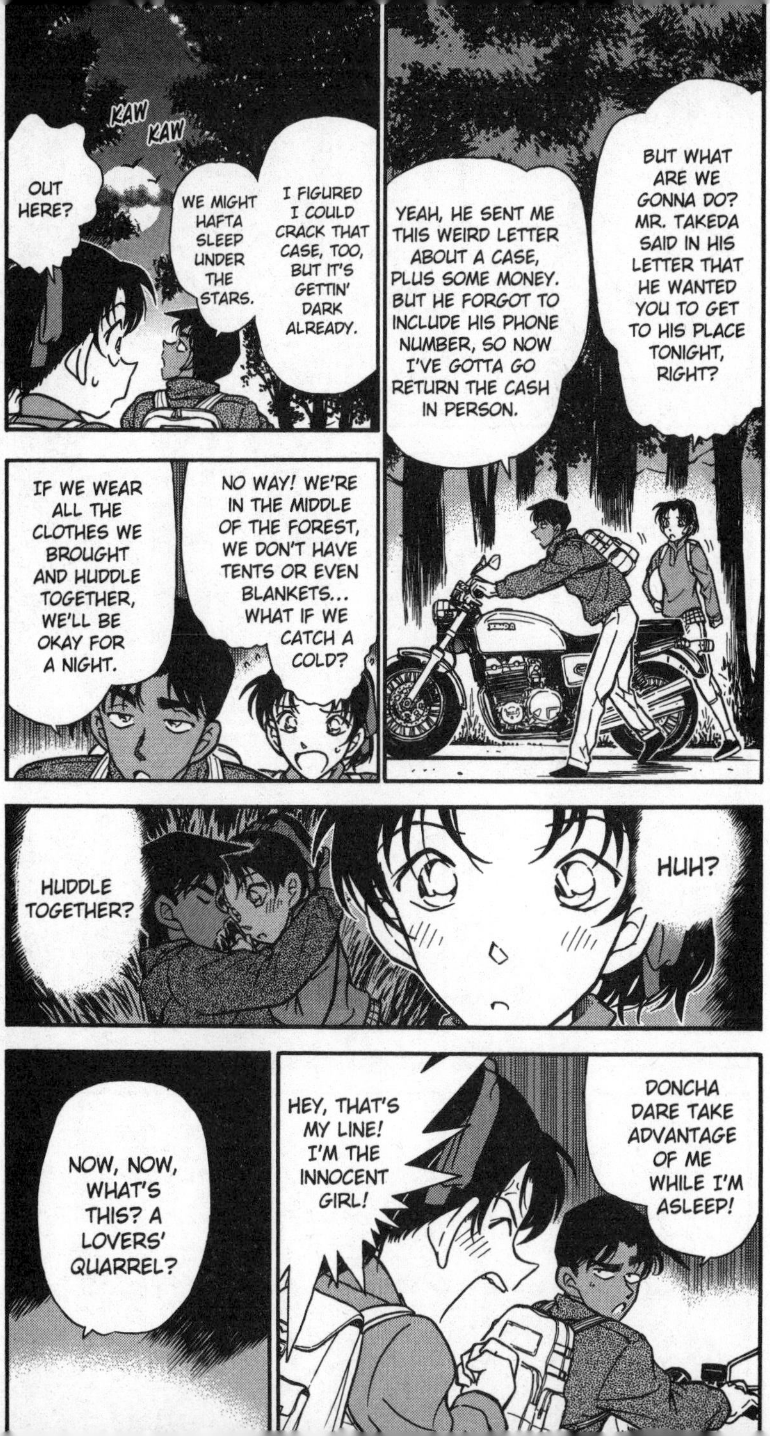

BUT WHAT ARE WE GONNA DO? MR. TAKEDA SAID IN HIS LETTER THAT HE WANTED YOU TO GET TO HIS PLACE TONIGHT, RIGHT?
YEAH, HE SENT ME THIS WEIRD LETTER ABOUT A CASE, PLUS SOME MONEY. BUT HE FORGOT TO INCLUDE HIS PHONE NUMBER, SO NOW I'VE GOTTA GO RETURN THE CASH IN PERSON.
KAW KAW
I FIGURED I COULD CRACK THAT CASE, TOO, BUT IT'S GETTIN' DARK ALREADY.
WE MIGHT HAFTA SLEEP UNDER THE STARS.
OUT HERE?
NO WAY! WE'RE IN THE MIDDLE OF THE FOREST, WE DON'T HAVE TENTS OR EVEN BLANKETS... WHAT IF WE CATCH A COLD?
IF WE WEAR ALL THE CLOTHES WE BROUGHT AND HUDDLE TOGETHER, WE'LL BE OKAY FOR A NIGHT.
HUH?
HUDDLE TOGETHER?
DONCHA DARE TAKE ADVANTAGE OF ME WHILE I'M ASLEEP!
HEY, THAT'S MY LINE! I'M THE INNOCENT GIRL!
NOW, NOW, WHAT'S THIS? A LOVERS' QUARREL?

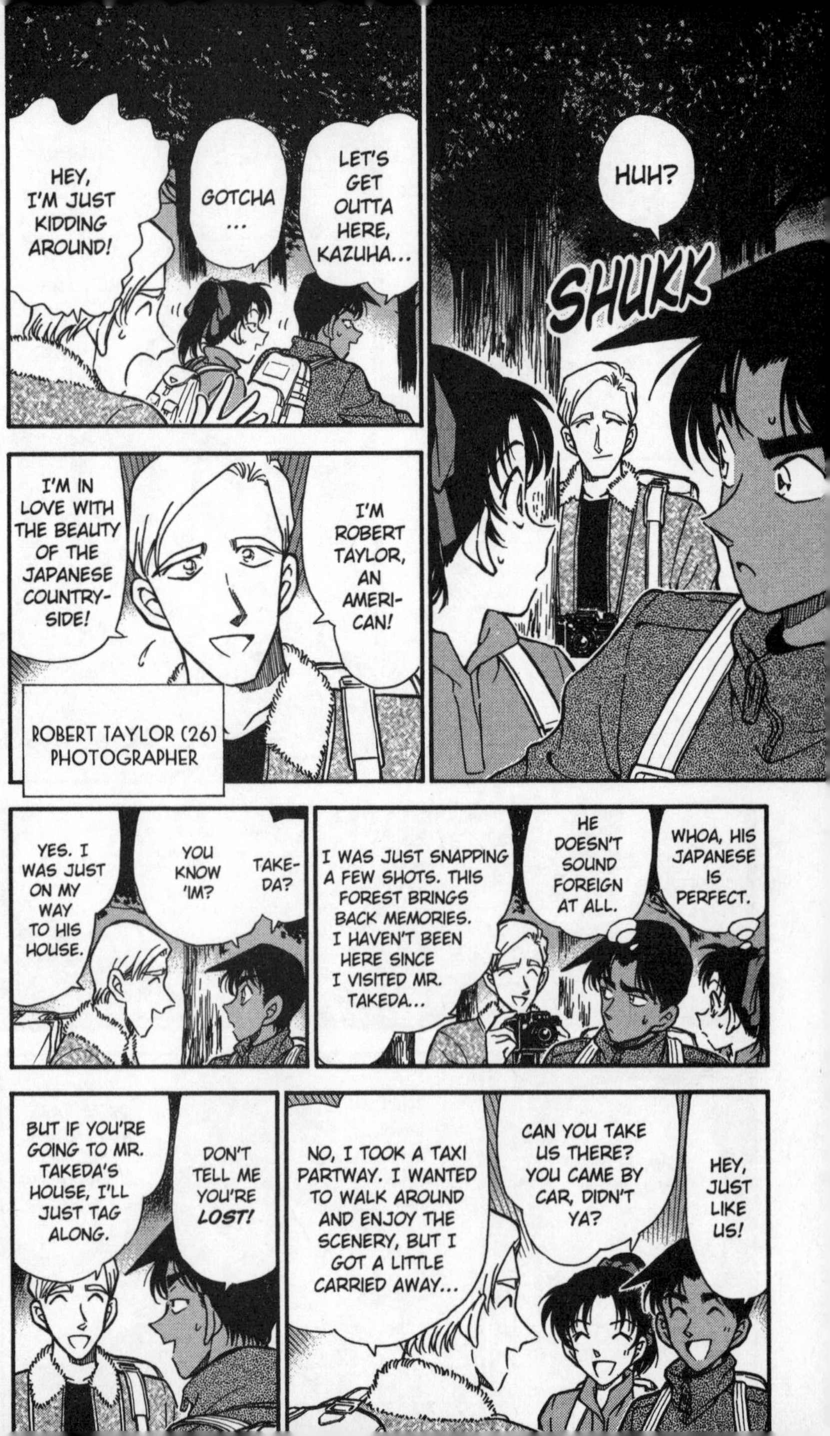
HUH?
SHUKK
LET'S GET OUTTA HERE, KAZUHA...
GOTCHA ...
HEY, I'M JUST KIDDING AROUND!
I'M ROBERT TAYLOR, AN AMERICAN!
I'M IN LOVE WITH THE BEAUTY OF THE JAPANESE COUNTRYSIDE!
ROBERT TAYLOR (26) PHOTOGRAPHER
WHOA, HIS JAPANESE IS PERFECT.
HE DOESN'T SOUND FOREIGN AT ALL.
I WAS JUST SNAPPING A FEW SHOTS. THIS FOREST BRINGS BACK MEMORIES. I HAVEN'T BEEN HERE SINCE I VISITED MR. TAKEDA...
TAKEDA?
YOU KNOW 'IM?
YES. I WAS JUST ON MY WAY TO HIS HOUSE.
HEY, JUST LIKE US!
CAN YOU TAKE US THERE? YOU CAME BY CAR, DIDN'T YA?
NO, I TOOK A TAXI PARTWAY. I WANTED TO WALK AROUND AND ENJOY THE SCENERY, BUT I GOT A LITTLE CARRIED AWAY...
DON'T TELL ME YOU'RE *LOST!*
BUT IF YOU'RE GOING TO MR. TAKEDA'S HOUSE, I'LL JUST TAG ALONG.

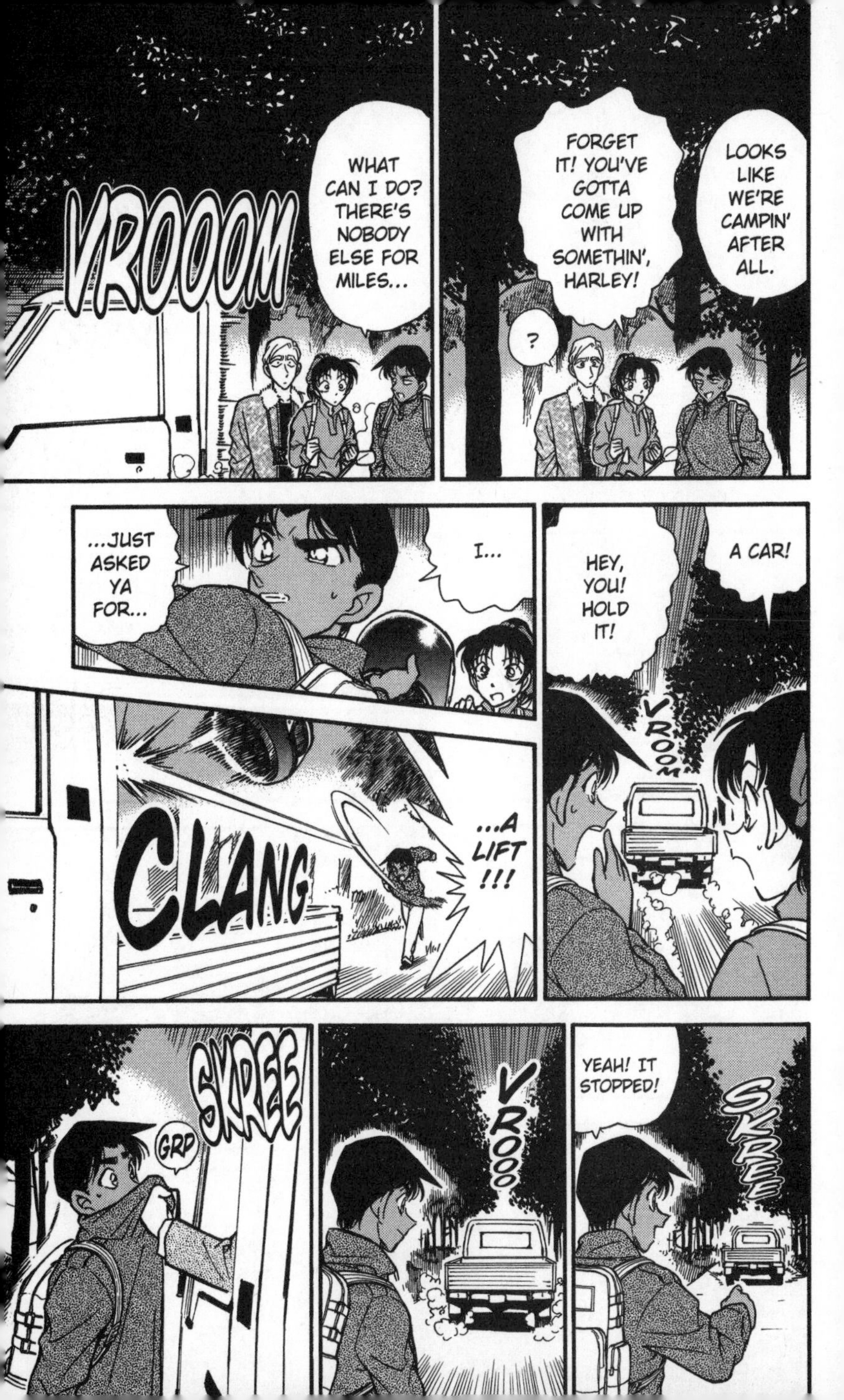
LOOKS LIKE WE'RE CAMPIN' AFTER ALL.
FORGET IT! YOU'VE GOTTA COME UP WITH SOMETHIN', HARLEY!
?
WHAT CAN I DO? THERE'S NOBODY ELSE FOR MILES...
VROOOM
A CAR!
HEY, YOU! HOLD IT!
VROOM
I...
...JUST ASKED YA FOR...
...A LIFT!!!
CLANG
YEAH! IT STOPPED!
SKREE
VROOO
SKREE
GRP

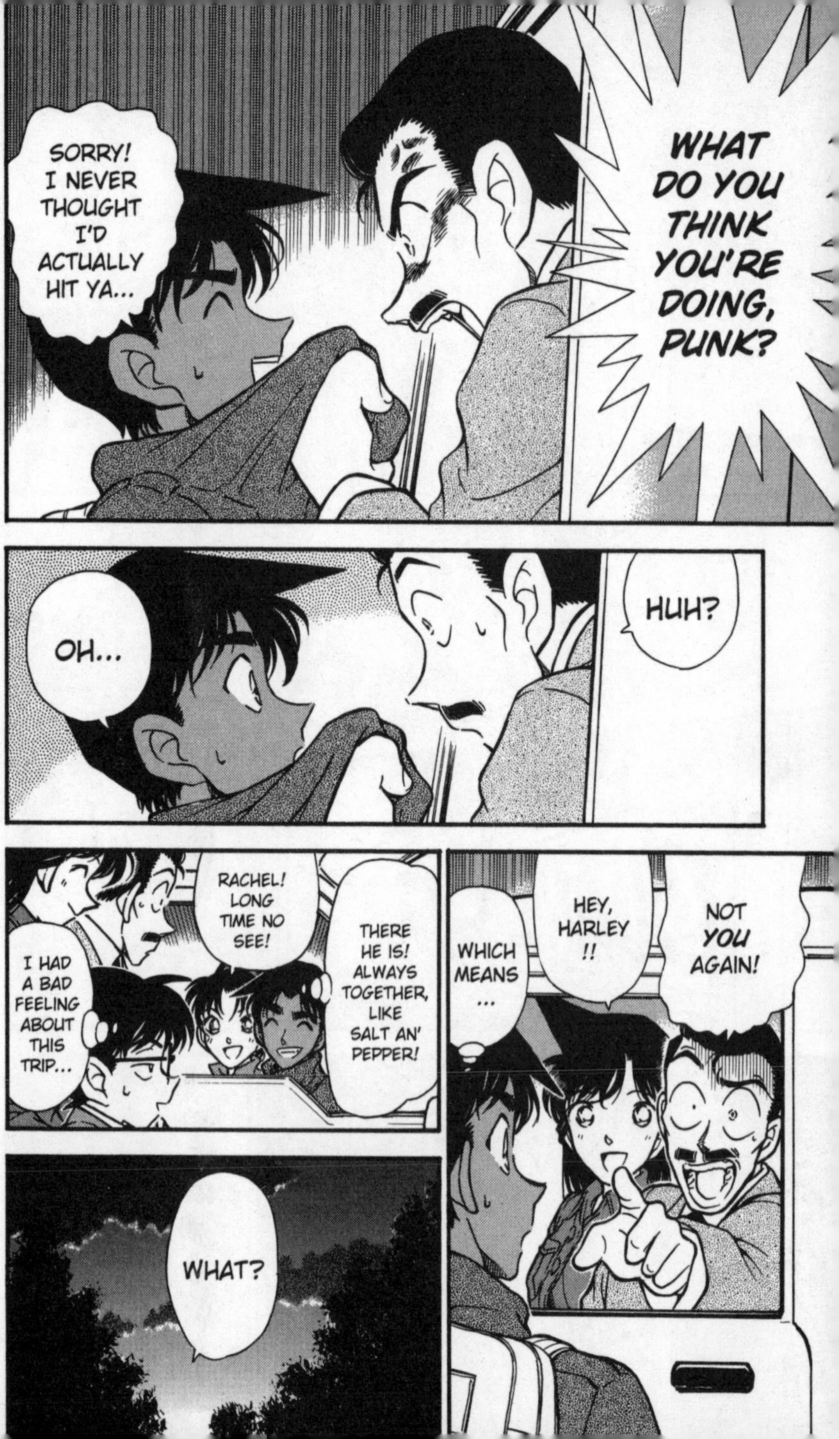
WHAT DO YOU THINK YOU'RE DOING, PUNK?
SORRY! I NEVER THOUGHT I'D ACTUALLY HIT YA...
HUH?
OH...
NOT YOU AGAIN!
HEY, HARLEY!!
WHICH MEANS...
THERE HE IS! ALWAYS TOGETHER, LIKE SALT AN' PEPPER!
RACHEL! LONG TIME NO SEE!
I HAD A BAD FEELING ABOUT THIS TRIP...
WHAT?

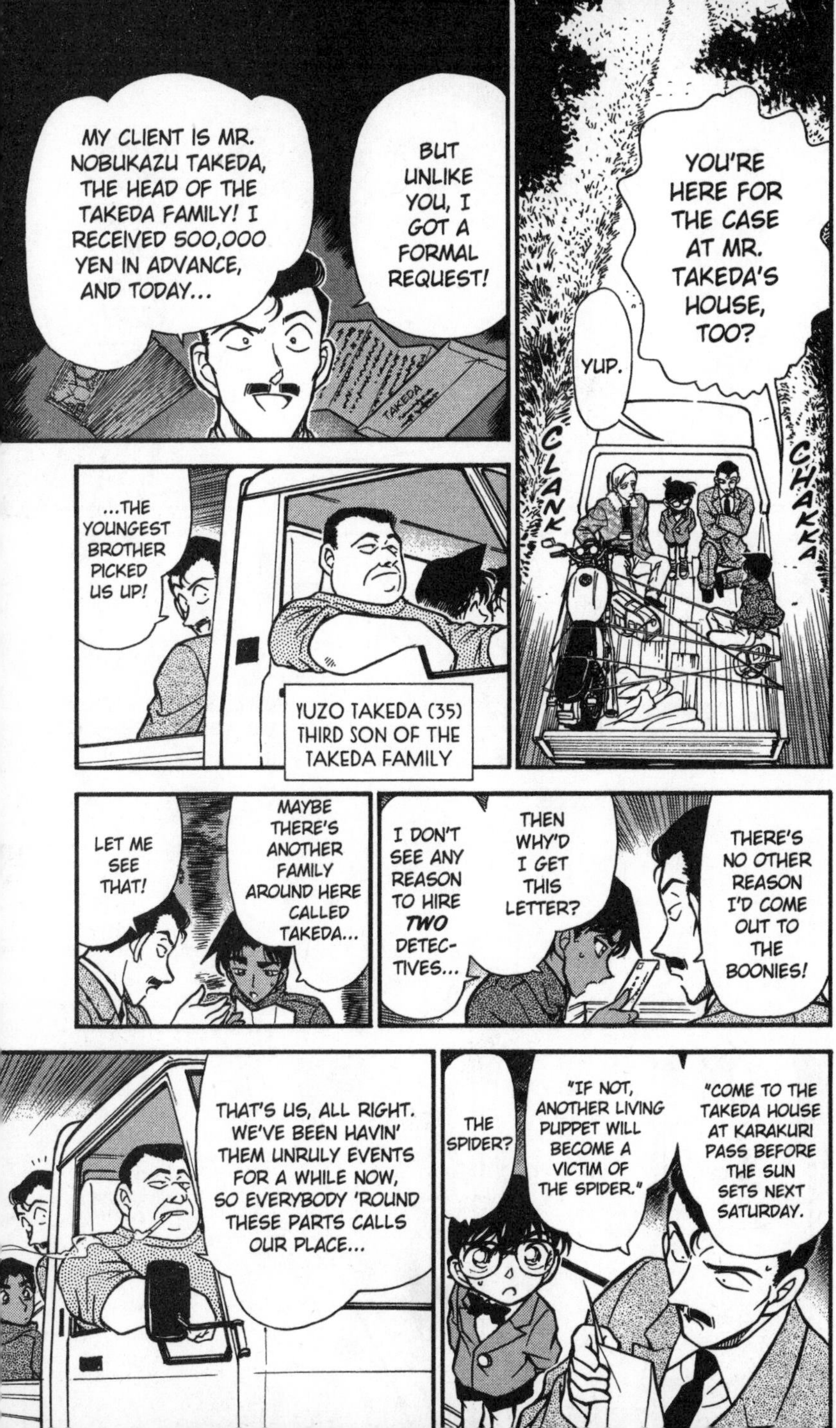
YOU'RE HERE FOR THE CASE AT MR. TAKEDA'S HOUSE, TOO?
YUP.
CHAKKA
CLANK
BUT UNLIKE YOU, I GOT A FORMAL REQUEST!
MY CLIENT IS MR. NOBUKAZU TAKEDA, THE HEAD OF THE TAKEDA FAMILY! I RECEIVED 500,000 YEN IN ADVANCE, AND TODAY...
...THE YOUNGEST BROTHER PICKED US UP!
YUZO TAKEDA (35) THIRD SON OF THE TAKEDA FAMILY
THERE'S NO OTHER REASON I'D COME OUT TO THE BOONIES!
THEN WHY'D I GET THIS LETTER?
I DON'T SEE ANY REASON TO HIRE *TWO* DETECTIVES...
MAYBE THERE'S ANOTHER FAMILY AROUND HERE CALLED TAKEDA...
LET ME SEE THAT!
"COME TO THE TAKEDA HOUSE AT KARAKURI PASS BEFORE THE SUN SETS NEXT SATURDAY.
"IF NOT, ANOTHER LIVING PUPPET WILL BECOME A VICTIM OF THE SPIDER."
THE SPIDER?
THAT'S US, ALL RIGHT. WE'VE BEEN HAVIN' THEM UNRULY EVENTS FOR A WHILE NOW, SO EVERYBODY 'ROUND THESE PARTS CALLS OUR PLACE...

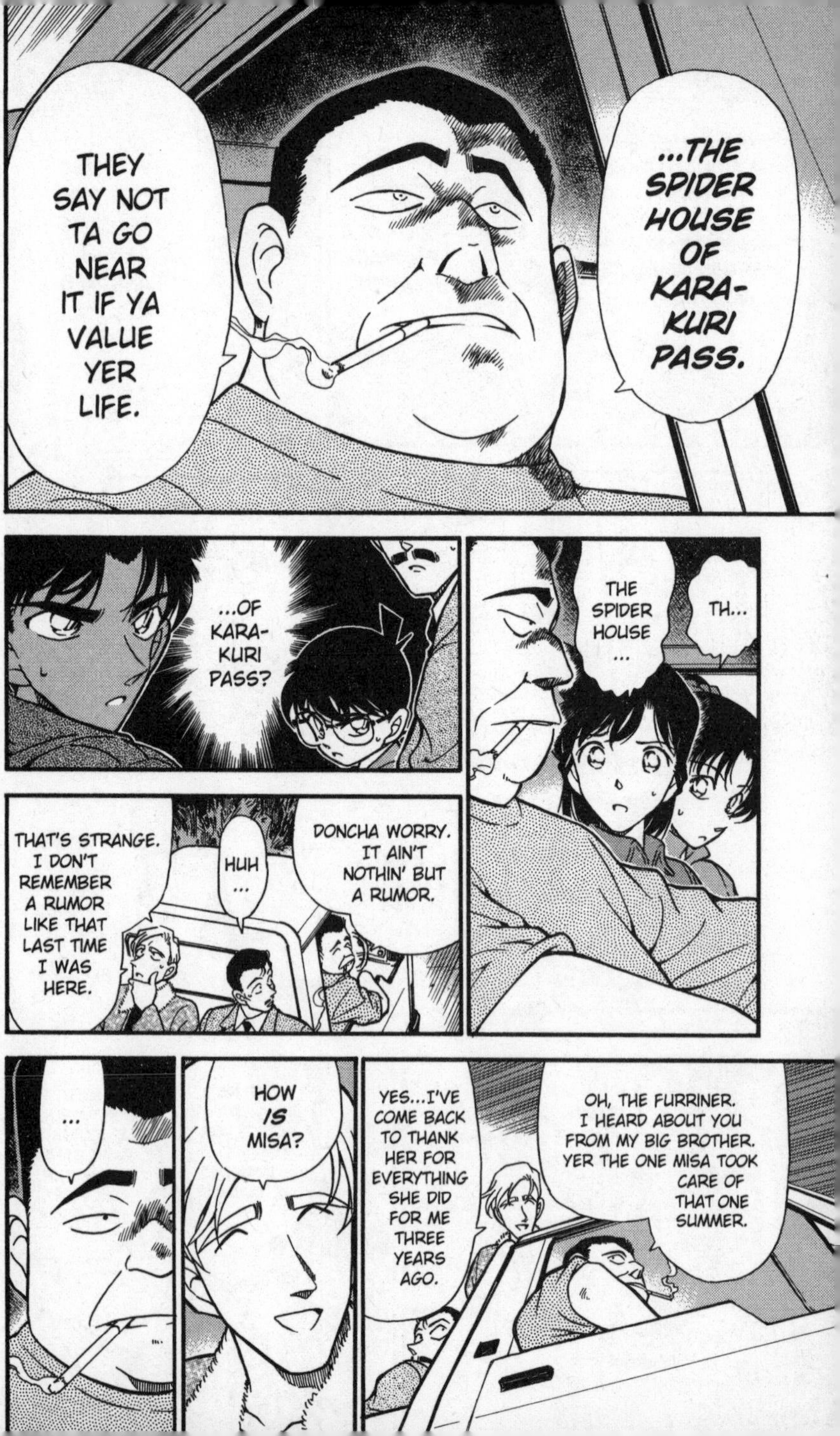
...THE SPIDER HOUSE OF KARAKURI PASS.
THEY SAY NOT TA GO NEAR IT IF YA VALUE YER LIFE.
TH...
THE SPIDER HOUSE...
...OF KARAKURI PASS?
DONCHA WORRY. IT AIN'T NOTHIN' BUT A RUMOR.
HUH...
THAT'S STRANGE. I DON'T REMEMBER A RUMOR LIKE THAT LAST TIME I WAS HERE.
OH, THE FURRINER. I HEARD ABOUT YOU FROM MY BIG BROTHER. YER THE ONE MISA TOOK CARE OF THAT ONE SUMMER.
YES...I'VE COME BACK TO THANK HER FOR EVERYTHING SHE DID FOR ME THREE YEARS AGO.
HOW *IS* MISA?
...

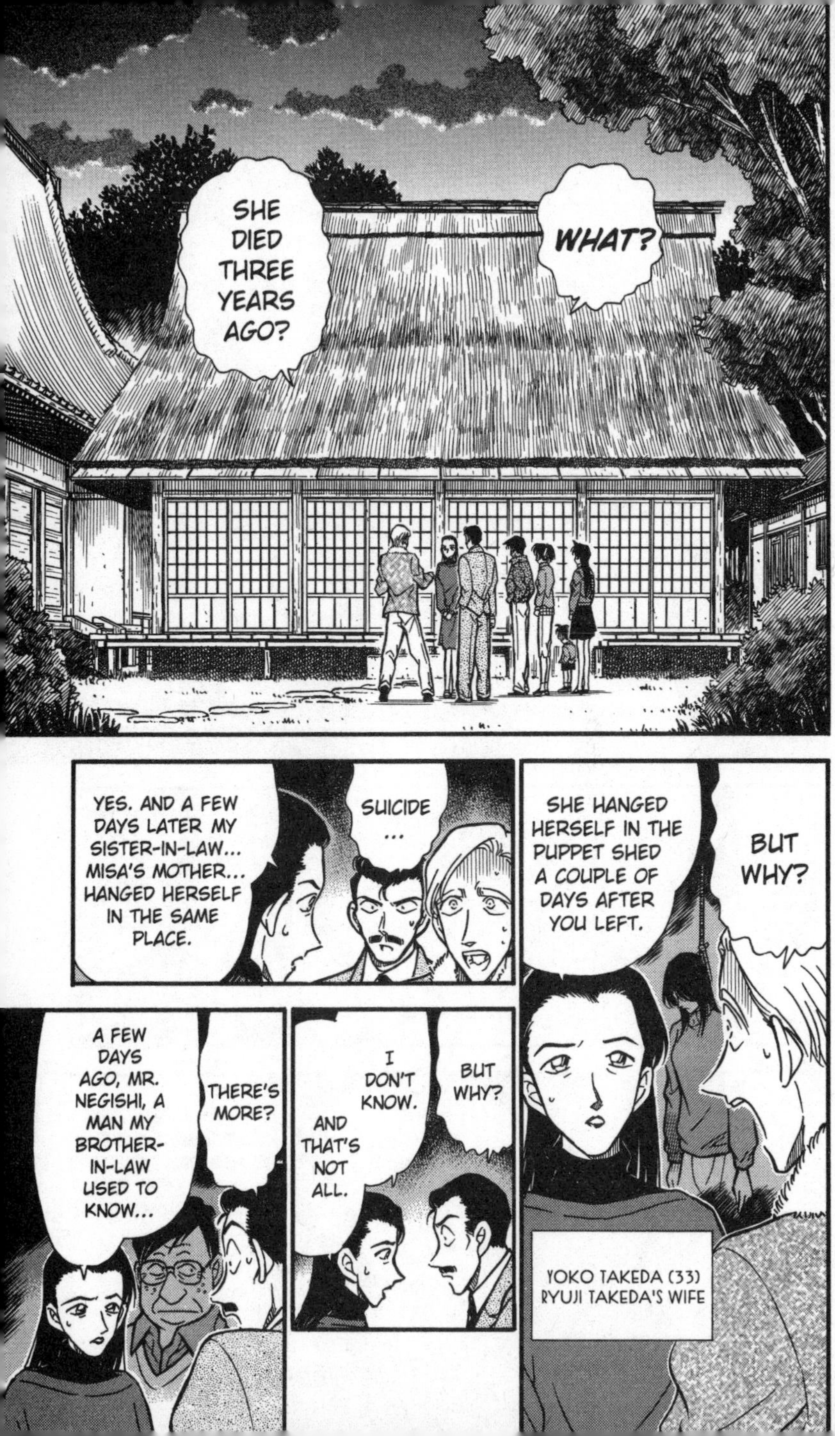
WHAT?
SHE DIED THREE YEARS AGO?
BUT WHY?
SHE HANGED HERSELF IN THE PUPPET SHED A COUPLE OF DAYS AFTER YOU LEFT.
YOKO TAKEDA (33) RYUJI TAKEDA'S WIFE
SUICIDE ...
YES. AND A FEW DAYS LATER MY SISTER-IN-LAW... MISA'S MOTHER... HANGED HERSELF IN THE SAME PLACE.
BUT WHY?
I DON'T KNOW.
AND THAT'S NOT ALL.
THERE'S MORE?
A FEW DAYS AGO, MR. NEGISHI, A MAN MY BROTHER-IN-LAW USED TO KNOW...

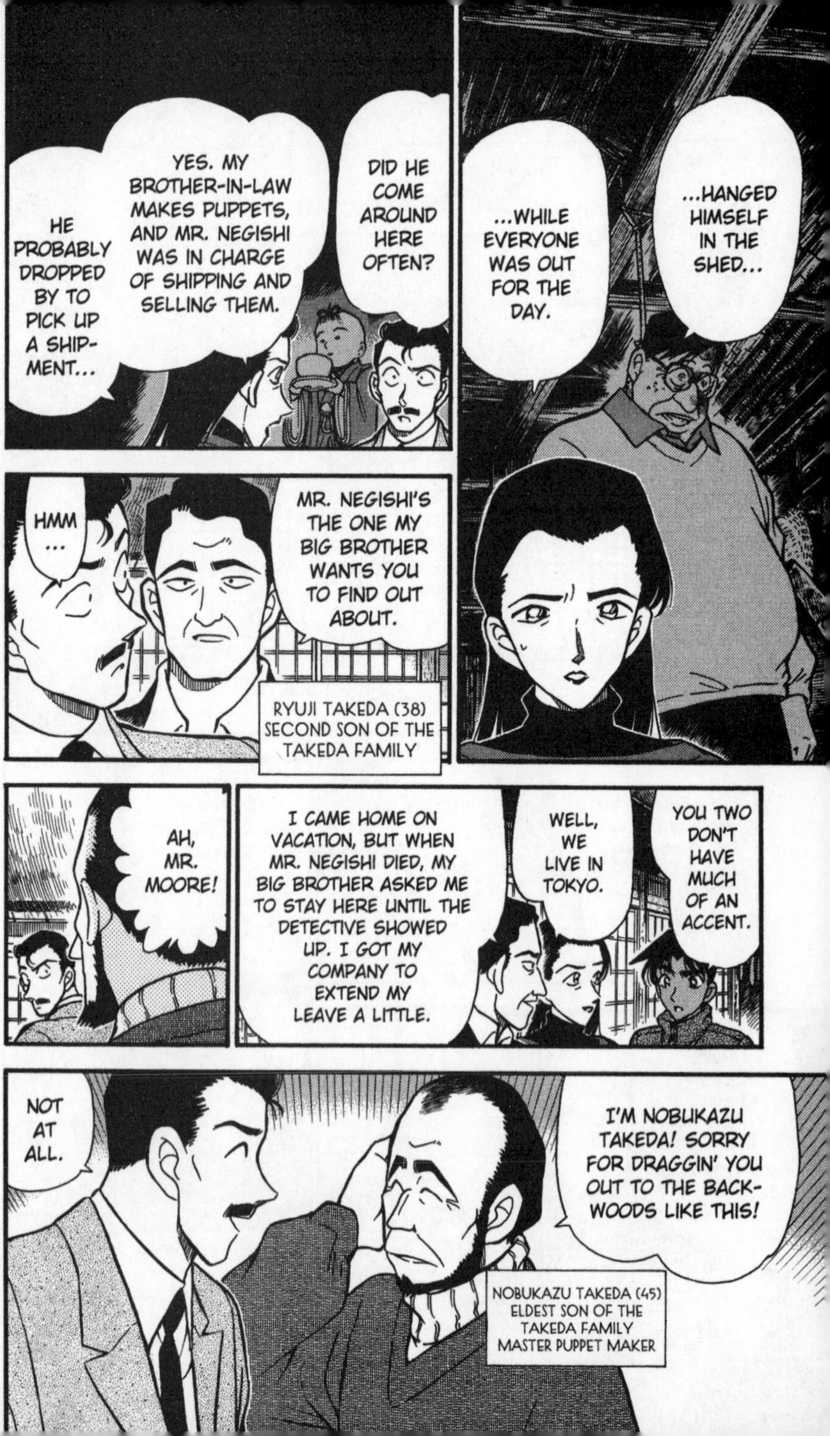
...HANGED HIMSELF IN THE SHED...
...WHILE EVERYONE WAS OUT FOR THE DAY.
DID HE COME AROUND HERE OFTEN?
YES. MY BROTHER-IN-LAW MAKES PUPPETS, AND MR. NEGISHI WAS IN CHARGE OF SHIPPING AND SELLING THEM.
HE PROBABLY DROPPED BY TO PICK UP A SHIPMENT...
MR. NEGISHI'S THE ONE MY BIG BROTHER WANTS YOU TO FIND OUT ABOUT.
HMM...
RYUJI TAKEDA (38) SECOND SON OF THE TAKEDA FAMILY
YOU TWO DON'T HAVE MUCH OF AN ACCENT.
WELL, WE LIVE IN TOKYO.
I CAME HOME ON VACATION, BUT WHEN MR. NEGISHI DIED, MY BIG BROTHER ASKED ME TO STAY HERE UNTIL THE DETECTIVE SHOWED UP. I GOT MY COMPANY TO EXTEND MY LEAVE A LITTLE.
AH, MR. MOORE!
I'M NOBUKAZU TAKEDA! SORRY FOR DRAGGIN' YOU OUT TO THE BACKWOODS LIKE THIS!
NOT AT ALL.
NOBUKAZU TAKEDA (45) ELDEST SON OF THE TAKEDA FAMILY MASTER PUPPET MAKER

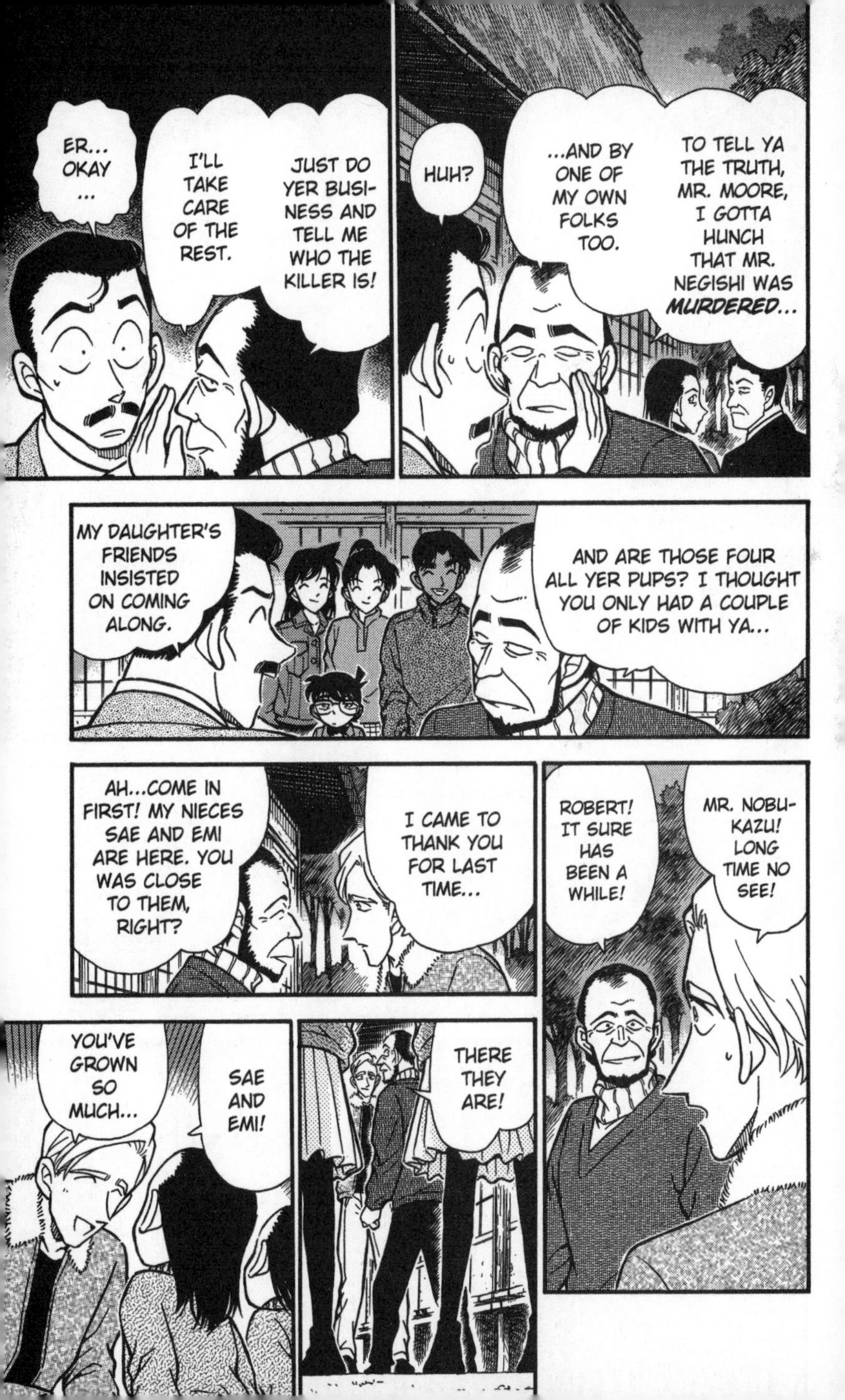
TO TELL YA THE TRUTH, MR. MOORE, I GOTTA HUNCH THAT MR. NEGISHI WAS MURDERED...
...AND BY ONE OF MY OWN FOLKS TOO.
HUH?
JUST DO YER BUSINESS AND TELL ME WHO THE KILLER IS!
I'LL TAKE CARE OF THE REST.
ER... OKAY ...
AND ARE THOSE FOUR ALL YER PUPS? I THOUGHT YOU ONLY HAD A COUPLE OF KIDS WITH YA...
MY DAUGHTER'S FRIENDS INSISTED ON COMING ALONG.
MR. NOBU-KAZU! LONG TIME NO SEE!
ROBERT! IT SURE HAS BEEN A WHILE!
I CAME TO THANK YOU FOR LAST TIME...
AH...COME IN FIRST! MY NIECES SAE AND EMI ARE HERE. YOU WAS CLOSE TO THEM, RIGHT?
THERE THEY ARE!
SAE AND EMI!
YOU'VE GROWN SO MUCH...

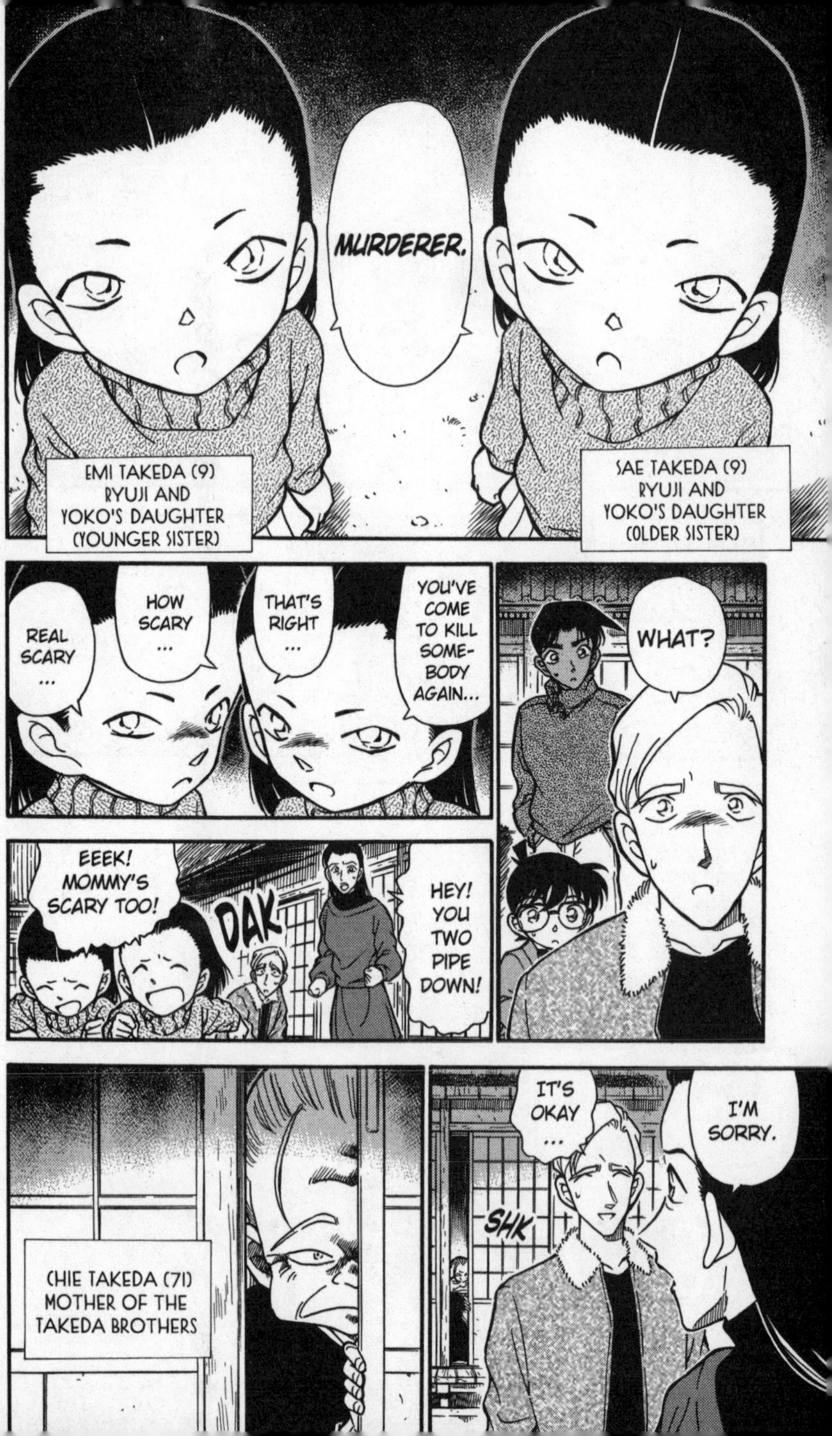
MURDERER.
SAE TAKEDA (9) RYUJI AND YOKO'S DAUGHTER (OLDER SISTER)
EMI TAKEDA (9) RYUJI AND YOKO'S DAUGHTER (YOUNGER SISTER)
WHAT?
YOU'VE COME TO KILL SOME-BODY AGAIN...
THAT'S RIGHT ...
HOW SCARY ...
REAL SCARY ...
HEY! YOU TWO PIPE DOWN!
DAK
EEEK! MOMMY'S SCARY TOO!
I'M SORRY.
IT'S OKAY ...
SHK
CHIE TAKEDA (71) MOTHER OF THE TAKEDA BROTHERS

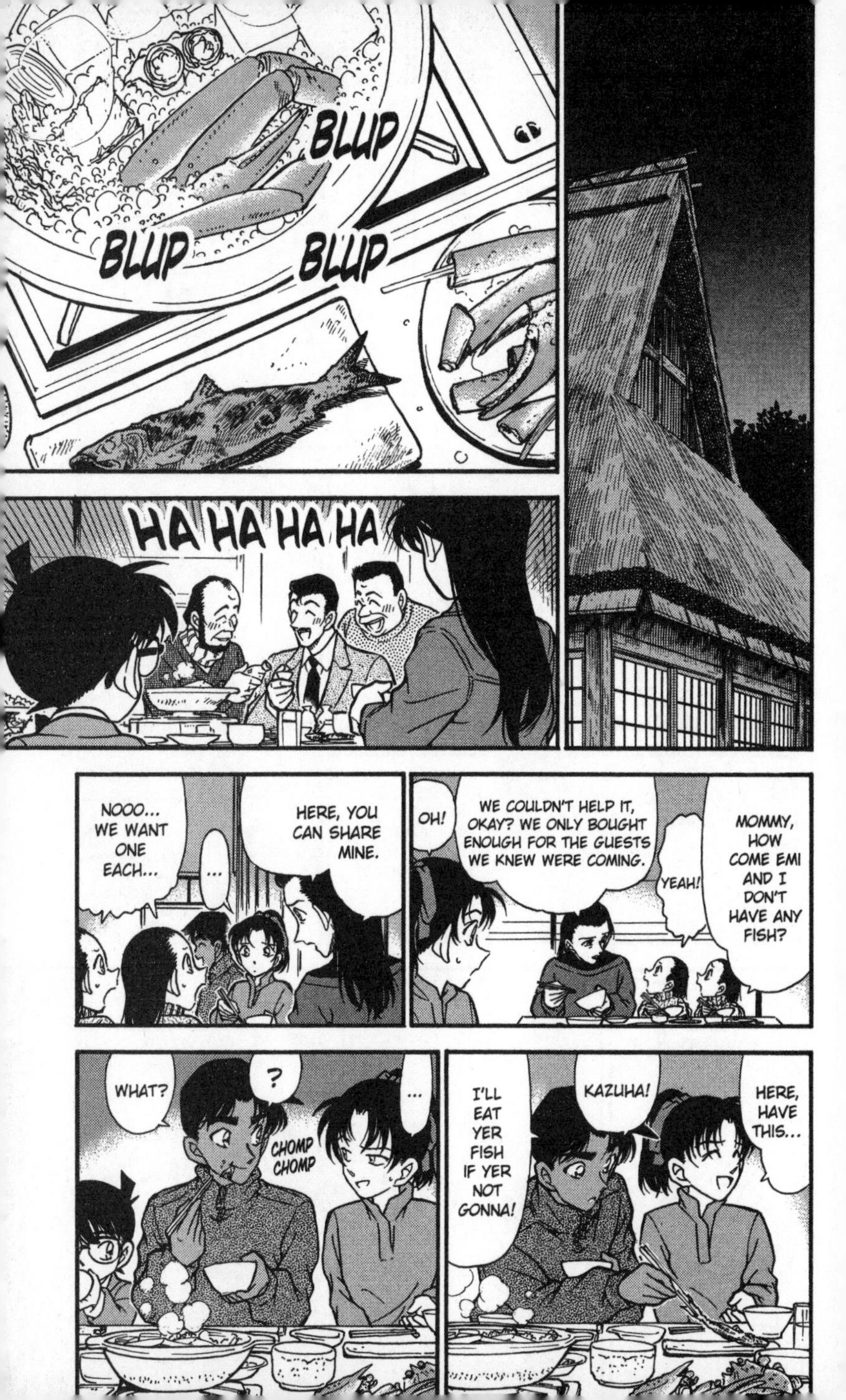
BLUP
BLUP
BLUP
HA HA HA HA
MOMMY, HOW COME EMI AND I DON'T HAVE ANY FISH?
YEAH!
WE COULDN'T HELP IT, OKAY? WE ONLY BOUGHT ENOUGH FOR THE GUESTS WE KNEW WERE COMING.
OH!
HERE, YOU CAN SHARE MINE.
...
NOOO... WE WANT ONE EACH...
HERE, HAVE THIS...
KAZUHA!
I'LL EAT YER FISH IF YER NOT GONNA!
...
?
CHOMP CHOMP
WHAT?

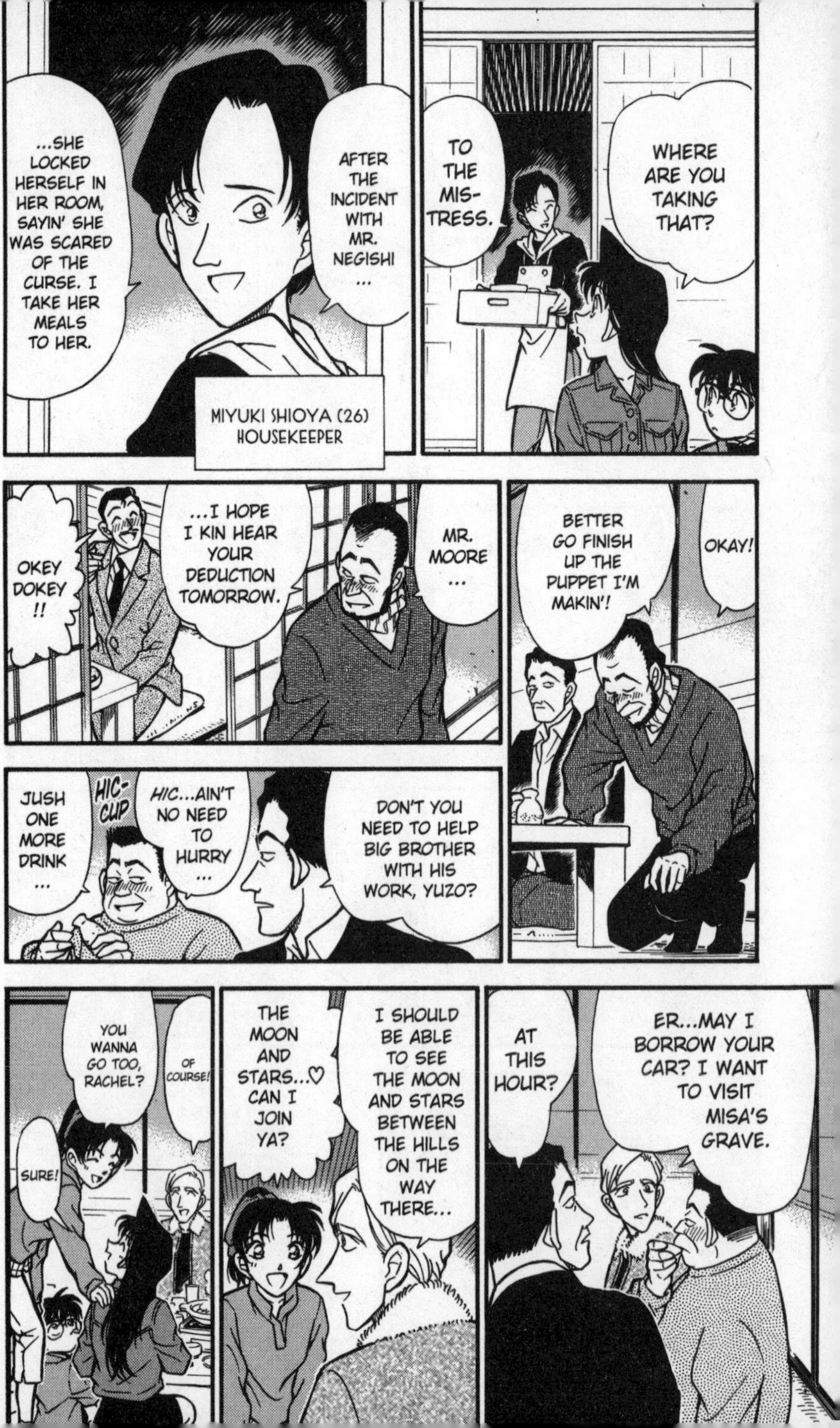
WHERE ARE YOU TAKING THAT?
TO THE MIS-TRESS.
AFTER THE INCIDENT WITH MR. NEGISHI...
...SHE LOCKED HERSELF IN HER ROOM, SAYIN' SHE WAS SCARED OF THE CURSE. I TAKE HER MEALS TO HER.
MIYUKI SHIOYA (26) HOUSEKEEPER
OKAY!
BETTER GO FINISH UP THE PUPPET I'M MAKIN'!
MR. MOORE...
...I HOPE I KIN HEAR YOUR DEDUCTION TOMORROW.
OKEY DOKEY!!
DON'T YOU NEED TO HELP BIG BROTHER WITH HIS WORK, YUZO?
HIC...AIN'T NO NEED TO HURRY...
HIC-CUP
JUSH ONE MORE DRINK...
ER...MAY I BORROW YOUR CAR? I WANT TO VISIT MISA'S GRAVE.
AT THIS HOUR?
I SHOULD BE ABLE TO SEE THE MOON AND STARS BETWEEN THE HILLS ON THE WAY THERE...
THE MOON AND STARS...♡ CAN I JOIN YA?
OF COURSE!
YOU WANNA GO TOO, RACHEL?
SURE!

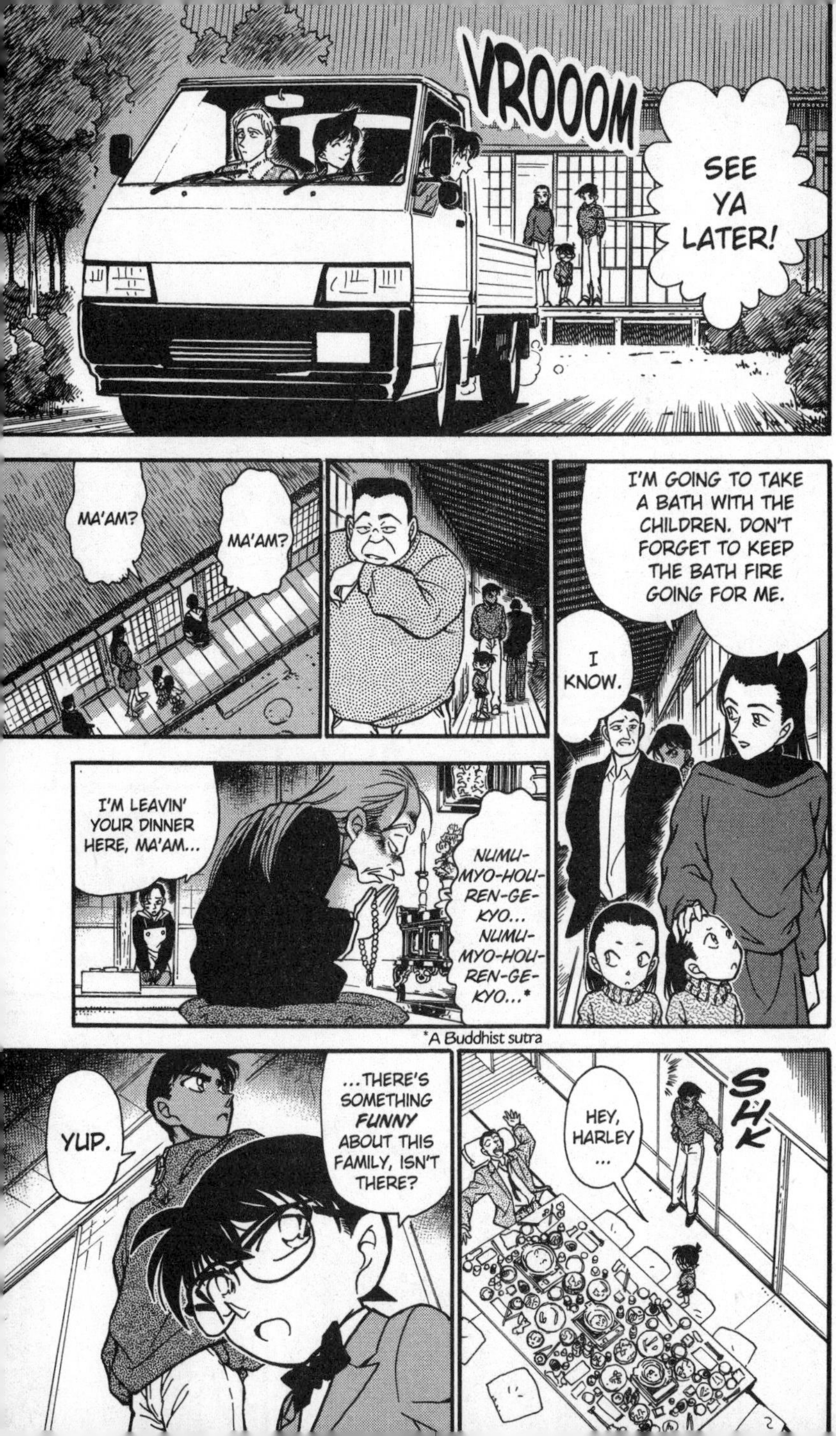
VROOOM
SEE YA LATER!
I'M GOING TO TAKE A BATH WITH THE CHILDREN. DON'T FORGET TO KEEP THE BATH FIRE GOING FOR ME.
I KNOW.
MA'AM?
MA'AM?
NUMU-MYO-HOU-REN-GE-KYO... NUMU-MYO-HOU-REN-GE-KYO...*
I'M LEAVIN' YOUR DINNER HERE, MA'AM...
*A Buddhist sutra
SHK
HEY, HARLEY ...
...THERE'S SOMETHING *FUNNY* ABOUT THIS FAMILY, ISN'T THERE?
YUP.

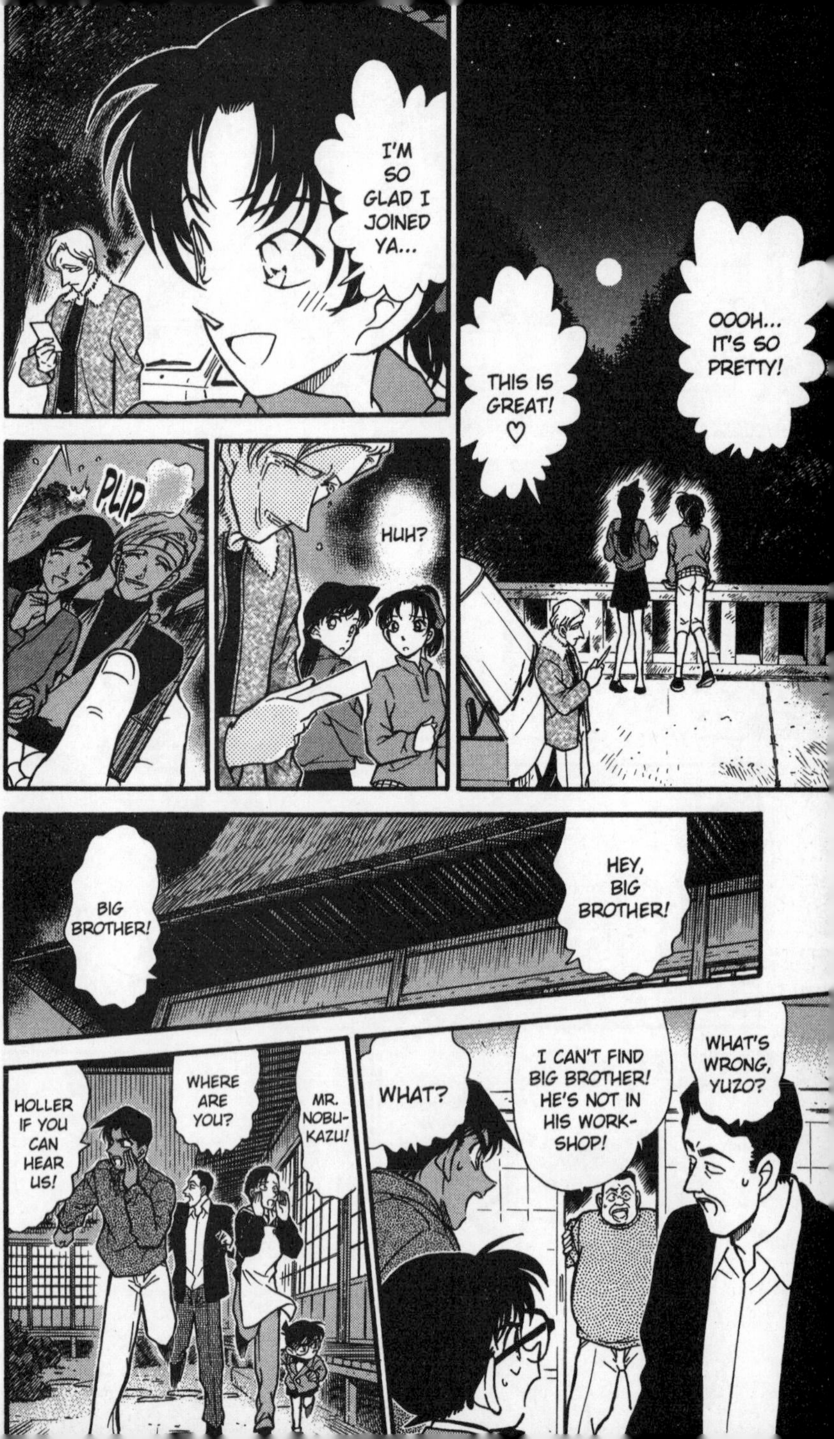
OOOH... IT'S SO PRETTY!
THIS IS GREAT! ♡
I'M SO GLAD I JOINED YA...
HUH?
PLIP
HEY, BIG BROTHER!
BIG BROTHER!
WHAT'S WRONG, YUZO?
I CAN'T FIND BIG BROTHER! HE'S NOT IN HIS WORK-SHOP!
WHAT?
MR. NOBU-KAZU!
WHERE ARE YOU?
HOLLER IF YOU CAN HEAR US!

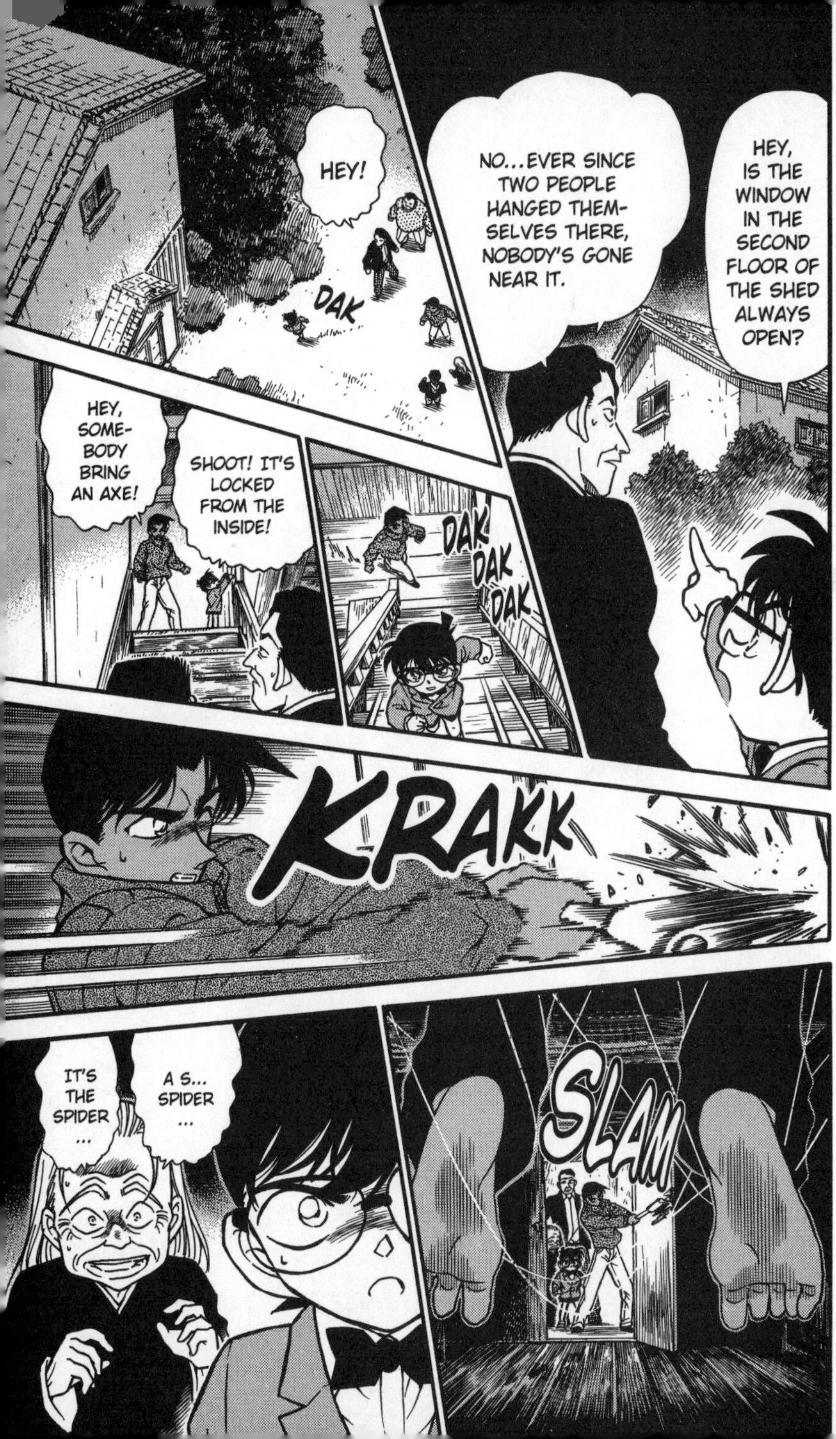
HEY, IS THE WINDOW IN THE SECOND FLOOR OF THE SHED ALWAYS OPEN?
NO...EVER SINCE TWO PEOPLE HANGED THEMSELVES THERE, NOBODY'S GONE NEAR IT.
HEY!
DAK
DAK DAK DAK
SHOOT! IT'S LOCKED FROM THE INSIDE!
HEY, SOMEBODY BRING AN AXE!
KRAKK
SLAM
A S... SPIDER ...
IT'S THE SPIDER ...

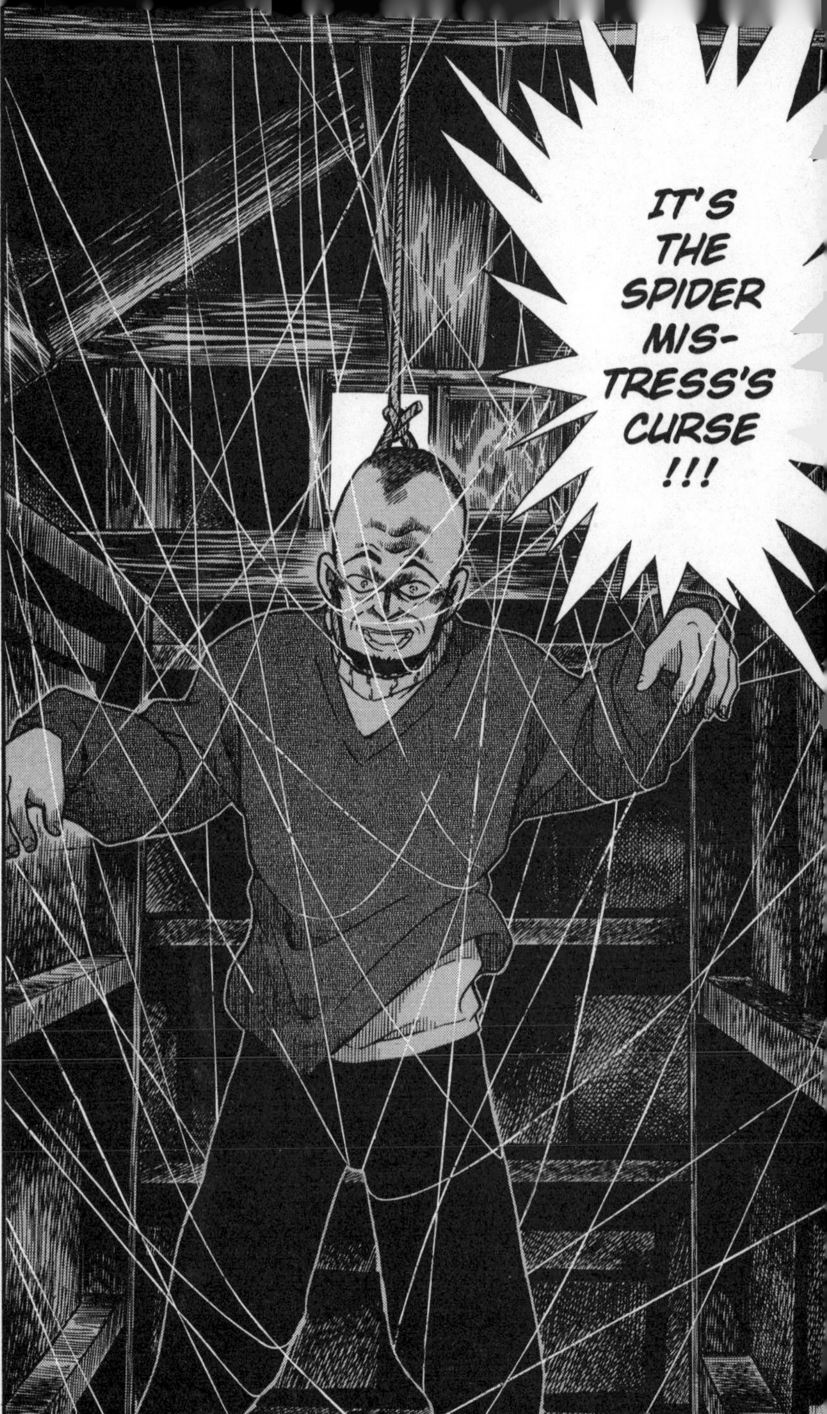
IT'S THE SPIDER MIS- TRESS'S CURSE !!!

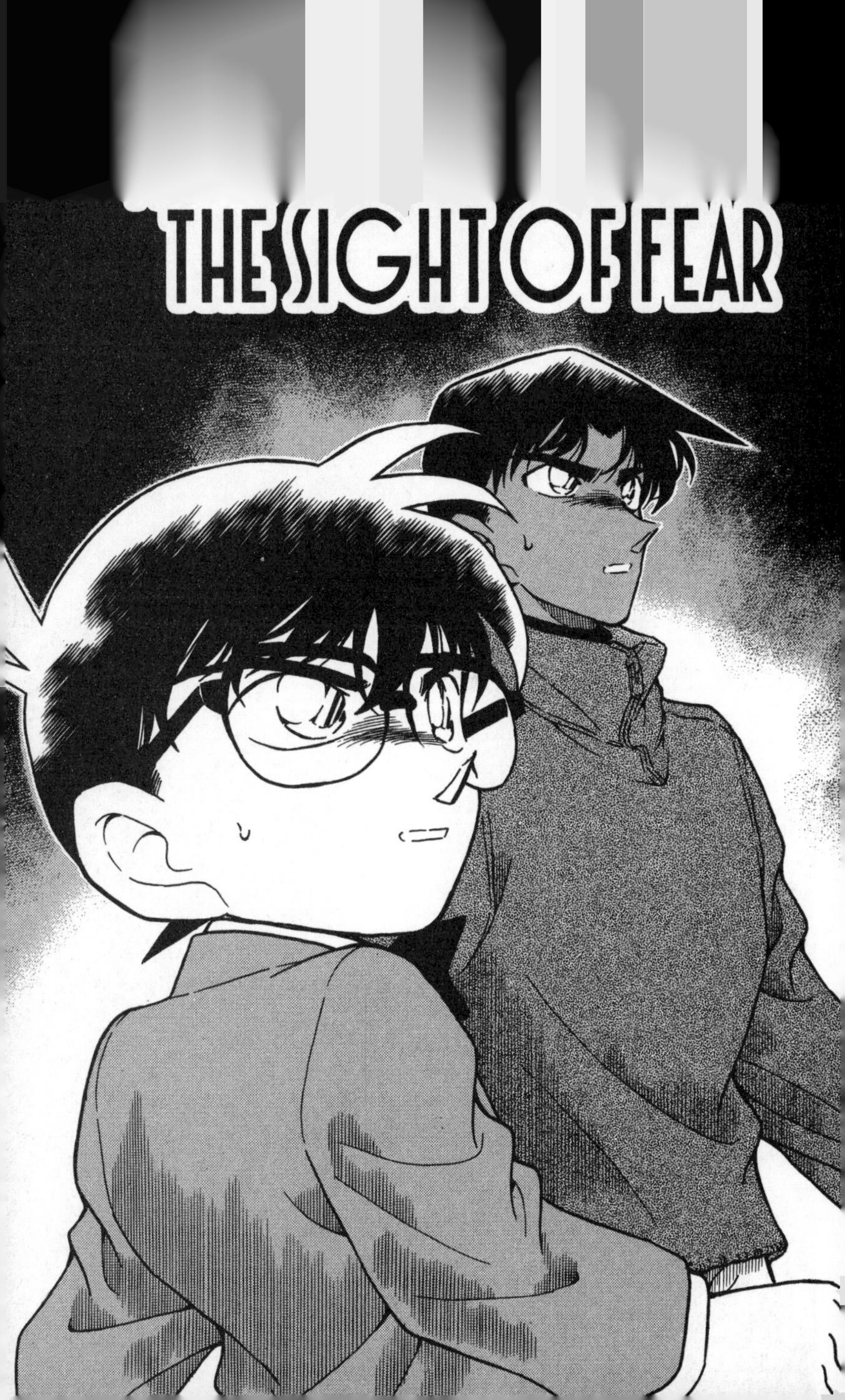
THE SIGHT OF FEAR

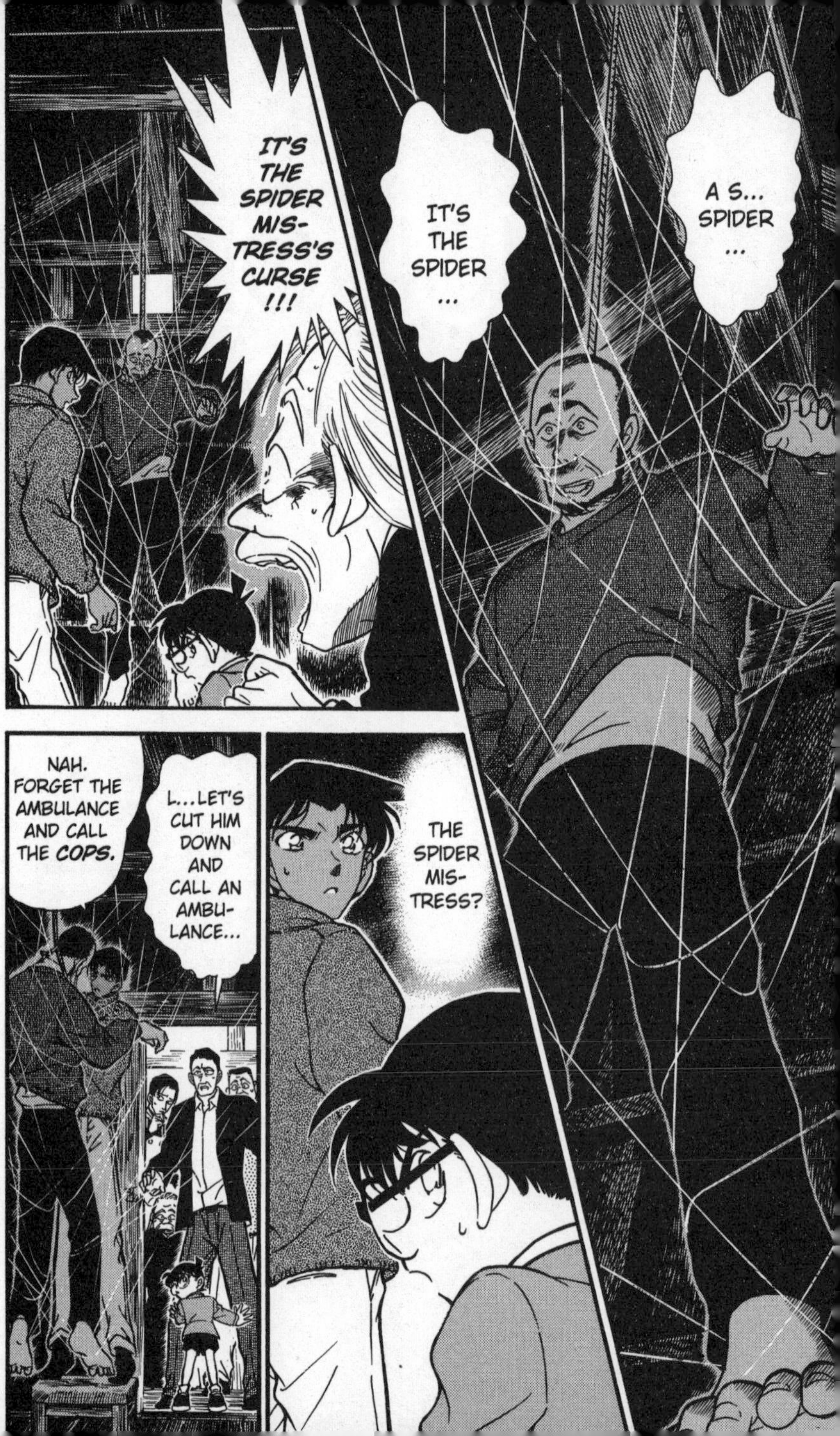
A S... SPIDER ...
IT'S THE SPIDER ...
IT'S THE SPIDER MIS-TRESS'S CURSE !!!
THE SPIDER MIS-TRESS?
L...LET'S CUT HIM DOWN AND CALL AN AMBU-LANCE...
NAH. FORGET THE AMBULANCE AND CALL THE **COPS.**

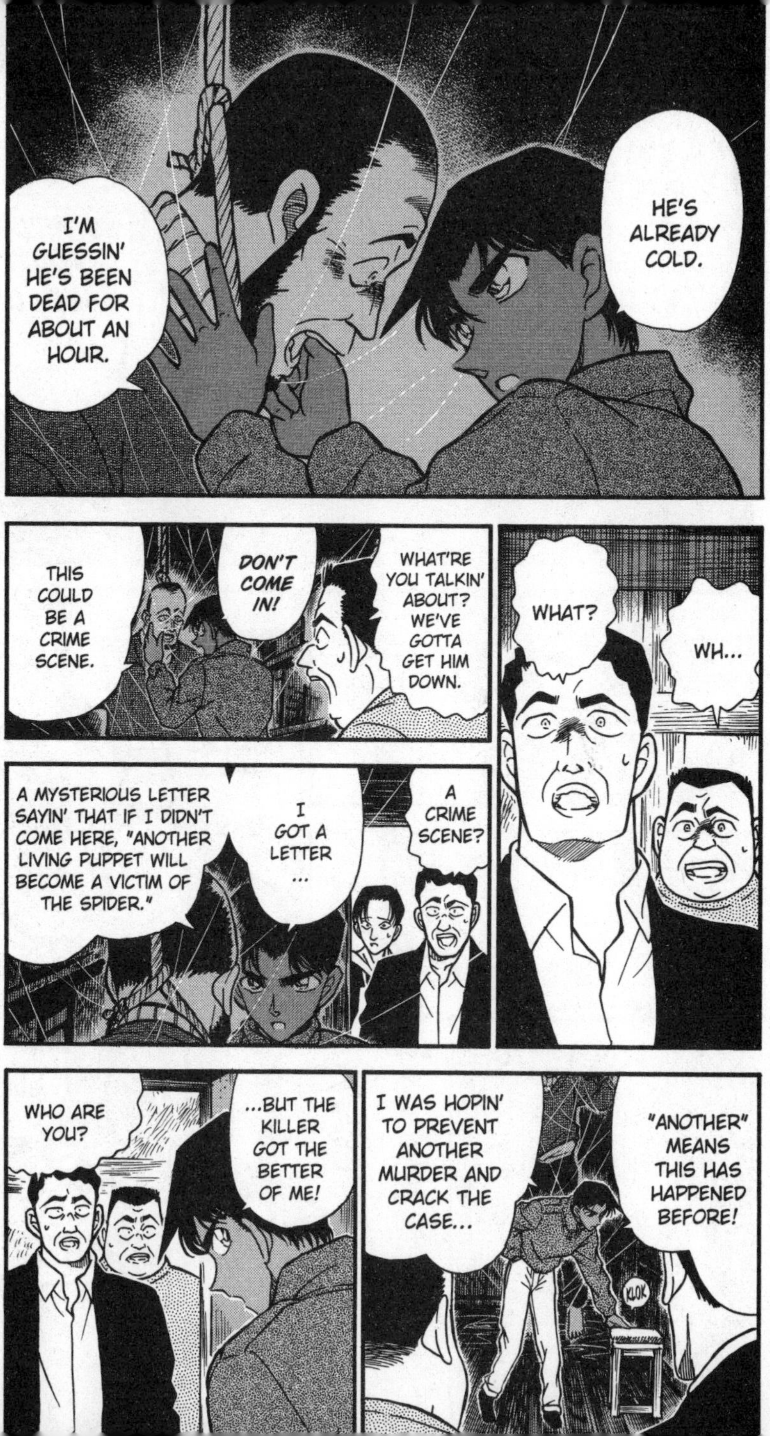
HE'S ALREADY COLD.
I'M GUESSIN' HE'S BEEN DEAD FOR ABOUT AN HOUR.
WH...
WHAT?
WHAT'RE YOU TALKIN' ABOUT? WE'VE GOTTA GET HIM DOWN.
DON'T COME IN!
THIS COULD BE A CRIME SCENE.
A CRIME SCENE?
I GOT A LETTER ...
A MYSTERIOUS LETTER SAYIN' THAT IF I DIDN'T COME HERE, "ANOTHER LIVING PUPPET WILL BECOME A VICTIM OF THE SPIDER."
"ANOTHER" MEANS THIS HAS HAPPENED BEFORE!
KLOK
I WAS HOPIN' TO PREVENT ANOTHER MURDER AND CRACK THE CASE...
...BUT THE KILLER GOT THE BETTER OF ME!
WHO ARE YOU?

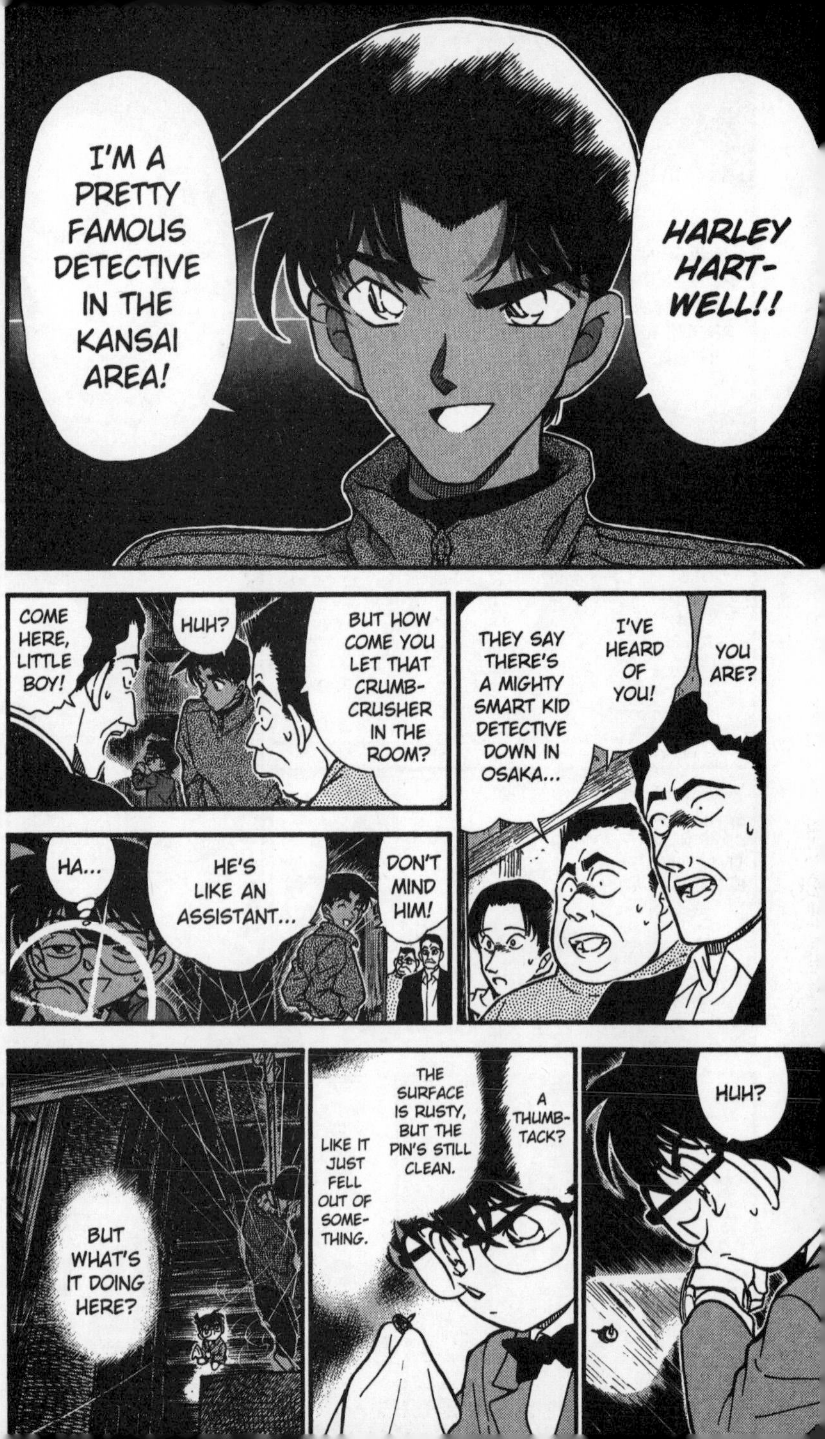
HARLEY HART-WELL!!
I'M A PRETTY FAMOUS DETECTIVE IN THE KANSAI AREA!
YOU ARE?
I'VE HEARD OF YOU!
THEY SAY THERE'S A MIGHTY SMART KID DETECTIVE DOWN IN OSAKA...
BUT HOW COME YOU LET THAT CRUMB-CRUSHER IN THE ROOM?
HUH?
COME HERE, LITTLE BOY!
DON'T MIND HIM!
HE'S LIKE AN ASSISTANT...
HA...
HUH?
A THUMB-TACK?
THE SURFACE IS RUSTY, BUT THE PIN'S STILL CLEAN.
LIKE IT JUST FELL OUT OF SOME-THING.
BUT WHAT'S IT DOING HERE?

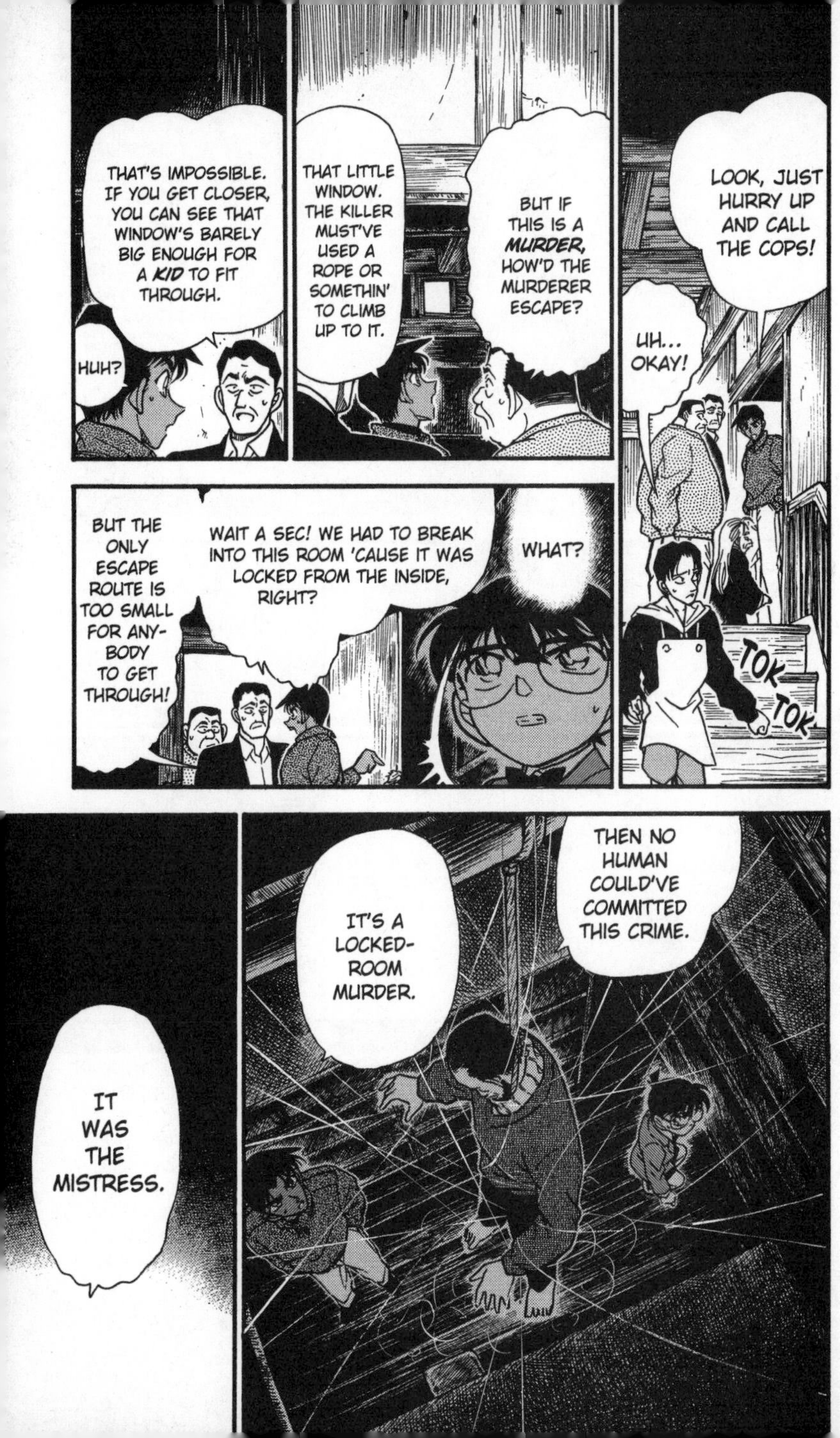
LOOK, JUST HURRY UP AND CALL THE COPS!
UH... OKAY!
TOK TOK
BUT IF THIS IS A MURDER, HOW'D THE MURDERER ESCAPE?
THAT LITTLE WINDOW. THE KILLER MUST'VE USED A ROPE OR SOMETHIN' TO CLIMB UP TO IT.
THAT'S IMPOSSIBLE. IF YOU GET CLOSER, YOU CAN SEE THAT WINDOW'S BARELY BIG ENOUGH FOR A KID TO FIT THROUGH.
HUH?
WHAT?
WAIT A SEC! WE HAD TO BREAK INTO THIS ROOM 'CAUSE IT WAS LOCKED FROM THE INSIDE, RIGHT?
BUT THE ONLY ESCAPE ROUTE IS TOO SMALL FOR ANYBODY TO GET THROUGH!
THEN NO HUMAN COULD'VE COMMITTED THIS CRIME.
IT'S A LOCKED-ROOM MURDER.
IT WAS THE MISTRESS.

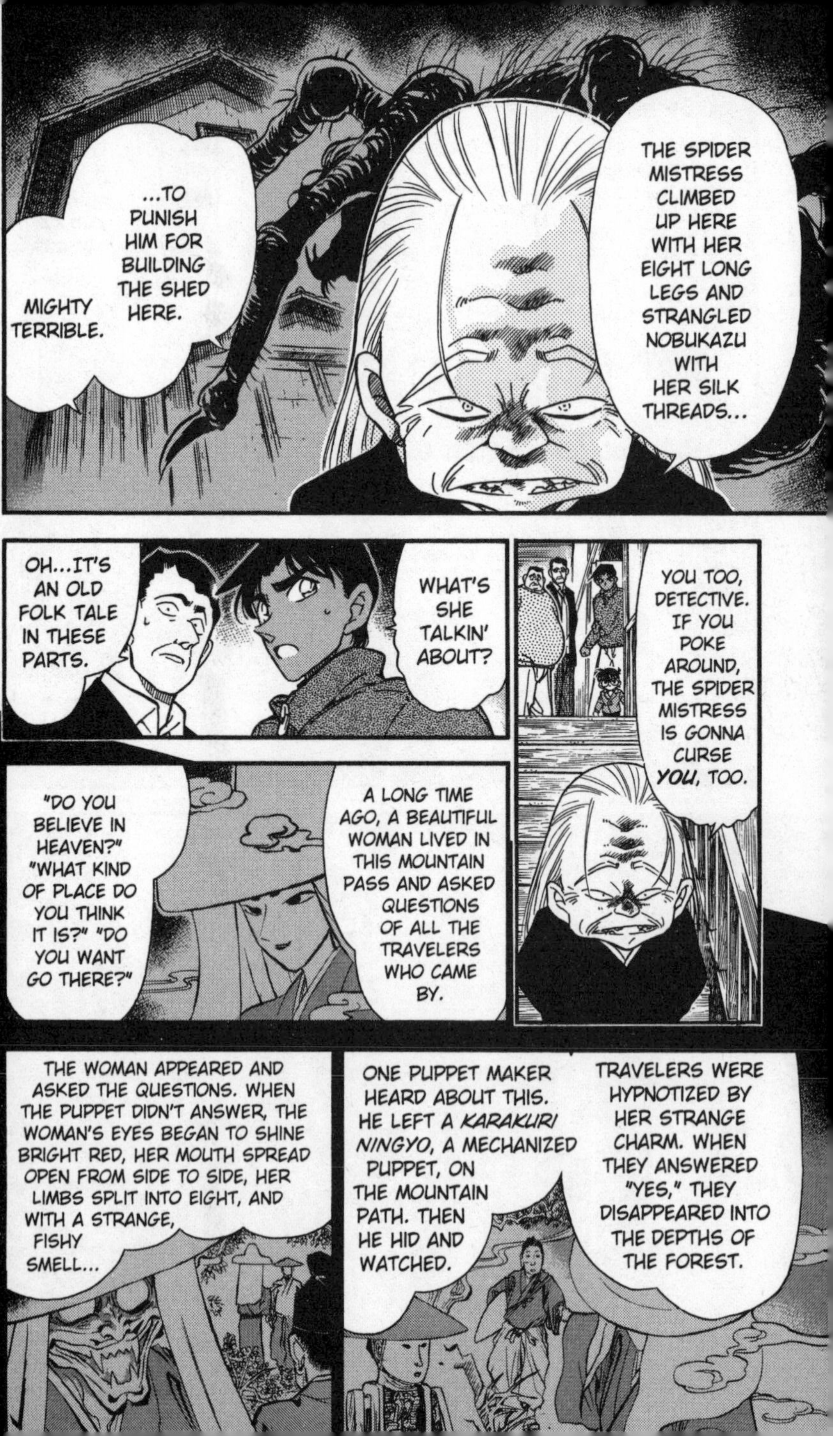
THE SPIDER MISTRESS CLIMBED UP HERE WITH HER EIGHT LONG LEGS AND STRANGLED NOBUKAZU WITH HER SILK THREADS...
...TO PUNISH HIM FOR BUILDING THE SHED HERE.
MIGHTY TERRIBLE.
YOU TOO, DETECTIVE. IF YOU POKE AROUND, THE SPIDER MISTRESS IS GONNA CURSE *YOU*, TOO.
WHAT'S SHE TALKIN' ABOUT?
OH...IT'S AN OLD FOLK TALE IN THESE PARTS.
A LONG TIME AGO, A BEAUTIFUL WOMAN LIVED IN THIS MOUNTAIN PASS AND ASKED QUESTIONS OF ALL THE TRAVELERS WHO CAME BY.
"DO YOU BELIEVE IN HEAVEN?" "WHAT KIND OF PLACE DO YOU THINK IT IS?" "DO YOU WANT GO THERE?"
TRAVELERS WERE HYPNOTIZED BY HER STRANGE CHARM. WHEN THEY ANSWERED "YES," THEY DISAPPEARED INTO THE DEPTHS OF THE FOREST.
ONE PUPPET MAKER HEARD ABOUT THIS. HE LEFT A *KARAKURI NINGYO*, A MECHANIZED PUPPET, ON THE MOUNTAIN PATH. THEN HE HID AND WATCHED.
THE WOMAN APPEARED AND ASKED THE QUESTIONS. WHEN THE PUPPET DIDN'T ANSWER, THE WOMAN'S EYES BEGAN TO SHINE BRIGHT RED, HER MOUTH SPREAD OPEN FROM SIDE TO SIDE, HER LIMBS SPLIT INTO EIGHT, AND WITH A STRANGE, FISHY SMELL...

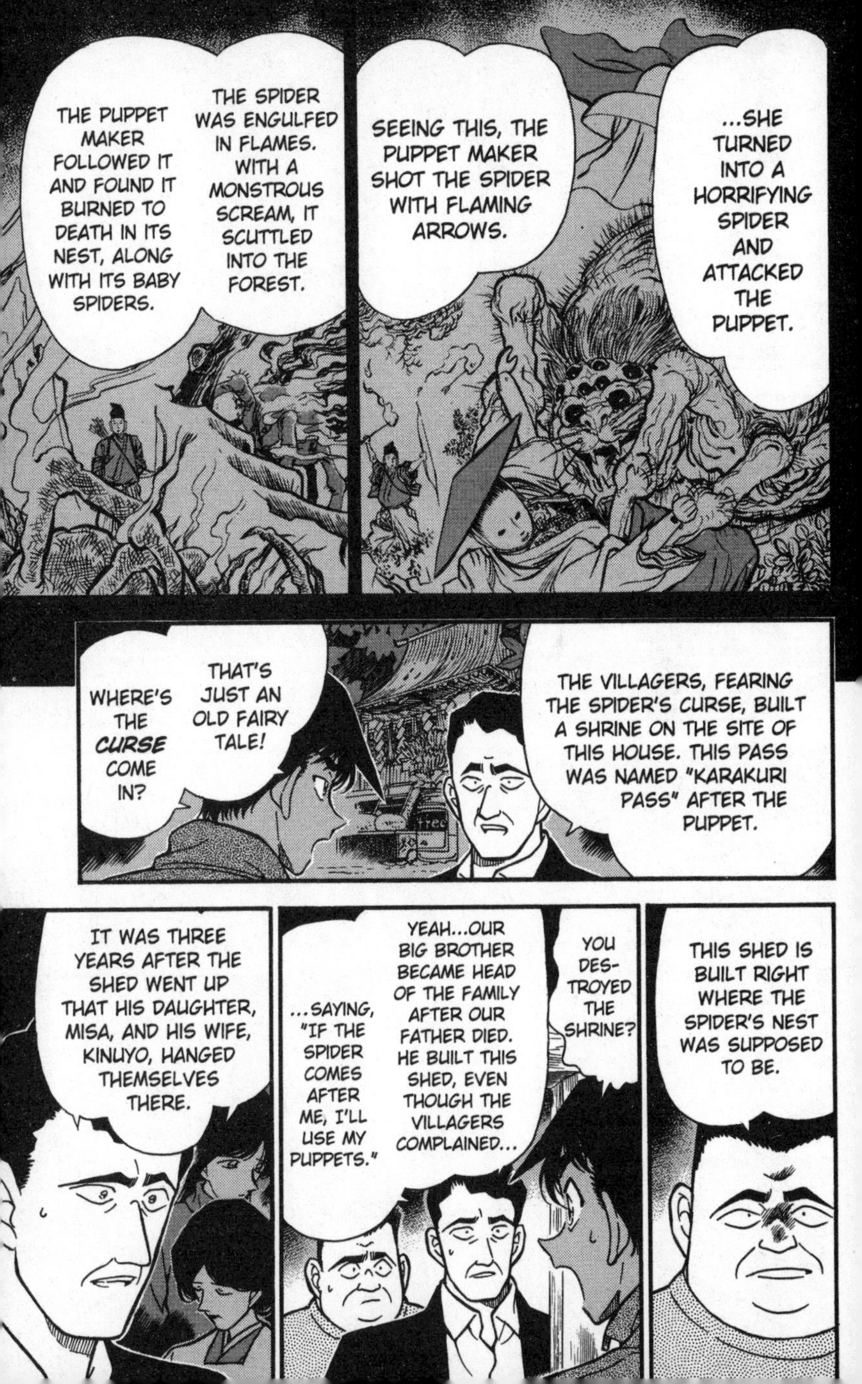

...SHE TURNED INTO A HORRIFYING SPIDER AND ATTACKED THE PUPPET.
SEEING THIS, THE PUPPET MAKER SHOT THE SPIDER WITH FLAMING ARROWS.
THE SPIDER WAS ENGULFED IN FLAMES. WITH A MONSTROUS SCREAM, IT SCUTTLED INTO THE FOREST.
THE PUPPET MAKER FOLLOWED IT AND FOUND IT BURNED TO DEATH IN ITS NEST, ALONG WITH ITS BABY SPIDERS.
THE VILLAGERS, FEARING THE SPIDER'S CURSE, BUILT A SHRINE ON THE SITE OF THIS HOUSE. THIS PASS WAS NAMED "KARAKURI PASS" AFTER THE PUPPET.
THAT'S JUST AN OLD FAIRY TALE!
WHERE'S THE *CURSE* COME IN?
THIS SHED IS BUILT RIGHT WHERE THE SPIDER'S NEST WAS SUPPOSED TO BE.
YOU DES-TROYED THE SHRINE?
YEAH...OUR BIG BROTHER BECAME HEAD OF THE FAMILY AFTER OUR FATHER DIED. HE BUILT THIS SHED, EVEN THOUGH THE VILLAGERS COMPLAINED...
...SAYING, "IF THE SPIDER COMES AFTER ME, I'LL USE MY PUPPETS."
IT WAS THREE YEARS AFTER THE SHED WENT UP THAT HIS DAUGHTER, MISA, AND HIS WIFE, KINUYO, HANGED THEMSELVES THERE.

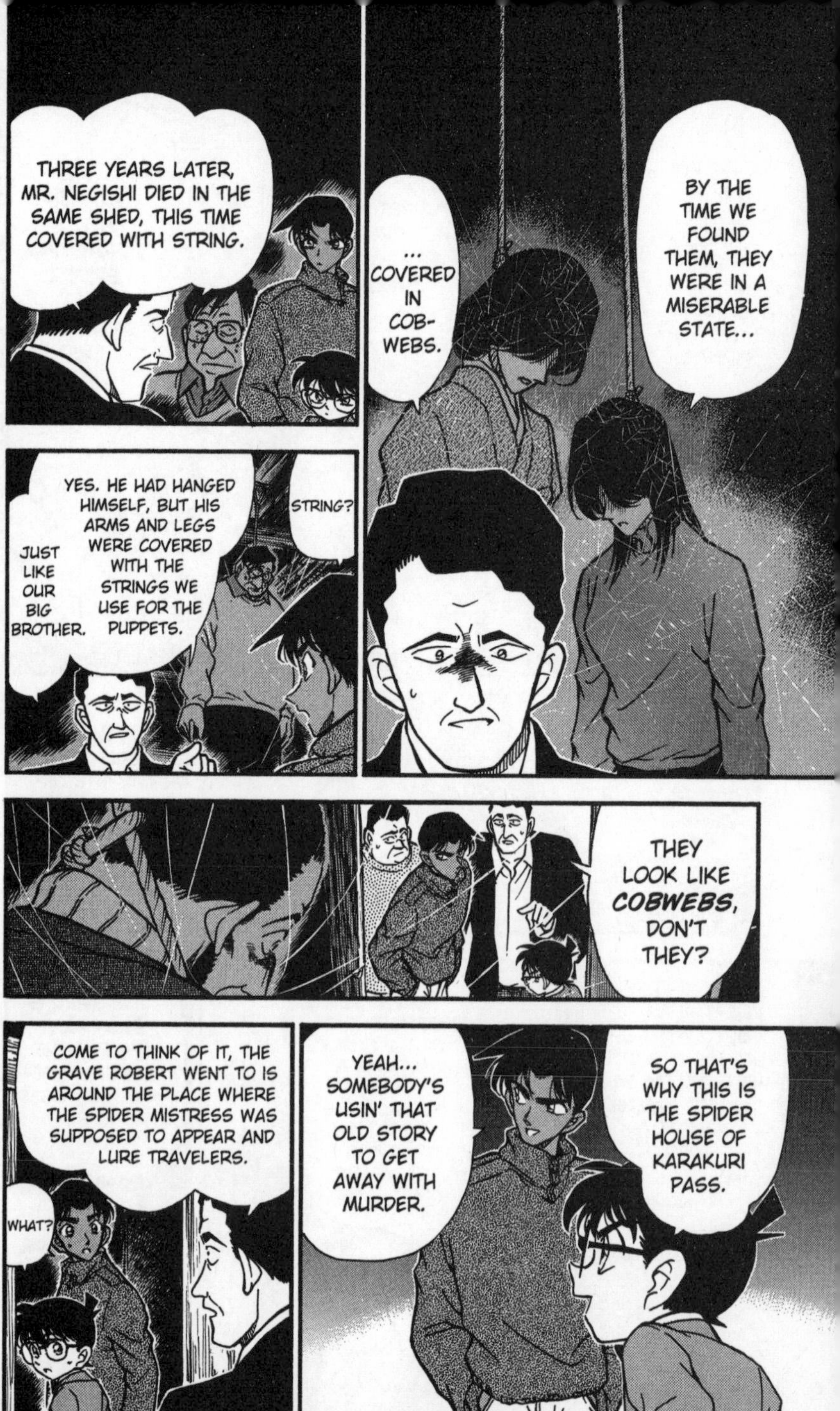
BY THE TIME WE FOUND THEM, THEY WERE IN A MISERABLE STATE...
... COVERED IN COB-WEBS.
THREE YEARS LATER, MR. NEGISHI DIED IN THE SAME SHED, THIS TIME COVERED WITH STRING.
STRING?
YES. HE HAD HANGED HIMSELF, BUT HIS ARMS AND LEGS WERE COVERED WITH THE STRINGS WE USE FOR THE PUPPETS.
JUST LIKE OUR BIG BROTHER.
THEY LOOK LIKE COBWEBS, DON'T THEY?
SO THAT'S WHY THIS IS THE SPIDER HOUSE OF KARAKURI PASS.
YEAH... SOMEBODY'S USIN' THAT OLD STORY TO GET AWAY WITH MURDER.
COME TO THINK OF IT, THE GRAVE ROBERT WENT TO IS AROUND THE PLACE WHERE THE SPIDER MISTRESS WAS SUPPOSED TO APPEAR AND LURE TRAVELERS.
WHAT?

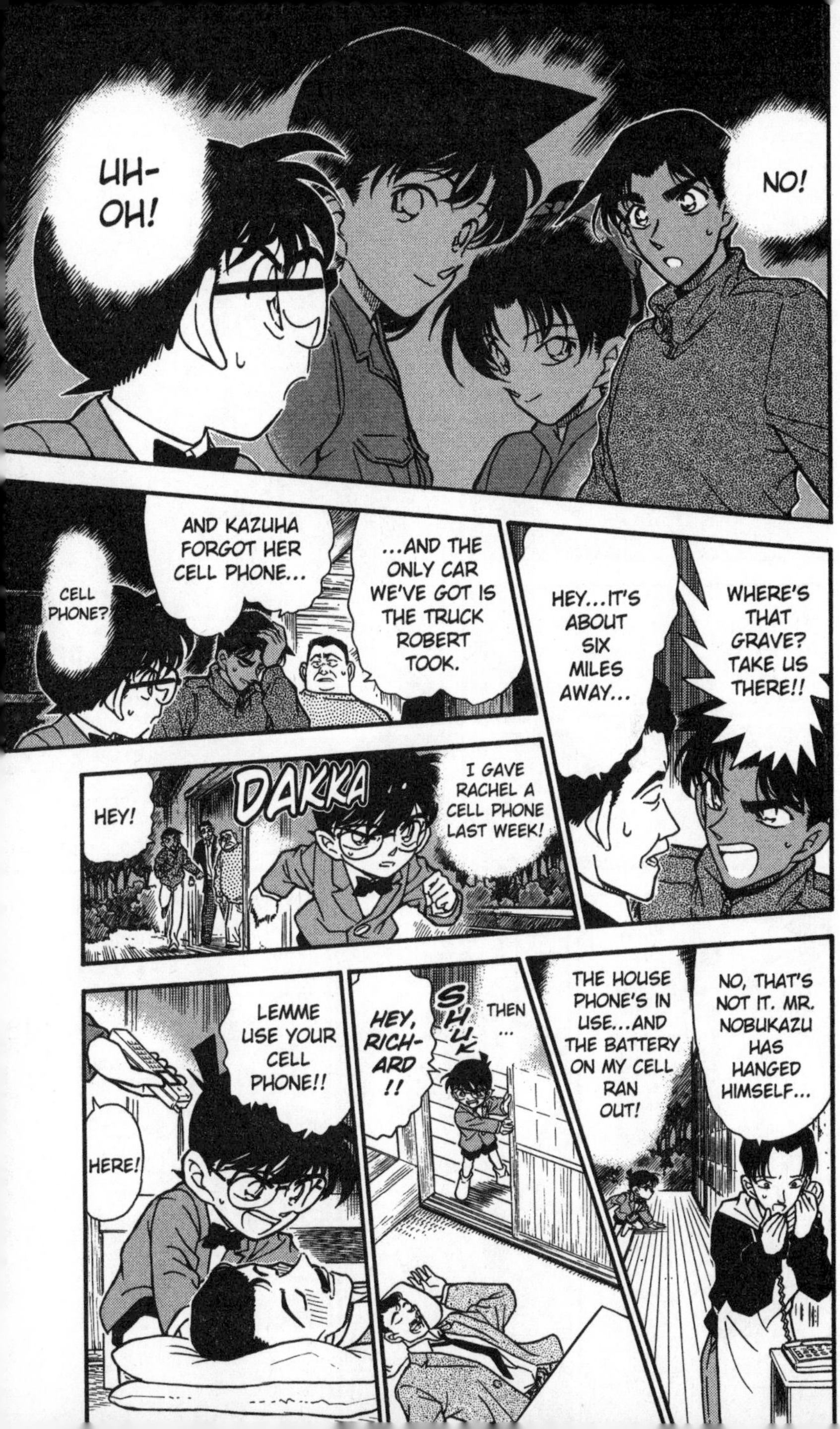
NO!
UH-OH!
WHERE'S THAT GRAVE? TAKE US THERE!!
HEY...IT'S ABOUT SIX MILES AWAY...
AND KAZUHA FORGOT HER CELL PHONE...
...AND THE ONLY CAR WE'VE GOT IS THE TRUCK ROBERT TOOK.
CELL PHONE?
I GAVE RACHEL A CELL PHONE LAST WEEK!
DAKKA
HEY!
NO, THAT'S NOT IT. MR. NOBUKAZU HAS HANGED HIMSELF...
THE HOUSE PHONE'S IN USE...AND THE BATTERY ON MY CELL RAN OUT!
THEN...
SHUK
HEY, RICHARD!!
LEMME USE YOUR CELL PHONE!!
HERE!

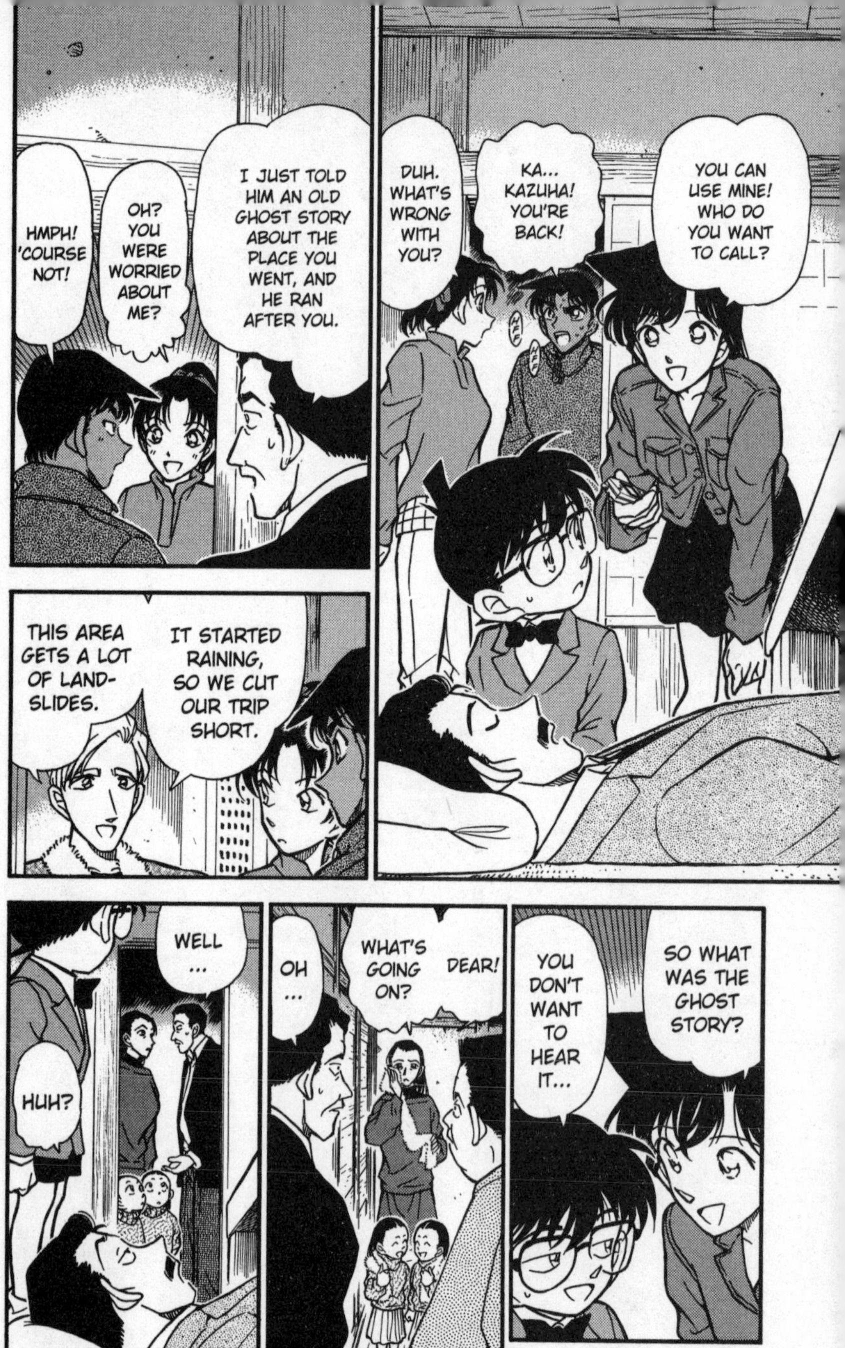
YOU CAN USE MINE! WHO DO YOU WANT TO CALL?
KA... KAZUHA! YOU'RE BACK!
DUH. WHAT'S WRONG WITH YOU?
I JUST TOLD HIM AN OLD GHOST STORY ABOUT THE PLACE YOU WENT, AND HE RAN AFTER YOU.
OH? YOU WERE WORRIED ABOUT ME?
HMPH! 'COURSE NOT!
IT STARTED RAINING, SO WE CUT OUR TRIP SHORT.
THIS AREA GETS A LOT OF LAND-SLIDES.
SO WHAT WAS THE GHOST STORY?
YOU DON'T WANT TO HEAR IT...
DEAR!
WHAT'S GOING ON?
OH ...
WELL ...
HUH?

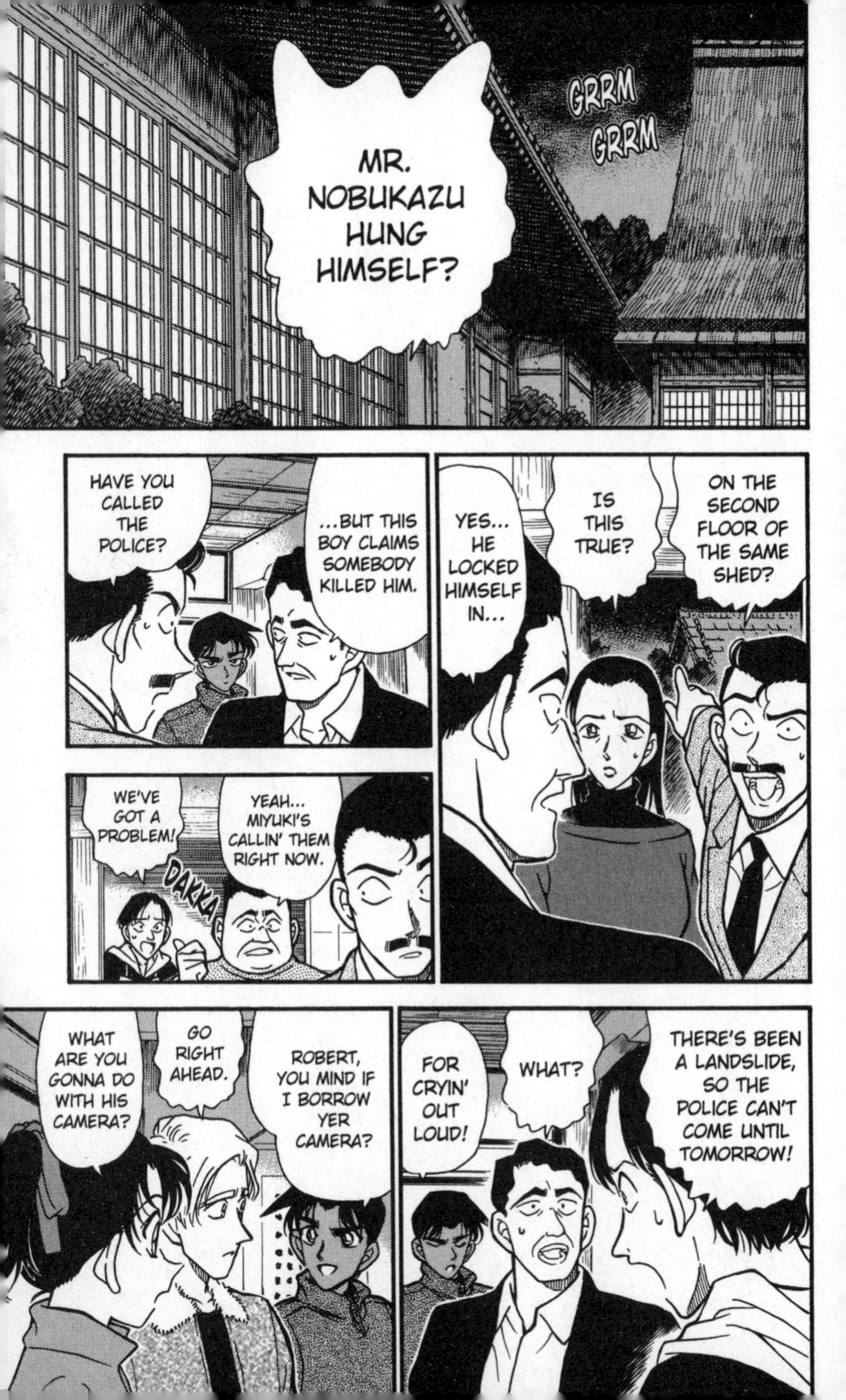
GRRM GRRM
MR. NOBUKAZU HUNG HIMSELF?
ON THE SECOND FLOOR OF THE SAME SHED?
IS THIS TRUE?
YES... HE LOCKED HIMSELF IN...
...BUT THIS BOY CLAIMS SOMEBODY KILLED HIM.
HAVE YOU CALLED THE POLICE?
YEAH... MIYUKI'S CALLIN' THEM RIGHT NOW.
DAKKA
WE'VE GOT A PROBLEM!
THERE'S BEEN A LANDSLIDE, SO THE POLICE CAN'T COME UNTIL TOMORROW!
WHAT?
FOR CRYIN' OUT LOUD!
ROBERT, YOU MIND IF I BORROW YER CAMERA?
GO RIGHT AHEAD.
WHAT ARE YOU GONNA DO WITH HIS CAMERA?

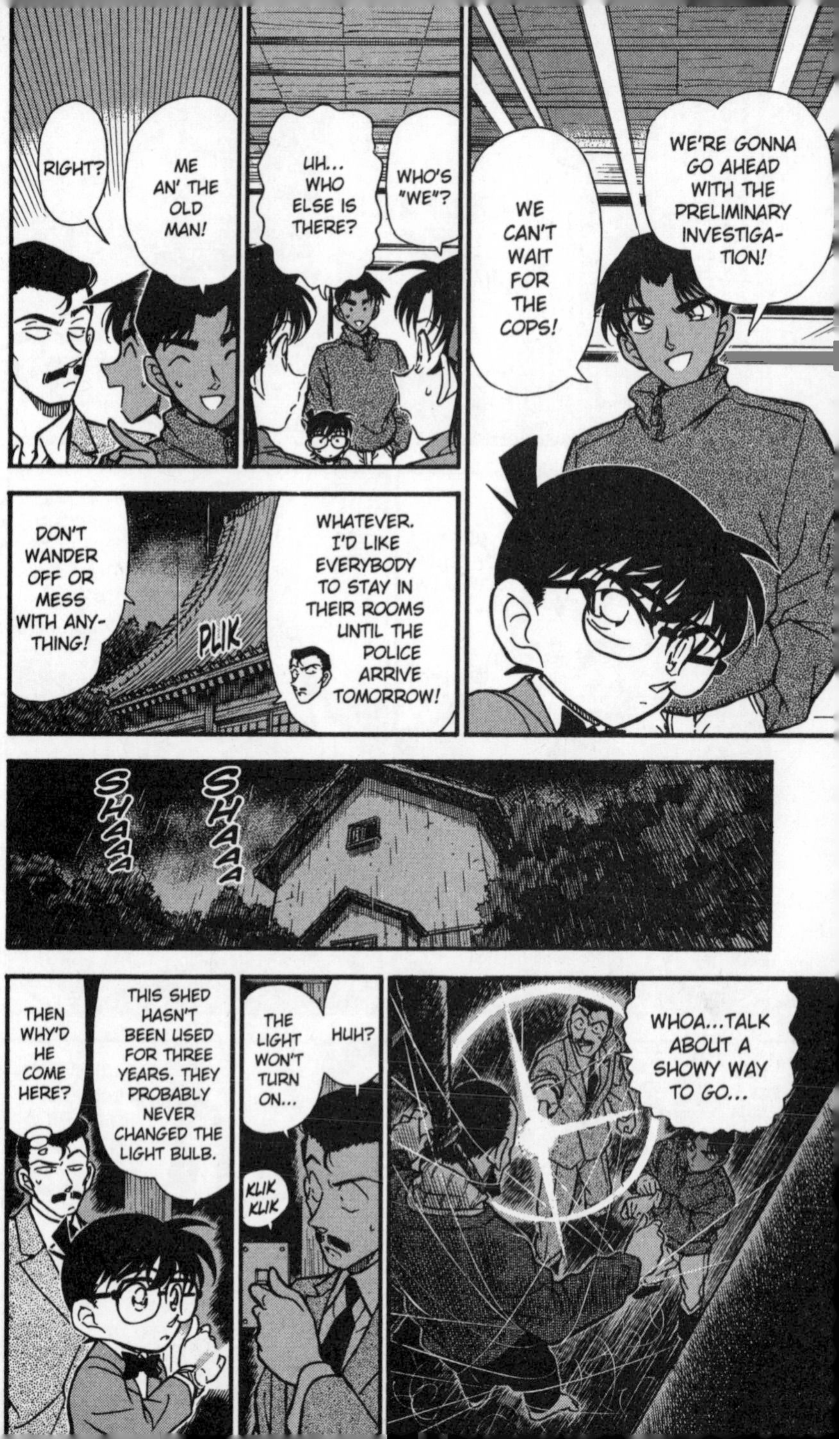
WE'RE GONNA GO AHEAD WITH THE PRELIMINARY INVESTIGA-TION!
WE CAN'T WAIT FOR THE COPS!
WHO'S "WE"?
UH... WHO ELSE IS THERE?
ME AN' THE OLD MAN!
RIGHT?
WHATEVER. I'D LIKE EVERYBODY TO STAY IN THEIR ROOMS UNTIL THE POLICE ARRIVE TOMORROW!
PLIK
DON'T WANDER OFF OR MESS WITH ANY-THING!
SHAAAA
SHAAAA
WHOA...TALK ABOUT A SHOWY WAY TO GO...
HUH?
THE LIGHT WON'T TURN ON...
KLIK KLIK
THIS SHED HASN'T BEEN USED FOR THREE YEARS. THEY PROBABLY NEVER CHANGED THE LIGHT BULB.
THEN WHY'D HE COME HERE?

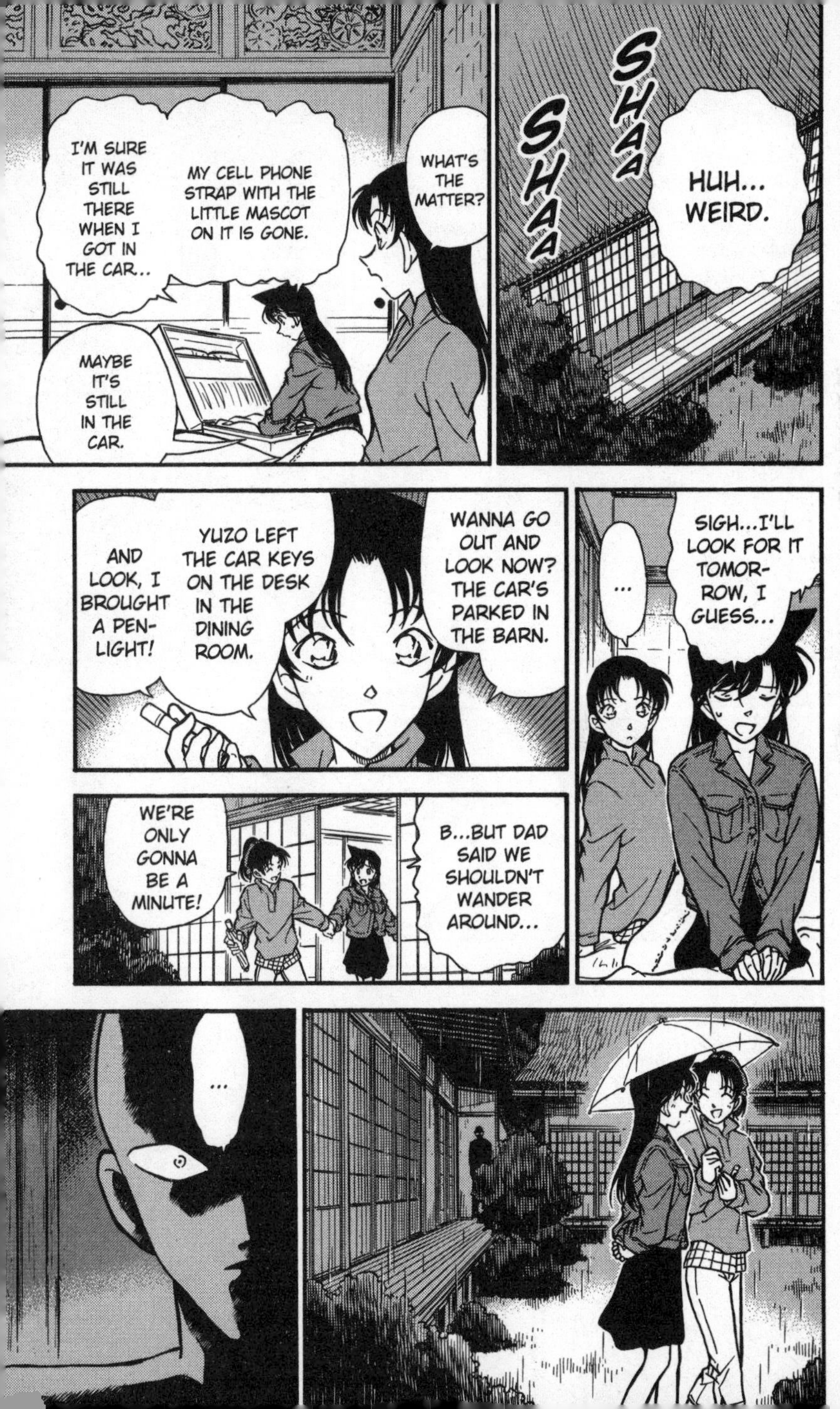
SHAA
SHAA
HUH... WEIRD.
WHAT'S THE MATTER?
MY CELL PHONE STRAP WITH THE LITTLE MASCOT ON IT IS GONE.
I'M SURE IT WAS STILL THERE WHEN I GOT IN THE CAR...
MAYBE IT'S STILL IN THE CAR.
SIGH...I'LL LOOK FOR IT TOMOR-ROW, I GUESS...
...
WANNA GO OUT AND LOOK NOW? THE CAR'S PARKED IN THE BARN.
YUZO LEFT THE CAR KEYS ON THE DESK IN THE DINING ROOM.
AND LOOK, I BROUGHT A PEN-LIGHT!
B...BUT DAD SAID WE SHOULDN'T WANDER AROUND...
WE'RE ONLY GONNA BE A MINUTE!
...

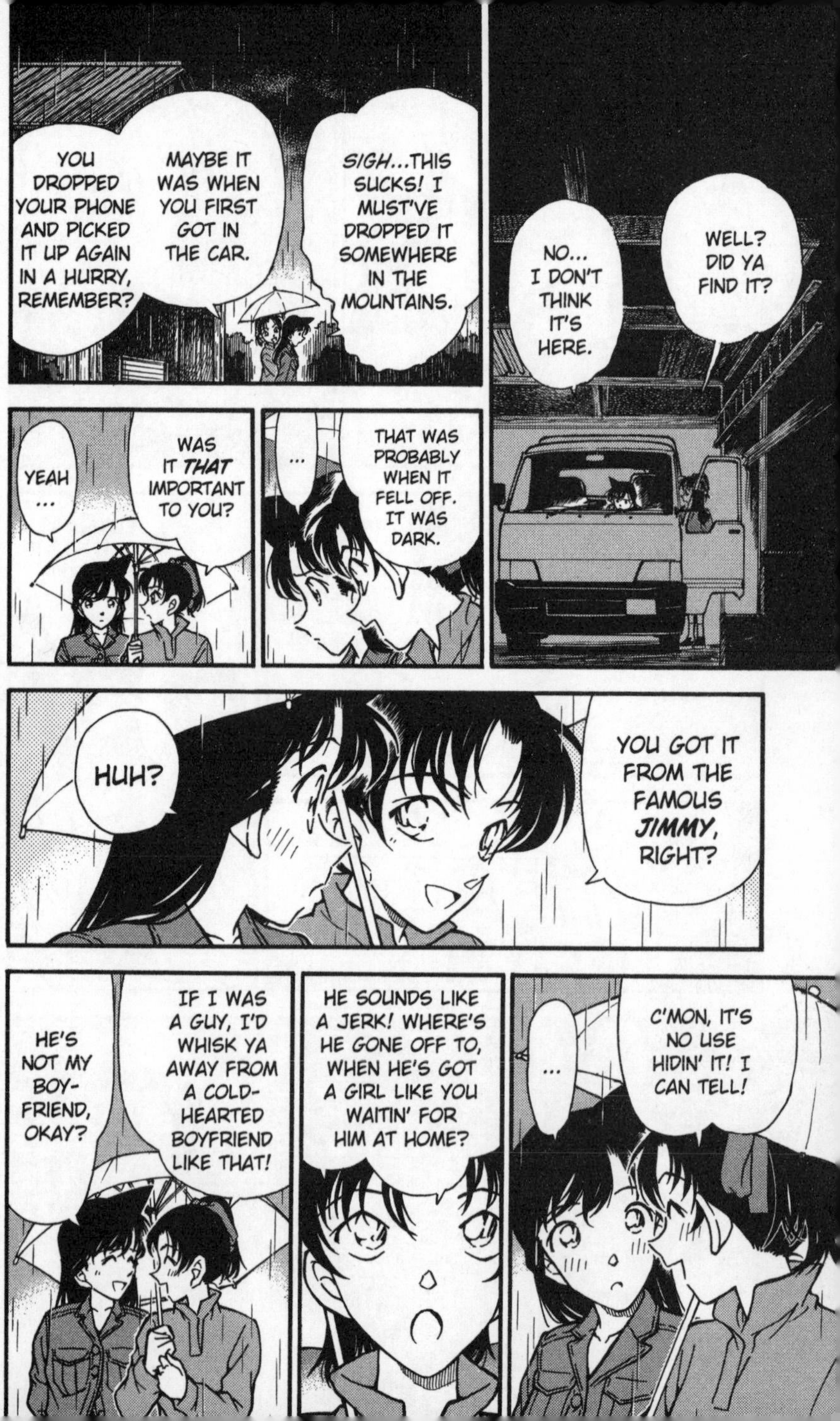
WELL? DID YA FIND IT?
NO... I DON'T THINK IT'S HERE.
SIGH...THIS SUCKS! I MUST'VE DROPPED IT SOMEWHERE IN THE MOUNTAINS.
MAYBE IT WAS WHEN YOU FIRST GOT IN THE CAR.
YOU DROPPED YOUR PHONE AND PICKED IT UP AGAIN IN A HURRY, REMEMBER?
THAT WAS PROBABLY WHEN IT FELL OFF. IT WAS DARK.
...
WAS IT ***THAT*** IMPORTANT TO YOU?
YEAH...
YOU GOT IT FROM THE FAMOUS ***JIMMY***, RIGHT?
HUH?
C'MON, IT'S NO USE HIDIN' IT! I CAN TELL!
...
HE SOUNDS LIKE A JERK! WHERE'S HE GONE OFF TO, WHEN HE'S GOT A GIRL LIKE YOU WAITIN' FOR HIM AT HOME?
IF I WAS A GUY, I'D WHISK YA AWAY FROM A COLD-HEARTED BOYFRIEND LIKE THAT!
HE'S NOT MY BOY-FRIEND, OKAY?

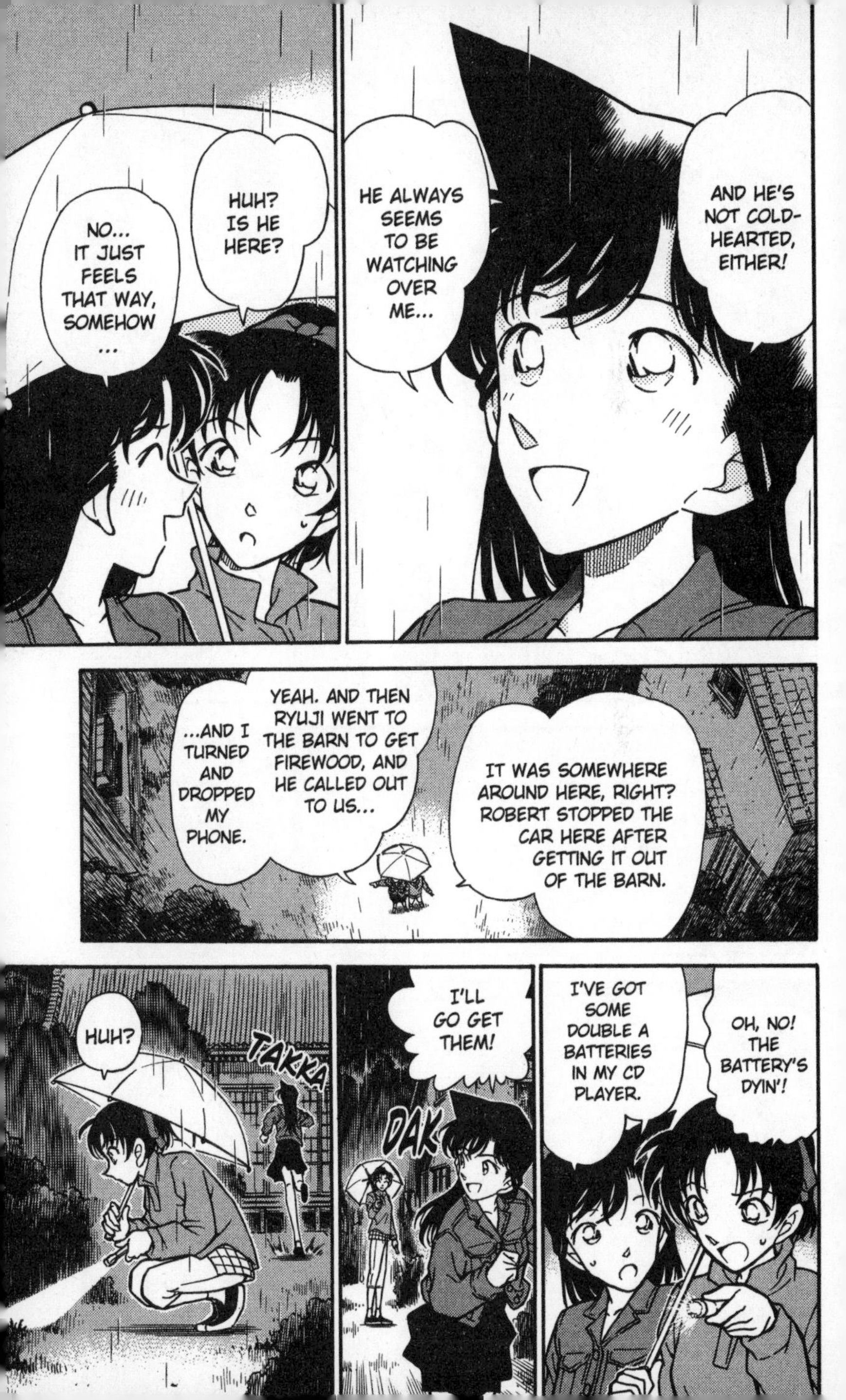
AND HE'S NOT COLD-HEARTED, EITHER!
HE ALWAYS SEEMS TO BE WATCHING OVER ME...
HUH? IS HE HERE?
NO... IT JUST FEELS THAT WAY, SOMEHOW...
IT WAS SOMEWHERE AROUND HERE, RIGHT? ROBERT STOPPED THE CAR HERE AFTER GETTING IT OUT OF THE BARN.
YEAH. AND THEN RYUJI WENT TO THE BARN TO GET FIREWOOD, AND HE CALLED OUT TO US...
...AND I TURNED AND DROPPED MY PHONE.
OH, NO! THE BATTERY'S DYIN'!
I'VE GOT SOME DOUBLE A BATTERIES IN MY CD PLAYER.
I'LL GO GET THEM!
DAK
TAKKA
HUH?

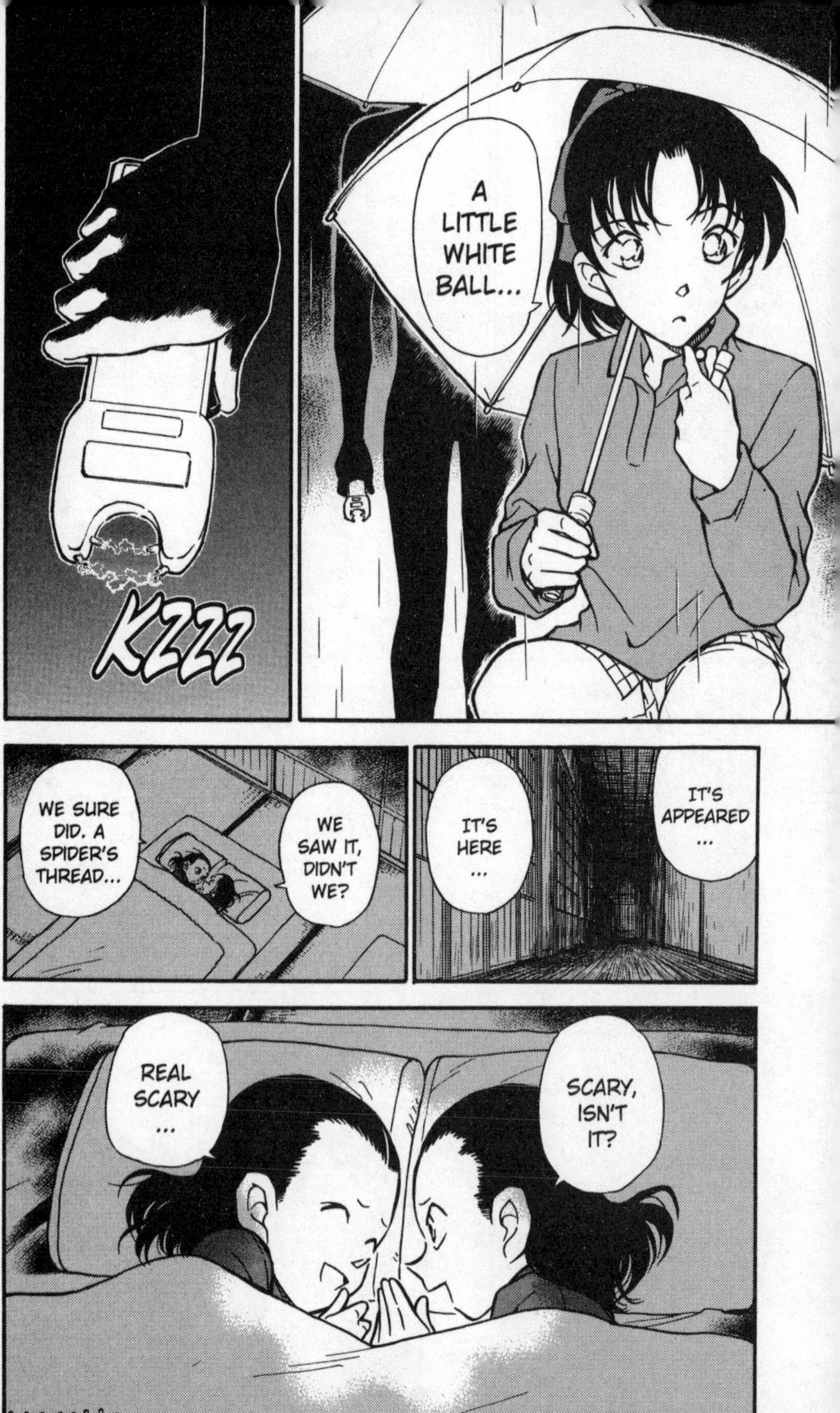
A LITTLE WHITE BALL...
KZZZ
IT'S APPEARED ...
IT'S HERE ...
WE SAW IT, DIDN'T WE?
WE SURE DID. A SPIDER'S THREAD...
SCARY, ISN'T IT?
REAL SCARY ...

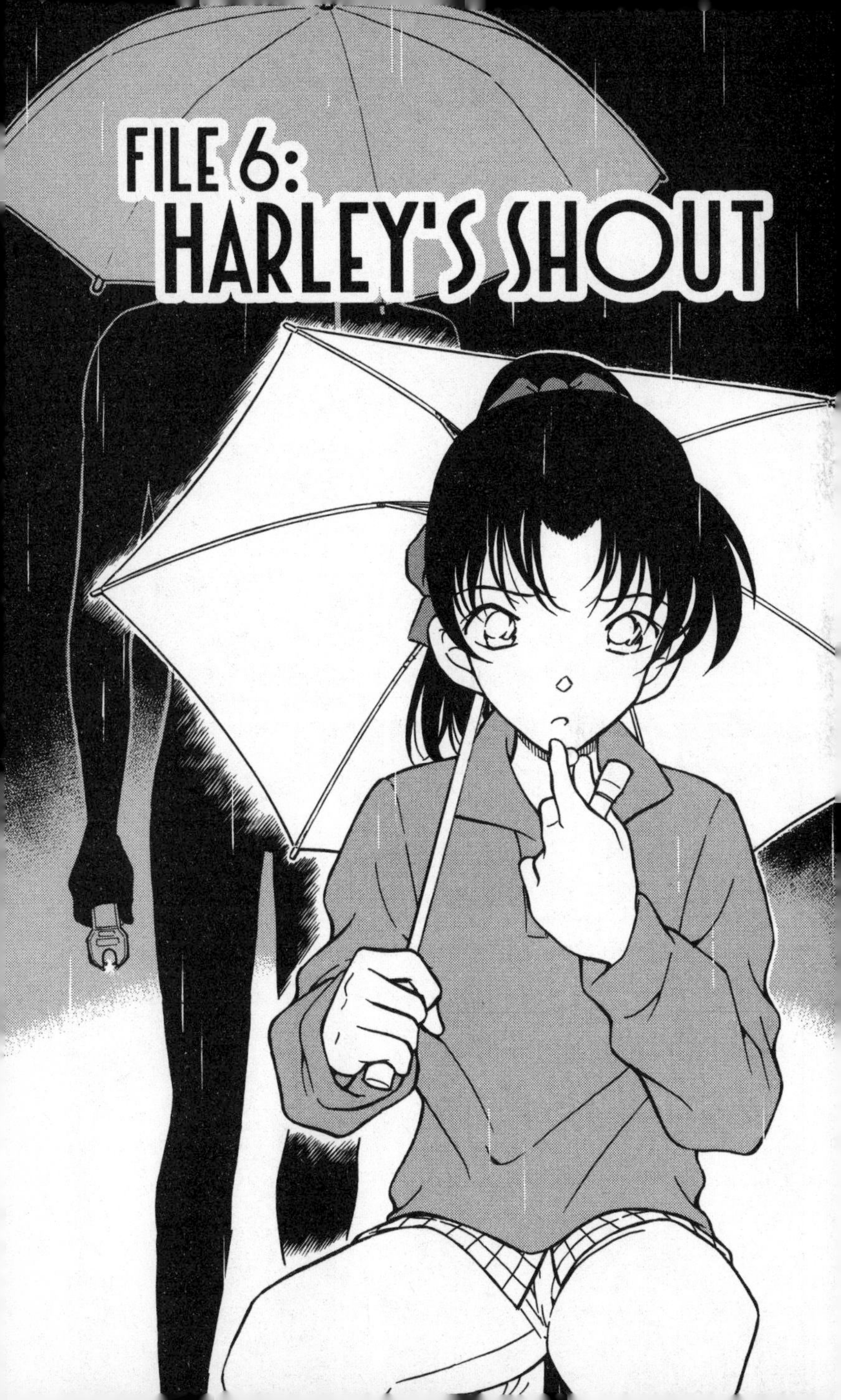
FILE 6:
HARLEY'S SHOUT

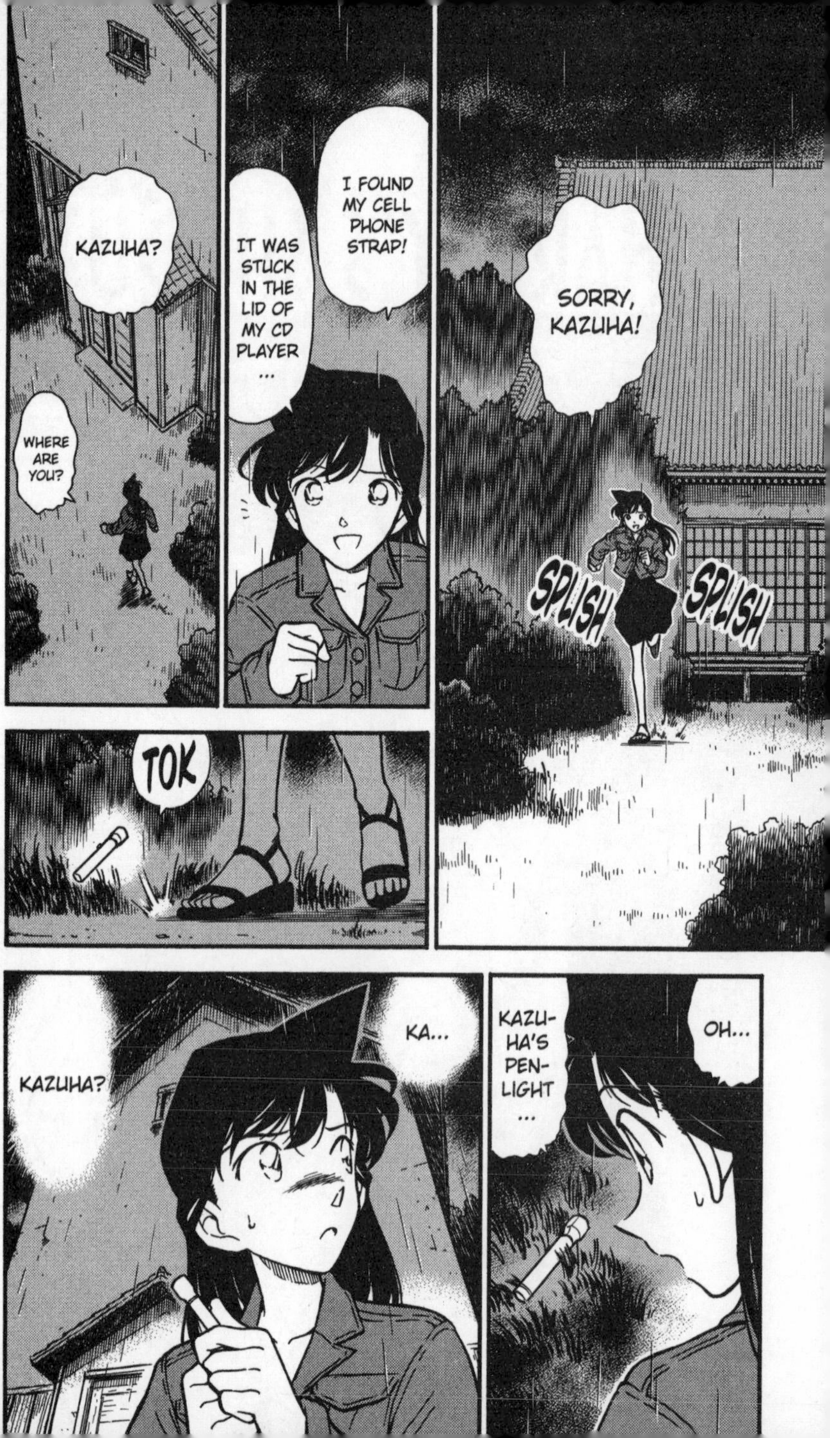

SORRY, KAZUHA!
SPLISH
SPLISH
I FOUND MY CELL PHONE STRAP!
IT WAS STUCK IN THE LID OF MY CD PLAYER ...
KAZUHA?
WHERE ARE YOU?
TOK
OH...
KAZU-HA'S PEN-LIGHT ...
KA...
KAZUHA?

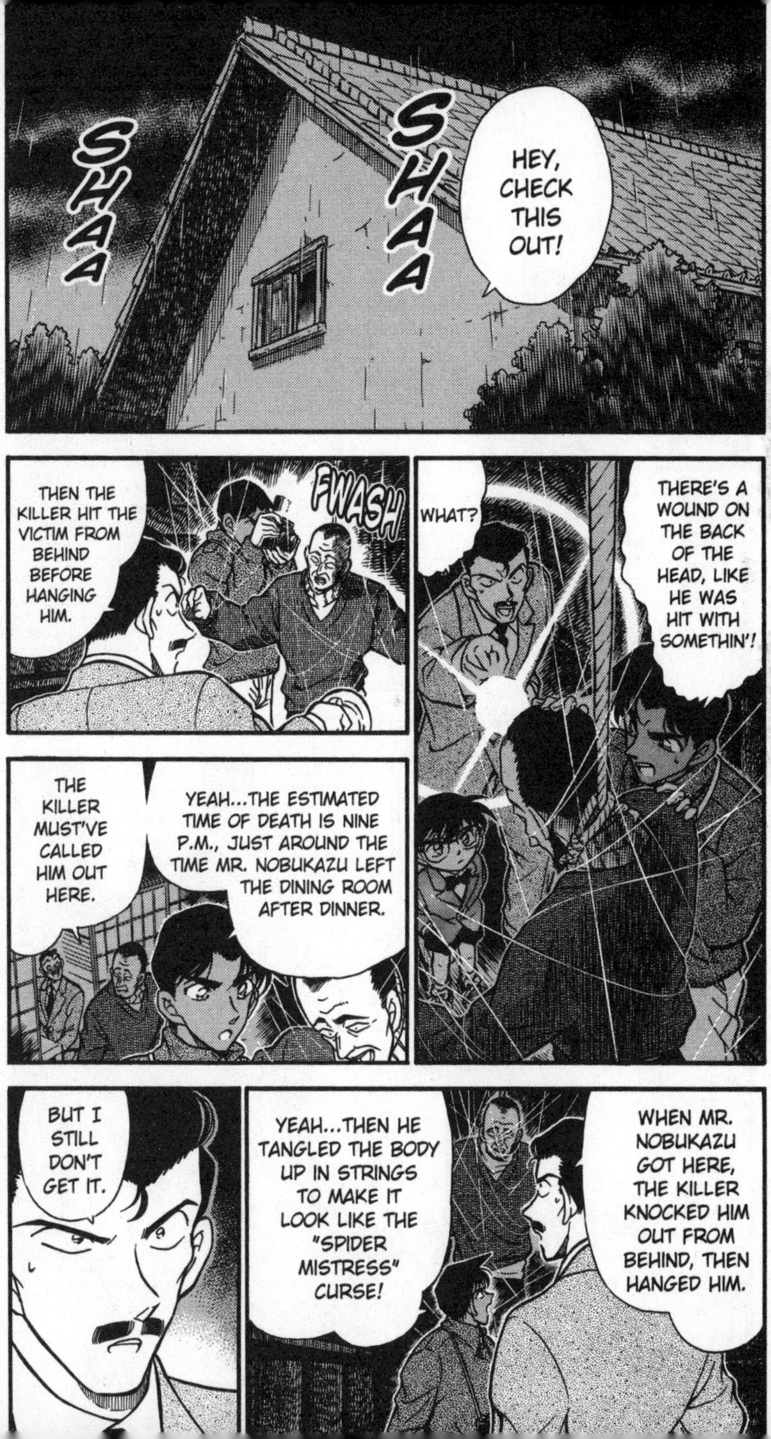
HEY, CHECK THIS OUT!
SHAA
SHAA
THERE'S A WOUND ON THE BACK OF THE HEAD, LIKE HE WAS HIT WITH SOMETHIN'!
WHAT?
FWASH
THEN THE KILLER HIT THE VICTIM FROM BEHIND BEFORE HANGING HIM.
YEAH...THE ESTIMATED TIME OF DEATH IS NINE P.M., JUST AROUND THE TIME MR. NOBUKAZU LEFT THE DINING ROOM AFTER DINNER.
THE KILLER MUST'VE CALLED HIM OUT HERE.
WHEN MR. NOBUKAZU GOT HERE, THE KILLER KNOCKED HIM OUT FROM BEHIND, THEN HANGED HIM.
YEAH...THEN HE TANGLED THE BODY UP IN STRINGS TO MAKE IT LOOK LIKE THE "SPIDER MISTRESS" CURSE!
BUT I STILL DON'T GET IT.

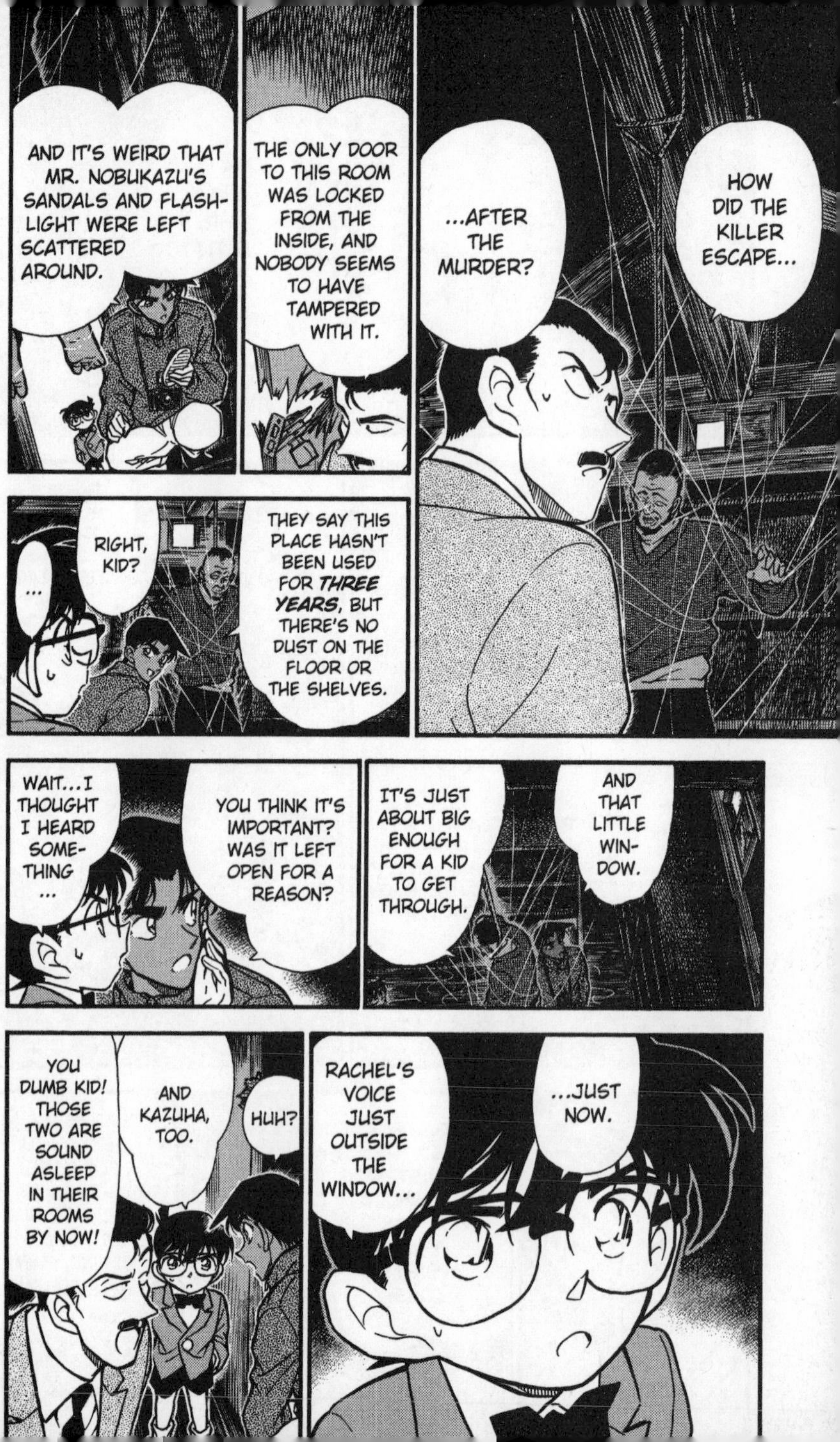
HOW DID THE KILLER ESCAPE...
...AFTER THE MURDER?
THE ONLY DOOR TO THIS ROOM WAS LOCKED FROM THE INSIDE, AND NOBODY SEEMS TO HAVE TAMPERED WITH IT.
AND IT'S WEIRD THAT MR. NOBUKAZU'S SANDALS AND FLASH-LIGHT WERE LEFT SCATTERED AROUND.
THEY SAY THIS PLACE HASN'T BEEN USED FOR THREE YEARS, BUT THERE'S NO DUST ON THE FLOOR OR THE SHELVES.
RIGHT, KID?
...
AND THAT LITTLE WIN-DOW.
IT'S JUST ABOUT BIG ENOUGH FOR A KID TO GET THROUGH.
YOU THINK IT'S IMPORTANT? WAS IT LEFT OPEN FOR A REASON?
WAIT...I THOUGHT I HEARD SOME-THING ...
RACHEL'S VOICE JUST OUTSIDE THE WINDOW...
...JUST NOW.
HUH?
AND KAZUHA, TOO.
YOU DUMB KID! THOSE TWO ARE SOUND ASLEEP IN THEIR ROOMS BY NOW!

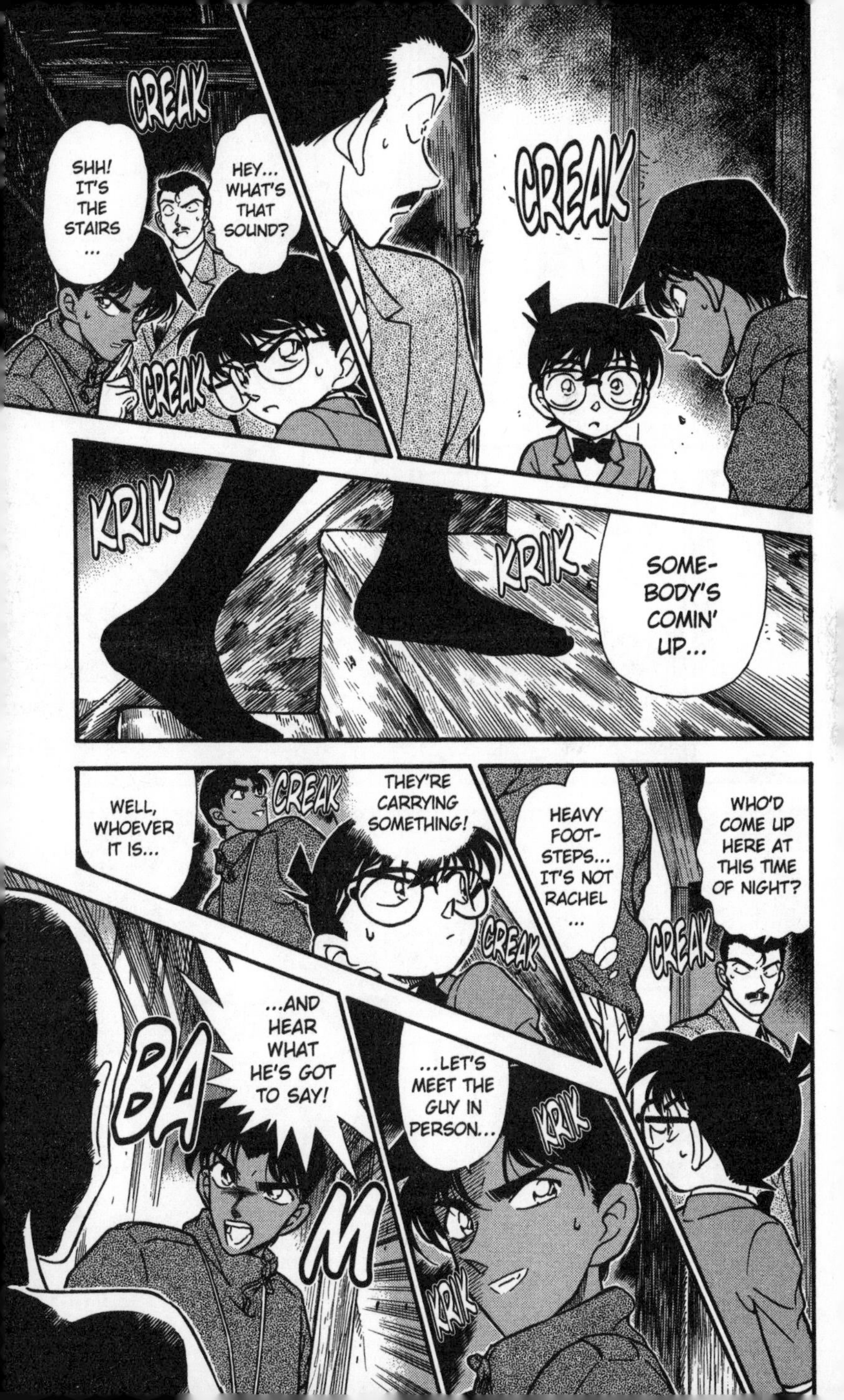
CREAK
HEY... WHAT'S THAT SOUND?
CREAK
SHH! IT'S THE STAIRS...
CREAK
SOME-BODY'S COMIN' UP...
KRIK
KRIK
WHO'D COME UP HERE AT THIS TIME OF NIGHT?
CREAK
HEAVY FOOT-STEPS... IT'S NOT RACHEL...
THEY'RE CARRYING SOMETHING!
CREAK
CREAK
WELL, WHOEVER IT IS...
...LET'S MEET THE GUY IN PERSON...
KRIK
KRIK
...AND HEAR WHAT HE'S GOT TO SAY!
BAM

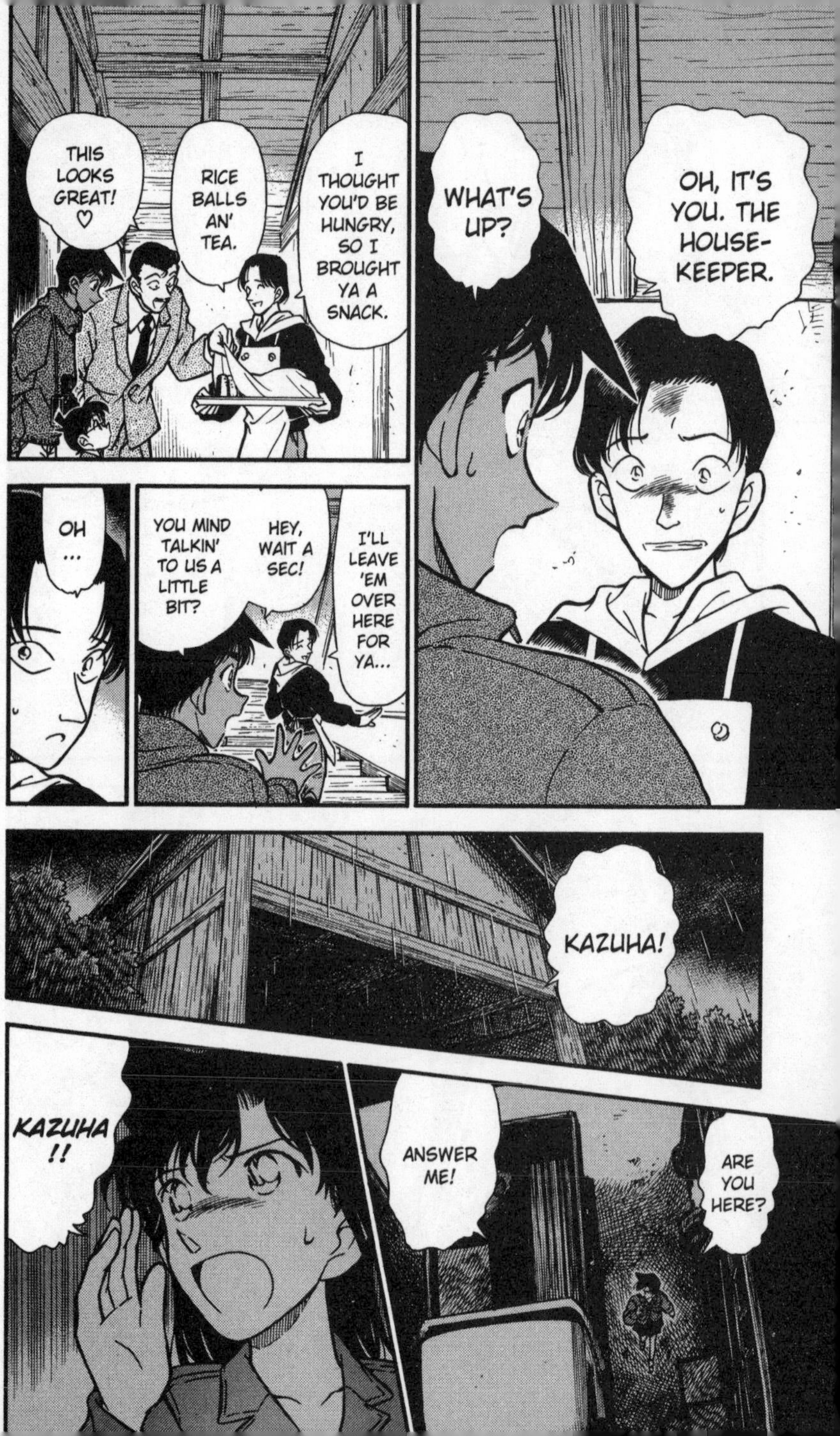
OH, IT'S YOU. THE HOUSE-KEEPER.
WHAT'S UP?
I THOUGHT YOU'D BE HUNGRY, SO I BROUGHT YA A SNACK.
RICE BALLS AN' TEA.
THIS LOOKS GREAT! ♡
I'LL LEAVE 'EM OVER HERE FOR YA...
HEY, WAIT A SEC!
YOU MIND TALKIN' TO US A LITTLE BIT?
OH ...
KAZUHA!
ARE YOU HERE?
ANSWER ME!
KAZUHA !!

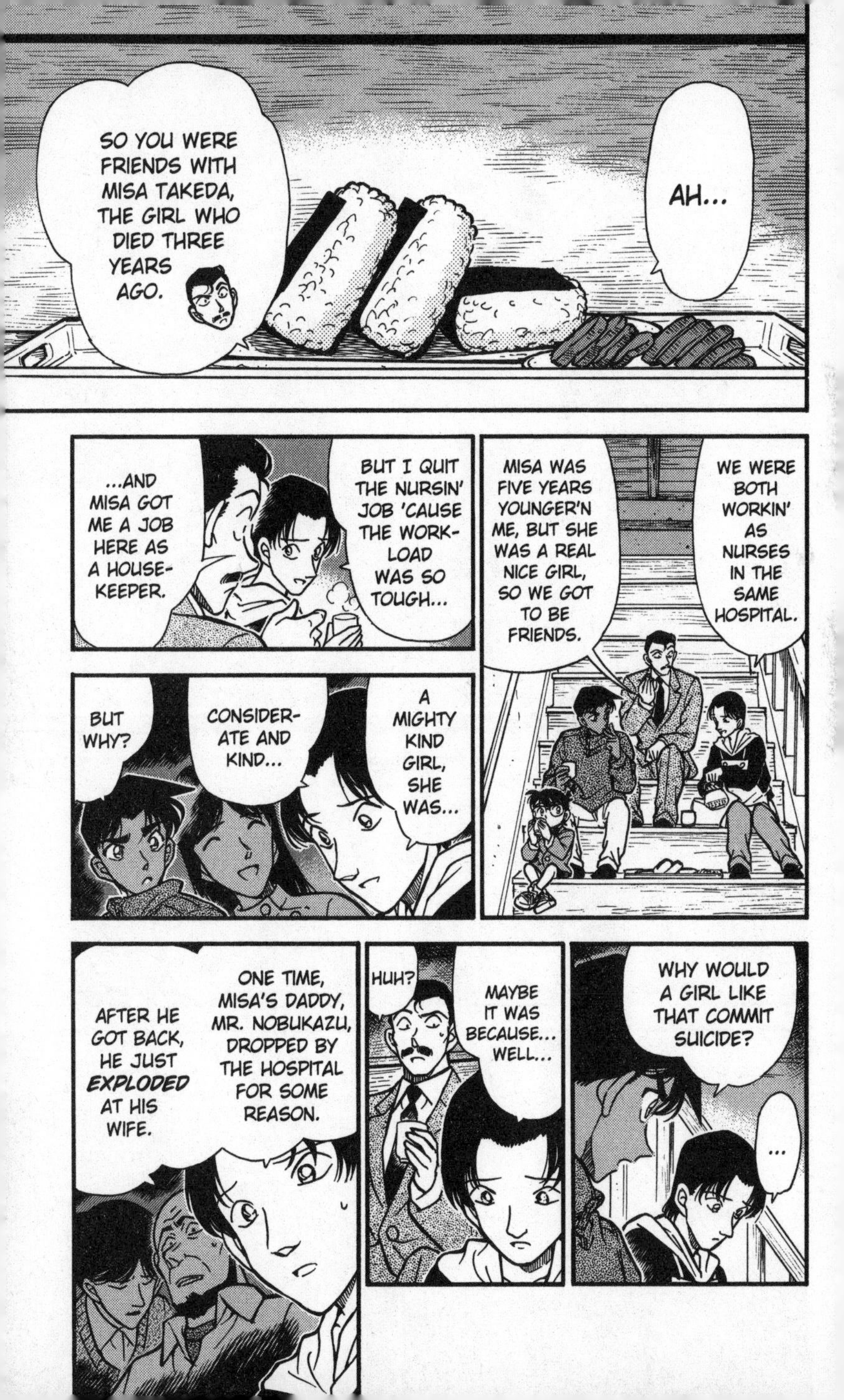
SO YOU WERE FRIENDS WITH MISA TAKEDA, THE GIRL WHO DIED THREE YEARS AGO.
AH...
WE WERE BOTH WORKIN' AS NURSES IN THE SAME HOSPITAL.
MISA WAS FIVE YEARS YOUNGER'N ME, BUT SHE WAS A REAL NICE GIRL, SO WE GOT TO BE FRIENDS.
BUT I QUIT THE NURSIN' JOB 'CAUSE THE WORK-LOAD WAS SO TOUGH...
...AND MISA GOT ME A JOB HERE AS A HOUSE-KEEPER.
A MIGHTY KIND GIRL, SHE WAS...
CONSIDER-ATE AND KIND...
BUT WHY?
WHY WOULD A GIRL LIKE THAT COMMIT SUICIDE?
...
MAYBE IT WAS BECAUSE... WELL...
HUH?
ONE TIME, MISA'S DADDY, MR. NOBUKAZU, DROPPED BY THE HOSPITAL FOR SOME REASON.
AFTER HE GOT BACK, HE JUST *EXPLODED* AT HIS WIFE.

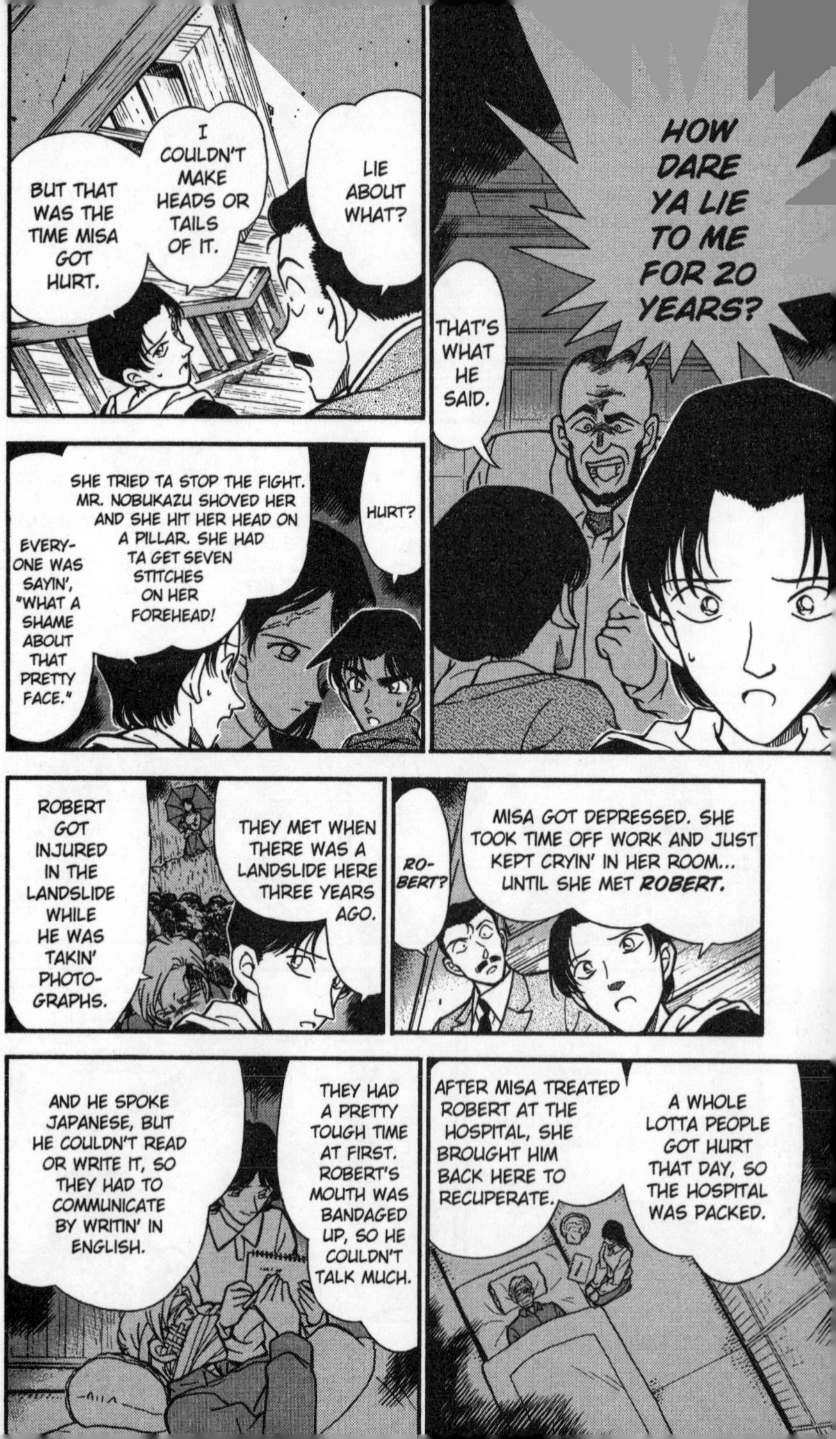
HOW DARE YA LIE TO ME FOR 20 YEARS?
THAT'S WHAT HE SAID.
LIE ABOUT WHAT?
I COULDN'T MAKE HEADS OR TAILS OF IT.
BUT THAT WAS THE TIME MISA GOT HURT.
HURT?
SHE TRIED TA STOP THE FIGHT. MR. NOBUKAZU SHOVED HER AND SHE HIT HER HEAD ON A PILLAR. SHE HAD TA GET SEVEN STITCHES ON HER FOREHEAD!
EVERYONE WAS SAYIN', "WHAT A SHAME ABOUT THAT PRETTY FACE."
MISA GOT DEPRESSED. SHE TOOK TIME OFF WORK AND JUST KEPT CRYIN' IN HER ROOM... UNTIL SHE MET ROBERT.
ROBERT?
THEY MET WHEN THERE WAS A LANDSLIDE HERE THREE YEARS AGO.
ROBERT GOT INJURED IN THE LANDSLIDE WHILE HE WAS TAKIN' PHOTOGRAPHS.
A WHOLE LOTTA PEOPLE GOT HURT THAT DAY, SO THE HOSPITAL WAS PACKED.
AFTER MISA TREATED ROBERT AT THE HOSPITAL, SHE BROUGHT HIM BACK HERE TO RECUPERATE.
THEY HAD A PRETTY TOUGH TIME AT FIRST. ROBERT'S MOUTH WAS BANDAGED UP, SO HE COULDN'T TALK MUCH.
AND HE SPOKE JAPANESE, BUT HE COULDN'T READ OR WRITE IT, SO THEY HAD TO COMMUNICATE BY WRITIN' IN ENGLISH.

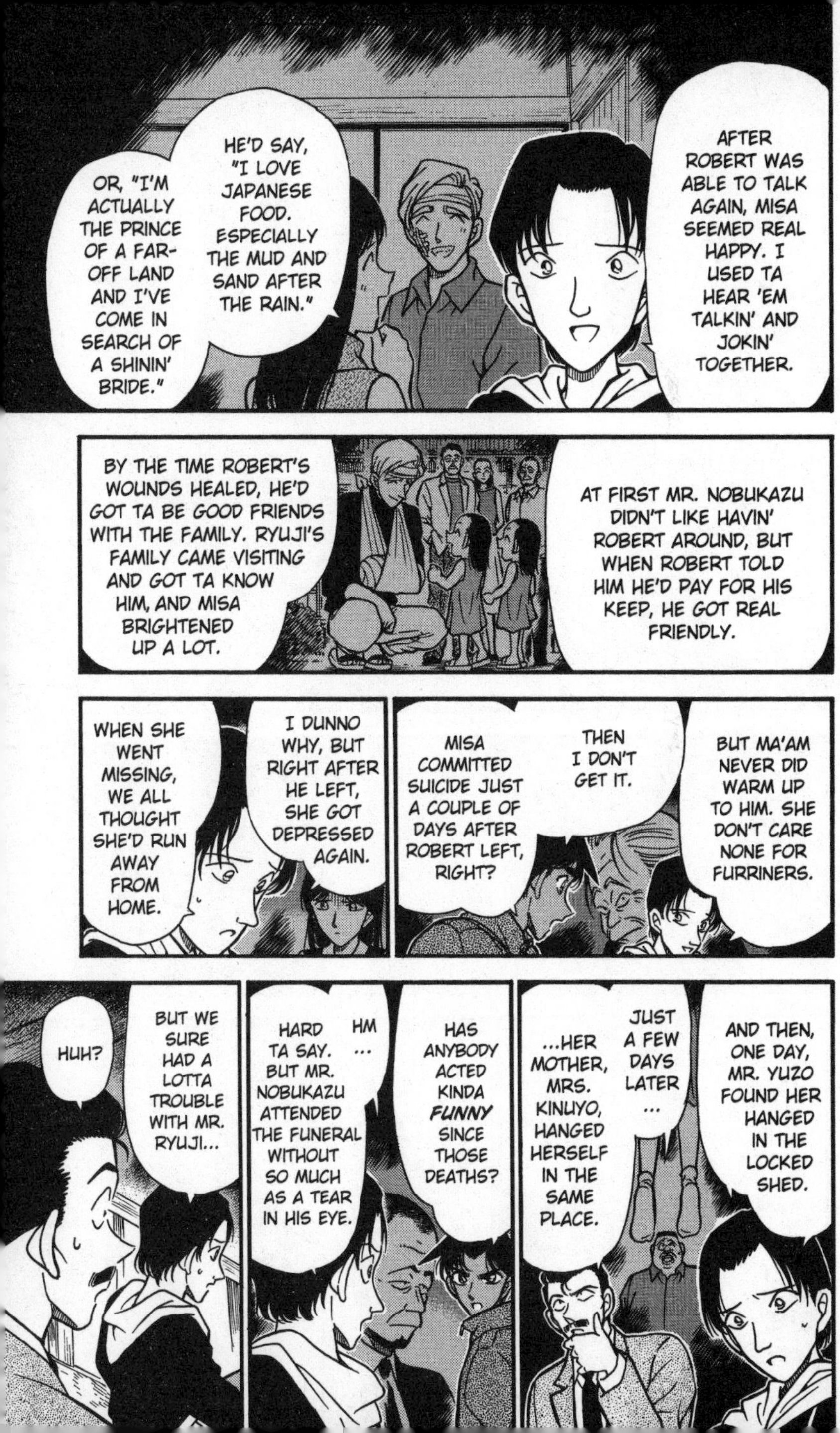
AFTER ROBERT WAS ABLE TO TALK AGAIN, MISA SEEMED REAL HAPPY. I USED TA HEAR 'EM TALKIN' AND JOKIN' TOGETHER.
HE'D SAY, "I LOVE JAPANESE FOOD. ESPECIALLY THE MUD AND SAND AFTER THE RAIN."
OR, "I'M ACTUALLY THE PRINCE OF A FAR-OFF LAND AND I'VE COME IN SEARCH OF A SHININ' BRIDE."
AT FIRST MR. NOBUKAZU DIDN'T LIKE HAVIN' ROBERT AROUND, BUT WHEN ROBERT TOLD HIM HE'D PAY FOR HIS KEEP, HE GOT REAL FRIENDLY.
BY THE TIME ROBERT'S WOUNDS HEALED, HE'D GOT TA BE GOOD FRIENDS WITH THE FAMILY. RYUJI'S FAMILY CAME VISITING AND GOT TA KNOW HIM, AND MISA BRIGHTENED UP A LOT.
BUT MA'AM NEVER DID WARM UP TO HIM. SHE DON'T CARE NONE FOR FURRINERS.
THEN I DON'T GET IT.
MISA COMMITTED SUICIDE JUST A COUPLE OF DAYS AFTER ROBERT LEFT, RIGHT?
I DUNNO WHY, BUT RIGHT AFTER HE LEFT, SHE GOT DEPRESSED AGAIN.
WHEN SHE WENT MISSING, WE ALL THOUGHT SHE'D RUN AWAY FROM HOME.
AND THEN, ONE DAY, MR. YUZO FOUND HER HANGED IN THE LOCKED SHED.
JUST A FEW DAYS LATER ...
...HER MOTHER, MRS. KINUYO, HANGED HERSELF IN THE SAME PLACE.
HAS ANYBODY ACTED KINDA *FUNNY* SINCE THOSE DEATHS?
HM ...
HARD TA SAY. BUT MR. NOBUKAZU ATTENDED THE FUNERAL WITHOUT SO MUCH AS A TEAR IN HIS EYE.
BUT WE SURE HAD A LOTTA TROUBLE WITH MR. RYUJI...
HUH?

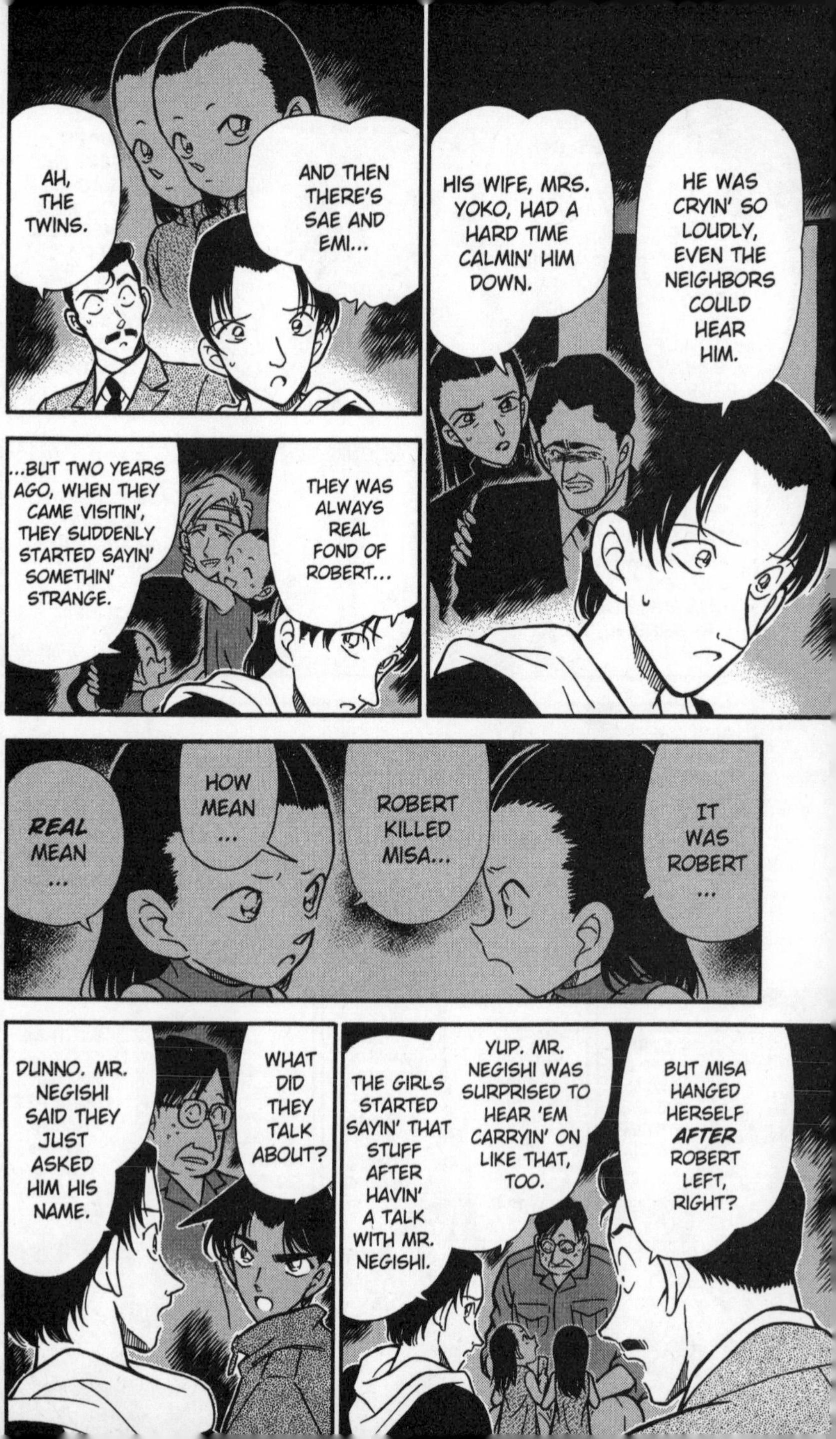
HE WAS CRYIN' SO LOUDLY, EVEN THE NEIGHBORS COULD HEAR HIM.
HIS WIFE, MRS. YOKO, HAD A HARD TIME CALMIN' HIM DOWN.
AND THEN THERE'S SAE AND EMI...
AH, THE TWINS.
THEY WAS ALWAYS REAL FOND OF ROBERT...
...BUT TWO YEARS AGO, WHEN THEY CAME VISITIN', THEY SUDDENLY STARTED SAYIN' SOMETHIN' STRANGE.
IT WAS ROBERT ...
ROBERT KILLED MISA...
HOW MEAN ...
REAL MEAN ...
BUT MISA HANGED HERSELF *AFTER* ROBERT LEFT, RIGHT?
YUP. MR. NEGISHI WAS SURPRISED TO HEAR 'EM CARRYIN' ON LIKE THAT, TOO.
THE GIRLS STARTED SAYIN' THAT STUFF AFTER HAVIN' A TALK WITH MR. NEGISHI.
WHAT DID THEY TALK ABOUT?
DUNNO. MR. NEGISHI SAID THEY JUST ASKED HIM HIS NAME.

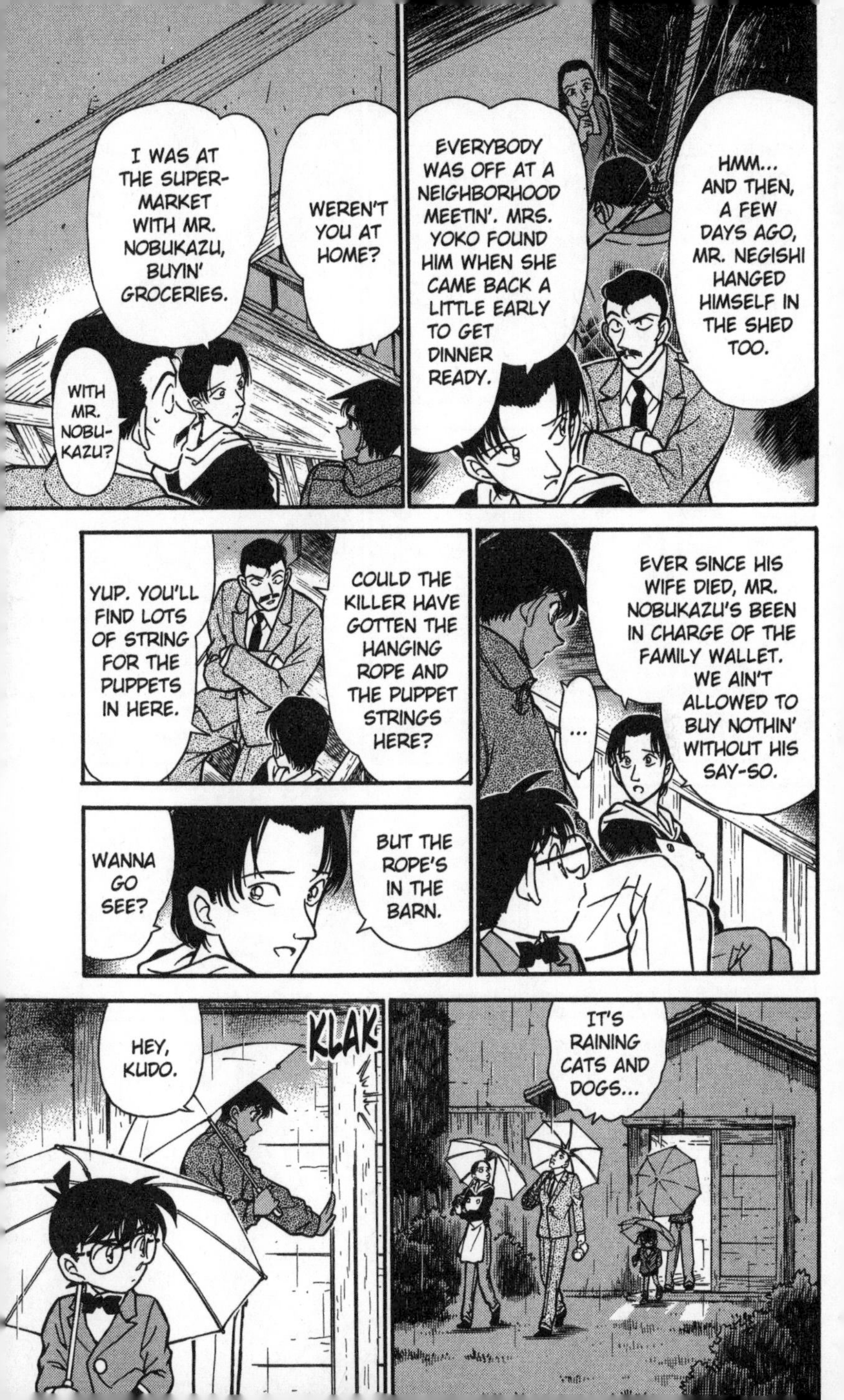
HMM... AND THEN, A FEW DAYS AGO, MR. NEGISHI HANGED HIMSELF IN THE SHED TOO.
EVERYBODY WAS OFF AT A NEIGHBORHOOD MEETIN'. MRS. YOKO FOUND HIM WHEN SHE CAME BACK A LITTLE EARLY TO GET DINNER READY.
WEREN'T YOU AT HOME?
I WAS AT THE SUPER-MARKET WITH MR. NOBUKAZU, BUYIN' GROCERIES.
WITH MR. NOBU-KAZU?
EVER SINCE HIS WIFE DIED, MR. NOBUKAZU'S BEEN IN CHARGE OF THE FAMILY WALLET. WE AIN'T ALLOWED TO BUY NOTHIN' WITHOUT HIS SAY-SO.
...
COULD THE KILLER HAVE GOTTEN THE HANGING ROPE AND THE PUPPET STRINGS HERE?
YUP. YOU'LL FIND LOTS OF STRING FOR THE PUPPETS IN HERE.
BUT THE ROPE'S IN THE BARN.
WANNA GO SEE?
IT'S RAINING CATS AND DOGS...
KLAK
HEY, KUDO.

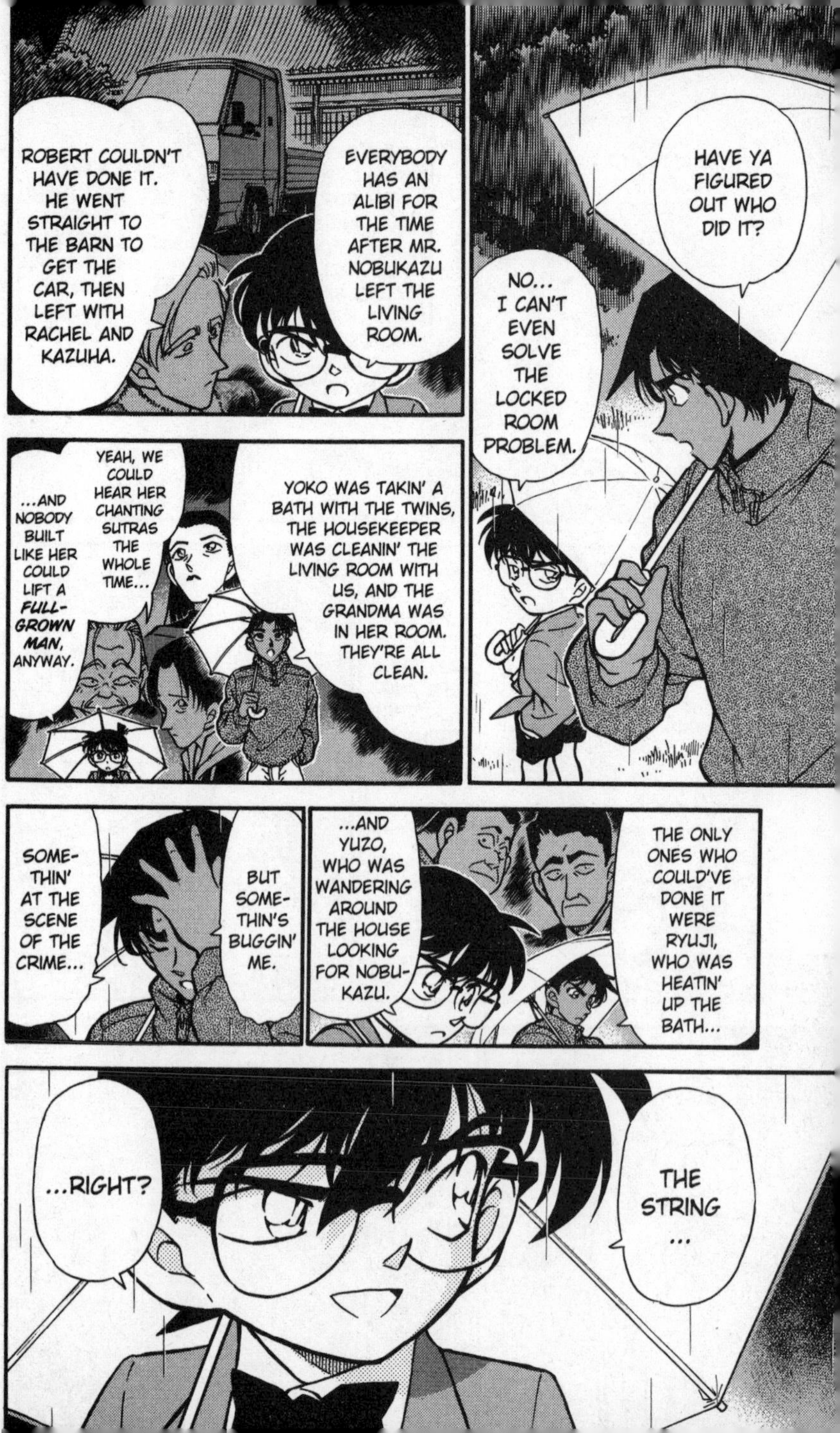
HAVE YA FIGURED OUT WHO DID IT?
NO... I CAN'T EVEN SOLVE THE LOCKED ROOM PROBLEM.
EVERYBODY HAS AN ALIBI FOR THE TIME AFTER MR. NOBUKAZU LEFT THE LIVING ROOM.
ROBERT COULDN'T HAVE DONE IT. HE WENT STRAIGHT TO THE BARN TO GET THE CAR, THEN LEFT WITH RACHEL AND KAZUHA.
YOKO WAS TAKIN' A BATH WITH THE TWINS, THE HOUSEKEEPER WAS CLEANIN' THE LIVING ROOM WITH US, AND THE GRANDMA WAS IN HER ROOM. THEY'RE ALL CLEAN.
YEAH, WE COULD HEAR HER CHANTING SUTRAS THE WHOLE TIME...
...AND NOBODY BUILT LIKE HER COULD LIFT A ***FULL-GROWN MAN***, ANYWAY.
THE ONLY ONES WHO COULD'VE DONE IT WERE RYUJI, WHO WAS HEATIN' UP THE BATH...
...AND YUZO, WHO WAS WANDERING AROUND THE HOUSE LOOKING FOR NOBUKAZU.
BUT SOMETHIN'S BUGGIN' ME.
SOMETHIN' AT THE SCENE OF THE CRIME...
THE STRING...
...RIGHT?

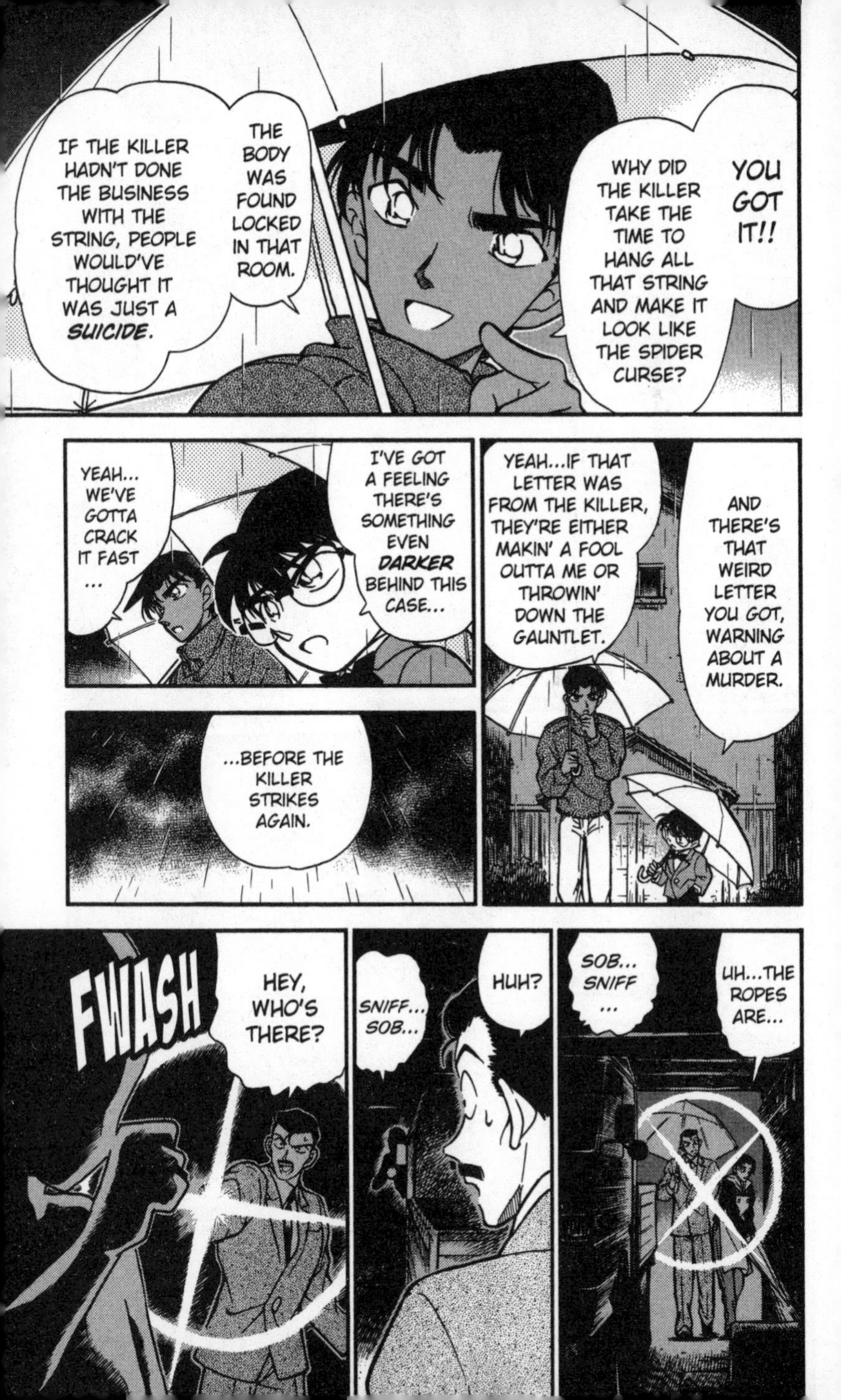
YOU GOT IT!!
WHY DID THE KILLER TAKE THE TIME TO HANG ALL THAT STRING AND MAKE IT LOOK LIKE THE SPIDER CURSE?
THE BODY WAS FOUND LOCKED IN THAT ROOM.
IF THE KILLER HADN'T DONE THE BUSINESS WITH THE STRING, PEOPLE WOULD'VE THOUGHT IT WAS JUST A *SUICIDE*.
AND THERE'S THAT WEIRD LETTER YOU GOT, WARNING ABOUT A MURDER.
YEAH...IF THAT LETTER WAS FROM THE KILLER, THEY'RE EITHER MAKIN' A FOOL OUTTA ME OR THROWIN' DOWN THE GAUNTLET.
I'VE GOT A FEELING THERE'S SOMETHING EVEN *DARKER* BEHIND THIS CASE...
YEAH... WE'VE GOTTA CRACK IT FAST ...
...BEFORE THE KILLER STRIKES AGAIN.
UH...THE ROPES ARE...
SOB... SNIFF ...
HUH?
SNIFF... SOB...
HEY, WHO'S THERE?
FWASH

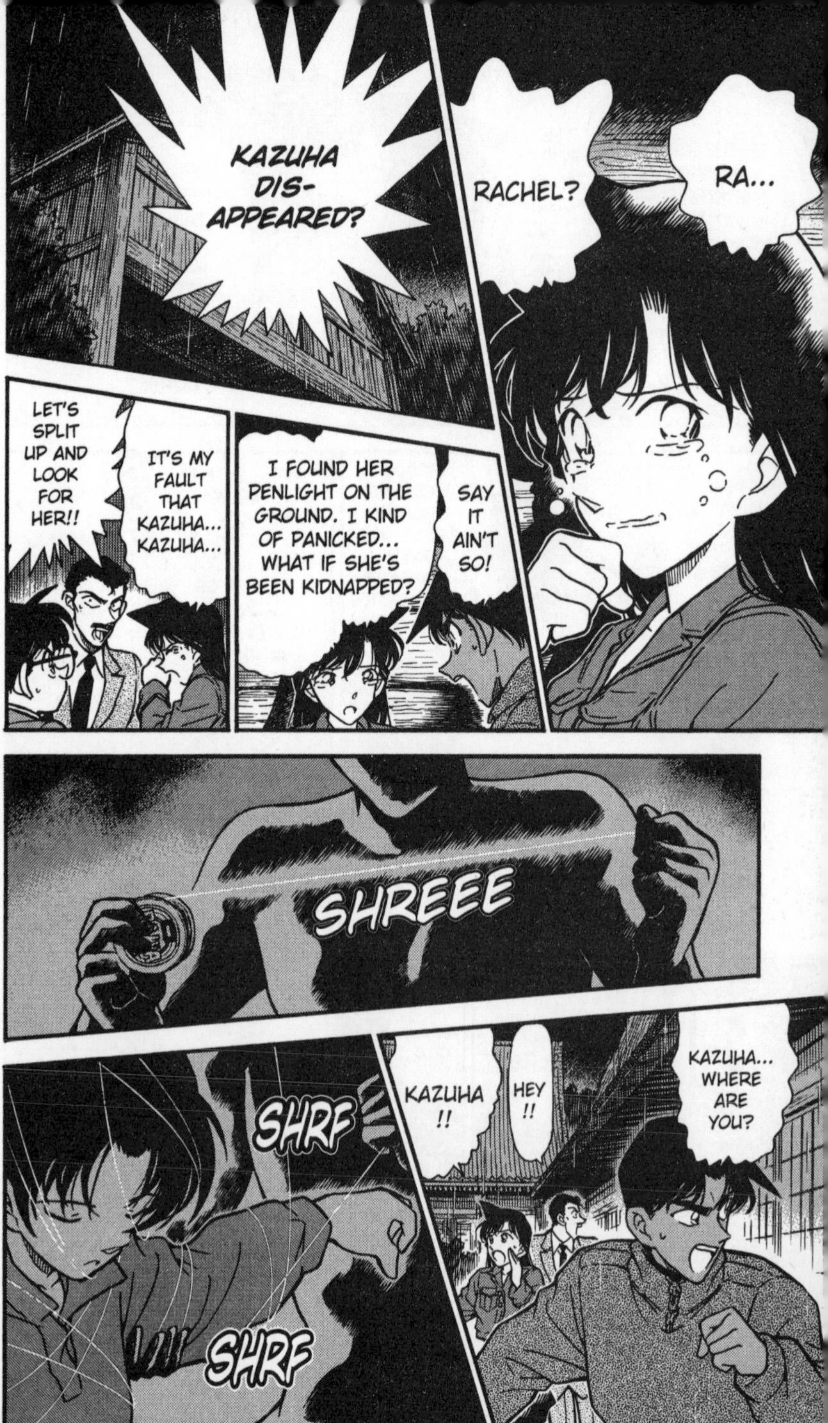
RA...
RACHEL?
KAZUHA DIS-APPEARED?
SAY IT AIN'T SO!
I FOUND HER PENLIGHT ON THE GROUND. I KIND OF PANICKED... WHAT IF SHE'S BEEN KIDNAPPED?
IT'S MY FAULT THAT KAZUHA... KAZUHA...
LET'S SPLIT UP AND LOOK FOR HER!!
SHREEE
KAZUHA... WHERE ARE YOU?
HEY !!
KAZUHA !!
SHRF
SHRF

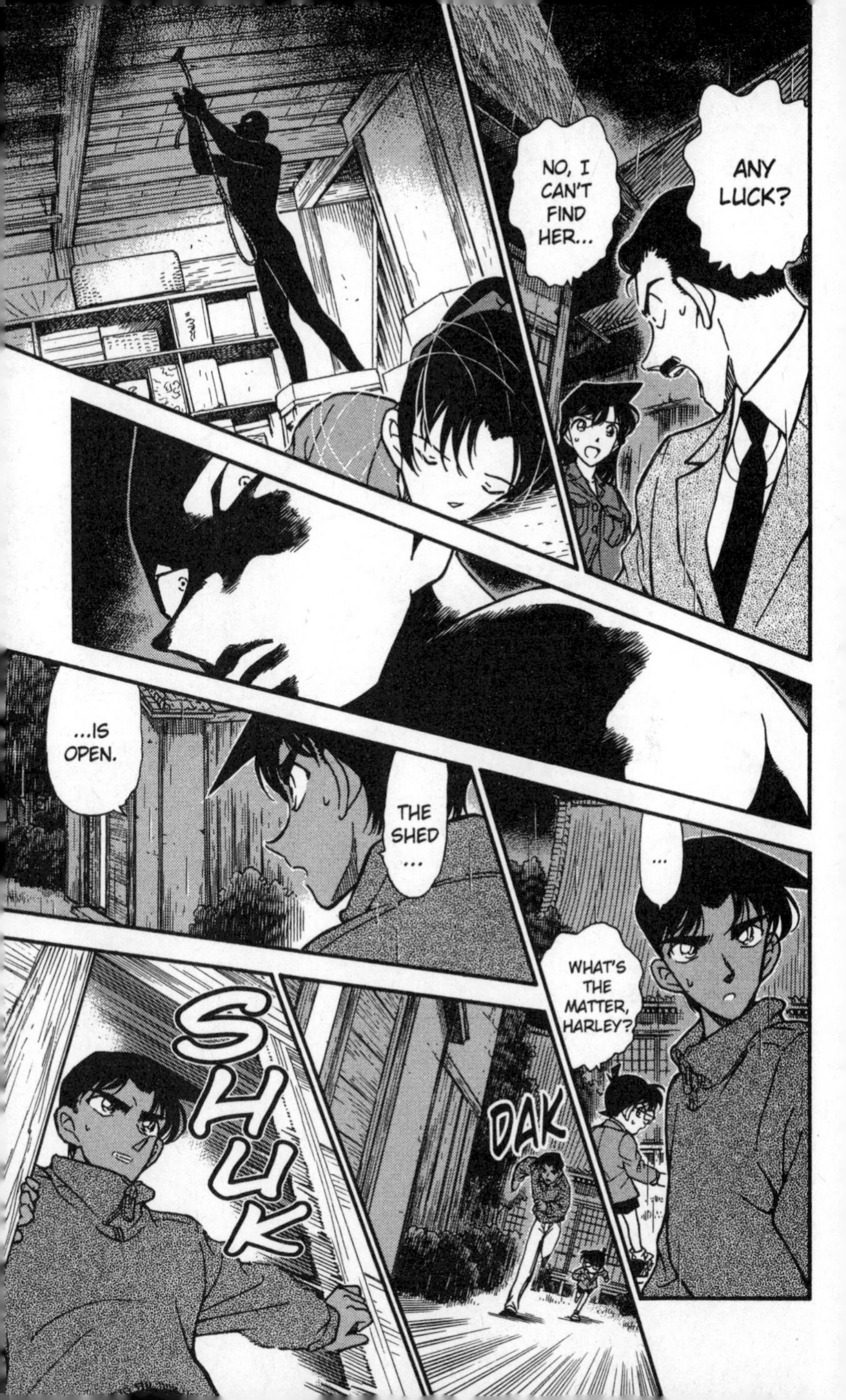
ANY LUCK?
NO, I CAN'T FIND HER...
...
THE SHED...
...IS OPEN.
WHAT'S THE MATTER, HARLEY?
DAK
SHUK

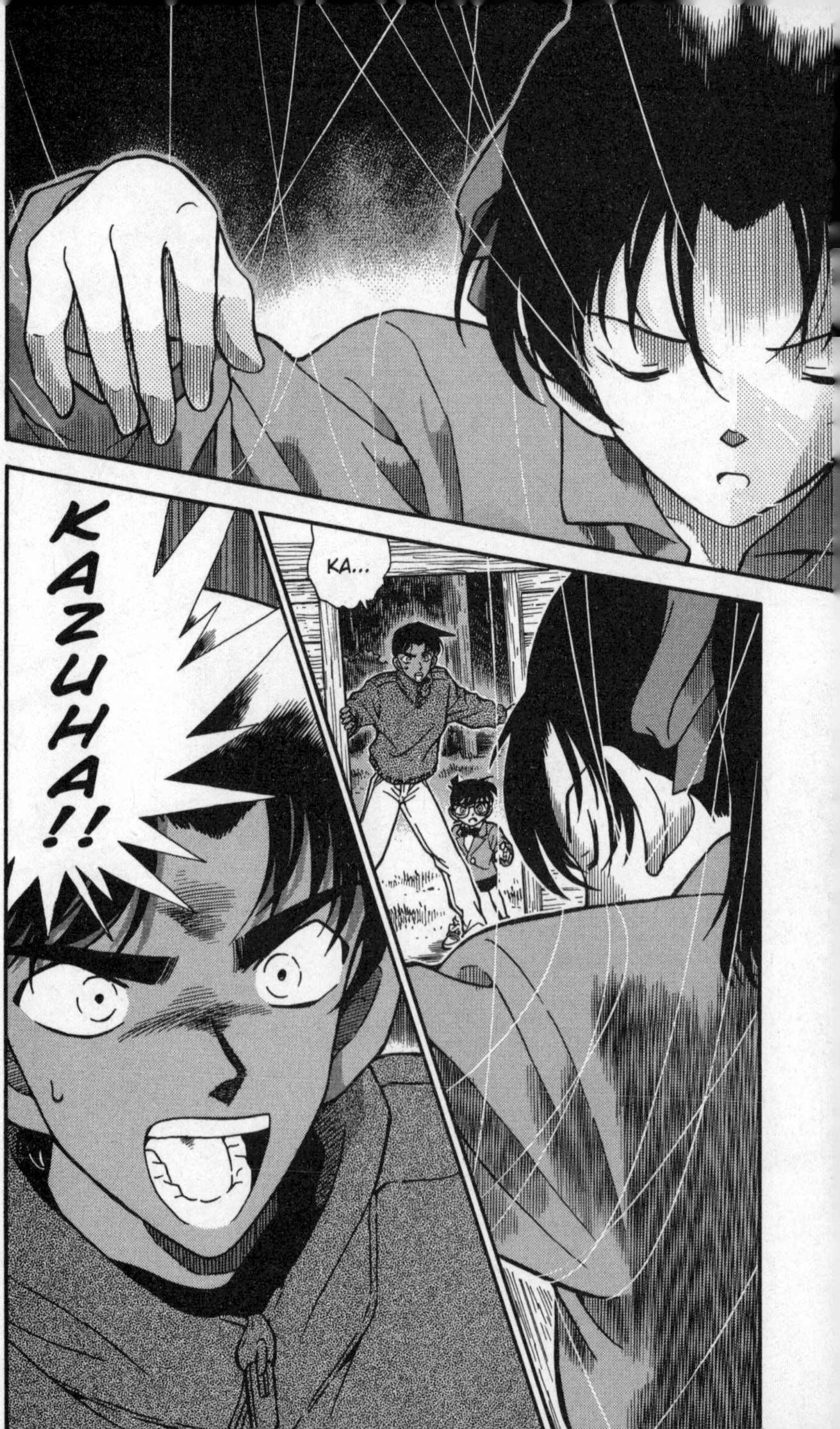
KA...
KAZUHA!!

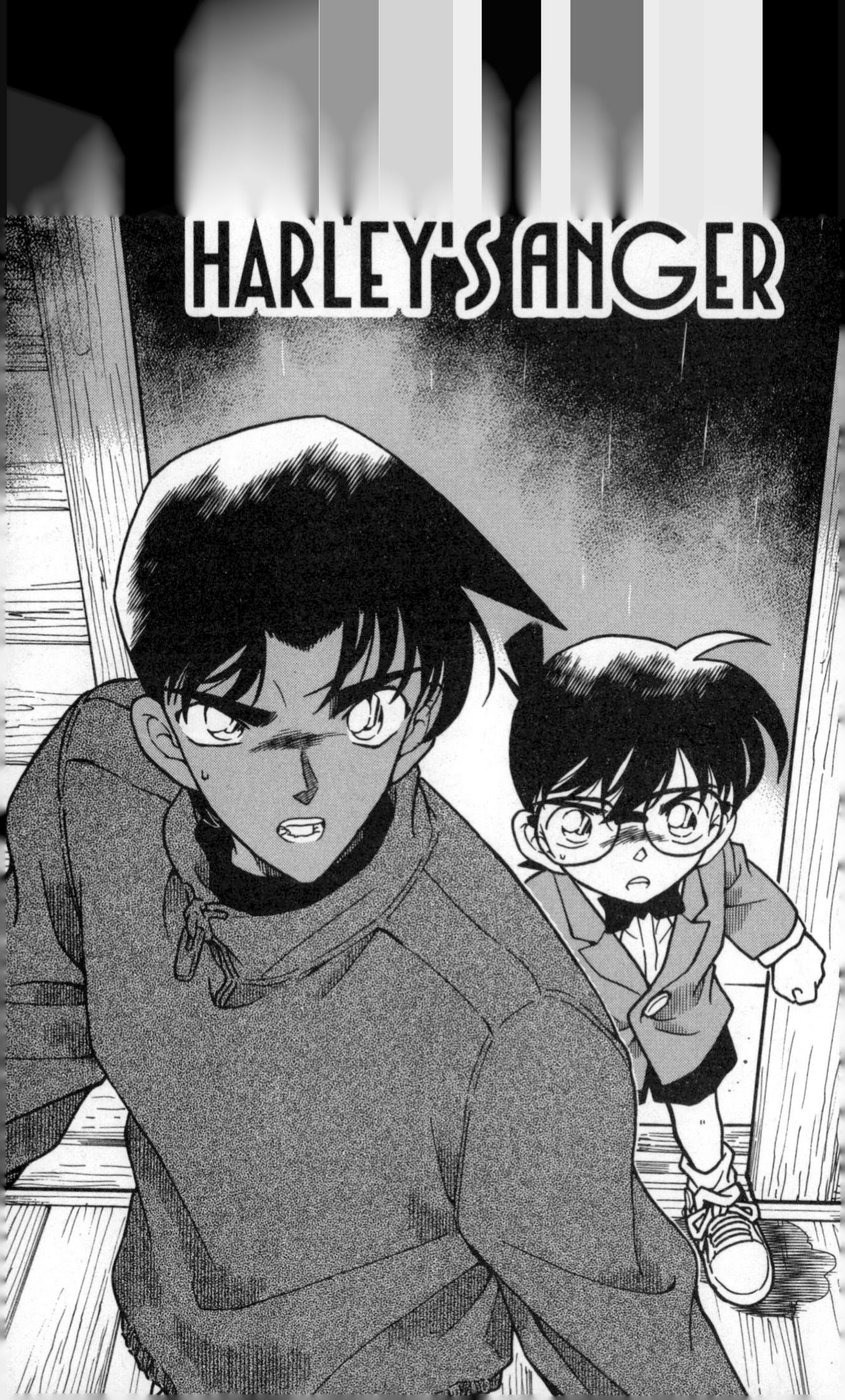
HARLEY'S ANGER

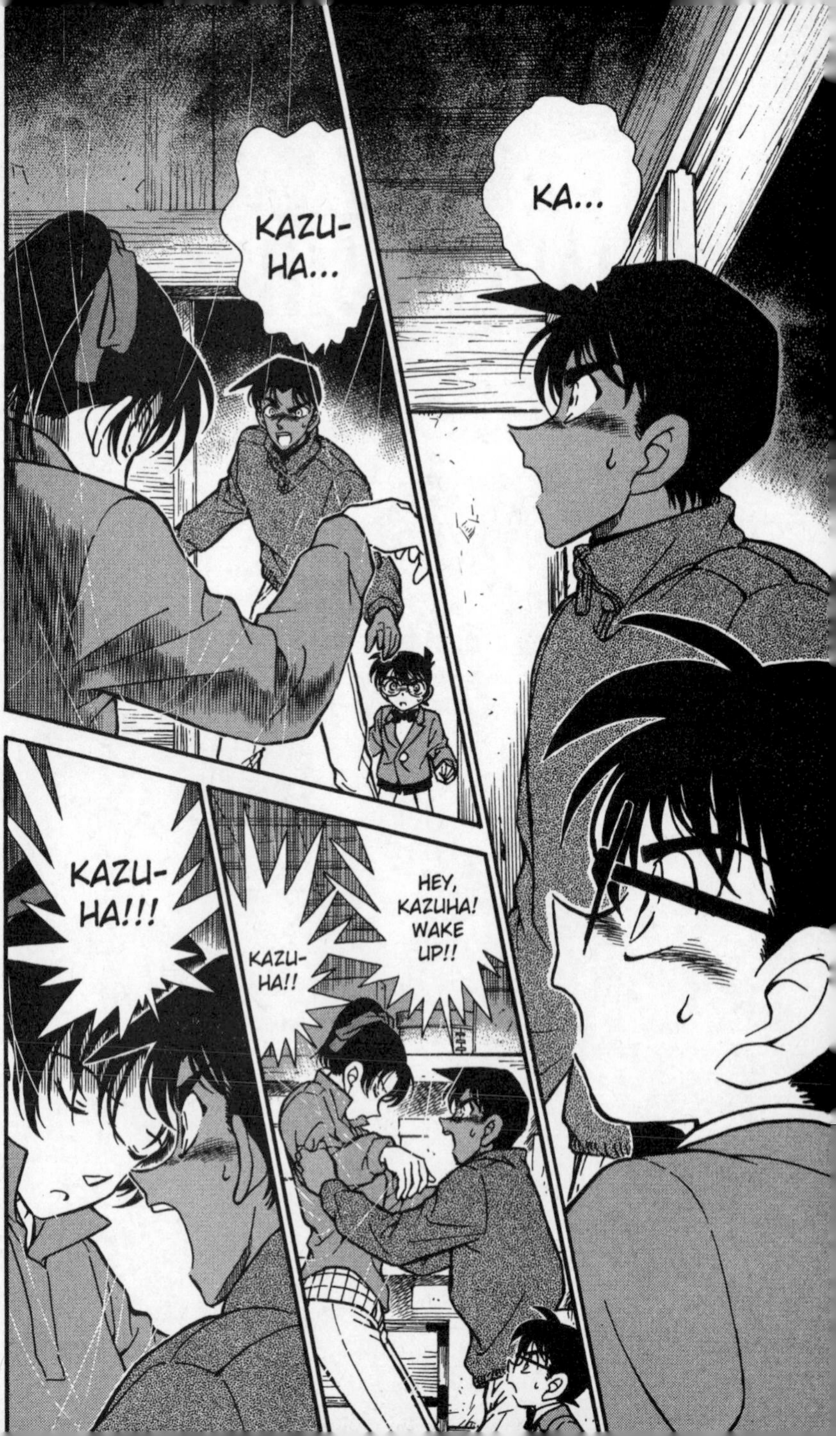
KA...
KAZU-HA...
HEY, KAZUHA! WAKE UP!!
KAZU-HA!!
KAZU-HA!!!

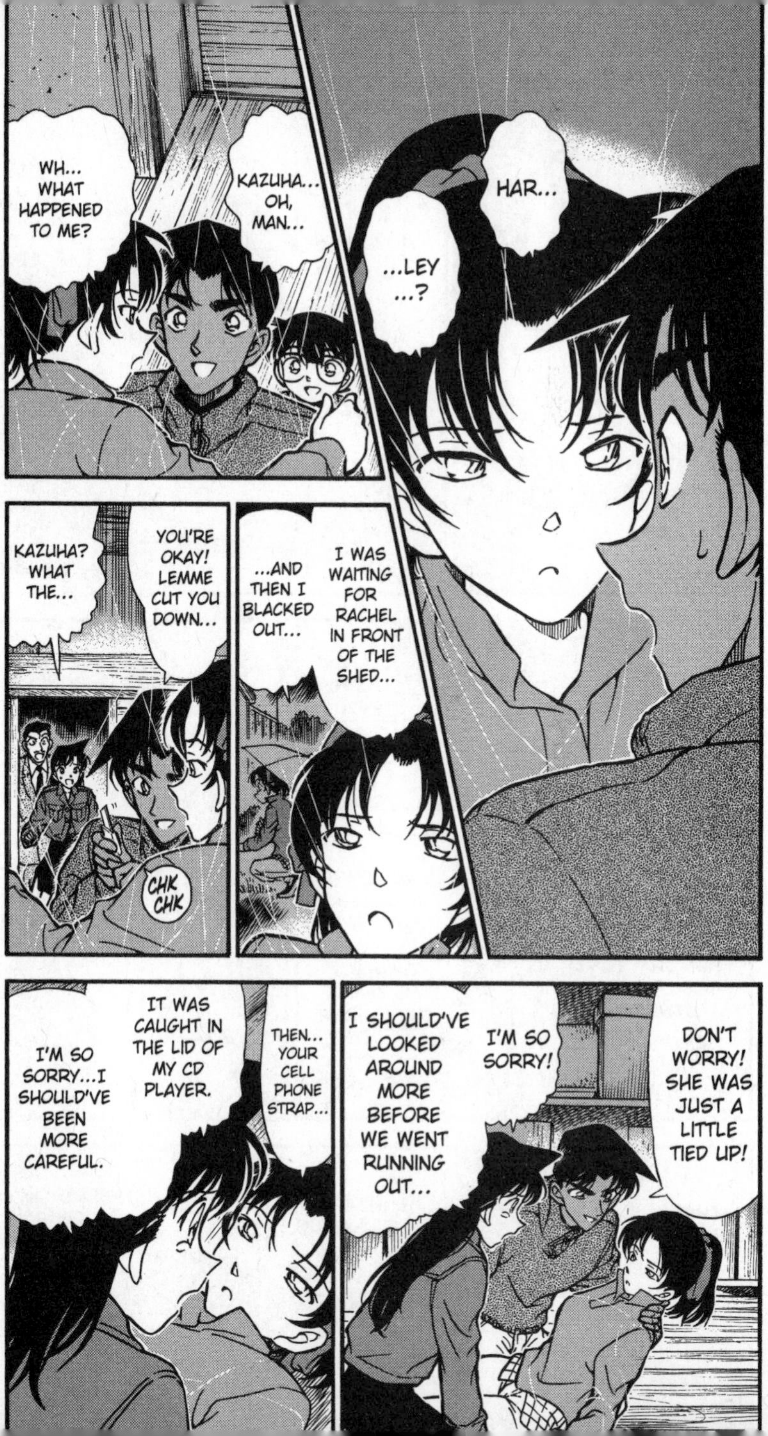
HAR...
...LEY ...?
KAZUHA... OH, MAN...
WH... WHAT HAPPENED TO ME?
I WAS WAITING FOR RACHEL IN FRONT OF THE SHED...
...AND THEN I BLACKED OUT...
YOU'RE OKAY! LEMME CUT YOU DOWN...
KAZUHA? WHAT THE...
CHK CHK
DON'T WORRY! SHE WAS JUST A LITTLE TIED UP!
I'M SO SORRY!
I SHOULD'VE LOOKED AROUND MORE BEFORE WE WENT RUNNING OUT...
THEN... YOUR CELL PHONE STRAP...
IT WAS CAUGHT IN THE LID OF MY CD PLAYER.
I'M SO SORRY...I SHOULD'VE BEEN MORE CAREFUL.

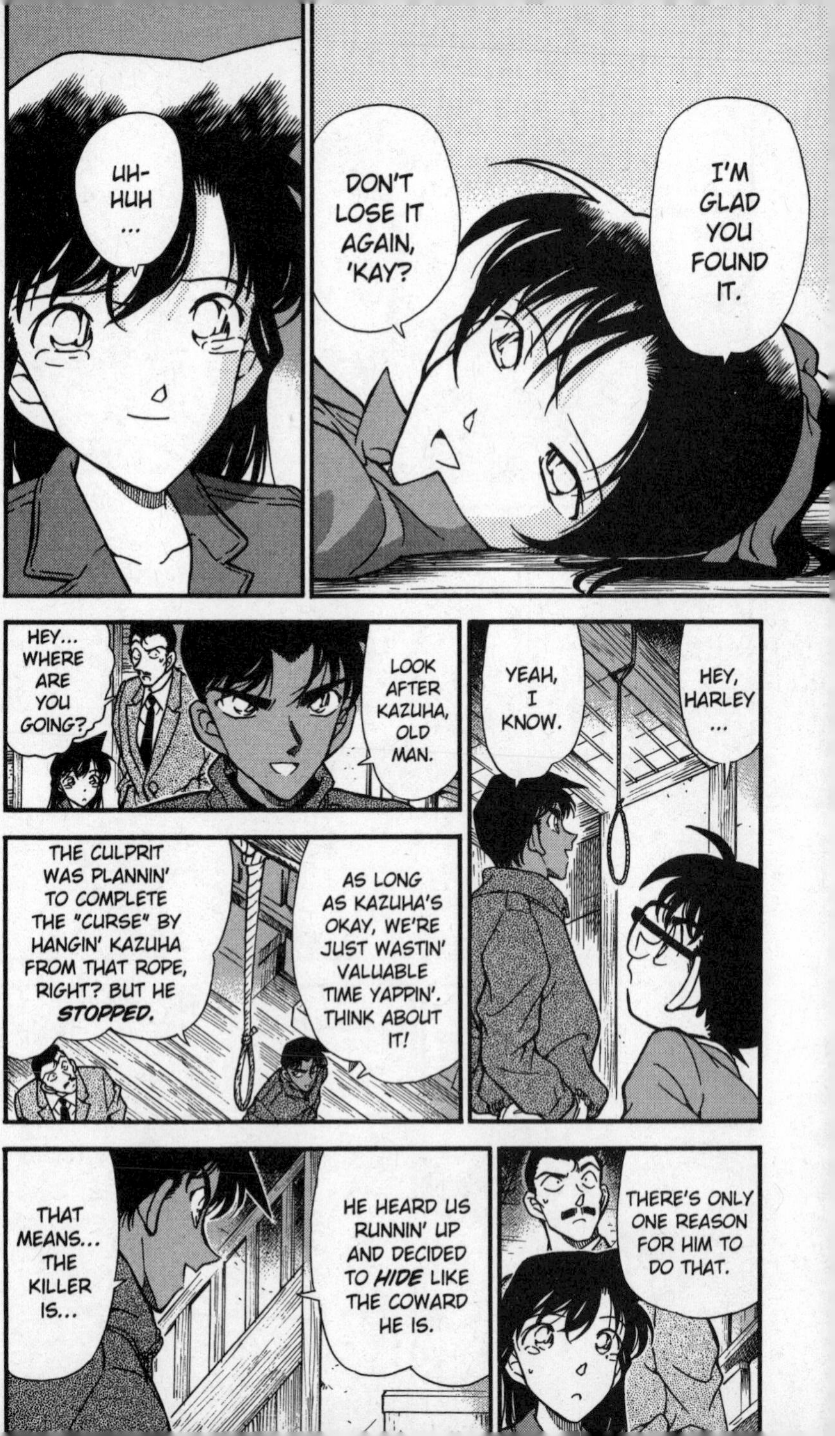
I'M GLAD YOU FOUND IT.
DON'T LOSE IT AGAIN, 'KAY?
UH-HUH...
HEY, HARLEY...
YEAH, I KNOW.
LOOK AFTER KAZUHA, OLD MAN.
HEY... WHERE ARE YOU GOING?
AS LONG AS KAZUHA'S OKAY, WE'RE JUST WASTIN' VALUABLE TIME YAPPIN'. THINK ABOUT IT!
THE CULPRIT WAS PLANNIN' TO COMPLETE THE "CURSE" BY HANGIN' KAZUHA FROM THAT ROPE, RIGHT? BUT HE STOPPED.
THERE'S ONLY ONE REASON FOR HIM TO DO THAT.
HE HEARD US RUNNIN' UP AND DECIDED TO HIDE LIKE THE COWARD HE IS.
THAT MEANS... THE KILLER IS...

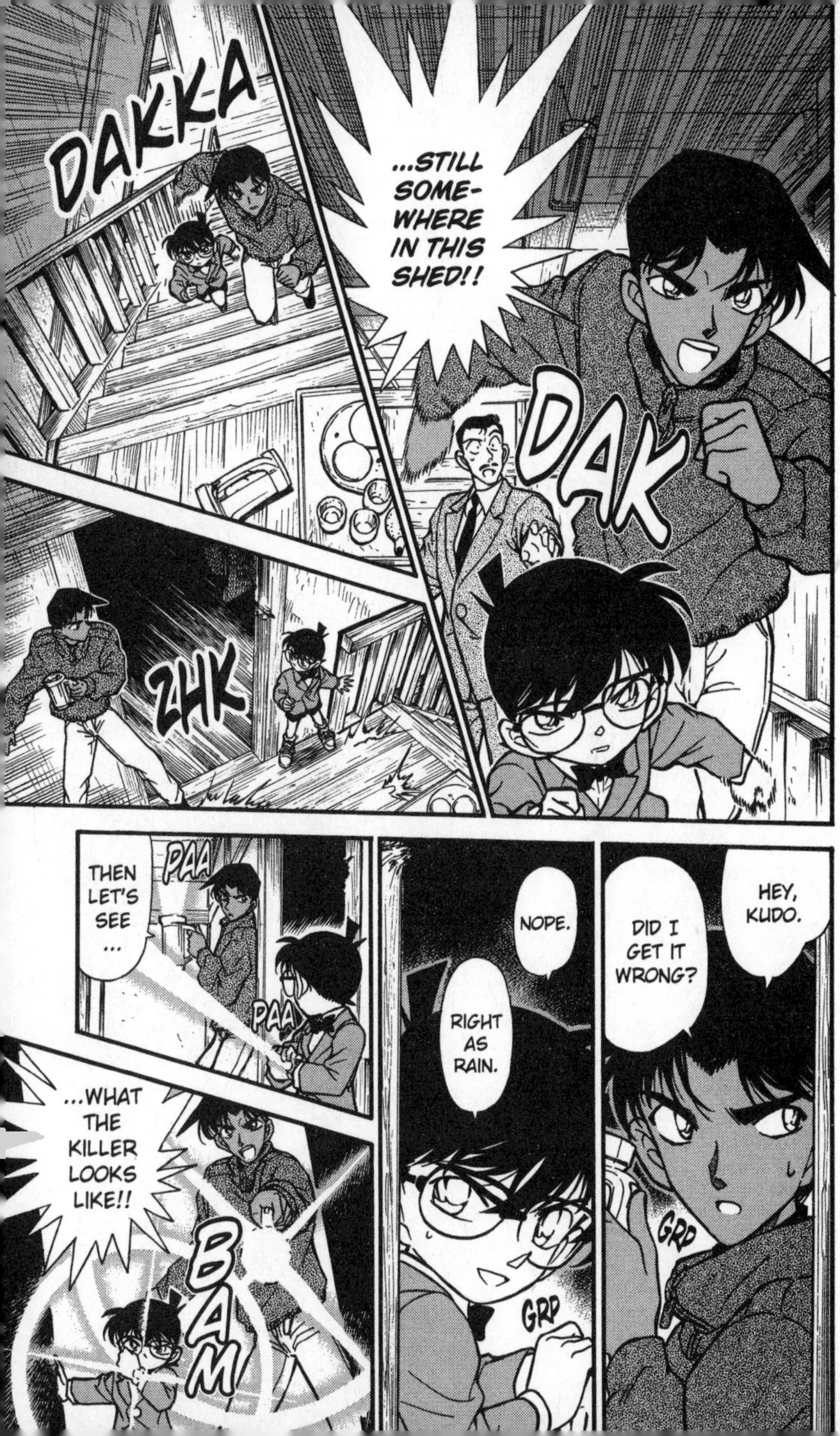
...STILL SOMEWHERE IN THIS SHED!!
DAK
DAKKA
ZHK
HEY, KUDO.
DID I GET IT WRONG?
GRP
NOPE.
RIGHT AS RAIN.
GRP
THEN LET'S SEE ...
PAA
PAA
...WHAT THE KILLER LOOKS LIKE!!
BAM

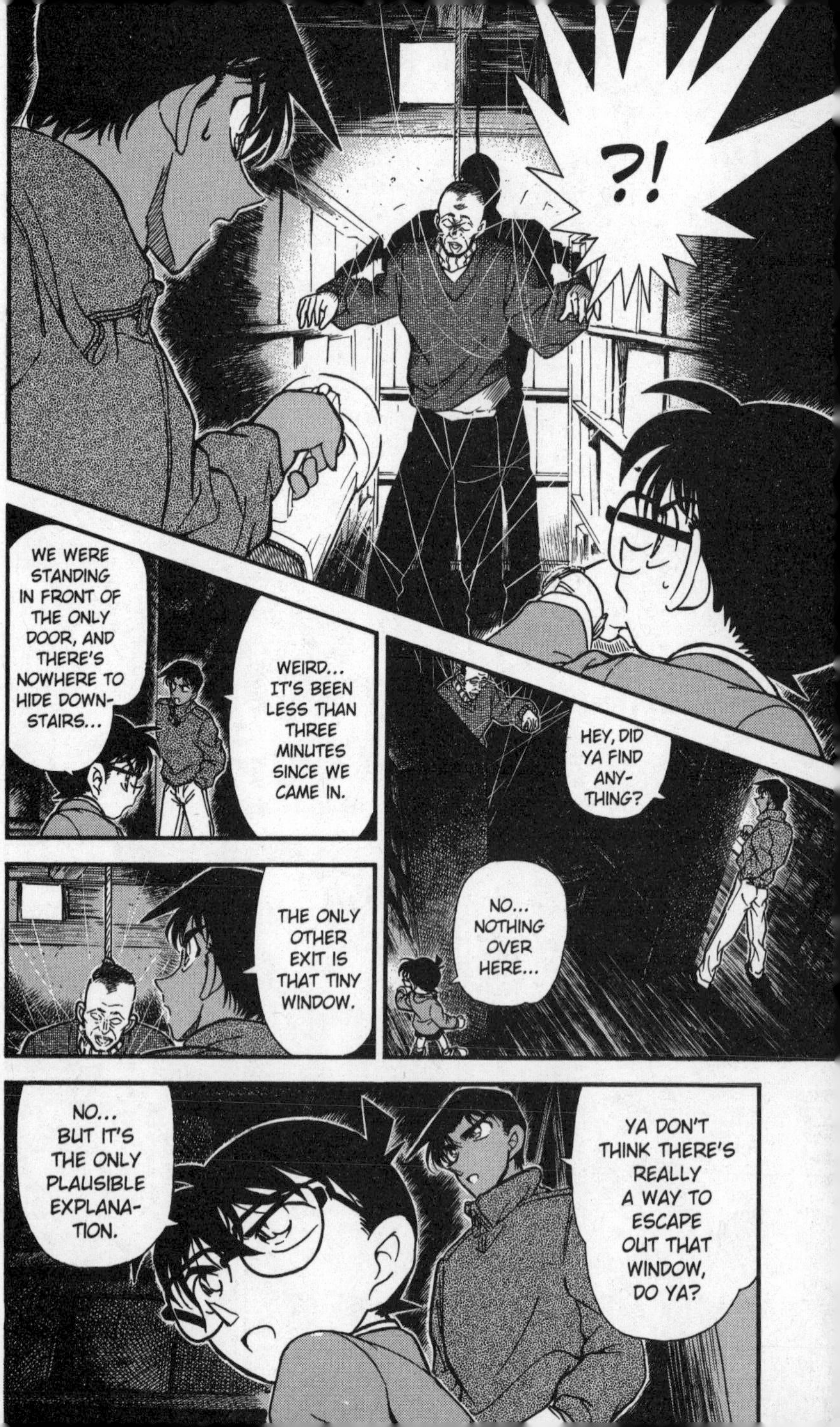
?!
HEY, DID YA FIND ANYTHING?
NO... NOTHING OVER HERE...
WEIRD... IT'S BEEN LESS THAN THREE MINUTES SINCE WE CAME IN.
WE WERE STANDING IN FRONT OF THE ONLY DOOR, AND THERE'S NOWHERE TO HIDE DOWN-STAIRS...
THE ONLY OTHER EXIT IS THAT TINY WINDOW.
YA DON'T THINK THERE'S REALLY A WAY TO ESCAPE OUT THAT WINDOW, DO YA?
NO... BUT IT'S THE ONLY PLAUSIBLE EXPLANATION.

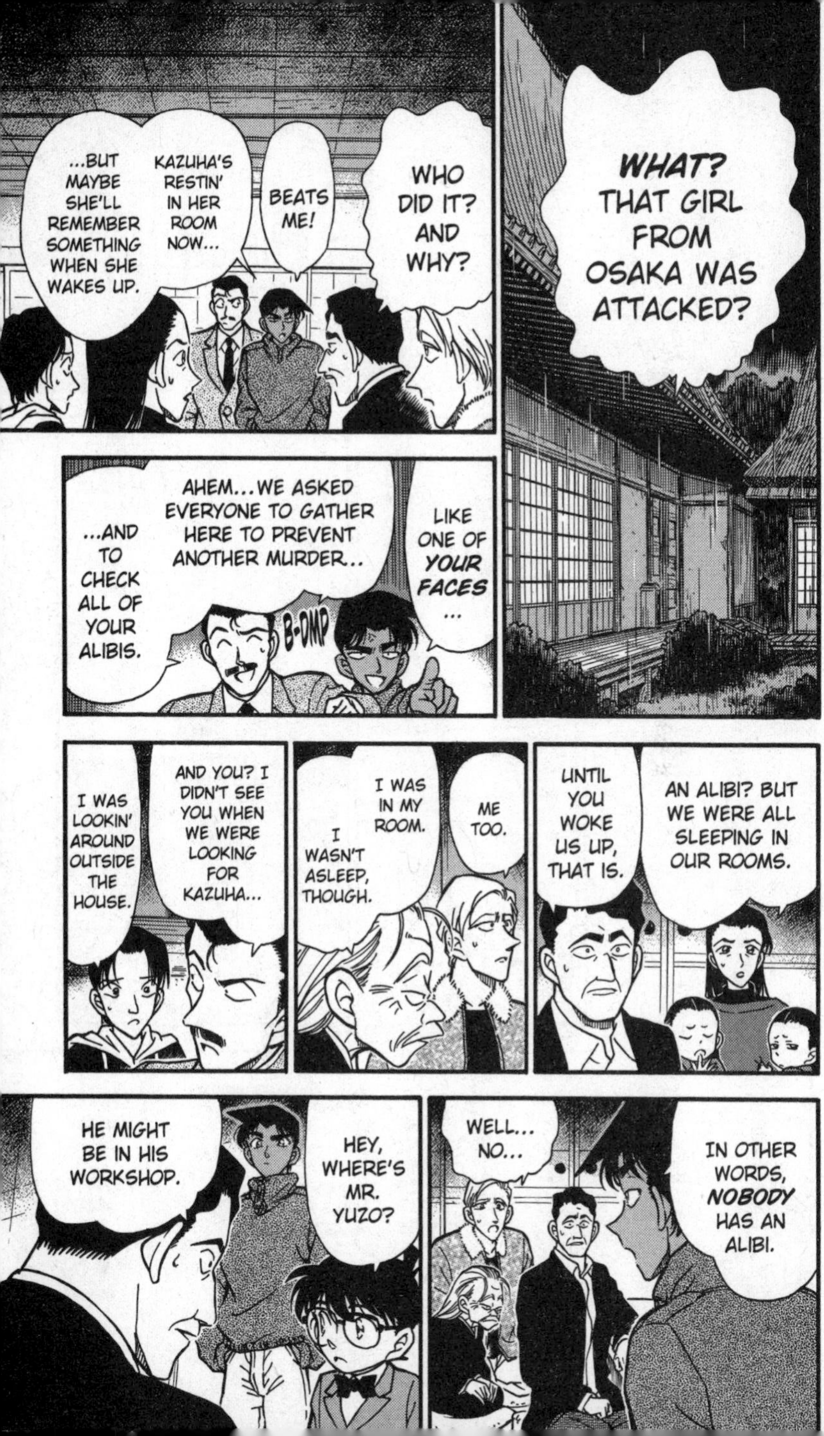
WHAT? THAT GIRL FROM OSAKA WAS ATTACKED?
WHO DID IT? AND WHY?
BEATS ME!
KAZUHA'S RESTIN' IN HER ROOM NOW...
...BUT MAYBE SHE'LL REMEMBER SOMETHING WHEN SHE WAKES UP.
AHEM... WE ASKED EVERYONE TO GATHER HERE TO PREVENT ANOTHER MURDER...
LIKE ONE OF YOUR FACES...
B-DMP
...AND TO CHECK ALL OF YOUR ALIBIS.
AN ALIBI? BUT WE WERE ALL SLEEPING IN OUR ROOMS.
UNTIL YOU WOKE US UP, THAT IS.
ME TOO.
I WAS IN MY ROOM.
I WASN'T ASLEEP, THOUGH.
AND YOU? I DIDN'T SEE YOU WHEN WE WERE LOOKING FOR KAZUHA...
I WAS LOOKIN' AROUND OUTSIDE THE HOUSE.
IN OTHER WORDS, NOBODY HAS AN ALIBI.
WELL... NO...
HEY, WHERE'S MR. YUZO?
HE MIGHT BE IN HIS WORKSHOP.

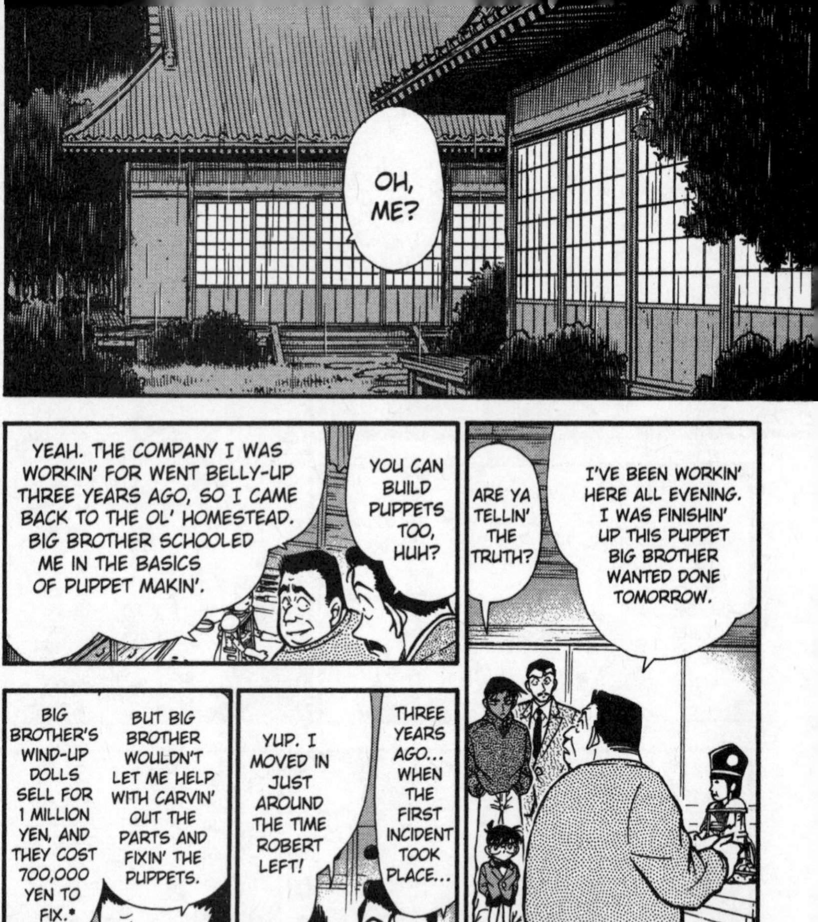
OH, ME?
I'VE BEEN WORKIN' HERE ALL EVENING. I WAS FINISHIN' UP THIS PUPPET BIG BROTHER WANTED DONE TOMORROW.
ARE YA TELLIN' THE TRUTH?
YOU CAN BUILD PUPPETS TOO, HUH?
YEAH. THE COMPANY I WAS WORKIN' FOR WENT BELLY-UP THREE YEARS AGO, SO I CAME BACK TO THE OL' HOMESTEAD. BIG BROTHER SCHOOLED ME IN THE BASICS OF PUPPET MAKIN'.
THREE YEARS AGO... WHEN THE FIRST INCIDENT TOOK PLACE...
YUP. I MOVED IN JUST AROUND THE TIME ROBERT LEFT!
BUT BIG BROTHER WOULDN'T LET ME HELP WITH CARVIN' OUT THE PARTS AND FIXIN' THE PUPPETS.
BIG BROTHER'S WIND-UP DOLLS SELL FOR 1 MILLION YEN, AND THEY COST 700,000 YEN TO FIX.*

*One million yen is about $9,000, and 700,000 yen is about $6,000.

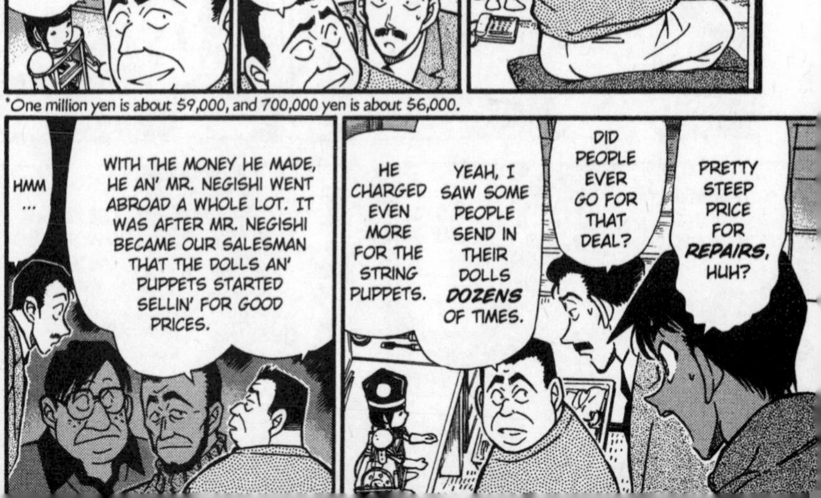
PRETTY STEEP PRICE FOR *REPAIRS*, HUH?
DID PEOPLE EVER GO FOR THAT DEAL?
YEAH, I SAW SOME PEOPLE SEND IN THEIR DOLLS *DOZENS* OF TIMES.
HE CHARGED EVEN MORE FOR THE STRING PUPPETS.
WITH THE MONEY HE MADE, HE AN' MR. NEGISHI WENT ABROAD A WHOLE LOT. IT WAS AFTER MR. NEGISHI BECAME OUR SALESMAN THAT THE DOLLS AN' PUPPETS STARTED SELLIN' FOR GOOD PRICES.
HMM ...

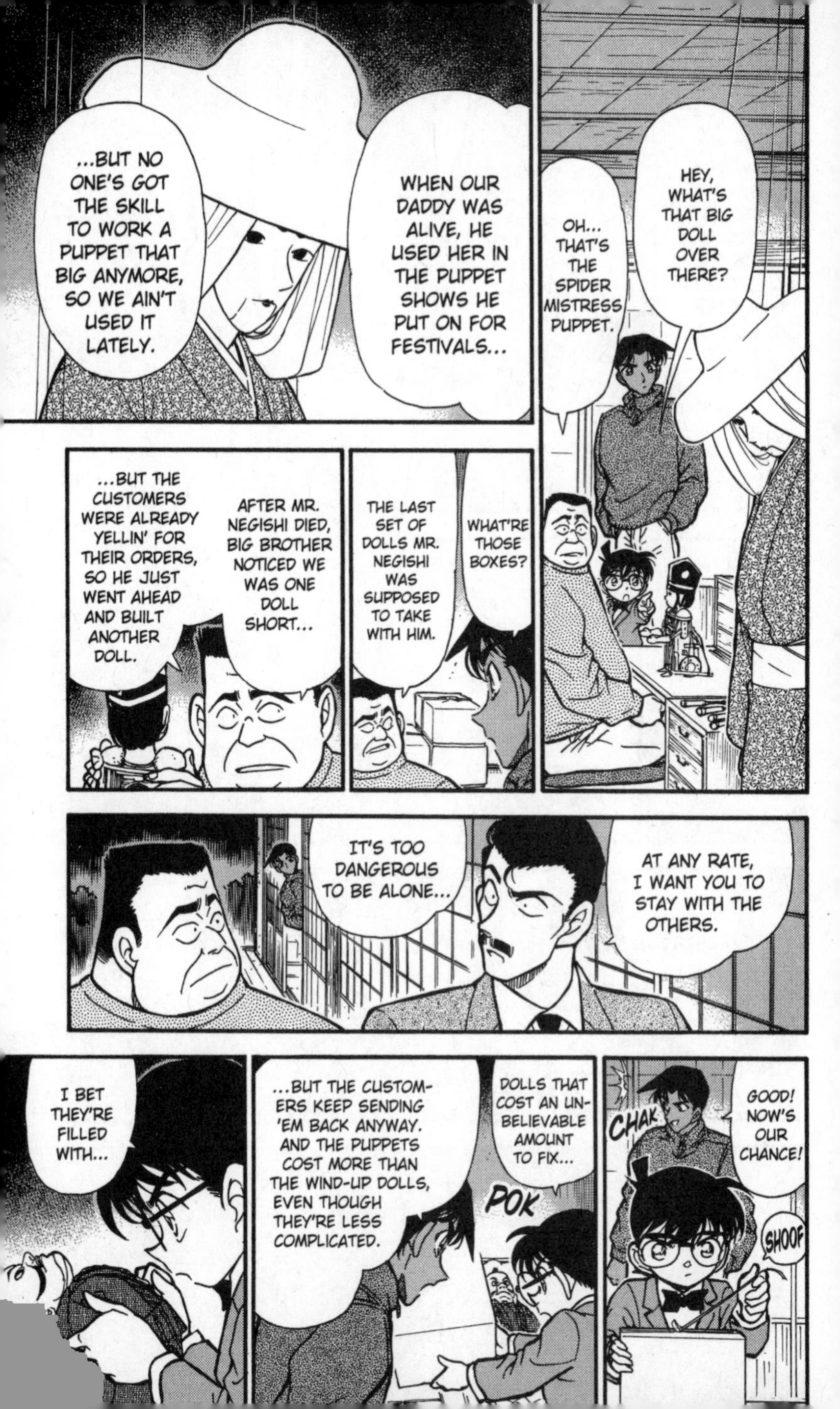
HEY, WHAT'S THAT BIG DOLL OVER THERE?
OH... THAT'S THE SPIDER MISTRESS PUPPET.
WHEN OUR DADDY WAS ALIVE, HE USED HER IN THE PUPPET SHOWS HE PUT ON FOR FESTIVALS...
...BUT NO ONE'S GOT THE SKILL TO WORK A PUPPET THAT BIG ANYMORE, SO WE AIN'T USED IT LATELY.
WHAT'RE THOSE BOXES?
THE LAST SET OF DOLLS MR. NEGISHI WAS SUPPOSED TO TAKE WITH HIM.
AFTER MR. NEGISHI DIED, BIG BROTHER NOTICED WE WAS ONE DOLL SHORT...
...BUT THE CUSTOMERS WERE ALREADY YELLIN' FOR THEIR ORDERS, SO HE JUST WENT AHEAD AND BUILT ANOTHER DOLL.
AT ANY RATE, I WANT YOU TO STAY WITH THE OTHERS.
IT'S TOO DANGEROUS TO BE ALONE...
GOOD! NOW'S OUR CHANCE!
CHAK
SHOOF
DOLLS THAT COST AN UN-BELIEVABLE AMOUNT TO FIX...
POK
...BUT THE CUSTOM-ERS KEEP SENDING 'EM BACK ANYWAY. AND THE PUPPETS COST MORE THAN THE WIND-UP DOLLS, EVEN THOUGH THEY'RE LESS COMPLICATED.
I BET THEY'RE FILLED WITH...

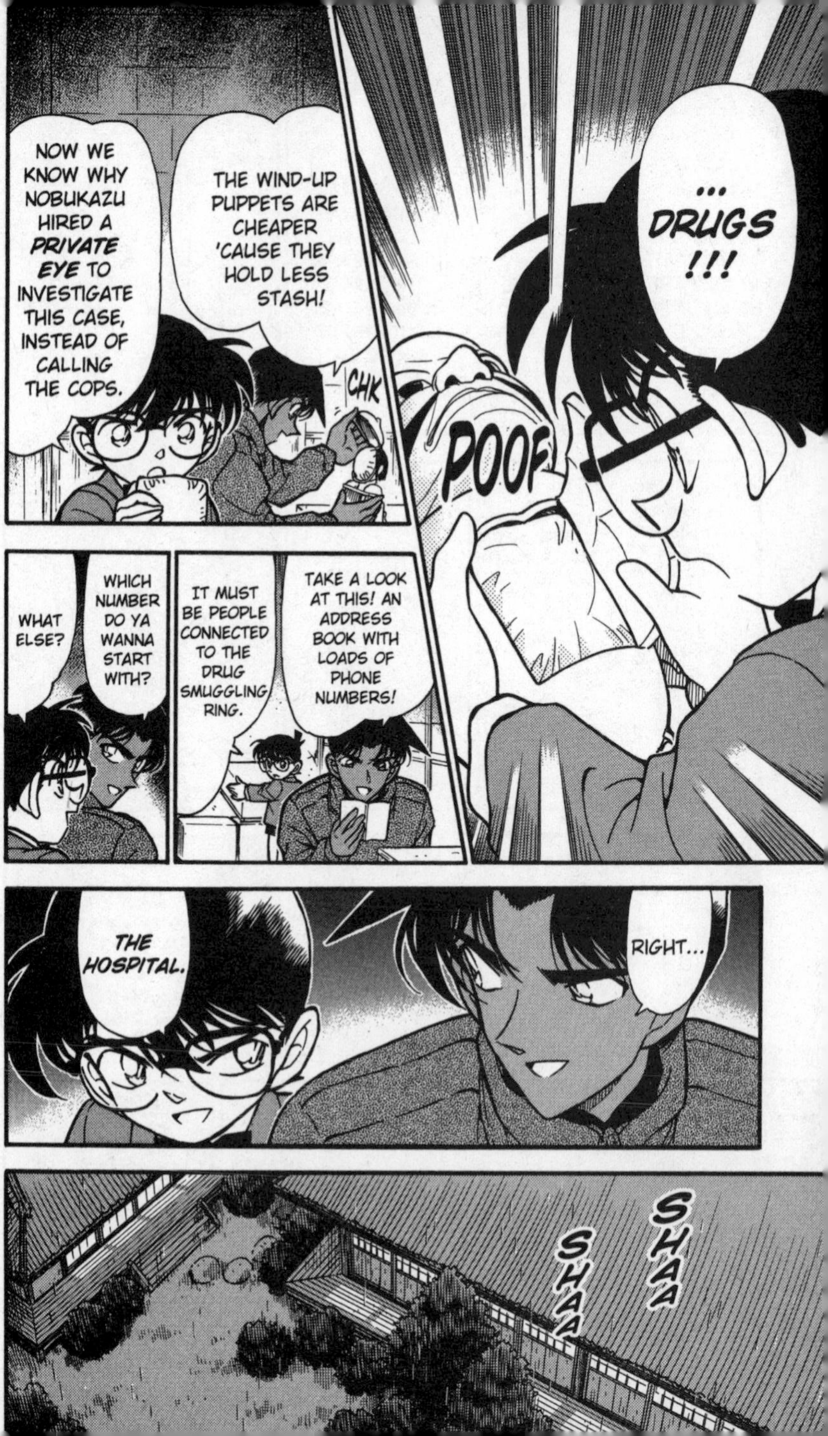
... DRUGS !!!
POOF
THE WIND-UP PUPPETS ARE CHEAPER 'CAUSE THEY HOLD LESS STASH!
CHK
NOW WE KNOW WHY NOBUKAZU HIRED A PRIVATE EYE TO INVESTIGATE THIS CASE, INSTEAD OF CALLING THE COPS.
TAKE A LOOK AT THIS! AN ADDRESS BOOK WITH LOADS OF PHONE NUMBERS!
IT MUST BE PEOPLE CONNECTED TO THE DRUG SMUGGLING RING.
WHICH NUMBER DO YA WANNA START WITH?
WHAT ELSE?
RIGHT...
THE HOSPITAL.
SHAA
SHAA

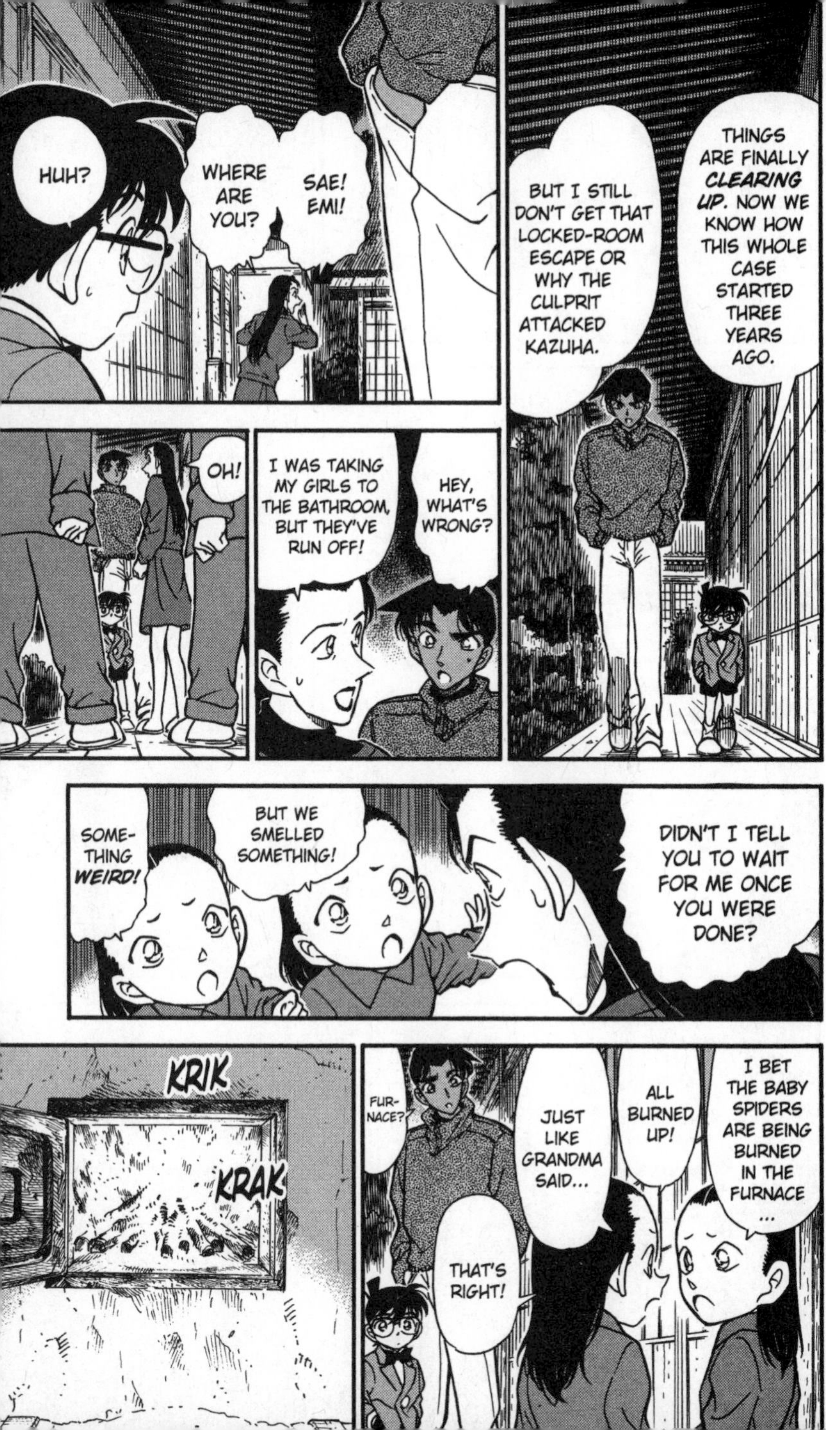
THINGS ARE FINALLY **CLEARING UP**. NOW WE KNOW HOW THIS WHOLE CASE STARTED THREE YEARS AGO.
BUT I STILL DON'T GET THAT LOCKED-ROOM ESCAPE OR WHY THE CULPRIT ATTACKED KAZUHA.
SAE! EMI!
WHERE ARE YOU?
HUH?
HEY, WHAT'S WRONG?
I WAS TAKING MY GIRLS TO THE BATHROOM, BUT THEY'VE RUN OFF!
OH!
DIDN'T I TELL YOU TO WAIT FOR ME ONCE YOU WERE DONE?
BUT WE SMELLED SOMETHING!
SOME-THING **WEIRD!**
I BET THE BABY SPIDERS ARE BEING BURNED IN THE FURNACE ...
ALL BURNED UP!
JUST LIKE GRANDMA SAID...
FUR-NACE?
THAT'S RIGHT!
KRIK
KRAK

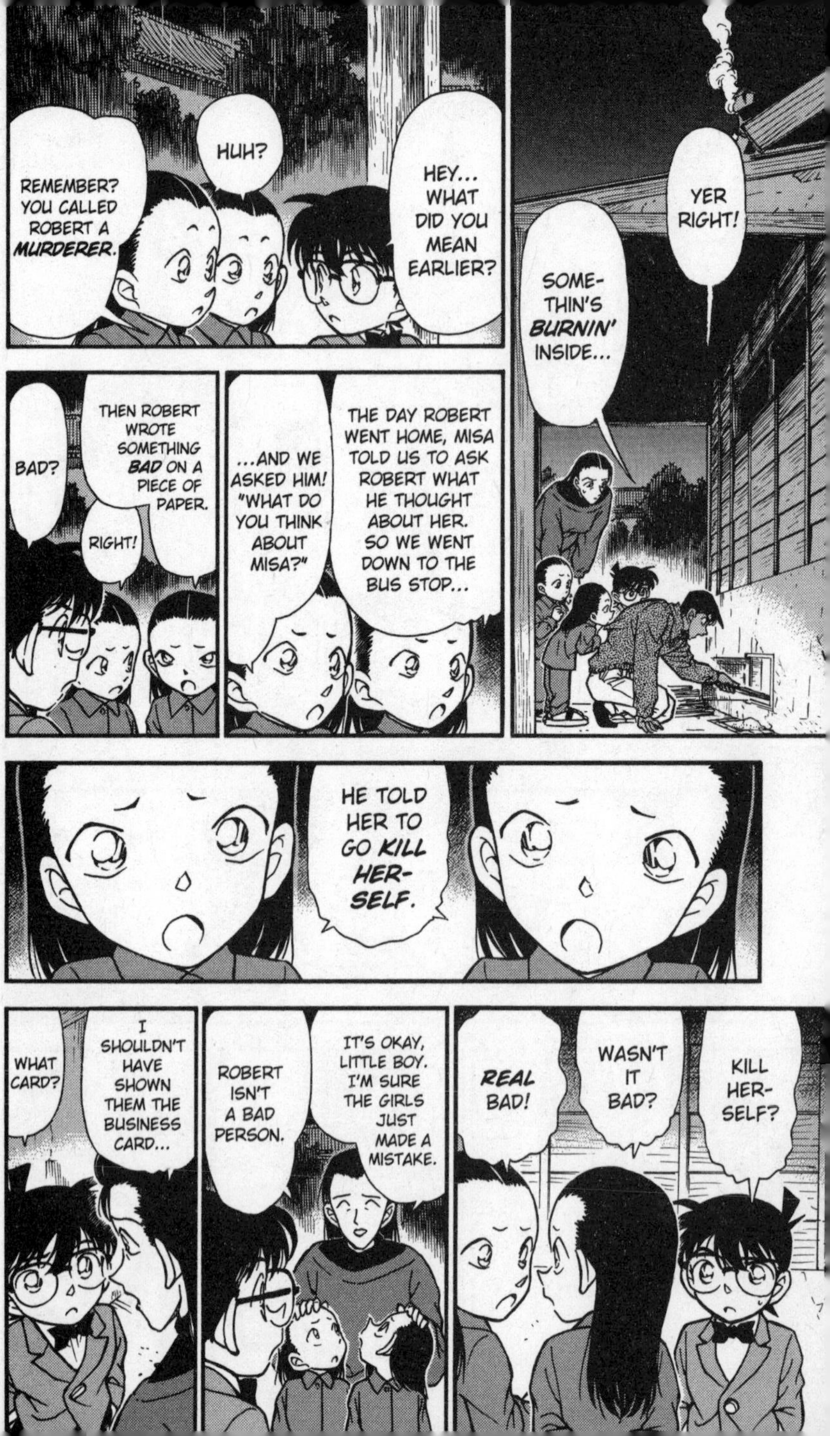
YER RIGHT!
SOME-THIN'S BURNIN' INSIDE...
HEY... WHAT DID YOU MEAN EARLIER?
HUH?
REMEMBER? YOU CALLED ROBERT A MURDERER.
THE DAY ROBERT WENT HOME, MISA TOLD US TO ASK ROBERT WHAT HE THOUGHT ABOUT HER. SO WE WENT DOWN TO THE BUS STOP...
...AND WE ASKED HIM! "WHAT DO YOU THINK ABOUT MISA?"
THEN ROBERT WROTE SOMETHING BAD ON A PIECE OF PAPER.
RIGHT!
BAD?
HE TOLD HER TO GO KILL HER-SELF.
KILL HER-SELF?
WASN'T IT BAD?
REAL BAD!
IT'S OKAY, LITTLE BOY. I'M SURE THE GIRLS JUST MADE A MISTAKE.
ROBERT ISN'T A BAD PERSON.
I SHOULDN'T HAVE SHOWN THEM THE BUSINESS CARD...
WHAT CARD?

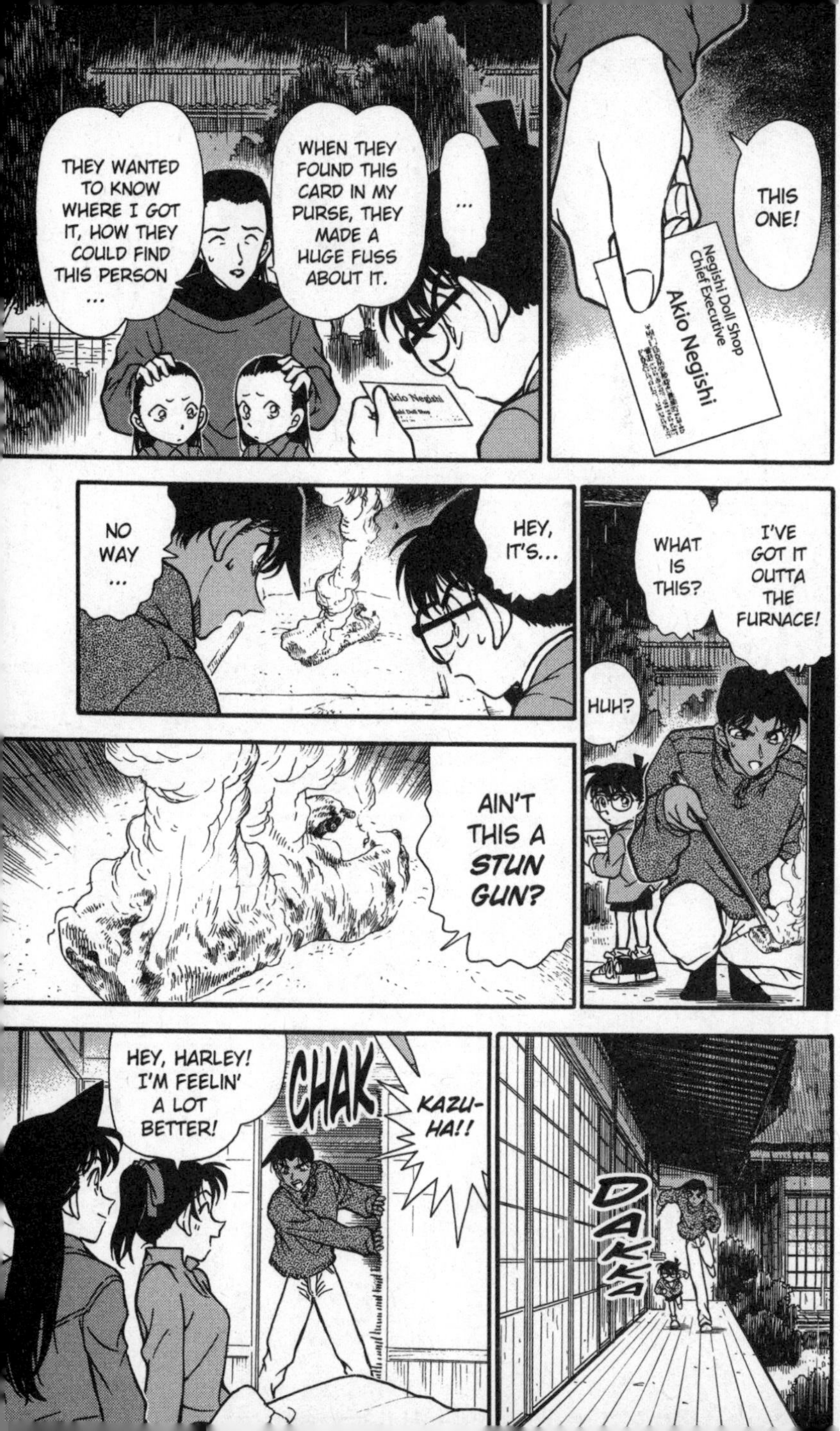
THIS ONE!
Negishi Doll Shop
Chief Executive
Akio Negishi
...
WHEN THEY FOUND THIS CARD IN MY PURSE, THEY MADE A HUGE FUSS ABOUT IT.
THEY WANTED TO KNOW WHERE I GOT IT, HOW THEY COULD FIND THIS PERSON ...
I'VE GOT IT OUTTA THE FURNACE!
WHAT IS THIS?
HUH?
HEY, IT'S...
NO WAY ...
AIN'T THIS A STUN GUN?
DAKKA
KAZU-HA!!
CHAK
HEY, HARLEY! I'M FEELIN' A LOT BETTER!

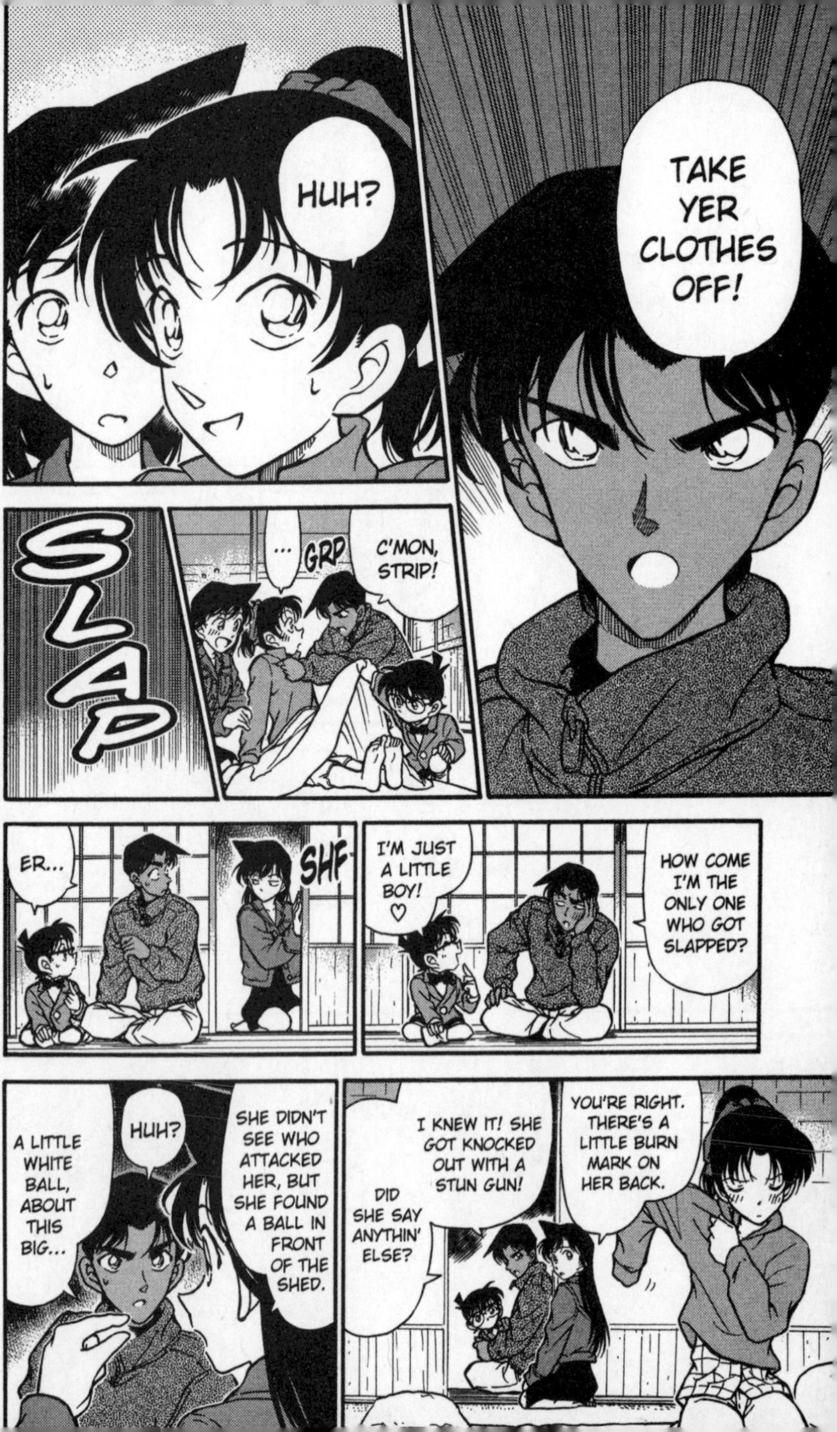
TAKE YER CLOTHES OFF!
HUH?
C'MON, STRIP!
GRP
...
SLAP
HOW COME I'M THE ONLY ONE WHO GOT SLAPPED?
I'M JUST A LITTLE BOY! ♡
SHF
ER...
YOU'RE RIGHT. THERE'S A LITTLE BURN MARK ON HER BACK.
I KNEW IT! SHE GOT KNOCKED OUT WITH A STUN GUN!
DID SHE SAY ANYTHIN' ELSE?
SHE DIDN'T SEE WHO ATTACKED HER, BUT SHE FOUND A BALL IN FRONT OF THE SHED.
HUH?
A LITTLE WHITE BALL, ABOUT THIS BIG...

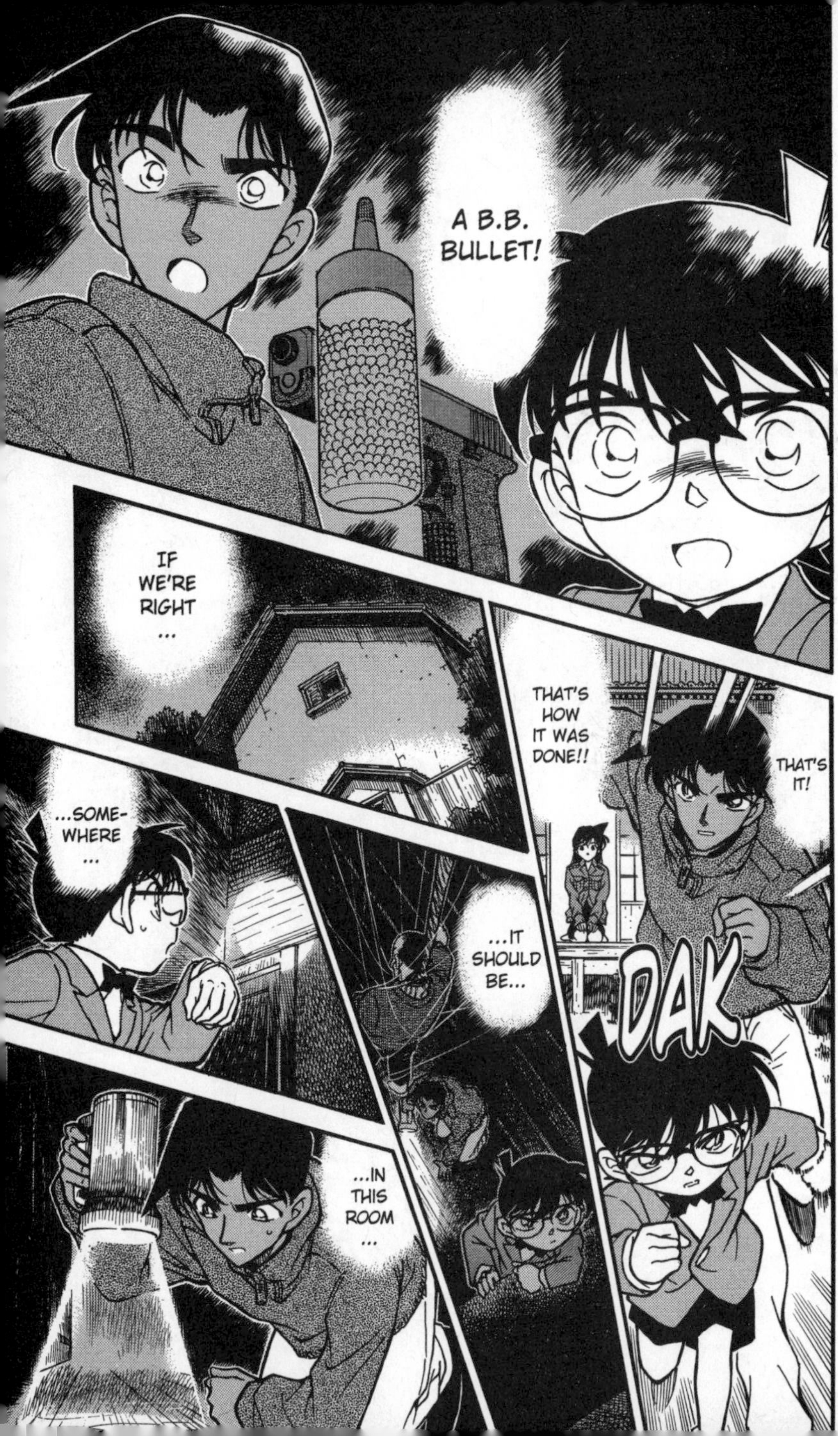
A B.B. BULLET!
THAT'S IT!
THAT'S HOW IT WAS DONE!!
DAK
IF WE'RE RIGHT ...
...IT SHOULD BE...
...SOME-WHERE ...
...IN THIS ROOM ...

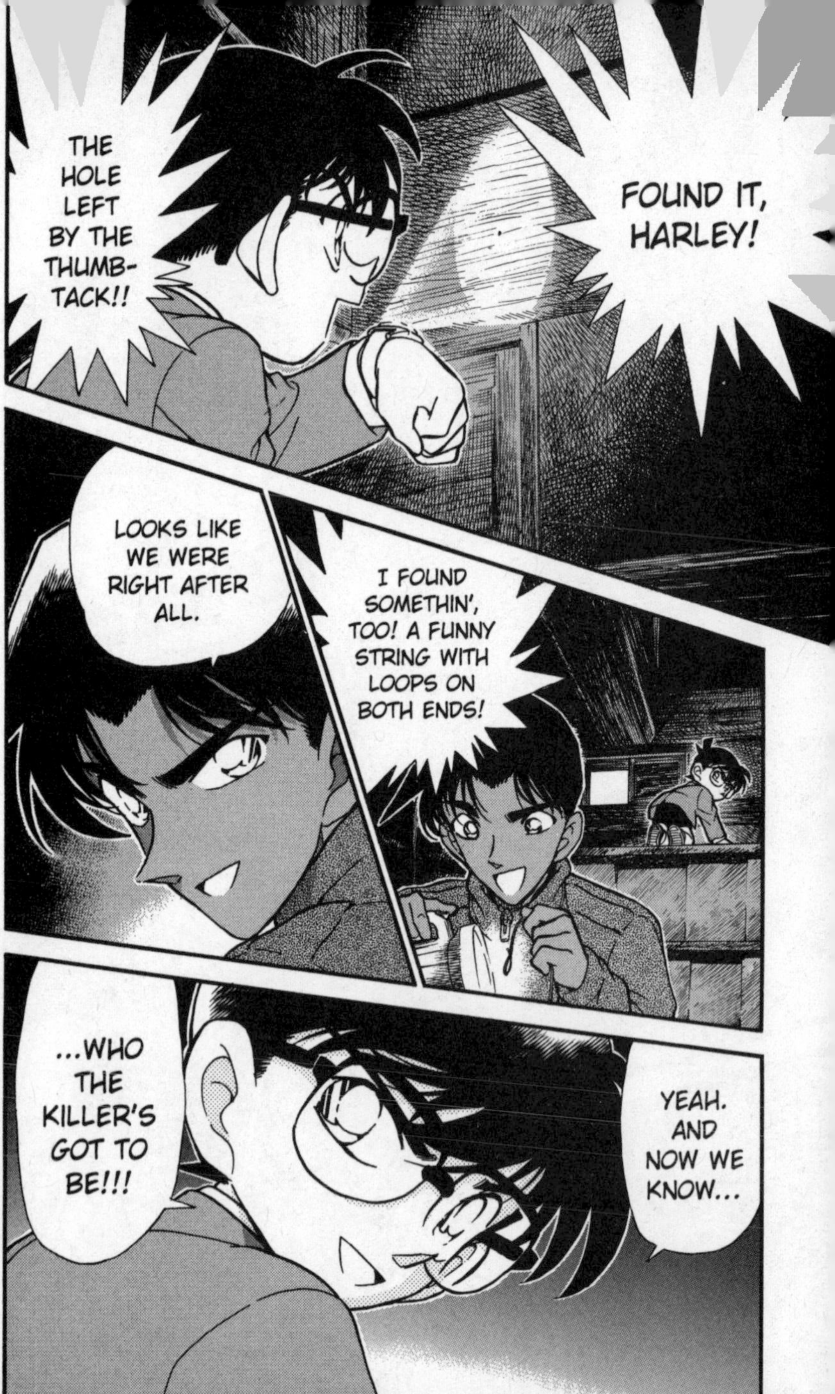
FOUND IT, HARLEY!
THE HOLE LEFT BY THE THUMB-TACK!!
I FOUND SOMETHIN', TOO! A FUNNY STRING WITH LOOPS ON BOTH ENDS!
LOOKS LIKE WE WERE RIGHT AFTER ALL.
YEAH. AND NOW WE KNOW...
...WHO THE KILLER'S GOT TO BE!!!

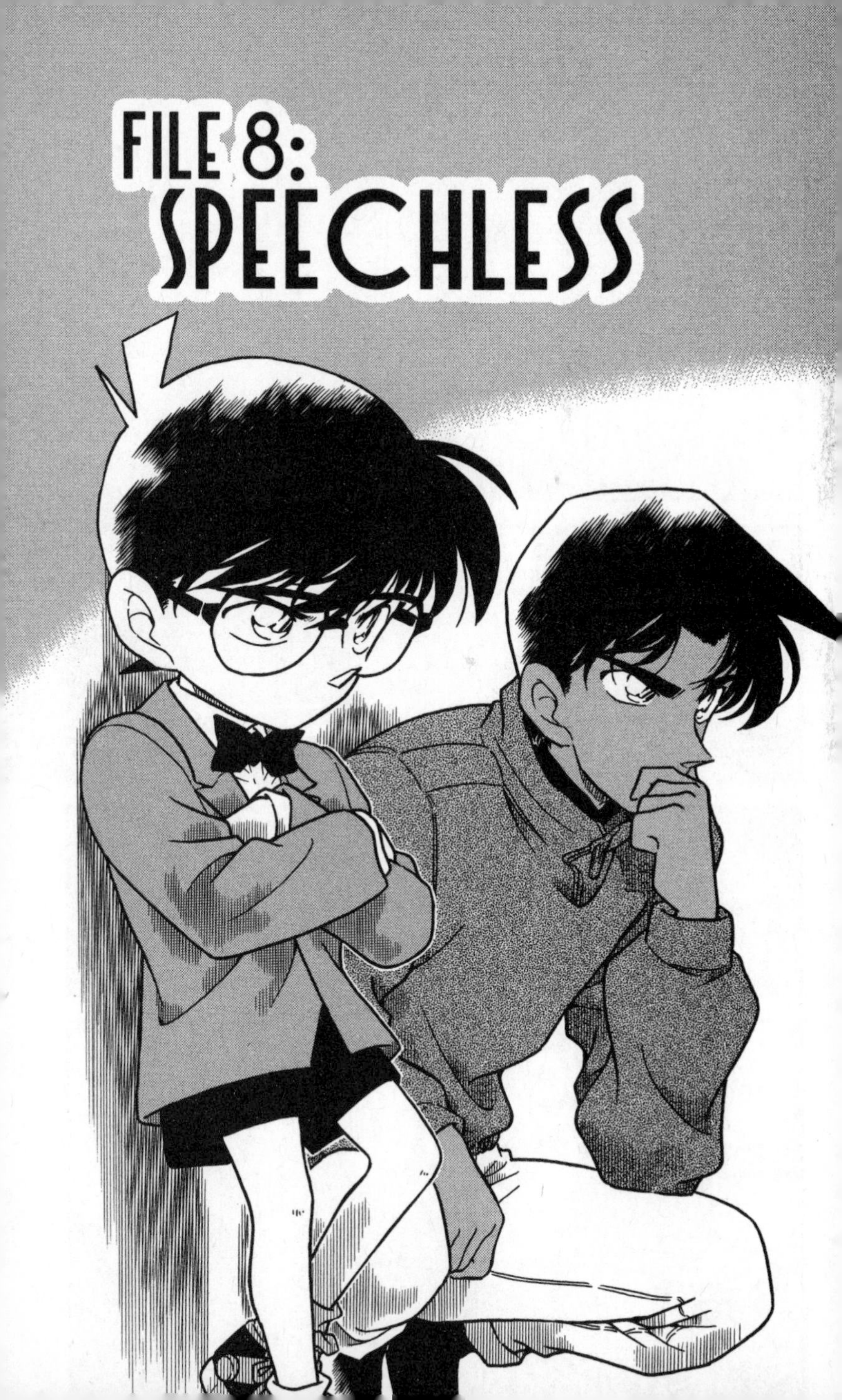

FILE 8:
SPEECHLESS

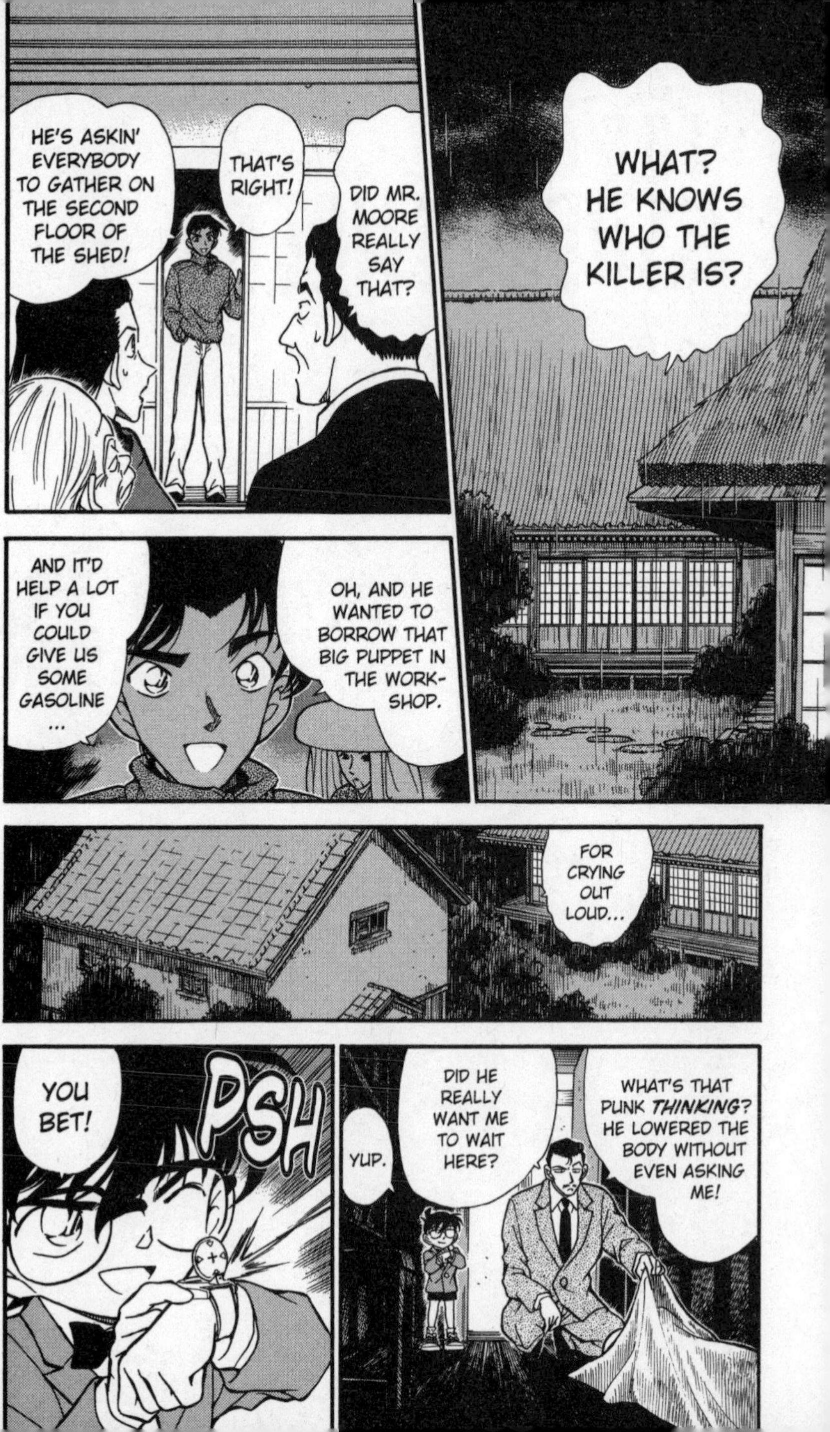
WHAT? HE KNOWS WHO THE KILLER IS?
DID MR. MOORE REALLY SAY THAT?
THAT'S RIGHT!
HE'S ASKIN' EVERYBODY TO GATHER ON THE SECOND FLOOR OF THE SHED!
OH, AND HE WANTED TO BORROW THAT BIG PUPPET IN THE WORK-SHOP.
AND IT'D HELP A LOT IF YOU COULD GIVE US SOME GASOLINE ...
FOR CRYING OUT LOUD...
WHAT'S THAT PUNK *THINKING*? HE LOWERED THE BODY WITHOUT EVEN ASKING ME!
DID HE REALLY WANT ME TO WAIT HERE?
YUP.
PSH
YOU BET!

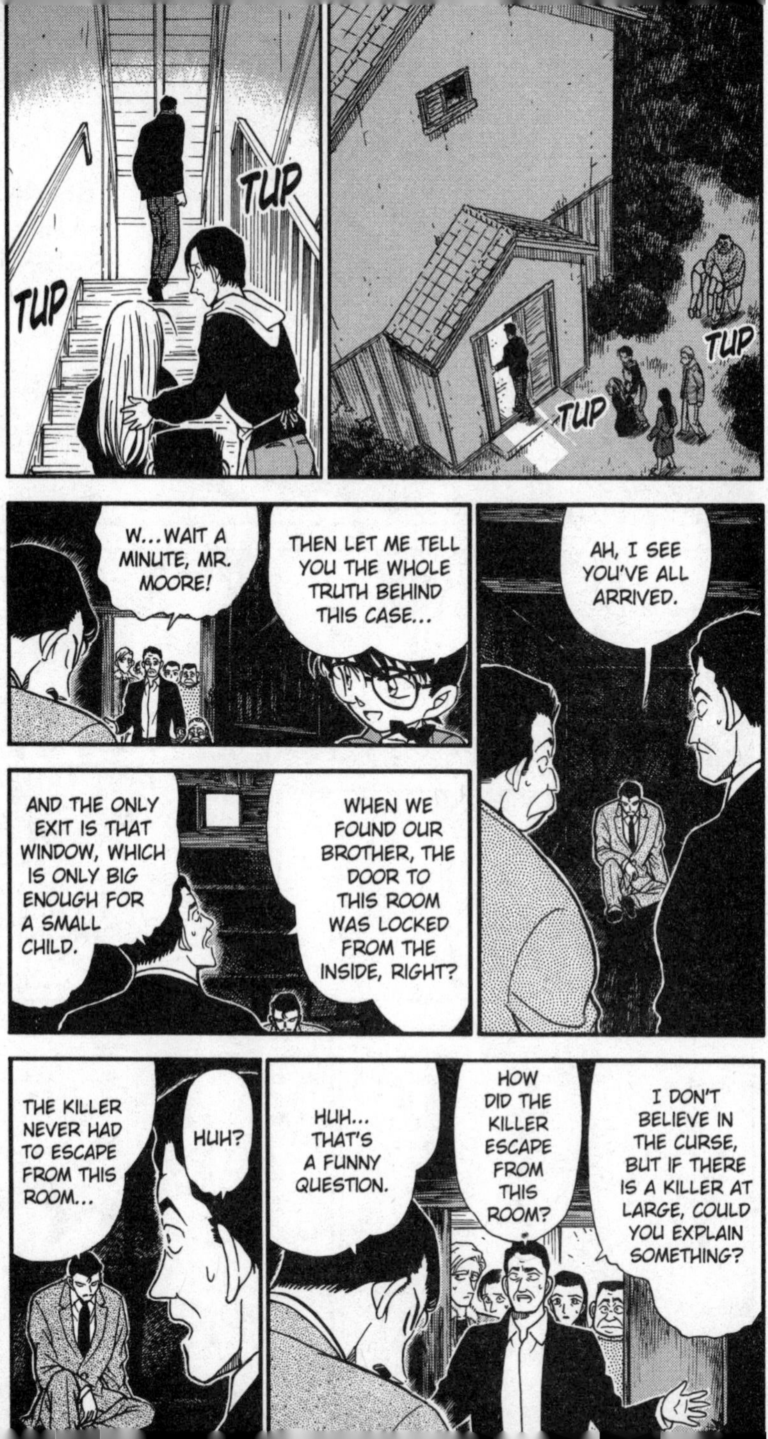
TUP
TUP
TUP
TUP
AH, I SEE YOU'VE ALL ARRIVED.
THEN LET ME TELL YOU THE WHOLE TRUTH BEHIND THIS CASE...
W...WAIT A MINUTE, MR. MOORE!
WHEN WE FOUND OUR BROTHER, THE DOOR TO THIS ROOM WAS LOCKED FROM THE INSIDE, RIGHT?
AND THE ONLY EXIT IS THAT WINDOW, WHICH IS ONLY BIG ENOUGH FOR A SMALL CHILD.
I DON'T BELIEVE IN THE CURSE, BUT IF THERE IS A KILLER AT LARGE, COULD YOU EXPLAIN SOMETHING?
HOW DID THE KILLER ESCAPE FROM THIS ROOM?
HUH... THAT'S A FUNNY QUESTION.
HUH?
THE KILLER NEVER HAD TO ESCAPE FROM THIS ROOM...

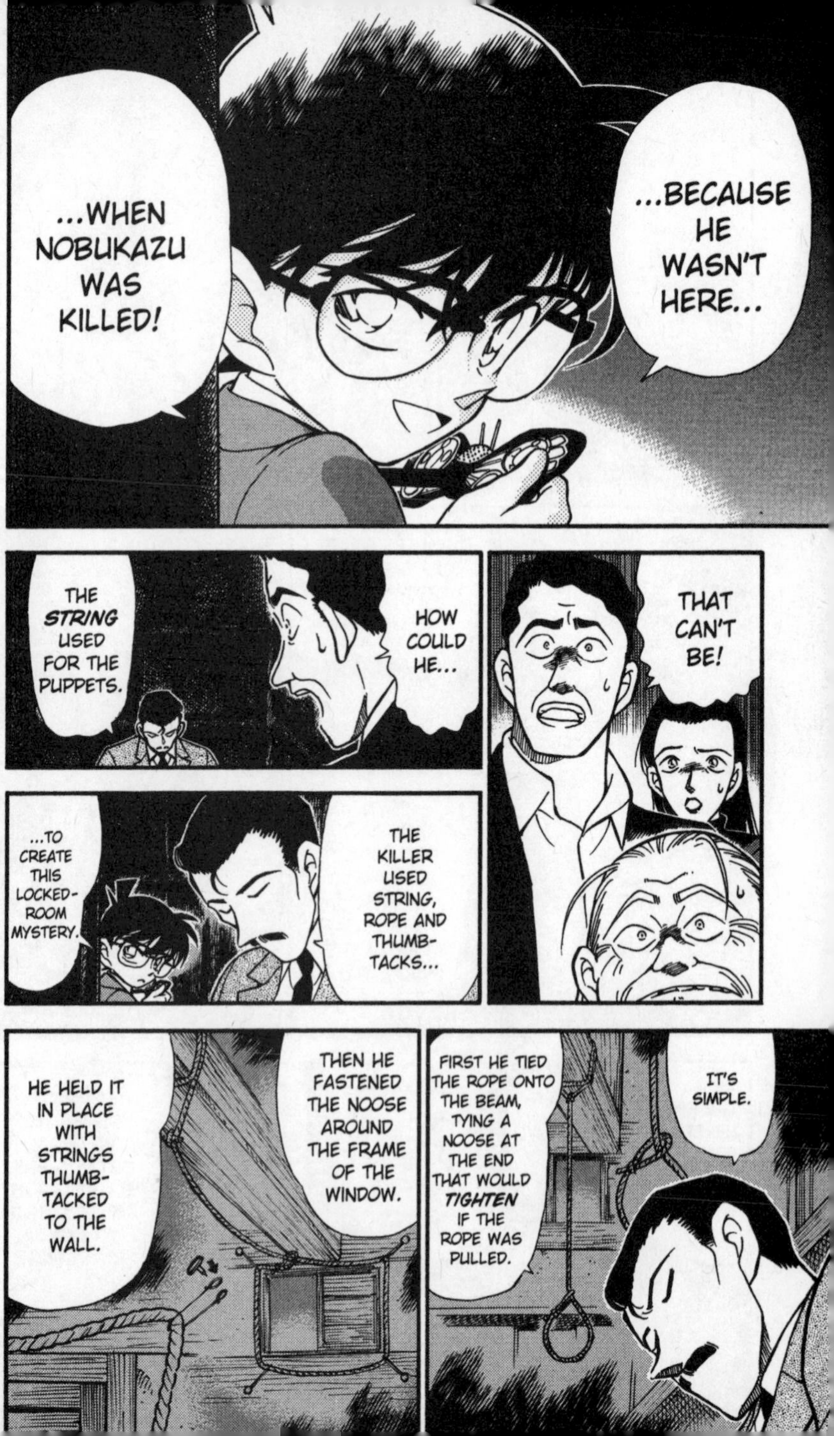
...BECAUSE HE WASN'T HERE...
...WHEN NOBUKAZU WAS KILLED!
THAT CAN'T BE!
HOW COULD HE...
THE *STRING* USED FOR THE PUPPETS.
THE KILLER USED STRING, ROPE AND THUMB-TACKS...
...TO CREATE THIS LOCKED-ROOM MYSTERY.
IT'S SIMPLE.
FIRST HE TIED THE ROPE ONTO THE BEAM, TYING A NOOSE AT THE END THAT WOULD *TIGHTEN* IF THE ROPE WAS PULLED.
THEN HE FASTENED THE NOOSE AROUND THE FRAME OF THE WINDOW.
HE HELD IT IN PLACE WITH STRINGS THUMB-TACKED TO THE WALL.

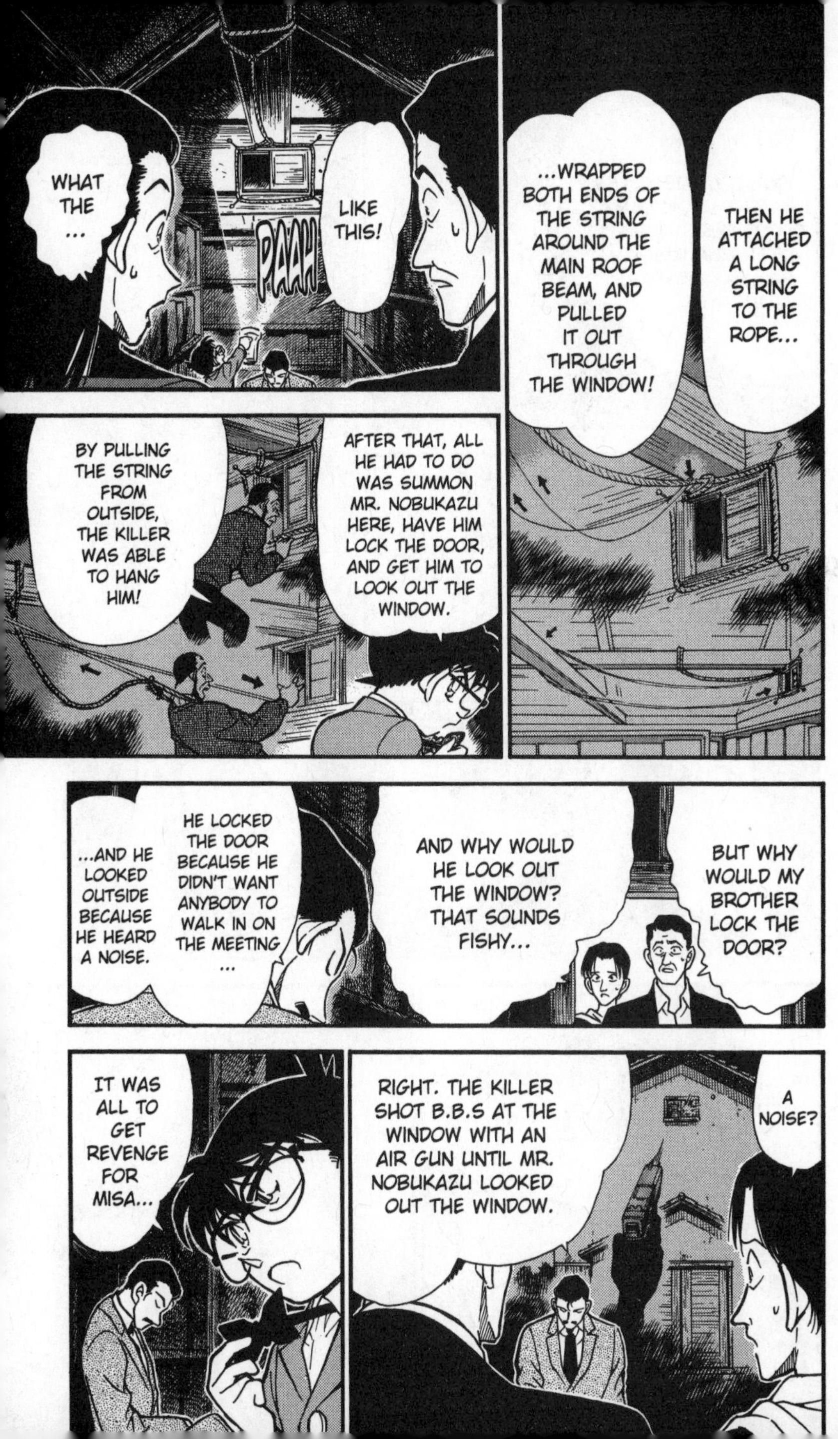
THEN HE ATTACHED A LONG STRING TO THE ROPE...
...WRAPPED BOTH ENDS OF THE STRING AROUND THE MAIN ROOF BEAM, AND PULLED IT OUT THROUGH THE WINDOW!
LIKE THIS!
PAAH
WHAT THE ...
AFTER THAT, ALL HE HAD TO DO WAS SUMMON MR. NOBUKAZU HERE, HAVE HIM LOCK THE DOOR, AND GET HIM TO LOOK OUT THE WINDOW.
BY PULLING THE STRING FROM OUTSIDE, THE KILLER WAS ABLE TO HANG HIM!
BUT WHY WOULD MY BROTHER LOCK THE DOOR?
AND WHY WOULD HE LOOK OUT THE WINDOW? THAT SOUNDS FISHY...
HE LOCKED THE DOOR BECAUSE HE DIDN'T WANT ANYBODY TO WALK IN ON THE MEETING ...
...AND HE LOOKED OUTSIDE BECAUSE HE HEARD A NOISE.
A NOISE?
RIGHT. THE KILLER SHOT B.B.S AT THE WINDOW WITH AN AIR GUN UNTIL MR. NOBUKAZU LOOKED OUT THE WINDOW.
IT WAS ALL TO GET REVENGE FOR MISA...

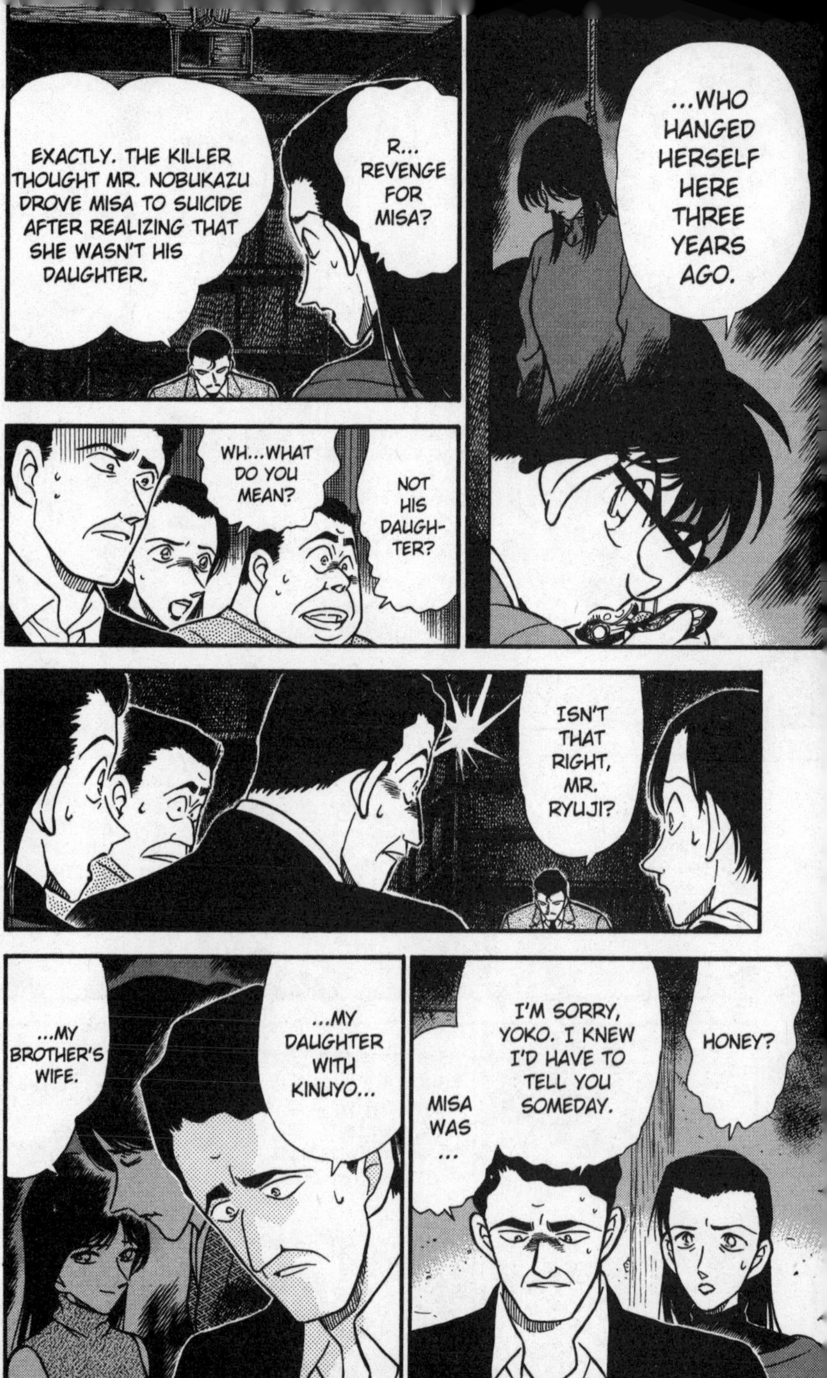
...WHO HANGED HERSELF HERE THREE YEARS AGO.
R... REVENGE FOR MISA?
EXACTLY. THE KILLER THOUGHT MR. NOBUKAZU DROVE MISA TO SUICIDE AFTER REALIZING THAT SHE WASN'T HIS DAUGHTER.
NOT HIS DAUGH-TER?
WH...WHAT DO YOU MEAN?
ISN'T THAT RIGHT, MR. RYUJI?
HONEY?
I'M SORRY, YOKO. I KNEW I'D HAVE TO TELL YOU SOMEDAY.
MISA WAS ...
...MY DAUGHTER WITH KINUYO...
...MY BROTHER'S WIFE.

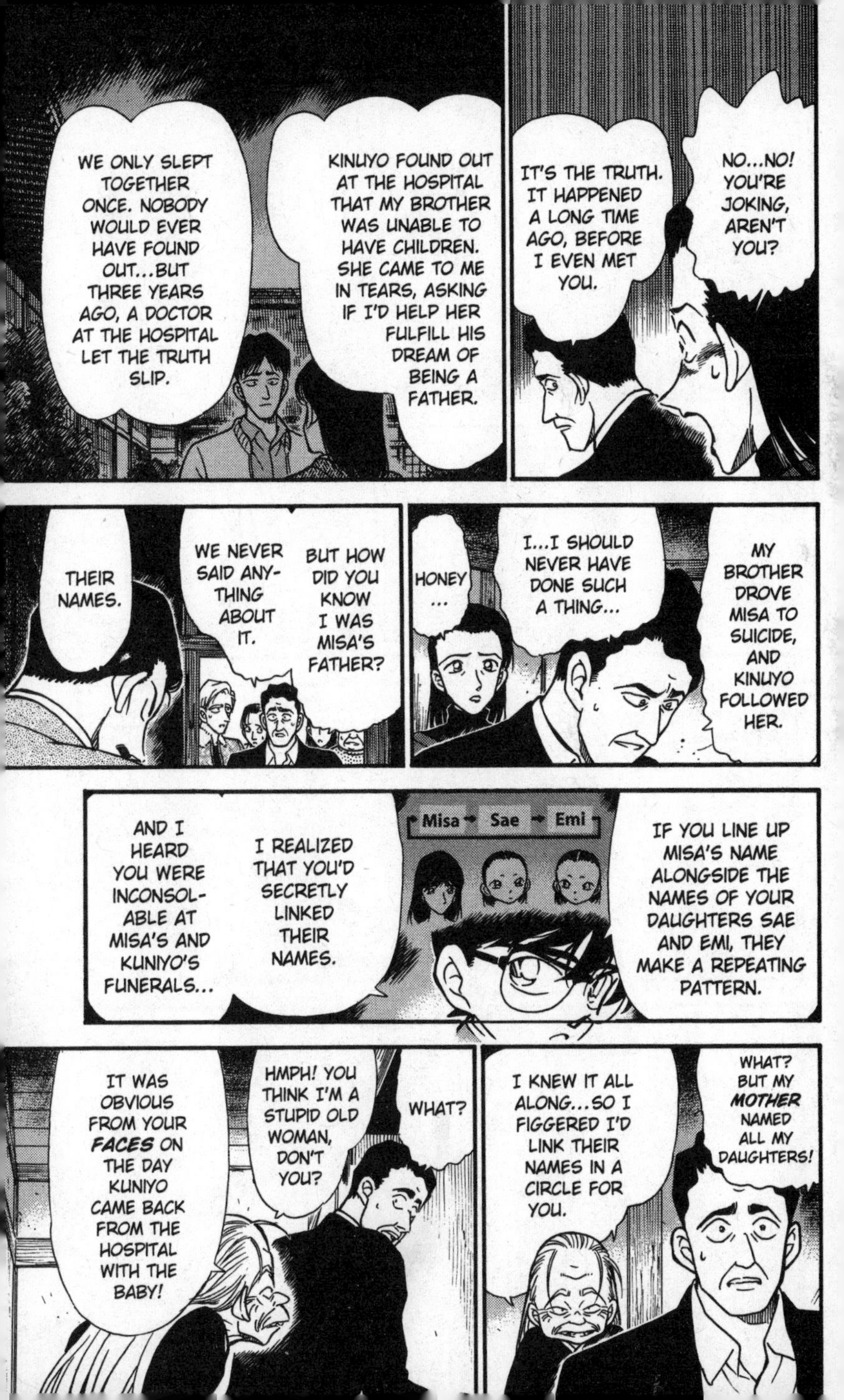
NO...NO! YOU'RE JOKING, AREN'T YOU?
IT'S THE TRUTH. IT HAPPENED A LONG TIME AGO, BEFORE I EVEN MET YOU.
KINUYO FOUND OUT AT THE HOSPITAL THAT MY BROTHER WAS UNABLE TO HAVE CHILDREN. SHE CAME TO ME IN TEARS, ASKING IF I'D HELP HER FULFILL HIS DREAM OF BEING A FATHER.
WE ONLY SLEPT TOGETHER ONCE. NOBODY WOULD EVER HAVE FOUND OUT...BUT THREE YEARS AGO, A DOCTOR AT THE HOSPITAL LET THE TRUTH SLIP.
MY BROTHER DROVE MISA TO SUICIDE, AND KINUYO FOLLOWED HER.
I...I SHOULD NEVER HAVE DONE SUCH A THING...
HONEY ...
BUT HOW DID YOU KNOW I WAS MISA'S FATHER?
WE NEVER SAID ANY-THING ABOUT IT.
THEIR NAMES.
IF YOU LINE UP MISA'S NAME ALONGSIDE THE NAMES OF YOUR DAUGHTERS SAE AND EMI, THEY MAKE A REPEATING PATTERN.
Misa → Sae → Emi
I REALIZED THAT YOU'D SECRETLY LINKED THEIR NAMES.
AND I HEARD YOU WERE INCONSOL-ABLE AT MISA'S AND KUNIYO'S FUNERALS...
WHAT? BUT MY ***MOTHER*** NAMED ALL MY DAUGHTERS!
I KNEW IT ALL ALONG...SO I FIGGERED I'D LINK THEIR NAMES IN A CIRCLE FOR YOU.
WHAT?
HMPH! YOU THINK I'M A STUPID OLD WOMAN, DON'T YOU?
IT WAS OBVIOUS FROM YOUR ***FACES*** ON THE DAY KUNIYO CAME BACK FROM THE HOSPITAL WITH THE BABY!

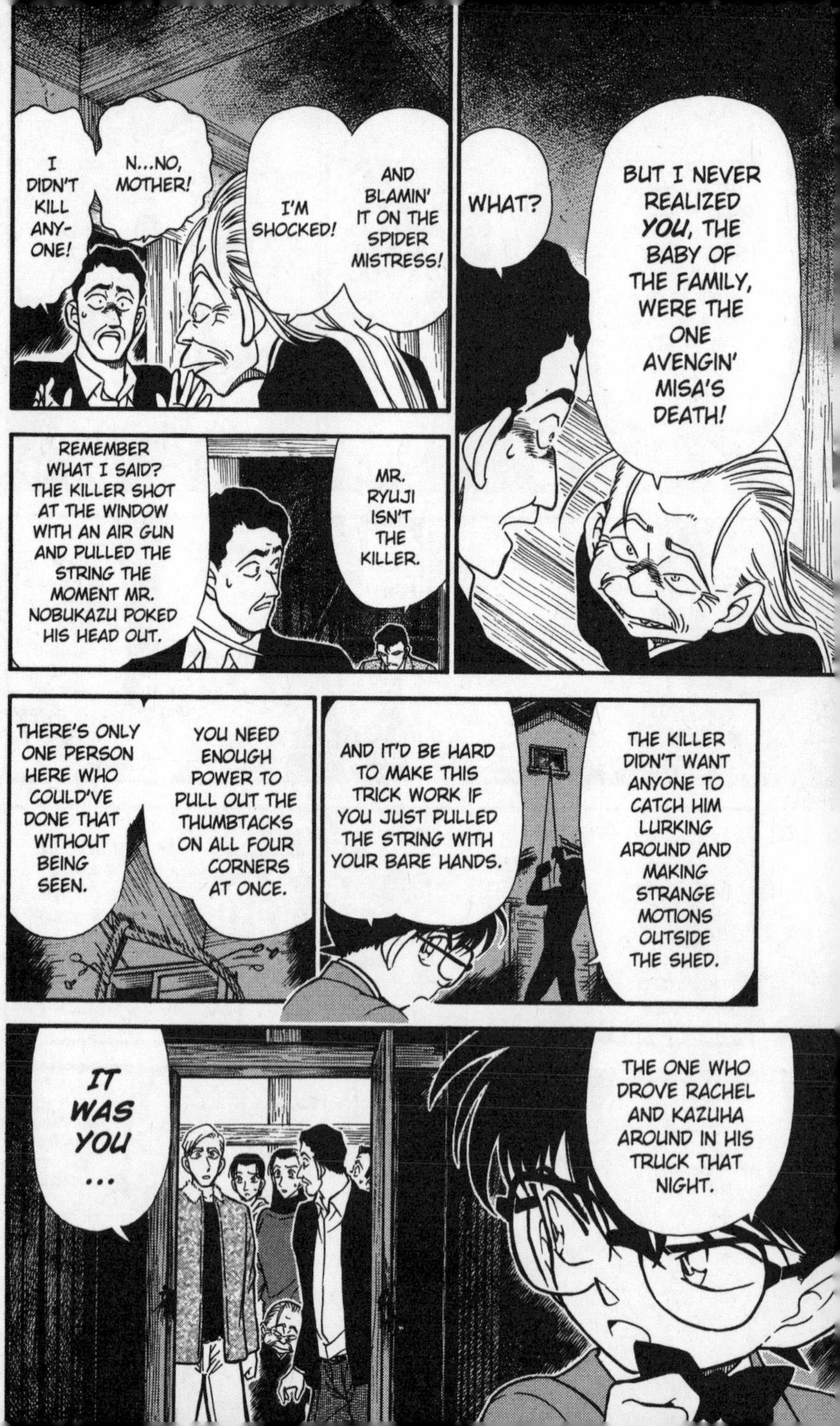
BUT I NEVER REALIZED *YOU*, THE BABY OF THE FAMILY, WERE THE ONE AVENGIN' MISA'S DEATH!
WHAT?
AND BLAMIN' IT ON THE SPIDER MISTRESS!
I'M SHOCKED!
N...NO, MOTHER!
I DIDN'T KILL ANY-ONE!
MR. RYUJI ISN'T THE KILLER.
REMEMBER WHAT I SAID? THE KILLER SHOT AT THE WINDOW WITH AN AIR GUN AND PULLED THE STRING THE MOMENT MR. NOBUKAZU POKED HIS HEAD OUT.
THE KILLER DIDN'T WANT ANYONE TO CATCH HIM LURKING AROUND AND MAKING STRANGE MOTIONS OUTSIDE THE SHED.
AND IT'D BE HARD TO MAKE THIS TRICK WORK IF YOU JUST PULLED THE STRING WITH YOUR BARE HANDS.
YOU NEED ENOUGH POWER TO PULL OUT THE THUMBTACKS ON ALL FOUR CORNERS AT ONCE.
THERE'S ONLY ONE PERSON HERE WHO COULD'VE DONE THAT WITHOUT BEING SEEN.
THE ONE WHO DROVE RACHEL AND KAZUHA AROUND IN HIS TRUCK THAT NIGHT.
IT WAS YOU...

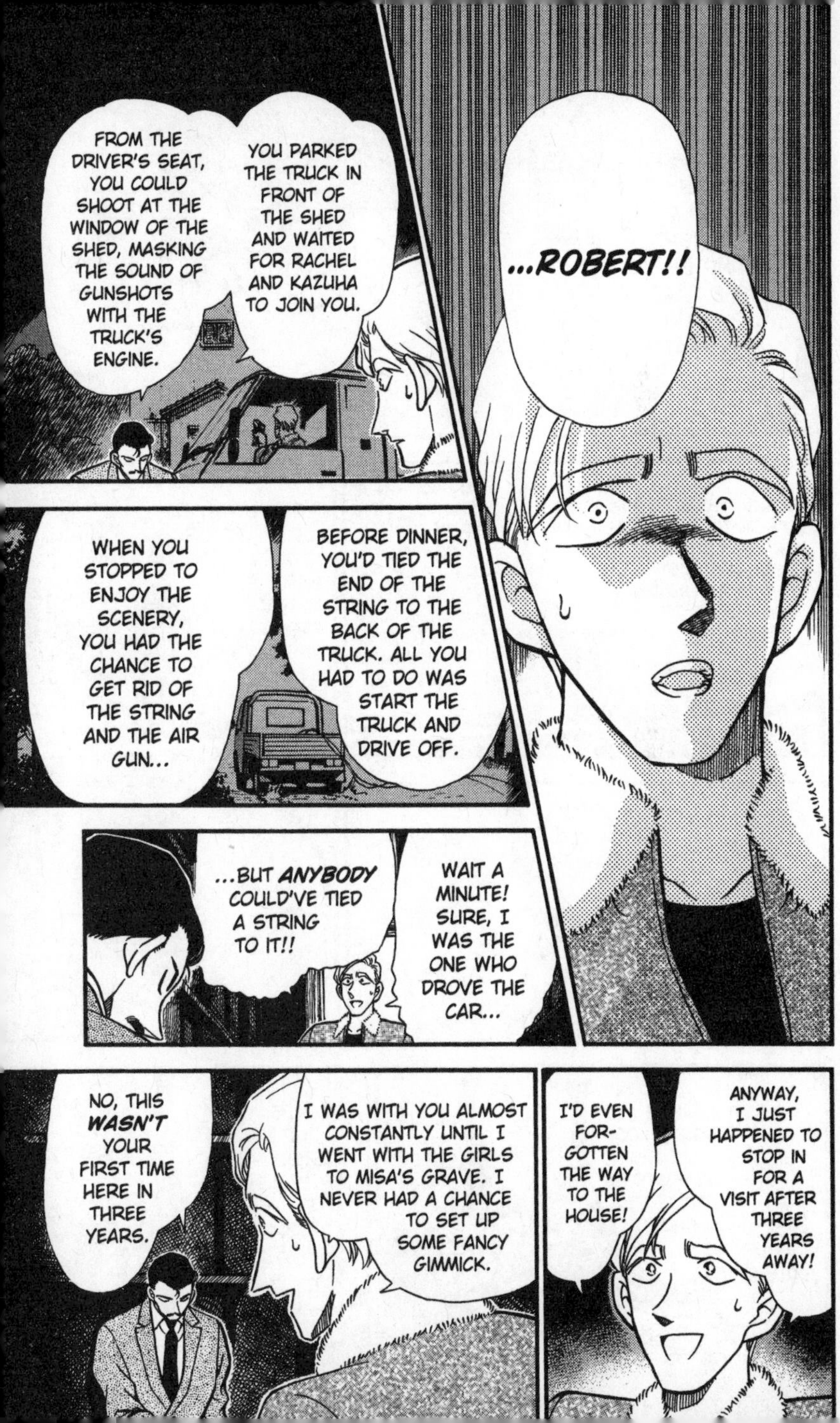
...ROBERT!!
YOU PARKED THE TRUCK IN FRONT OF THE SHED AND WAITED FOR RACHEL AND KAZUHA TO JOIN YOU.
FROM THE DRIVER'S SEAT, YOU COULD SHOOT AT THE WINDOW OF THE SHED, MASKING THE SOUND OF GUNSHOTS WITH THE TRUCK'S ENGINE.
BEFORE DINNER, YOU'D TIED THE END OF THE STRING TO THE BACK OF THE TRUCK. ALL YOU HAD TO DO WAS START THE TRUCK AND DRIVE OFF.
WHEN YOU STOPPED TO ENJOY THE SCENERY, YOU HAD THE CHANCE TO GET RID OF THE STRING AND THE AIR GUN...
WAIT A MINUTE! SURE, I WAS THE ONE WHO DROVE THE CAR...
...BUT ANYBODY COULD'VE TIED A STRING TO IT!!
ANYWAY, I JUST HAPPENED TO STOP IN FOR A VISIT AFTER THREE YEARS AWAY!
I'D EVEN FOR-GOTTEN THE WAY TO THE HOUSE!
I WAS WITH YOU ALMOST CONSTANTLY UNTIL I WENT WITH THE GIRLS TO MISA'S GRAVE. I NEVER HAD A CHANCE TO SET UP SOME FANCY GIMMICK.
NO, THIS WASN'T YOUR FIRST TIME HERE IN THREE YEARS.

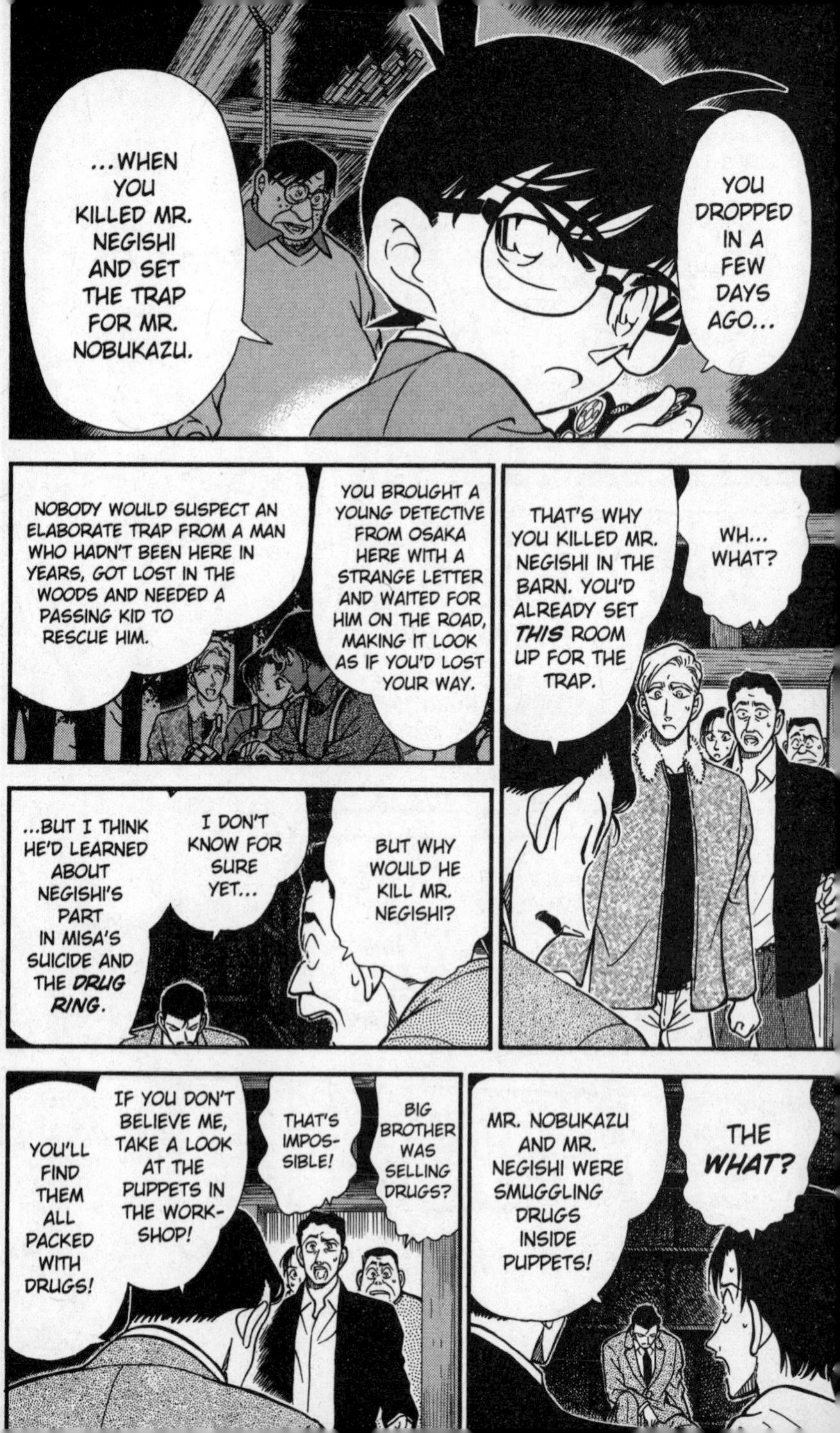
YOU DROPPED IN A FEW DAYS AGO...
...WHEN YOU KILLED MR. NEGISHI AND SET THE TRAP FOR MR. NOBUKAZU.
WH... WHAT?
THAT'S WHY YOU KILLED MR. NEGISHI IN THE BARN. YOU'D ALREADY SET *THIS* ROOM UP FOR THE TRAP.
YOU BROUGHT A YOUNG DETECTIVE FROM OSAKA HERE WITH A STRANGE LETTER AND WAITED FOR HIM ON THE ROAD, MAKING IT LOOK AS IF YOU'D LOST YOUR WAY.
NOBODY WOULD SUSPECT AN ELABORATE TRAP FROM A MAN WHO HADN'T BEEN HERE IN YEARS, GOT LOST IN THE WOODS AND NEEDED A PASSING KID TO RESCUE HIM.
BUT WHY WOULD HE KILL MR. NEGISHI?
I DON'T KNOW FOR SURE YET...
...BUT I THINK HE'D LEARNED ABOUT NEGISHI'S PART IN MISA'S SUICIDE AND THE *DRUG RING*.
THE *WHAT?*
MR. NOBUKAZU AND MR. NEGISHI WERE SMUGGLING DRUGS INSIDE PUPPETS!
BIG BROTHER WAS SELLING DRUGS?
THAT'S IMPOSSIBLE!
IF YOU DON'T BELIEVE ME, TAKE A LOOK AT THE PUPPETS IN THE WORKSHOP!
YOU'LL FIND THEM ALL PACKED WITH DRUGS!

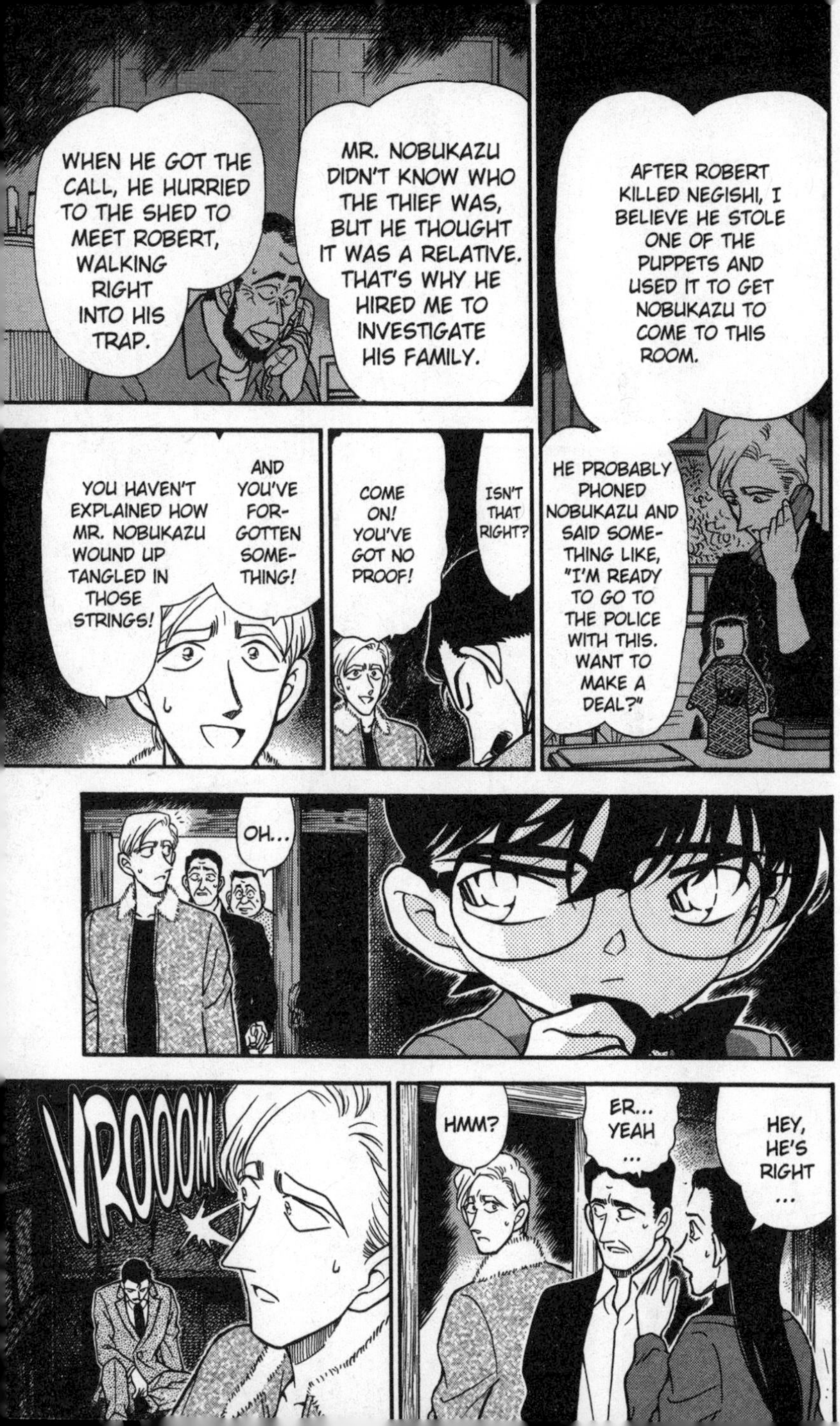
AFTER ROBERT KILLED NEGISHI, I BELIEVE HE STOLE ONE OF THE PUPPETS AND USED IT TO GET NOBUKAZU TO COME TO THIS ROOM.
HE PROBABLY PHONED NOBUKAZU AND SAID SOMETHING LIKE, "I'M READY TO GO TO THE POLICE WITH THIS. WANT TO MAKE A DEAL?"
MR. NOBUKAZU DIDN'T KNOW WHO THE THIEF WAS, BUT HE THOUGHT IT WAS A RELATIVE. THAT'S WHY HE HIRED ME TO INVESTIGATE HIS FAMILY.
WHEN HE GOT THE CALL, HE HURRIED TO THE SHED TO MEET ROBERT, WALKING RIGHT INTO HIS TRAP.
ISN'T THAT RIGHT?
COME ON! YOU'VE GOT NO PROOF!
AND YOU'VE FORGOTTEN SOMETHING!
YOU HAVEN'T EXPLAINED HOW MR. NOBUKAZU WOUND UP TANGLED IN THOSE STRINGS!
OH...
HEY, HE'S RIGHT...
ER... YEAH...
HMM?
VROOOM

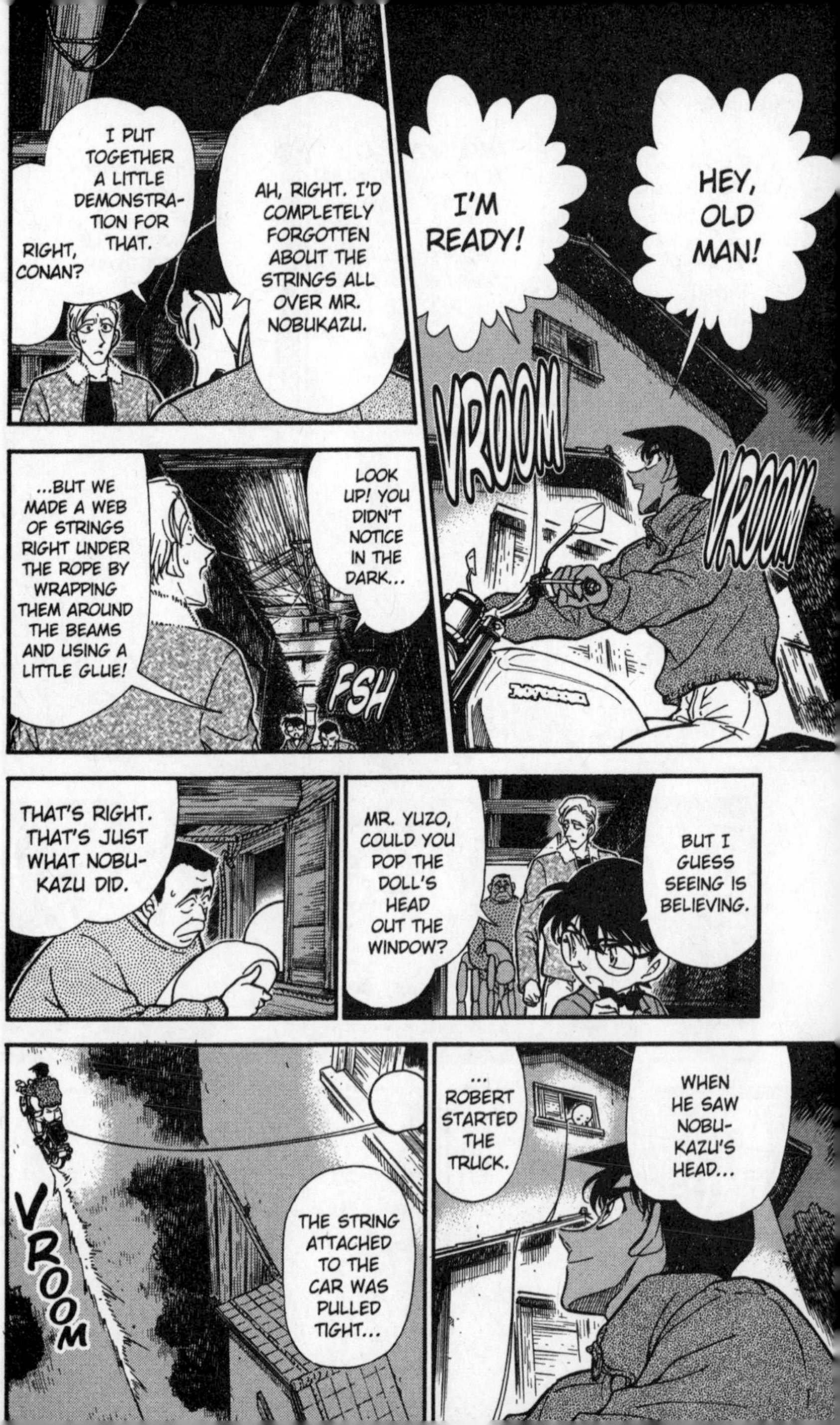

HEY, OLD MAN!
I'M READY!
VROOM
VROOM
AH, RIGHT. I'D COMPLETELY FORGOTTEN ABOUT THE STRINGS ALL OVER MR. NOBUKAZU.
I PUT TOGETHER A LITTLE DEMONSTRA-TION FOR THAT.
RIGHT, CONAN?
LOOK UP! YOU DIDN'T NOTICE IN THE DARK...
...BUT WE MADE A WEB OF STRINGS RIGHT UNDER THE ROPE BY WRAPPING THEM AROUND THE BEAMS AND USING A LITTLE GLUE!
FSH
BUT I GUESS SEEING IS BELIEVING.
MR. YUZO, COULD YOU POP THE DOLL'S HEAD OUT THE WINDOW?
THAT'S RIGHT. THAT'S JUST WHAT NOBU-KAZU DID.
WHEN HE SAW NOBU-KAZU'S HEAD...
...ROBERT STARTED THE TRUCK.
THE STRING ATTACHED TO THE CAR WAS PULLED TIGHT...
VROOM

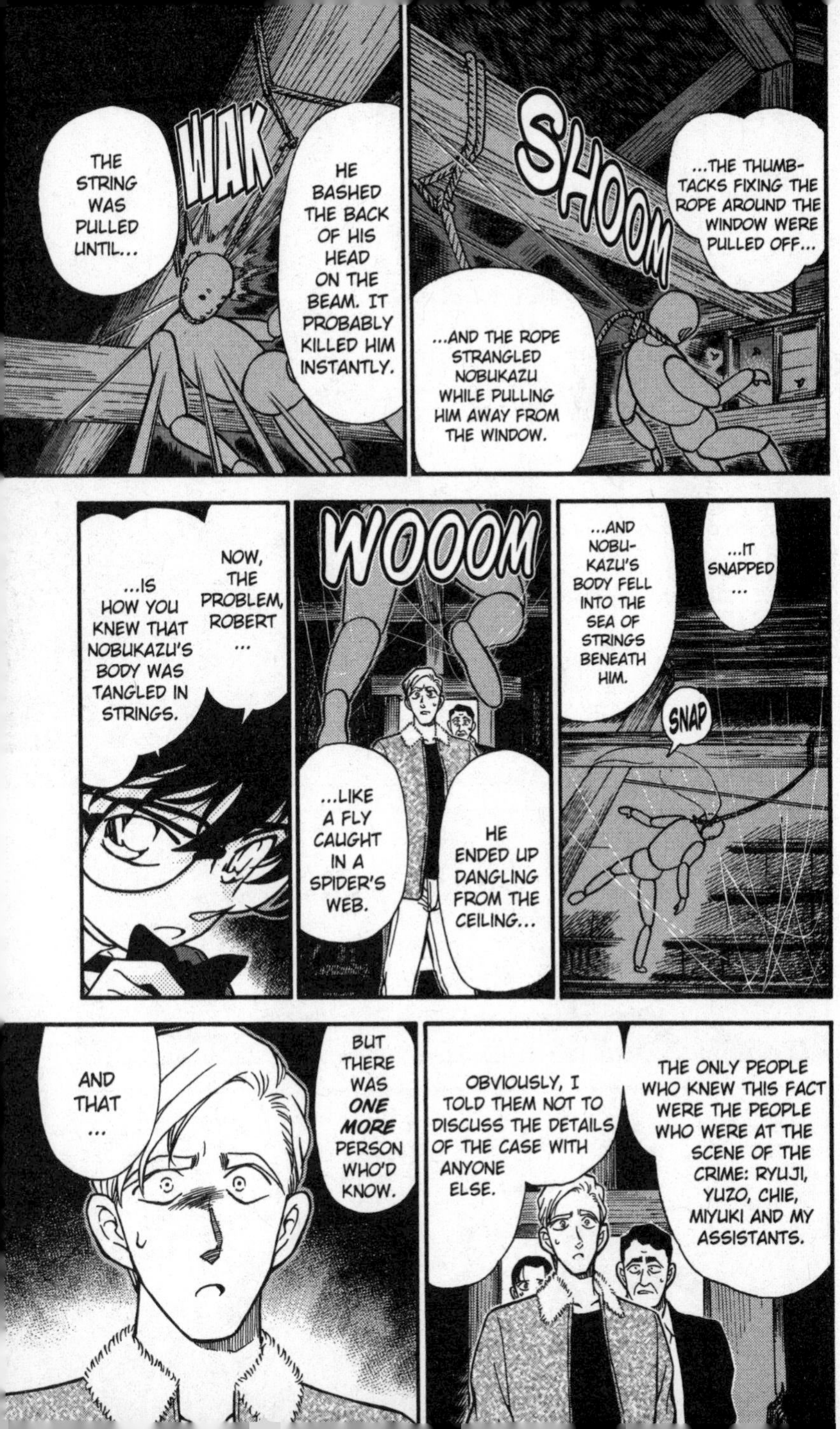
...THE THUMB-TACKS FIXING THE ROPE AROUND THE WINDOW WERE PULLED OFF...
SHOOM
...AND THE ROPE STRANGLED NOBUKAZU WHILE PULLING HIM AWAY FROM THE WINDOW.
HE BASHED THE BACK OF HIS HEAD ON THE BEAM. IT PROBABLY KILLED HIM INSTANTLY.
WAK
THE STRING WAS PULLED UNTIL...
...IT SNAPPED...
...AND NOBU-KAZU'S BODY FELL INTO THE SEA OF STRINGS BENEATH HIM.
SNAP
WOOOM
HE ENDED UP DANGLING FROM THE CEILING...
...LIKE A FLY CAUGHT IN A SPIDER'S WEB.
NOW, THE PROBLEM, ROBERT...
...IS HOW YOU KNEW THAT NOBUKAZU'S BODY WAS TANGLED IN STRINGS.
THE ONLY PEOPLE WHO KNEW THIS FACT WERE THE PEOPLE WHO WERE AT THE SCENE OF THE CRIME: RYUJI, YUZO, CHIE, MIYUKI AND MY ASSISTANTS.
OBVIOUSLY, I TOLD THEM NOT TO DISCUSS THE DETAILS OF THE CASE WITH ANYONE ELSE.
BUT THERE WAS ONE MORE PERSON WHO'D KNOW.
AND THAT...

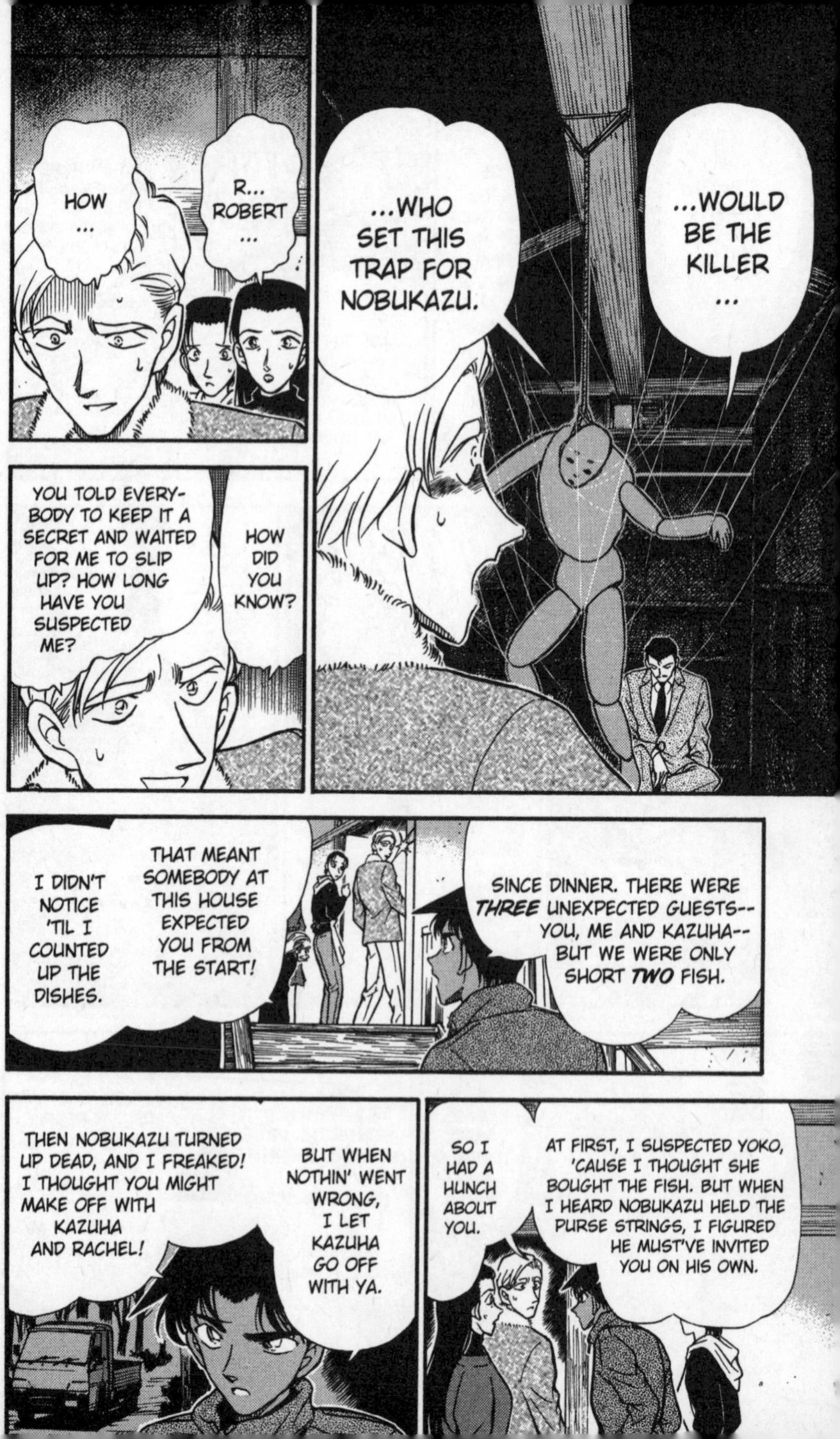

...WHO SET THIS TRAP FOR NOBUKAZU.
...WOULD BE THE KILLER ...
R... ROBERT ...
HOW ...
HOW DID YOU KNOW?
YOU TOLD EVERYBODY TO KEEP IT A SECRET AND WAITED FOR ME TO SLIP UP? HOW LONG HAVE YOU SUSPECTED ME?
SINCE DINNER. THERE WERE *THREE* UNEXPECTED GUESTS--YOU, ME AND KAZUHA--BUT WE WERE ONLY SHORT *TWO* FISH.
THAT MEANT SOMEBODY AT THIS HOUSE EXPECTED YOU FROM THE START!
I DIDN'T NOTICE 'TIL I COUNTED UP THE DISHES.
AT FIRST, I SUSPECTED YOKO, 'CAUSE I THOUGHT SHE BOUGHT THE FISH. BUT WHEN I HEARD NOBUKAZU HELD THE PURSE STRINGS, I FIGURED HE MUST'VE INVITED YOU ON HIS OWN.
SO I HAD A HUNCH ABOUT YOU.
BUT WHEN NOTHIN' WENT WRONG, I LET KAZUHA GO OFF WITH YA.
THEN NOBUKAZU TURNED UP DEAD, AND I FREAKED! I THOUGHT YOU MIGHT MAKE OFF WITH KAZUHA AND RACHEL!

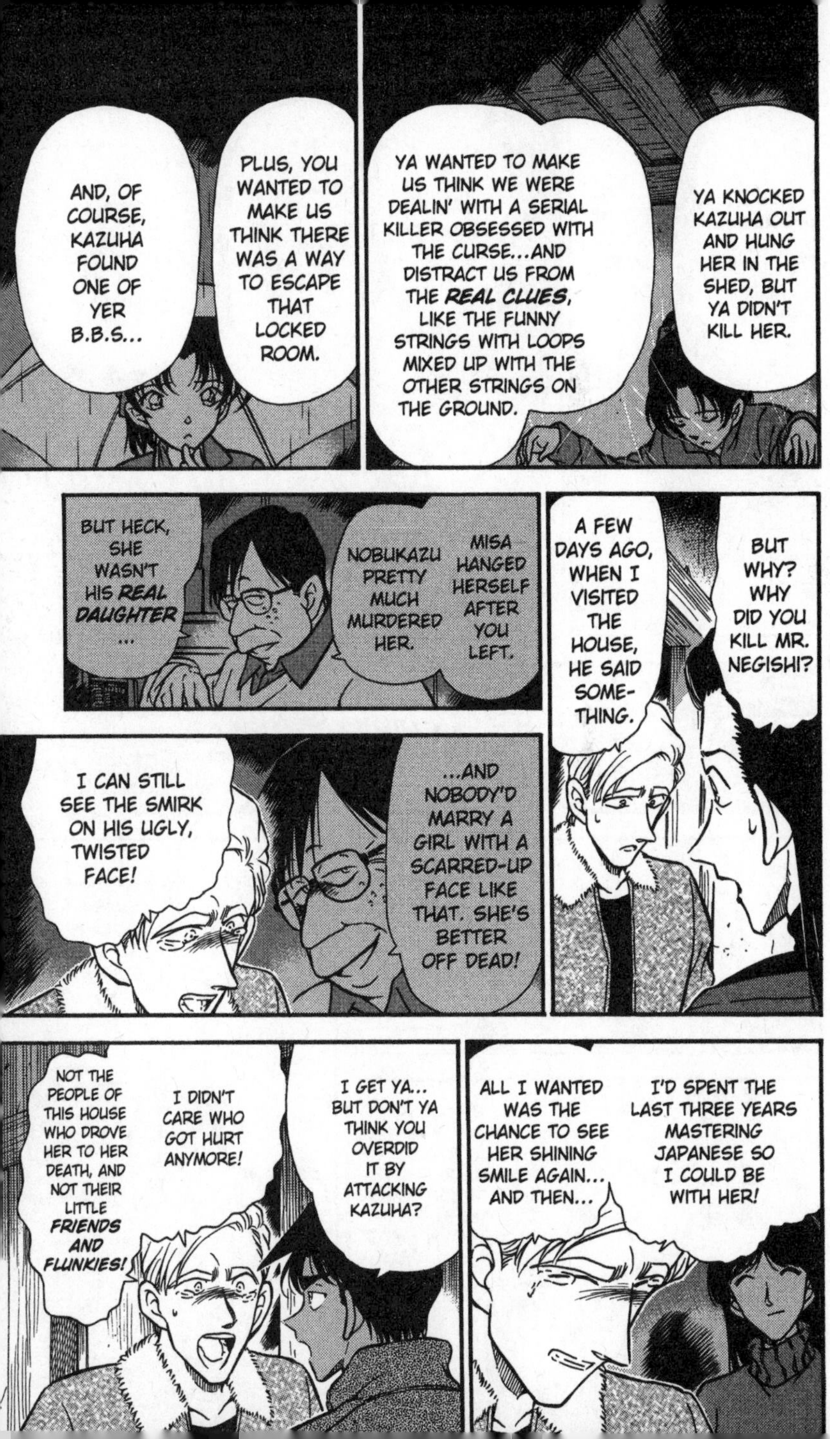

YA KNOCKED KAZUHA OUT AND HUNG HER IN THE SHED, BUT YA DIDN'T KILL HER.
YA WANTED TO MAKE US THINK WE WERE DEALIN' WITH A SERIAL KILLER OBSESSED WITH THE CURSE...AND DISTRACT US FROM THE ***REAL CLUES***, LIKE THE FUNNY STRINGS WITH LOOPS MIXED UP WITH THE OTHER STRINGS ON THE GROUND.
PLUS, YOU WANTED TO MAKE US THINK THERE WAS A WAY TO ESCAPE THAT LOCKED ROOM.
AND, OF COURSE, KAZUHA FOUND ONE OF YER B.B.S...
BUT WHY? WHY DID YOU KILL MR. NEGISHI?
A FEW DAYS AGO, WHEN I VISITED THE HOUSE, HE SAID SOME-THING.
MISA HANGED HERSELF AFTER YOU LEFT.
NOBUKAZU PRETTY MUCH MURDERED HER.
BUT HECK, SHE WASN'T HIS ***REAL DAUGHTER***...
...AND NOBODY'D MARRY A GIRL WITH A SCARRED-UP FACE LIKE THAT. SHE'S BETTER OFF DEAD!
I CAN STILL SEE THE SMIRK ON HIS UGLY, TWISTED FACE!
I'D SPENT THE LAST THREE YEARS MASTERING JAPANESE SO I COULD BE WITH HER!
ALL I WANTED WAS THE CHANCE TO SEE HER SHINING SMILE AGAIN... AND THEN...
I GET YA... BUT DON'T YA THINK YOU OVERDID IT BY ATTACKING KAZUHA?
I DIDN'T CARE WHO GOT HURT ANYMORE!
NOT THE PEOPLE OF THIS HOUSE WHO DROVE HER TO HER DEATH, AND NOT THEIR LITTLE ***FRIENDS AND FLUNKIES!***

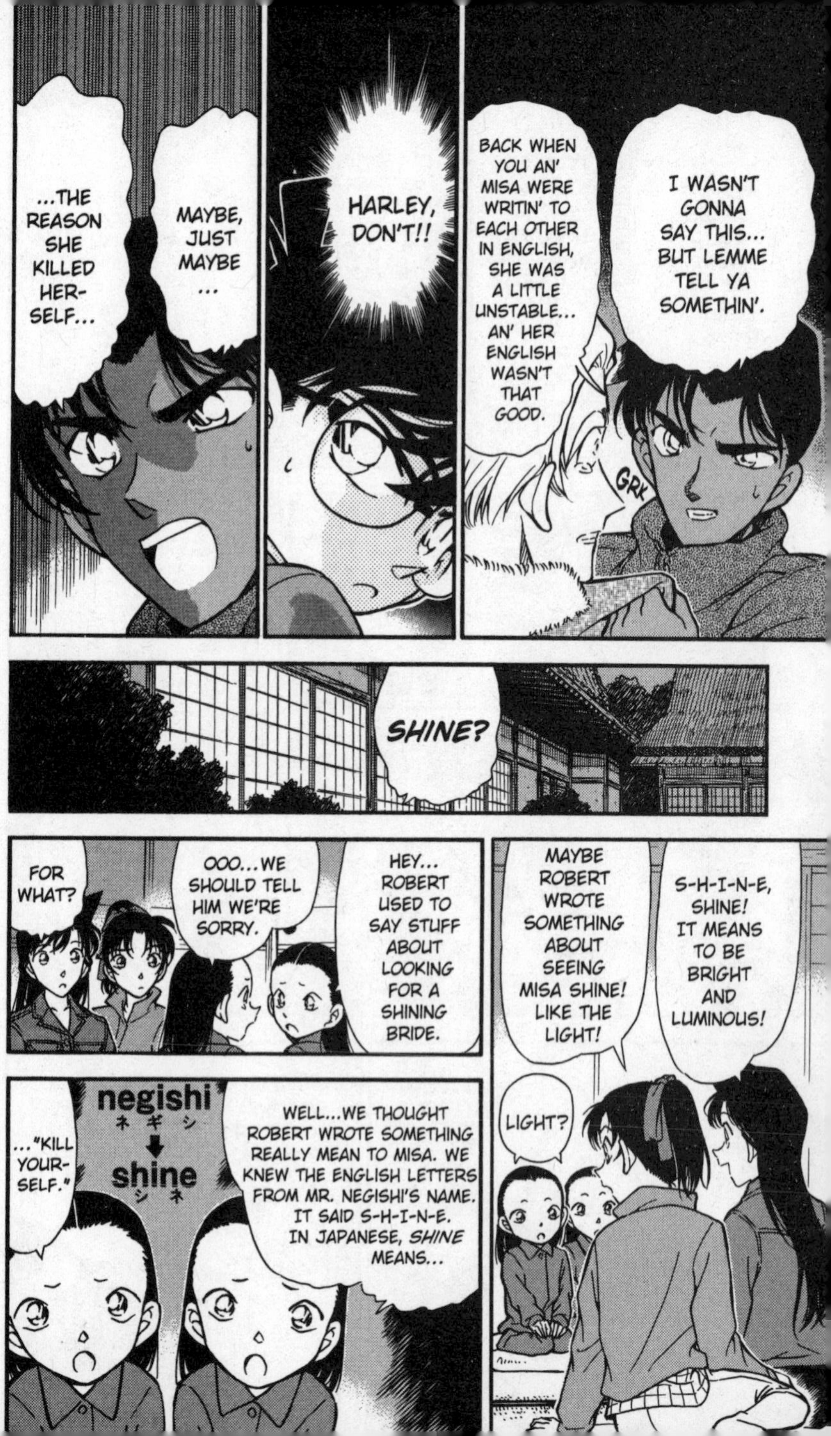
I WASN'T GONNA SAY THIS... BUT LEMME TELL YA SOMETHIN'.
BACK WHEN YOU AN' MISA WERE WRITIN' TO EACH OTHER IN ENGLISH, SHE WAS A LITTLE UNSTABLE... AN' HER ENGLISH WASN'T THAT GOOD.
GRK
HARLEY, DON'T!!
MAYBE, JUST MAYBE ...
...THE REASON SHE KILLED HER-SELF...
SHINE?
S-H-I-N-E, SHINE! IT MEANS TO BE BRIGHT AND LUMINOUS!
MAYBE ROBERT WROTE SOMETHING ABOUT SEEING MISA SHINE! LIKE THE LIGHT!
LIGHT?
HEY... ROBERT USED TO SAY STUFF ABOUT LOOKING FOR A SHINING BRIDE.
OOO...WE SHOULD TELL HIM WE'RE SORRY.
FOR WHAT?
WELL...WE THOUGHT ROBERT WROTE SOMETHING REALLY MEAN TO MISA. WE KNEW THE ENGLISH LETTERS FROM MR. NEGISHI'S NAME. IT SAID S-H-I-N-E. IN JAPANESE, *SHINE* MEANS...
negishi
ネギシ
shine
シネ
..."KILL YOURSELF."

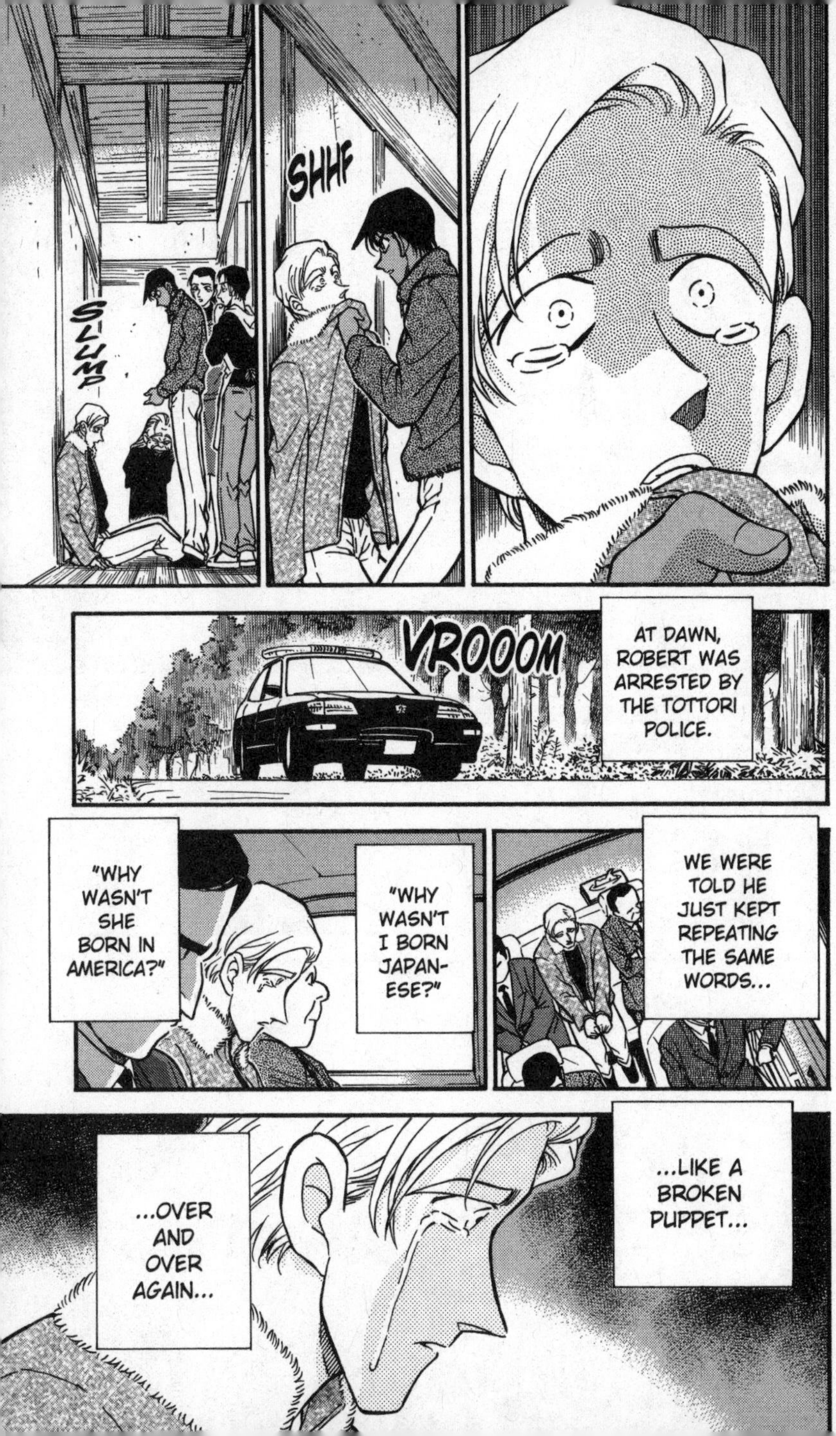
SHHF
SLUMP
AT DAWN, ROBERT WAS ARRESTED BY THE TOTTORI POLICE.
VROOOM
WE WERE TOLD HE JUST KEPT REPEATING THE SAME WORDS...
"WHY WASN'T I BORN JAPANESE?"
"WHY WASN'T SHE BORN IN AMERICA?"
...LIKE A BROKEN PUPPET...
...OVER AND OVER AGAIN...

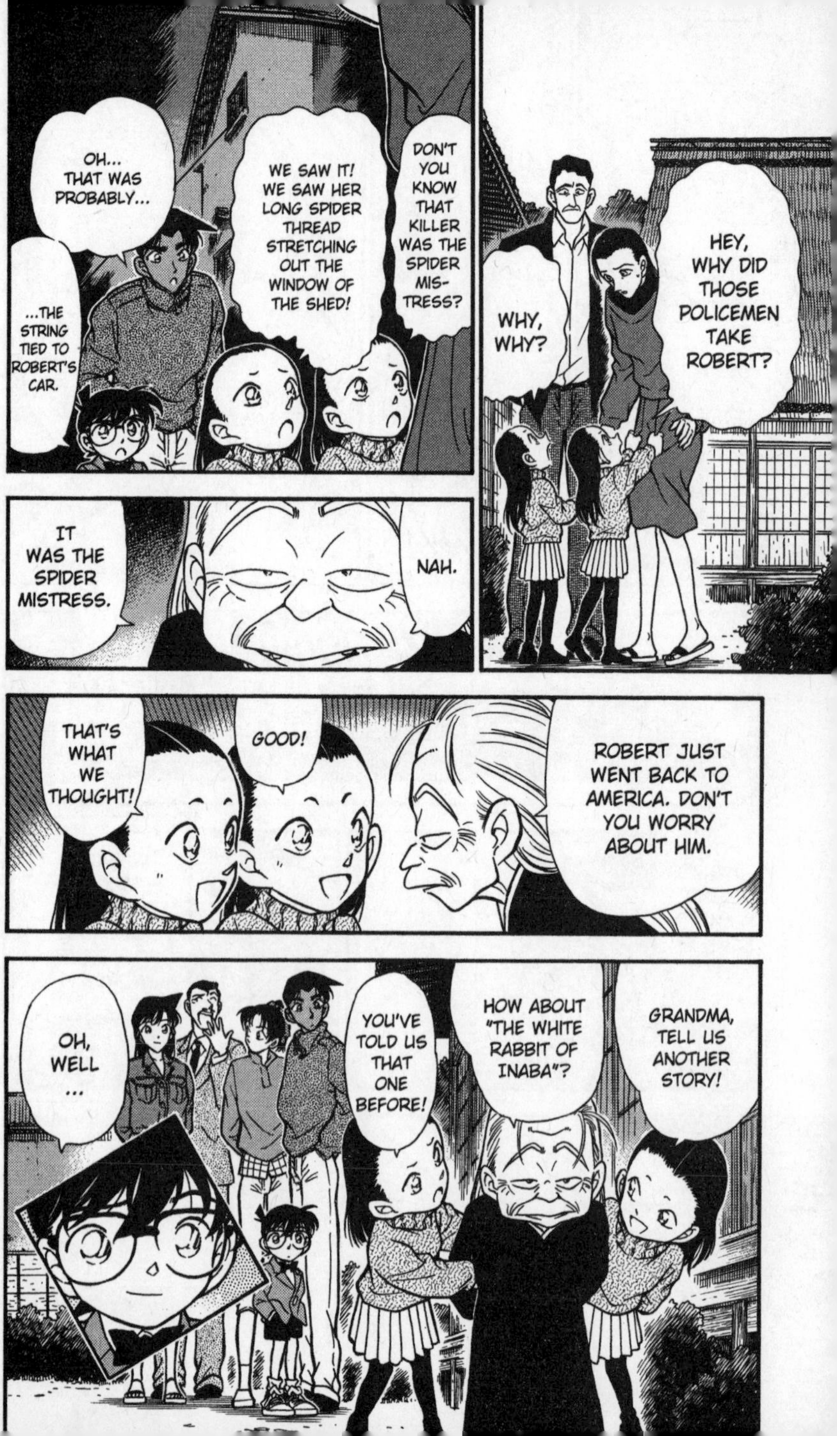
HEY, WHY DID THOSE POLICEMEN TAKE ROBERT?
WHY, WHY?
DON'T YOU KNOW THAT KILLER WAS THE SPIDER MISTRESS?
WE SAW IT! WE SAW HER LONG SPIDER THREAD STRETCHING OUT THE WINDOW OF THE SHED!
OH... THAT WAS PROBABLY...
...THE STRING TIED TO ROBERT'S CAR.
NAH.
IT WAS THE SPIDER MISTRESS.
ROBERT JUST WENT BACK TO AMERICA. DON'T YOU WORRY ABOUT HIM.
GOOD!
THAT'S WHAT WE THOUGHT!
GRANDMA, TELL US ANOTHER STORY!
HOW ABOUT "THE WHITE RABBIT OF INABA"?
YOU'VE TOLD US THAT ONE BEFORE!
OH, WELL ...

FILE 9: THE WOUNDED DETECTIVE LEAGUE

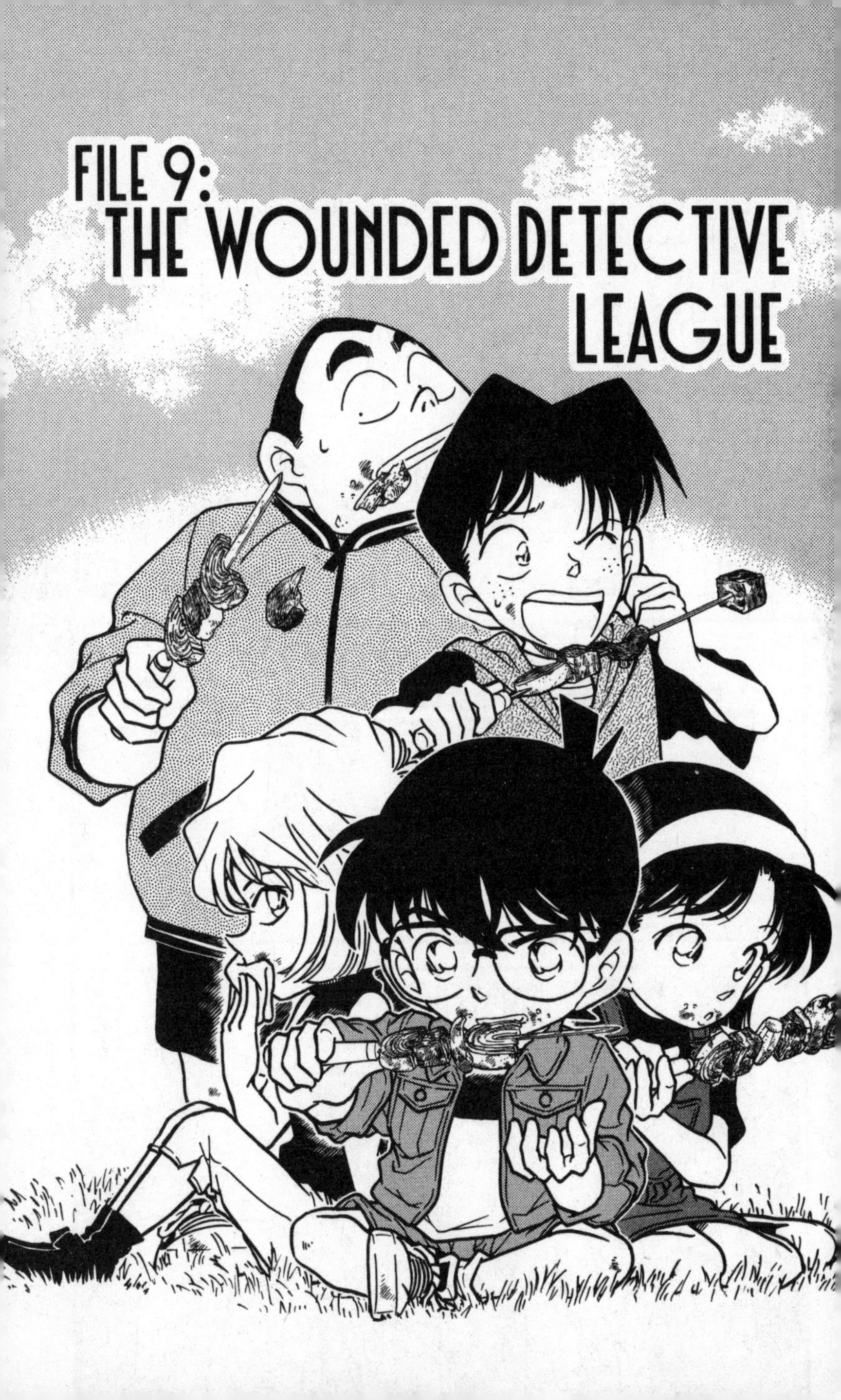

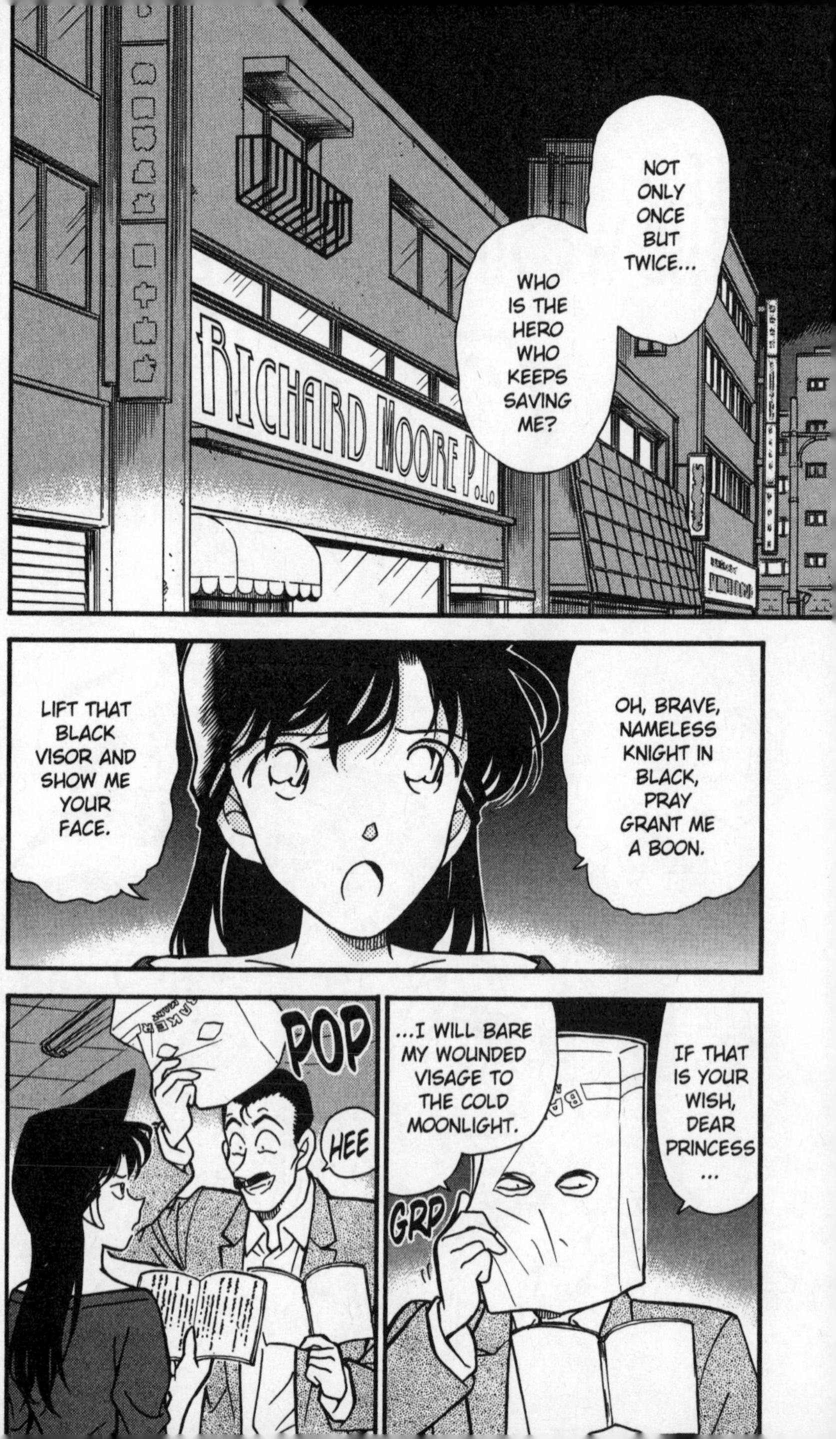
NOT ONLY ONCE BUT TWICE...
WHO IS THE HERO WHO KEEPS SAVING ME?
RICHARD MOORE P.I.
OH, BRAVE, NAMELESS KNIGHT IN BLACK, PRAY GRANT ME A BOON.
LIFT THAT BLACK VISOR AND SHOW ME YOUR FACE.
IF THAT IS YOUR WISH, DEAR PRINCESS...
...I WILL BARE MY WOUNDED VISAGE TO THE COLD MOONLIGHT.
GRP
POP
HEE

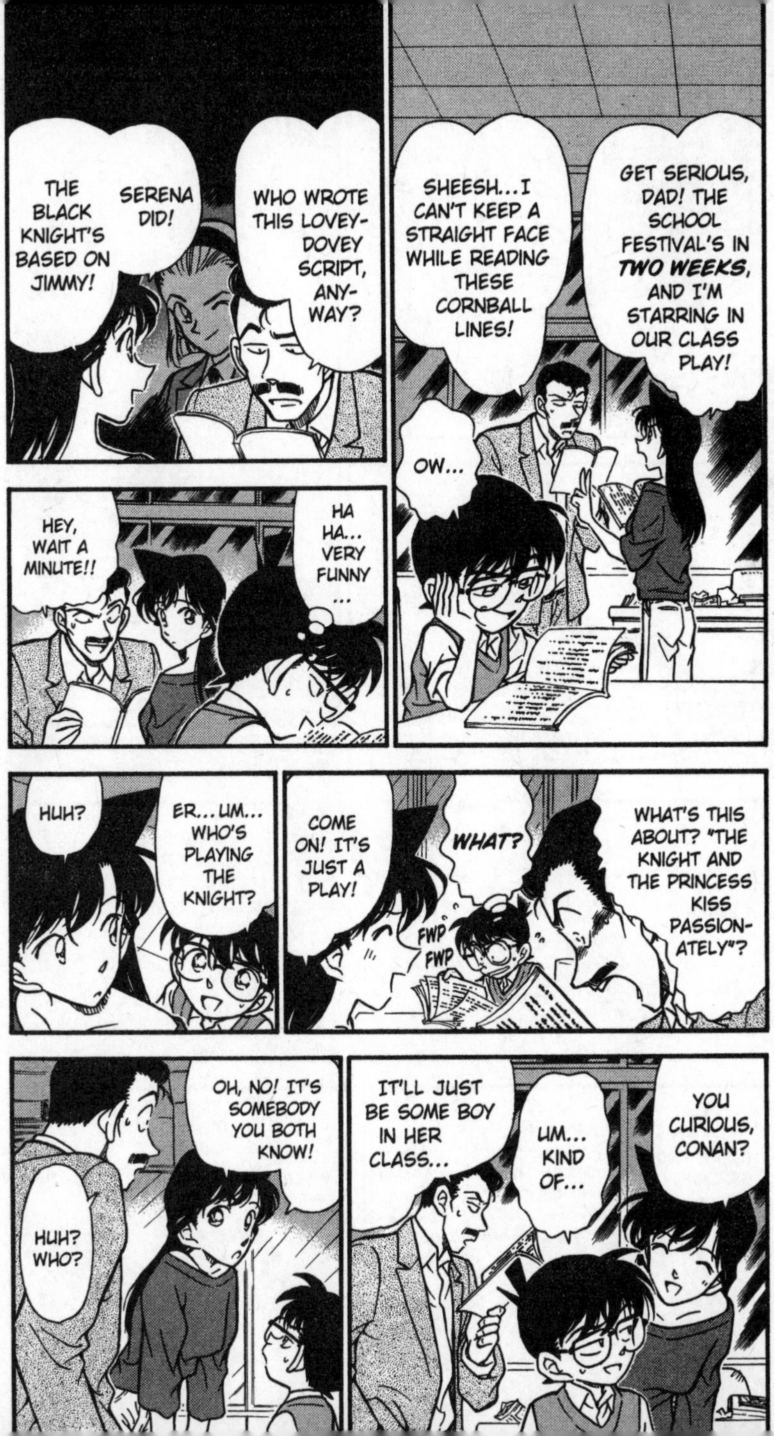
GET SERIOUS, DAD! THE SCHOOL FESTIVAL'S IN **TWO WEEKS**, AND I'M STARRING IN OUR CLASS PLAY!
SHEESH...I CAN'T KEEP A STRAIGHT FACE WHILE READING THESE CORNBALL LINES!
OW...
WHO WROTE THIS LOVEY-DOVEY SCRIPT, ANYWAY?
SERENA DID!
THE BLACK KNIGHT'S BASED ON JIMMY!
HA HA... VERY FUNNY ...
HEY, WAIT A MINUTE!!
WHAT'S THIS ABOUT? "THE KNIGHT AND THE PRINCESS KISS PASSIONATELY"?
WHAT?
FWP
FWP
COME ON! IT'S JUST A PLAY!
ER...UM... WHO'S PLAYING THE KNIGHT?
HUH?
YOU CURIOUS, CONAN?
UM... KIND OF...
IT'LL JUST BE SOME BOY IN HER CLASS...
OH, NO! IT'S SOMEBODY YOU BOTH KNOW!
HUH? WHO?

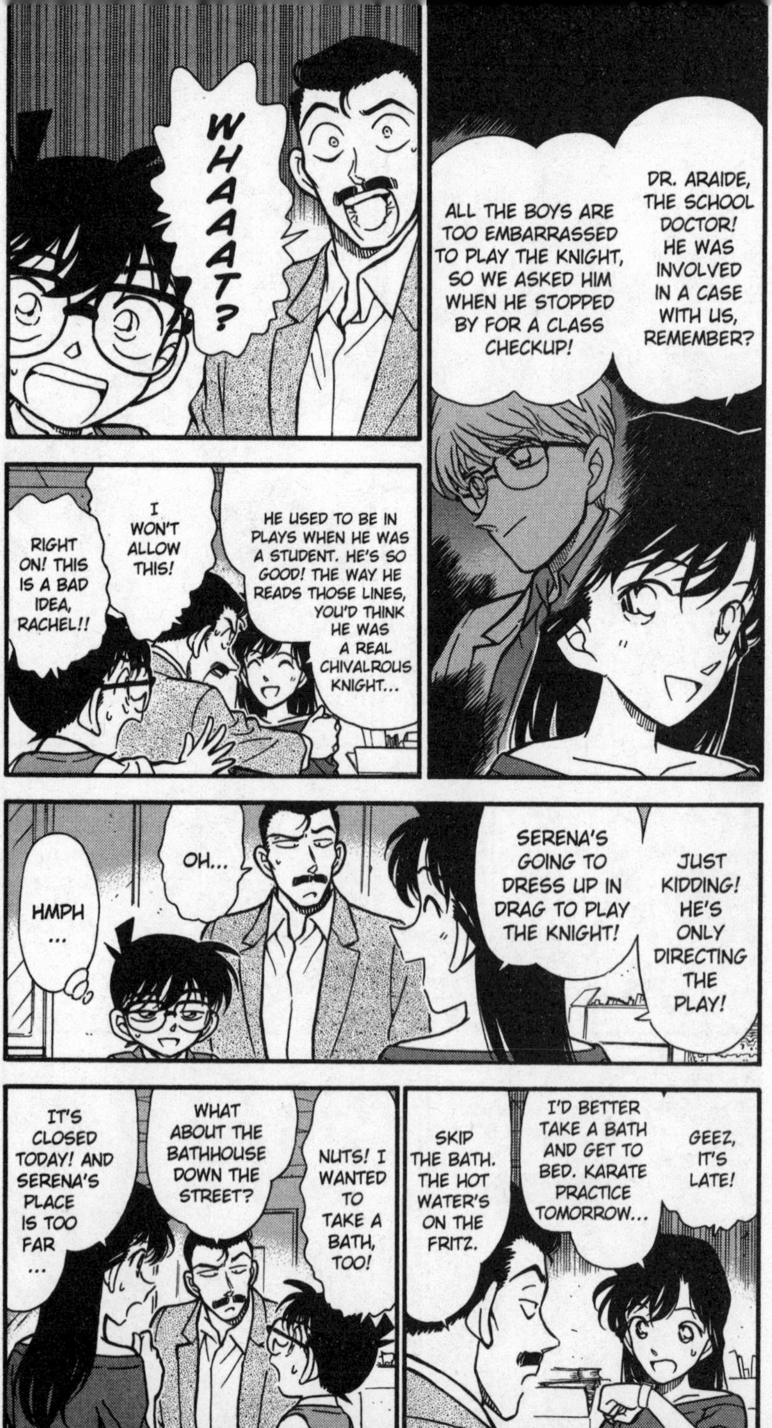
DR. ARAIDE, THE SCHOOL DOCTOR! HE WAS INVOLVED IN A CASE WITH US, REMEMBER?
ALL THE BOYS ARE TOO EMBARRASSED TO PLAY THE KNIGHT, SO WE ASKED HIM WHEN HE STOPPED BY FOR A CLASS CHECKUP!
WHAAAAT?
HE USED TO BE IN PLAYS WHEN HE WAS A STUDENT. HE'S SO GOOD! THE WAY HE READS THOSE LINES, YOU'D THINK HE WAS A REAL CHIVALROUS KNIGHT...
I WON'T ALLOW THIS!
RIGHT ON! THIS IS A BAD IDEA, RACHEL!!
SERENA'S GOING TO DRESS UP IN DRAG TO PLAY THE KNIGHT!
JUST KIDDING! HE'S ONLY DIRECTING THE PLAY!
OH...
HMPH ...
GEEZ, IT'S LATE!
I'D BETTER TAKE A BATH AND GET TO BED. KARATE PRACTICE TOMORROW...
SKIP THE BATH. THE HOT WATER'S ON THE FRITZ.
NUTS! I WANTED TO TAKE A BATH, TOO!
WHAT ABOUT THE BATHHOUSE DOWN THE STREET?
IT'S CLOSED TODAY! AND SERENA'S PLACE IS TOO FAR ...

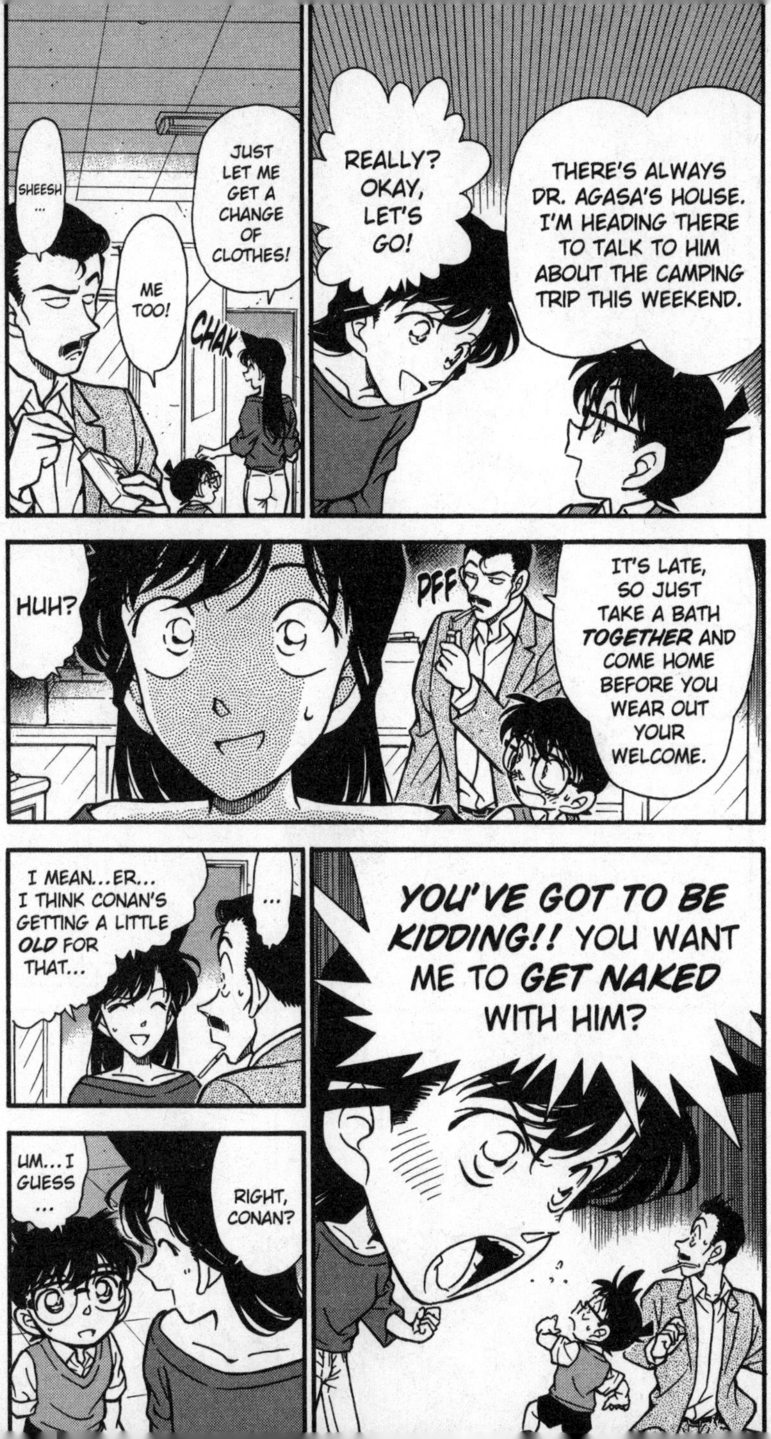
THERE'S ALWAYS DR. AGASA'S HOUSE. I'M HEADING THERE TO TALK TO HIM ABOUT THE CAMPING TRIP THIS WEEKEND.
REALLY? OKAY, LET'S GO!
JUST LET ME GET A CHANGE OF CLOTHES!
SHEESH...
ME TOO!
CHAK
IT'S LATE, SO JUST TAKE A BATH TOGETHER AND COME HOME BEFORE YOU WEAR OUT YOUR WELCOME.
PFF
HUH?
YOU'VE GOT TO BE KIDDING!! YOU WANT ME TO GET NAKED WITH HIM?
...
I MEAN...ER... I THINK CONAN'S GETTING A LITTLE OLD FOR THAT...
RIGHT, CONAN?
UM...I GUESS...

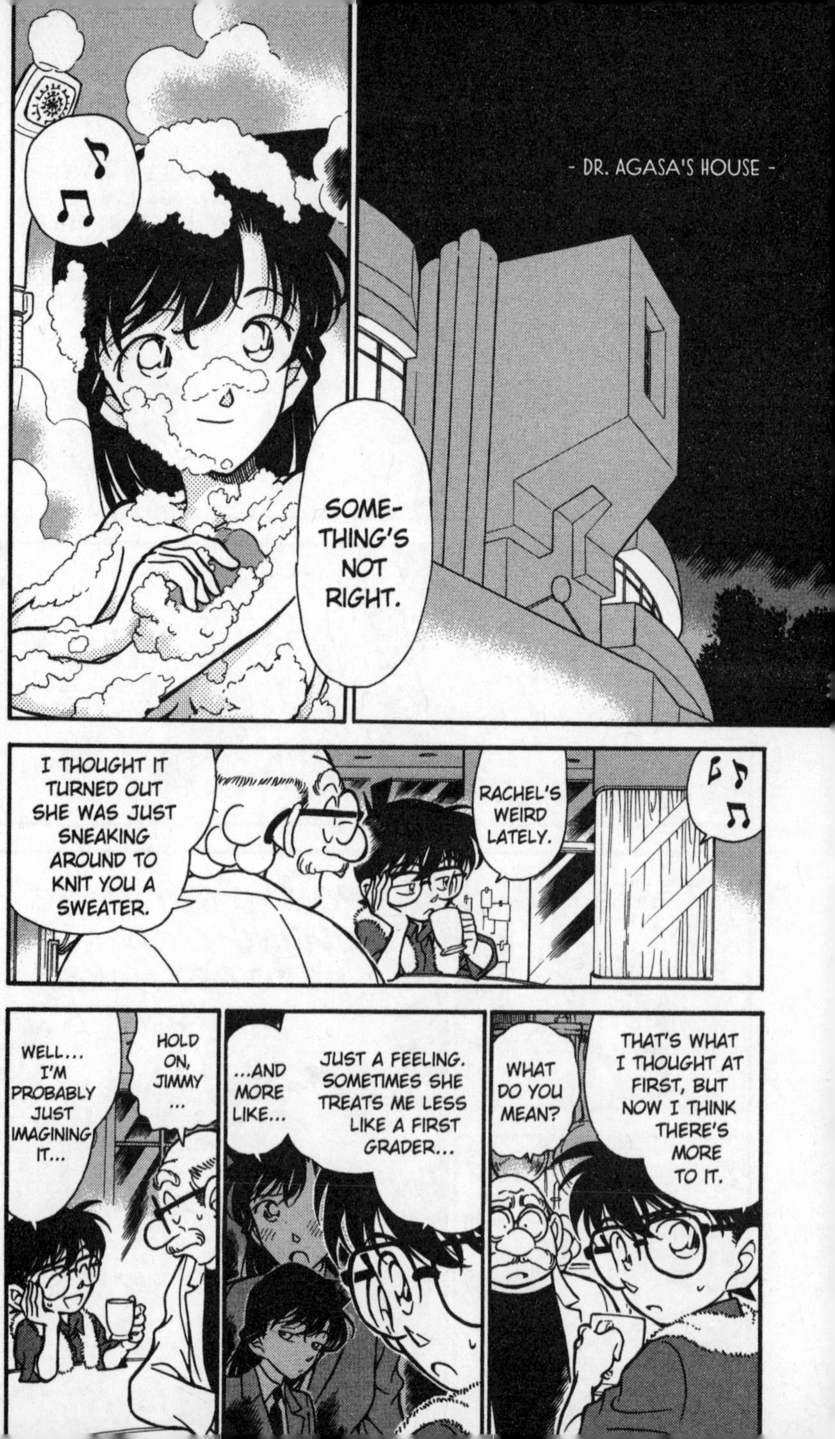
- DR. AGASA'S HOUSE -
SOMETHING'S NOT RIGHT.
RACHEL'S WEIRD LATELY.
I THOUGHT IT TURNED OUT SHE WAS JUST SNEAKING AROUND TO KNIT YOU A SWEATER.
THAT'S WHAT I THOUGHT AT FIRST, BUT NOW I THINK THERE'S MORE TO IT.
WHAT DO YOU MEAN?
JUST A FEELING. SOMETIMES SHE TREATS ME LESS LIKE A FIRST GRADER...
...AND MORE LIKE...
HOLD ON, JIMMY...
WELL... I'M PROBABLY JUST IMAGINING IT...

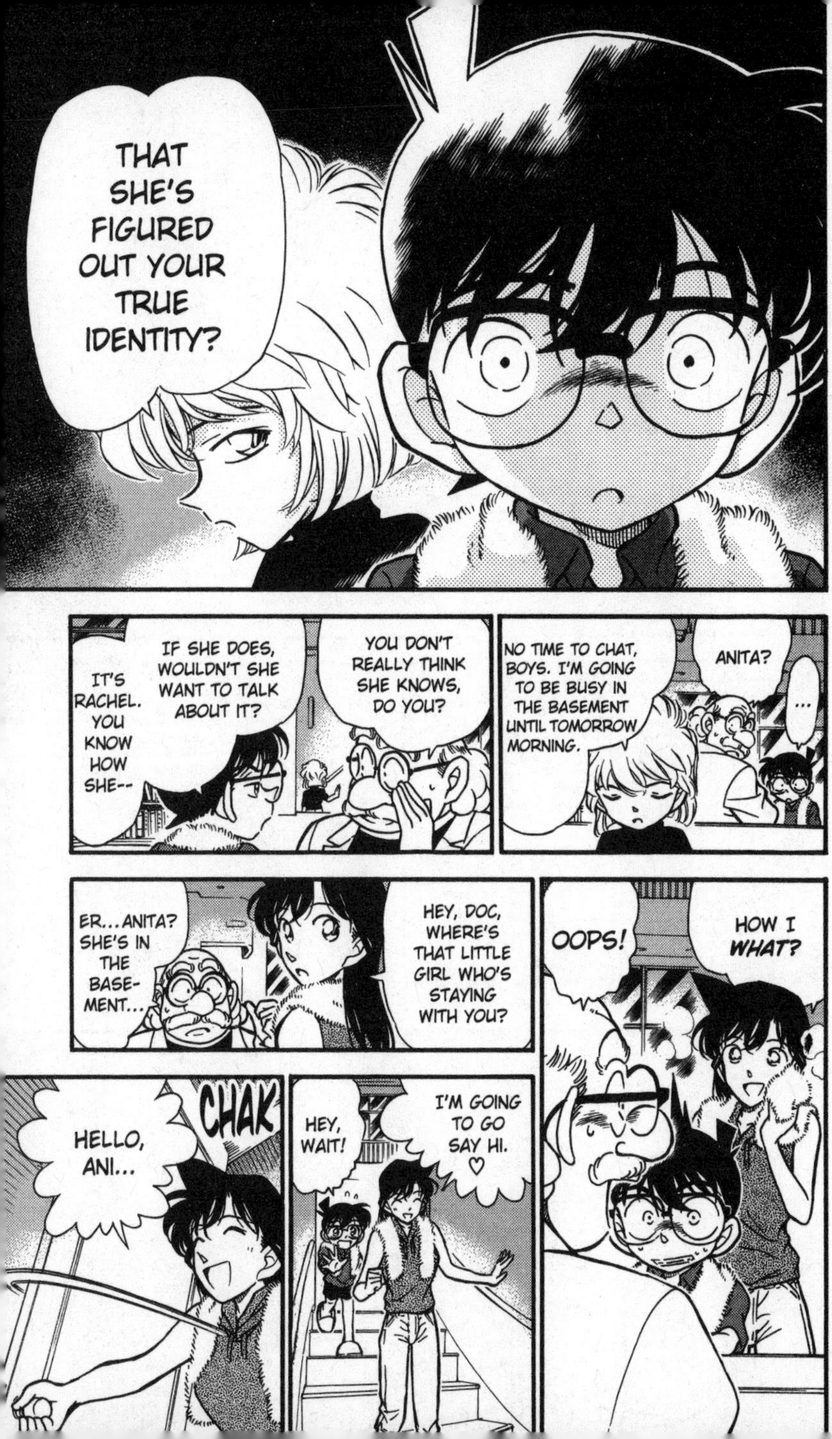
THAT SHE'S FIGURED OUT YOUR TRUE IDENTITY?
ANITA?
...
NO TIME TO CHAT, BOYS. I'M GOING TO BE BUSY IN THE BASEMENT UNTIL TOMORROW MORNING.
YOU DON'T REALLY THINK SHE KNOWS, DO YOU?
IF SHE DOES, WOULDN'T SHE WANT TO TALK ABOUT IT?
IT'S RACHEL. YOU KNOW HOW SHE--
HOW I *WHAT?*
OOPS!
HEY, DOC, WHERE'S THAT LITTLE GIRL WHO'S STAYING WITH YOU?
ER...ANITA? SHE'S IN THE BASE-MENT...
I'M GOING TO GO SAY HI. ♡
HEY, WAIT!
CHAK
HELLO, ANI...

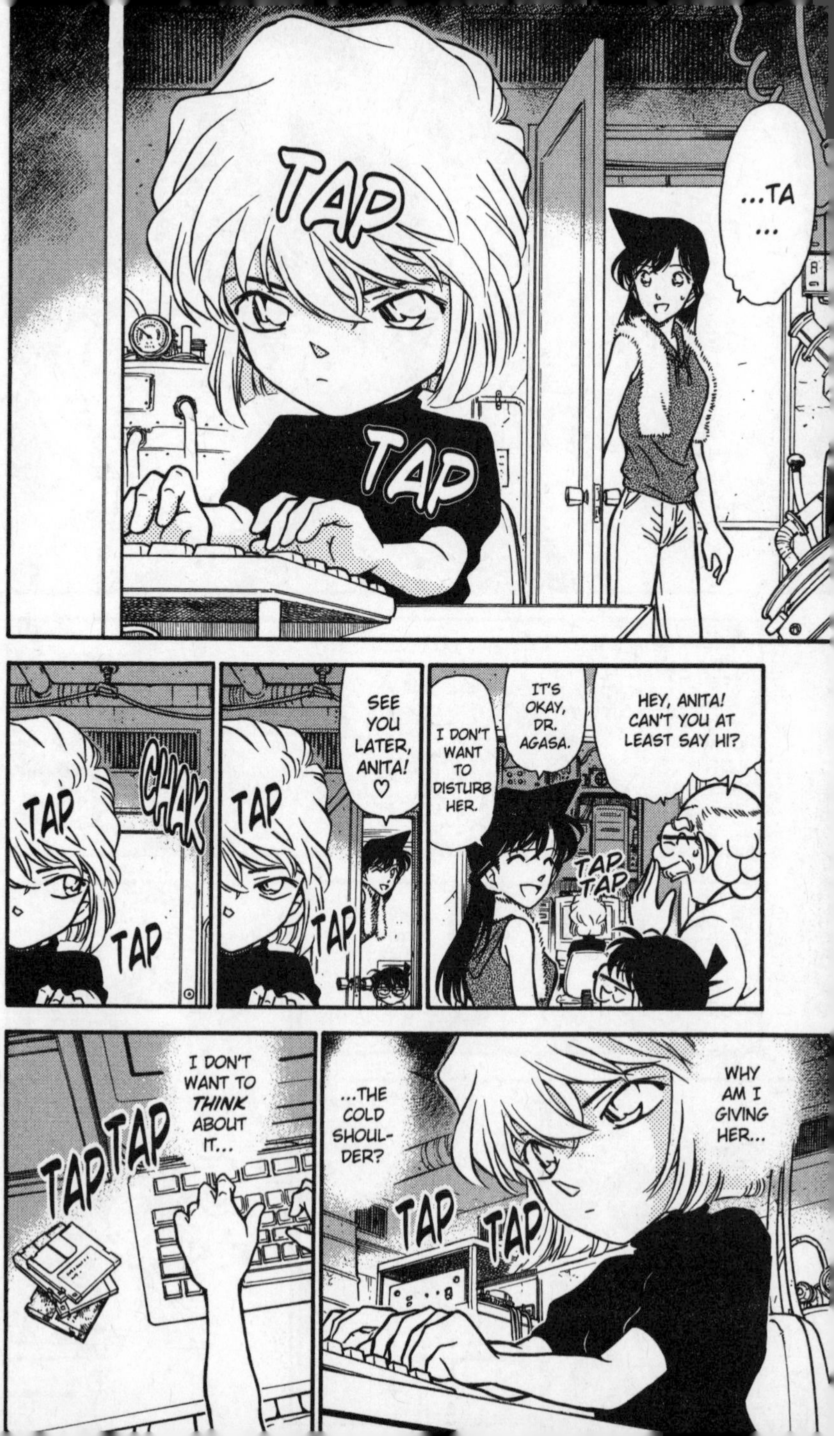
...TA ...
TAP
TAP
HEY, ANITA! CAN'T YOU AT LEAST SAY HI?
IT'S OKAY, DR. AGASA.
I DON'T WANT TO DISTURB HER.
TAP TAP
SEE YOU LATER, ANITA! ♡
TAP
TAP
CHAK
TAP
TAP
WHY AM I GIVING HER...
...THE COLD SHOULDER?
TAP
TAP
I DON'T WANT TO *THINK* ABOUT IT...
TAP TAP

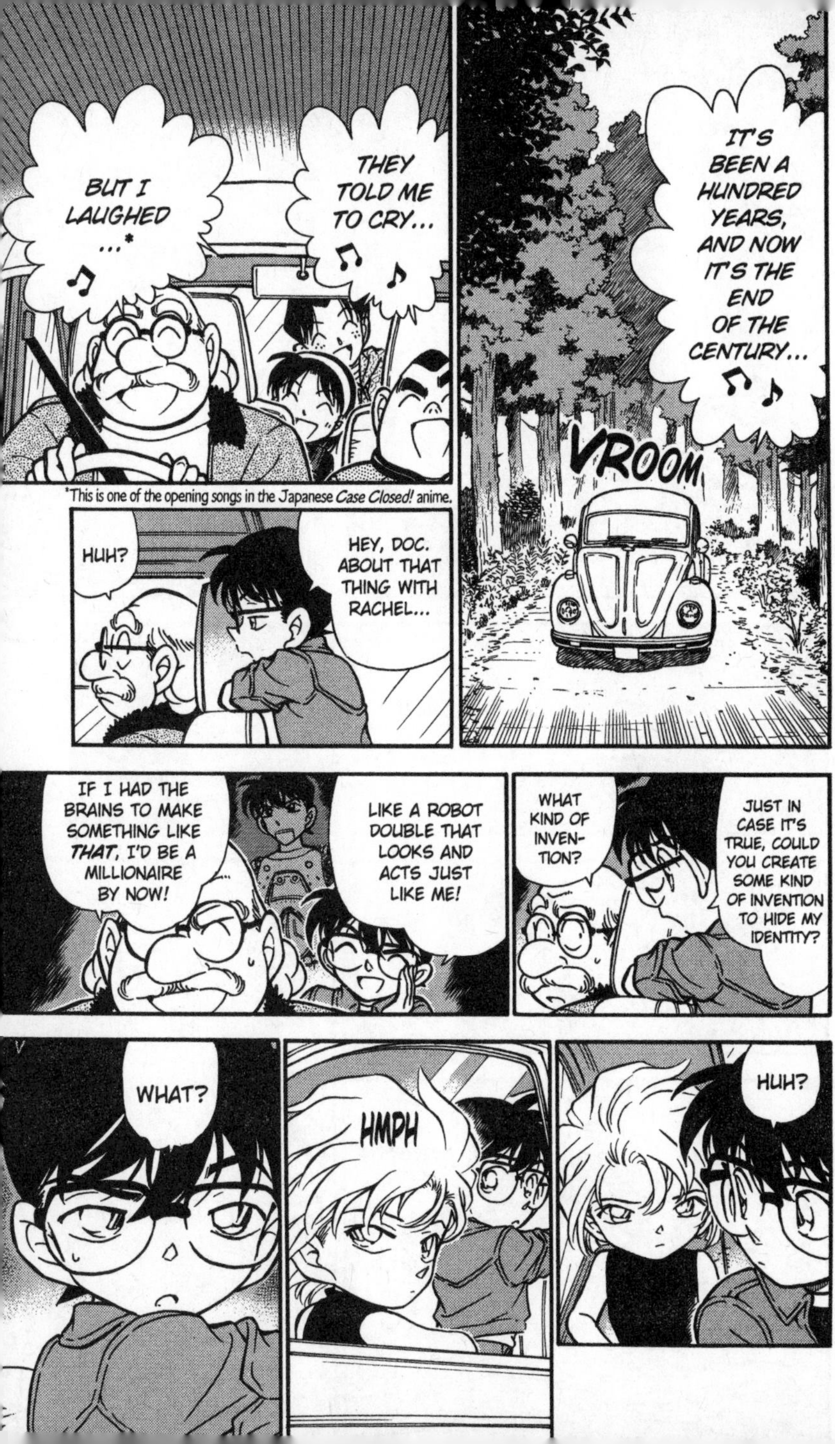
IT'S BEEN A HUNDRED YEARS, AND NOW IT'S THE END OF THE CENTURY... ♫ ♪
VROOM
THEY TOLD ME TO CRY... ♫ ♪
BUT I LAUGHED ...* ♫
HEY, DOC. ABOUT THAT THING WITH RACHEL...
HUH?
JUST IN CASE IT'S TRUE, COULD YOU CREATE SOME KIND OF INVENTION TO HIDE MY IDENTITY?
WHAT KIND OF INVEN-TION?
LIKE A ROBOT DOUBLE THAT LOOKS AND ACTS JUST LIKE ME!
IF I HAD THE BRAINS TO MAKE SOMETHING LIKE *THAT*, I'D BE A MILLIONAIRE BY NOW!
...
HUH?
HMPH
WHAT?

*This is one of the opening songs in the Japanese *Case Closed!* anime.

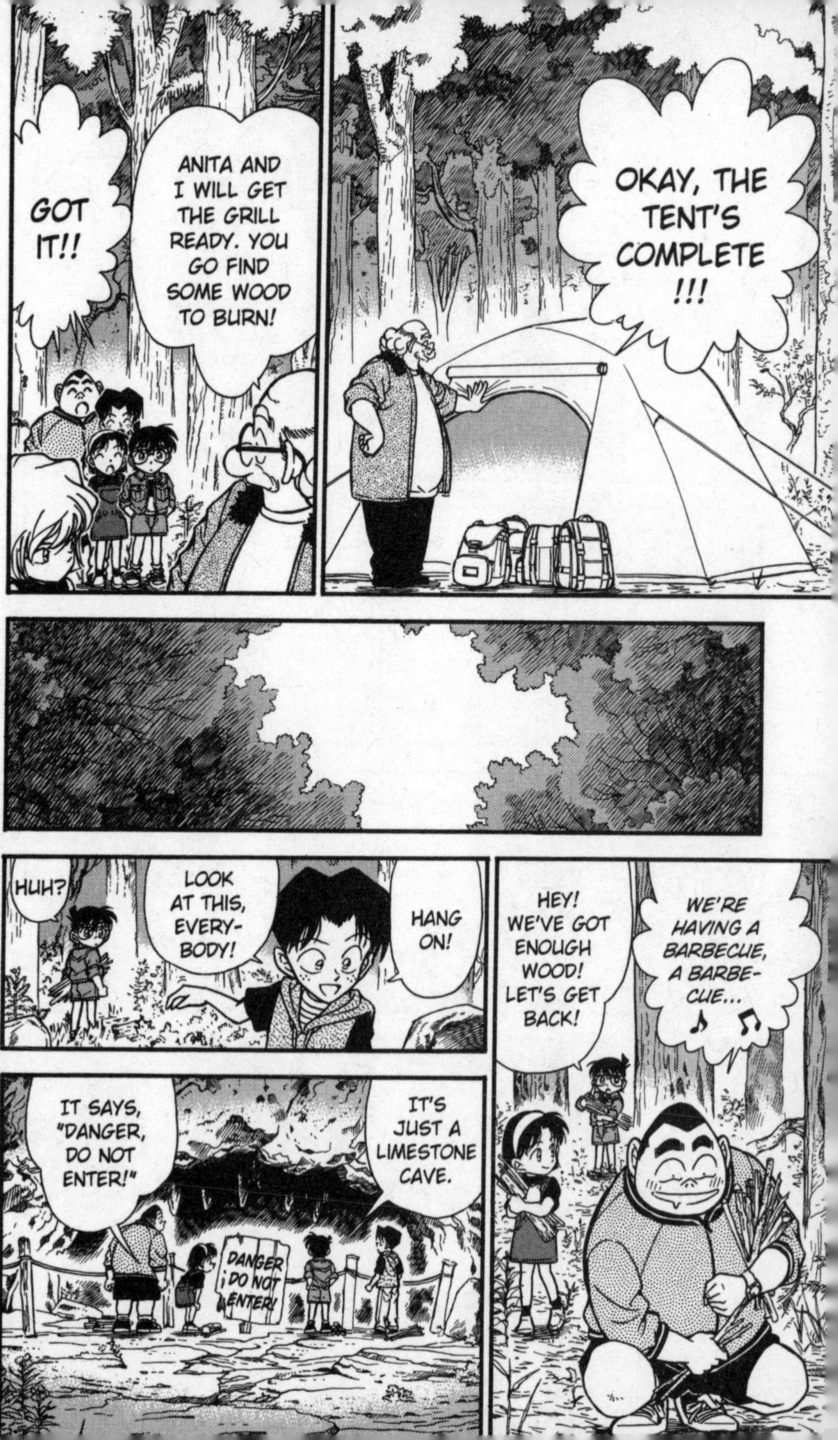
OKAY, THE TENT'S COMPLETE !!!
ANITA AND I WILL GET THE GRILL READY. YOU GO FIND SOME WOOD TO BURN!
GOT IT!!
WE'RE HAVING A BARBECUE, A BARBE-CUE... ♪ ♫
HEY! WE'VE GOT ENOUGH WOOD! LET'S GET BACK!
HANG ON!
LOOK AT THIS, EVERY-BODY!
HUH?
IT'S JUST A LIMESTONE CAVE.
IT SAYS, "DANGER, DO NOT ENTER!"
DANGER DO NOT ENTER!

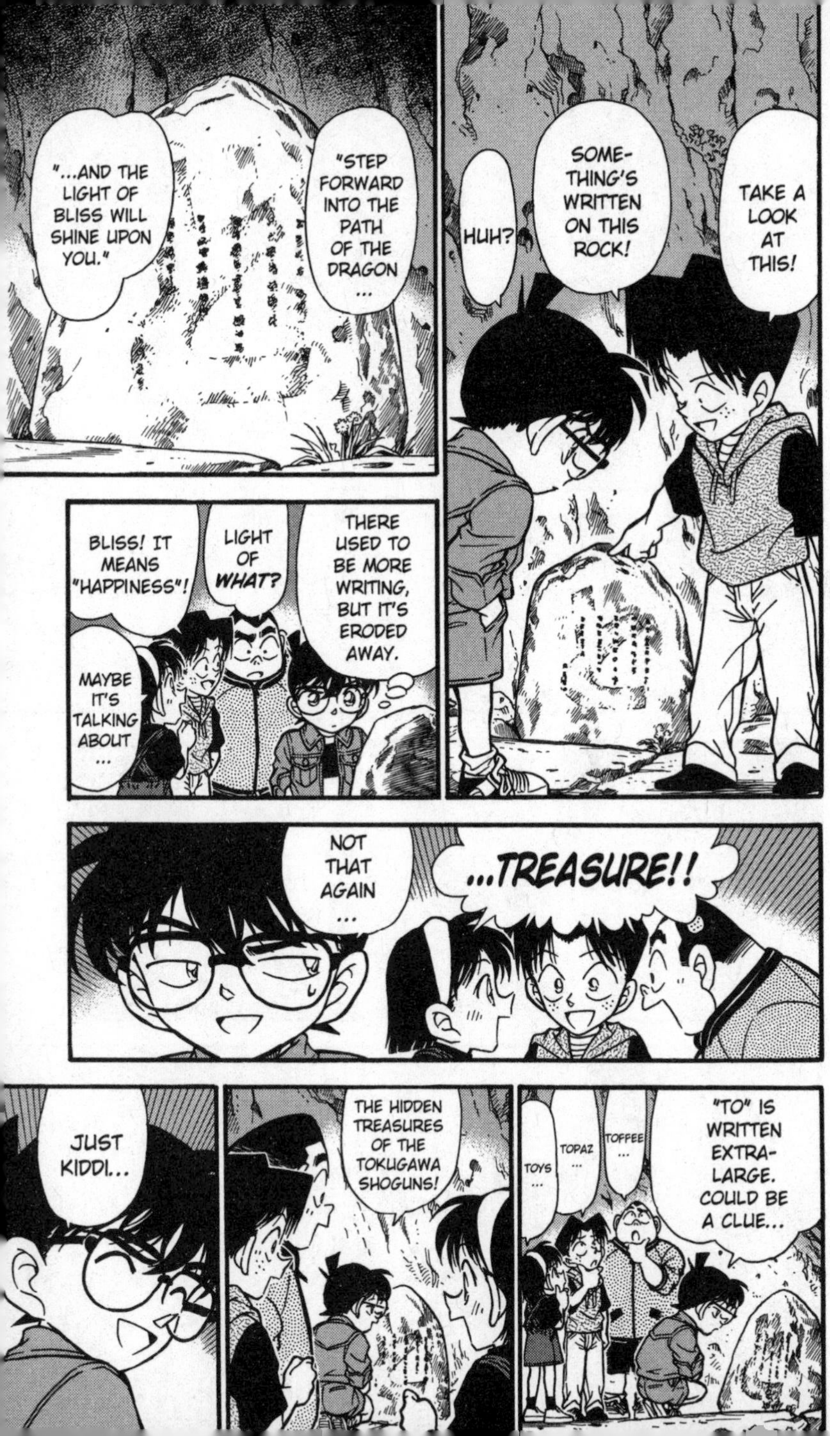
TAKE A LOOK AT THIS!
SOME-THING'S WRITTEN ON THIS ROCK!
HUH?
"STEP FORWARD INTO THE PATH OF THE DRAGON ...
"...AND THE LIGHT OF BLISS WILL SHINE UPON YOU."
THERE USED TO BE MORE WRITING, BUT IT'S ERODED AWAY.
LIGHT OF *WHAT?*
BLISS! IT MEANS "HAPPINESS"!
MAYBE IT'S TALKING ABOUT ...
...TREASURE!!
NOT THAT AGAIN ...
"TO" IS WRITTEN EXTRA-LARGE. COULD BE A CLUE...
TOFFEE ...
TOPAZ ...
TOYS ...
THE HIDDEN TREASURES OF THE TOKUGAWA SHOGUNS!
JUST KIDDI...

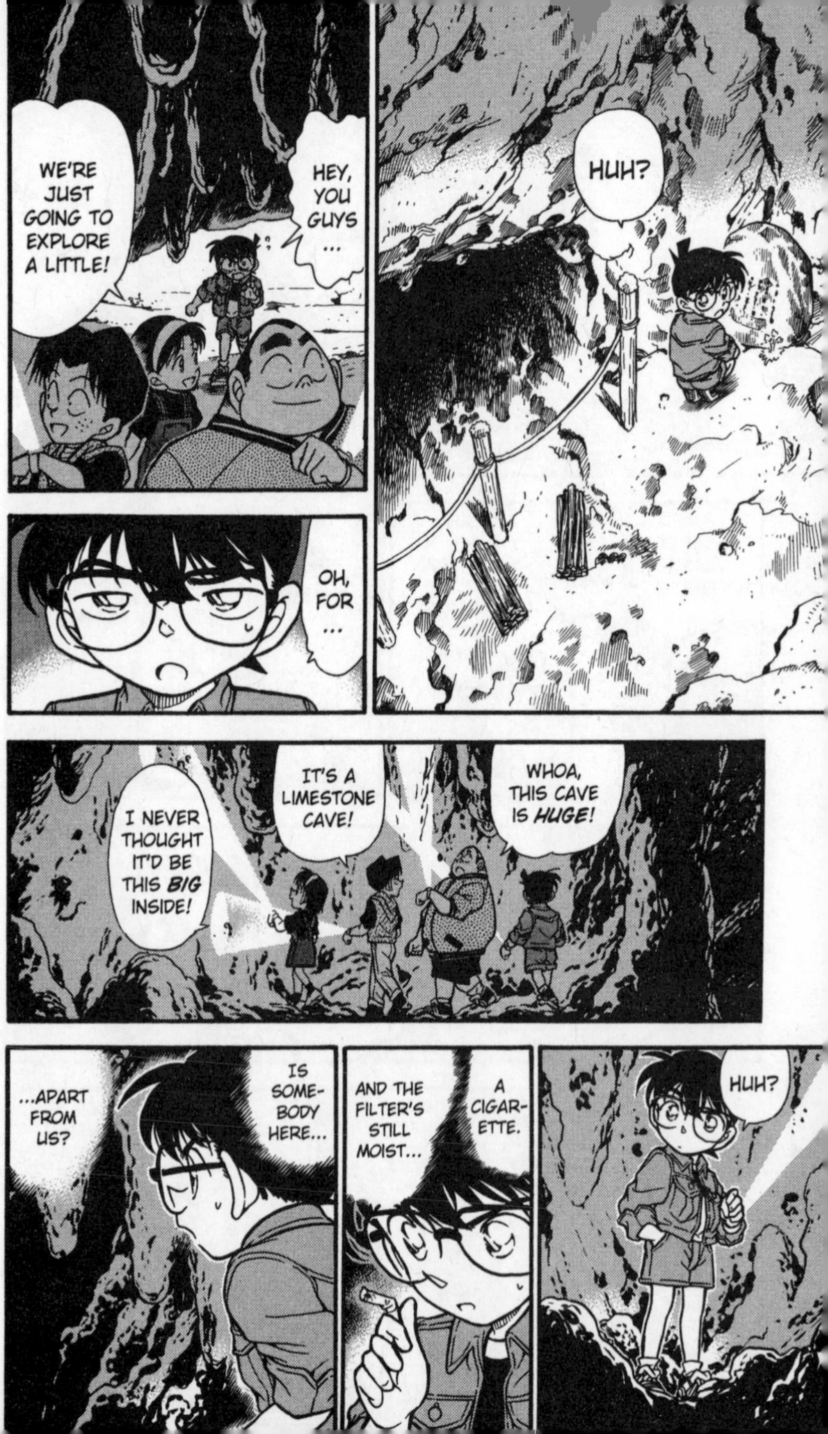
HUH?
HEY, YOU GUYS...
WE'RE JUST GOING TO EXPLORE A LITTLE!
OH, FOR...
WHOA, THIS CAVE IS *HUGE*!
IT'S A LIMESTONE CAVE!
I NEVER THOUGHT IT'D BE THIS *BIG* INSIDE!
HUH?
A CIGARETTE.
AND THE FILTER'S STILL MOIST...
IS SOMEBODY HERE...
...APART FROM US?

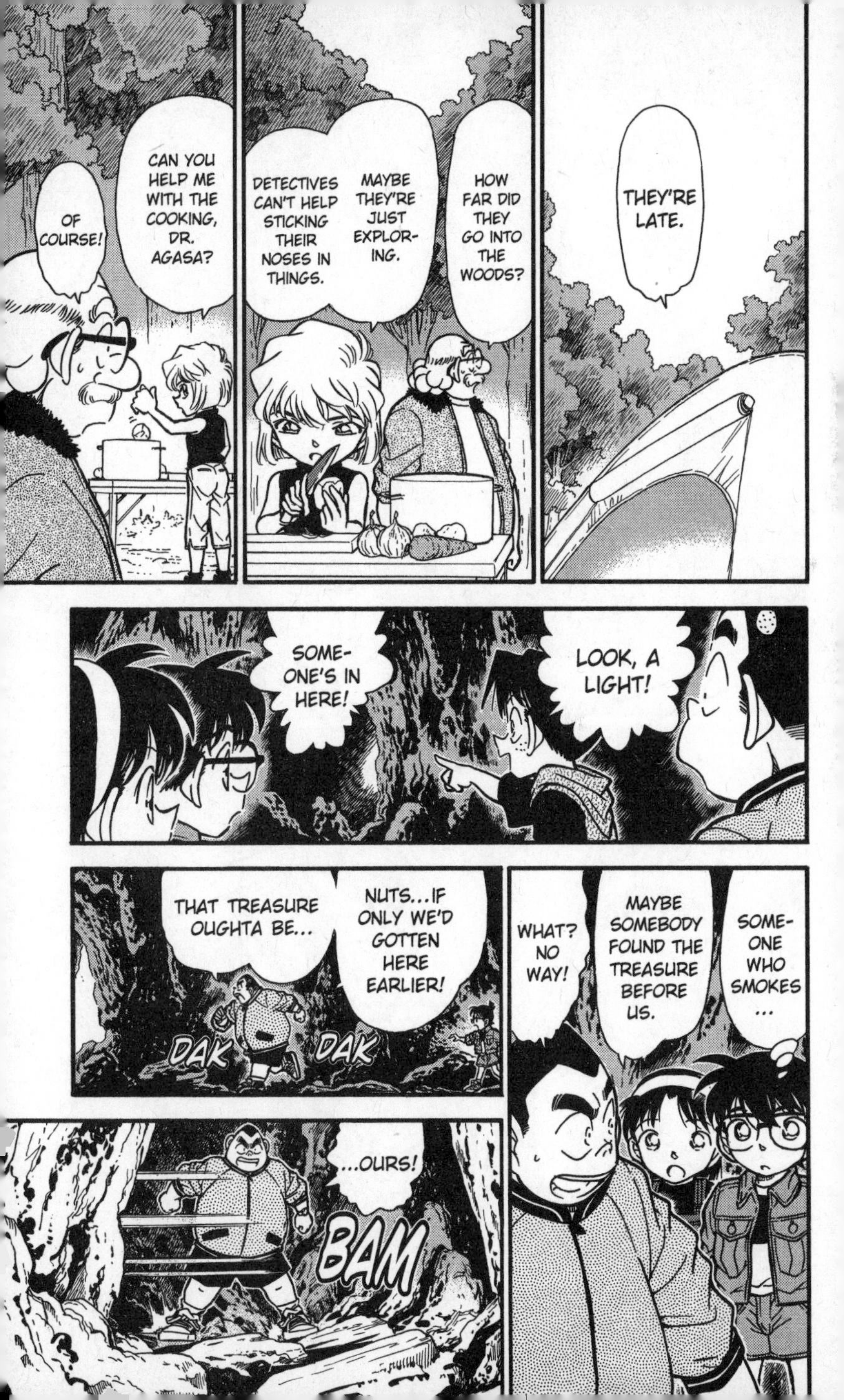
THEY'RE LATE.
HOW FAR DID THEY GO INTO THE WOODS?
MAYBE THEY'RE JUST EXPLOR-ING.
DETECTIVES CAN'T HELP STICKING THEIR NOSES IN THINGS.
CAN YOU HELP ME WITH THE COOKING, DR. AGASA?
OF COURSE!
LOOK, A LIGHT!
SOME-ONE'S IN HERE!
SOME-ONE WHO SMOKES...
MAYBE SOMEBODY FOUND THE TREASURE BEFORE US.
WHAT? NO WAY!
NUTS...IF ONLY WE'D GOTTEN HERE EARLIER!
THAT TREASURE OUGHTA BE...
DAK
DAK
...OURS!
BAM

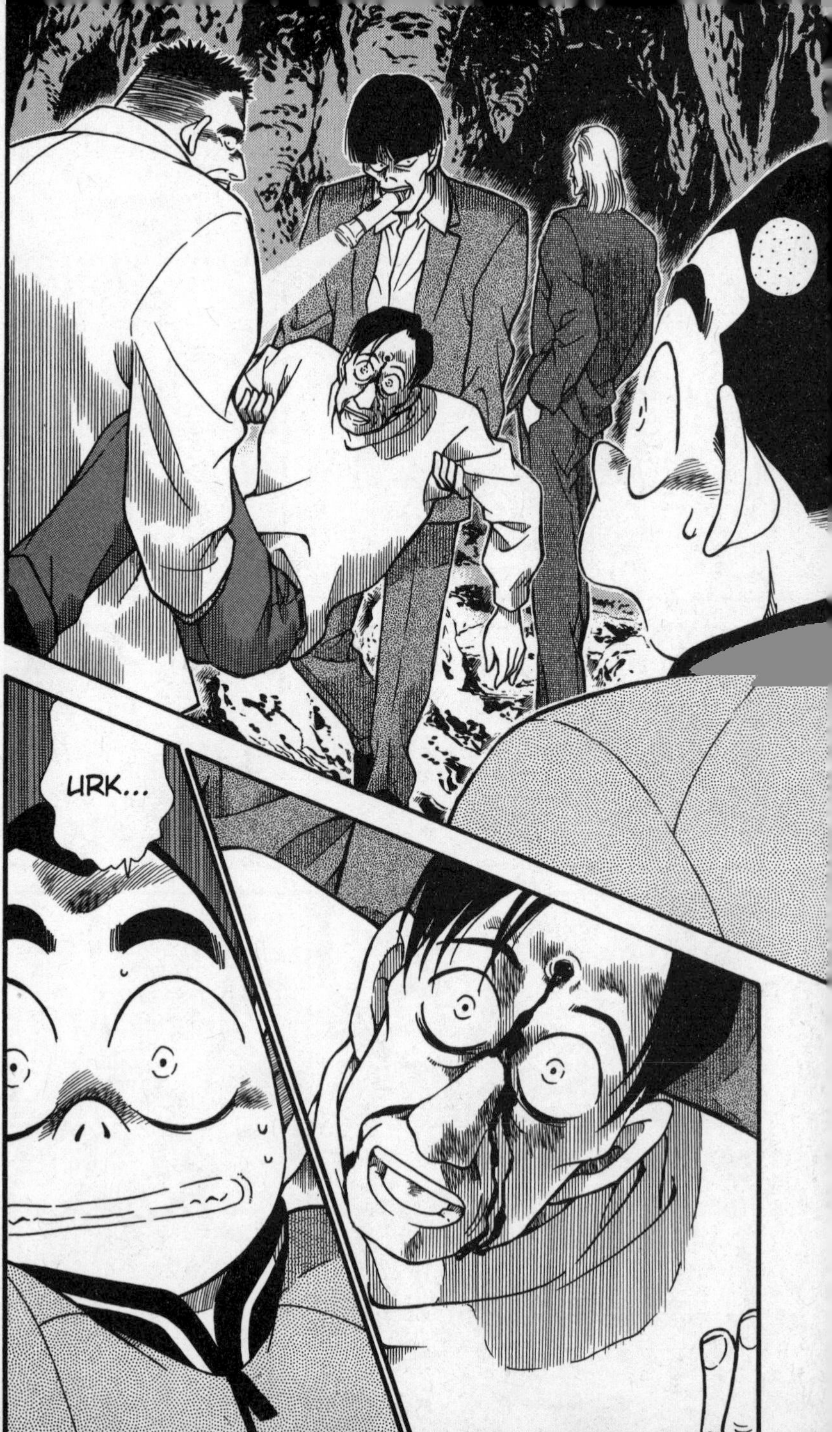
URK...

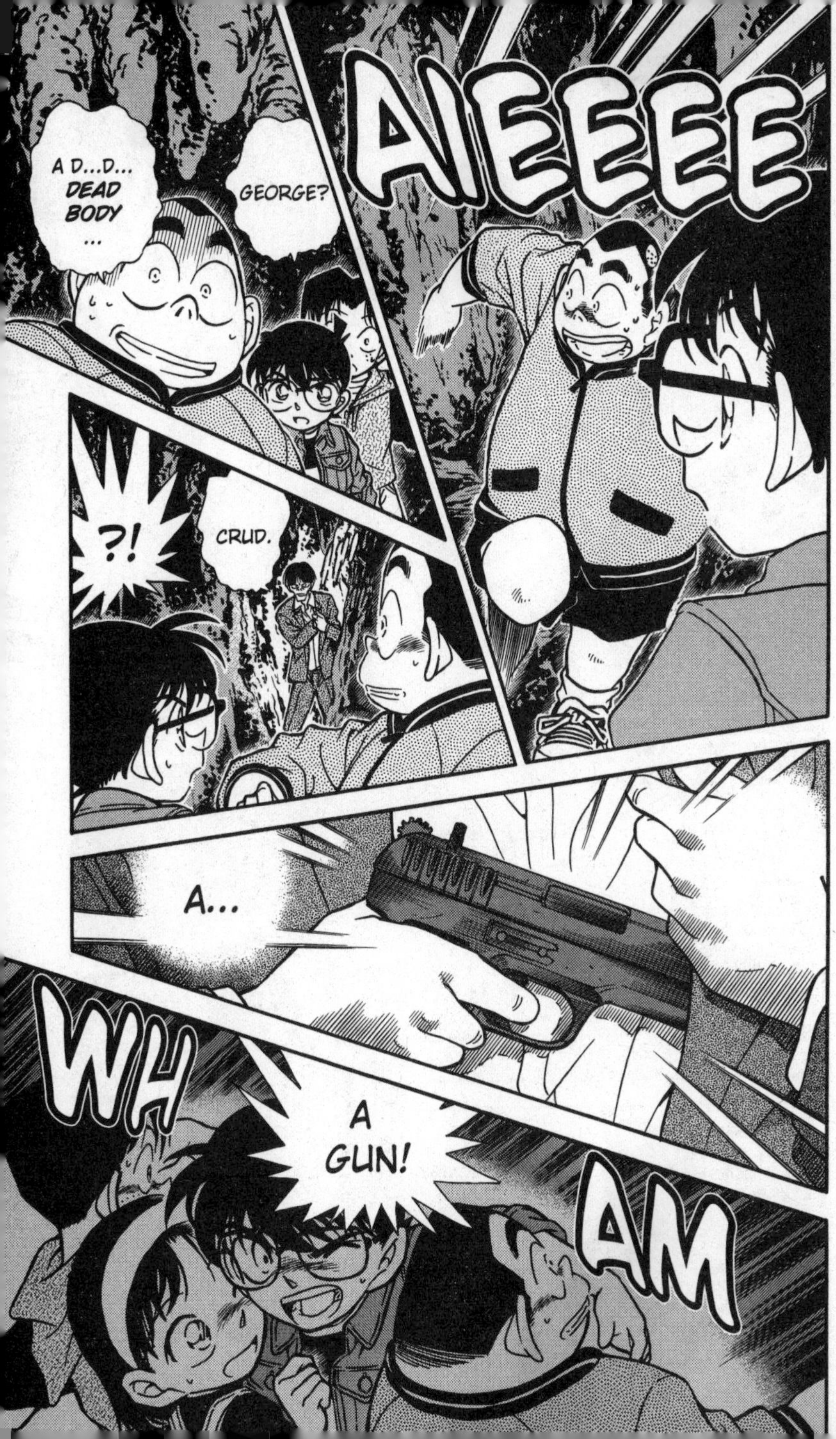
AIEEEE
GEORGE?
A D...D... DEAD BODY ...
CRUD.
?!
A...
WHAM
A GUN!

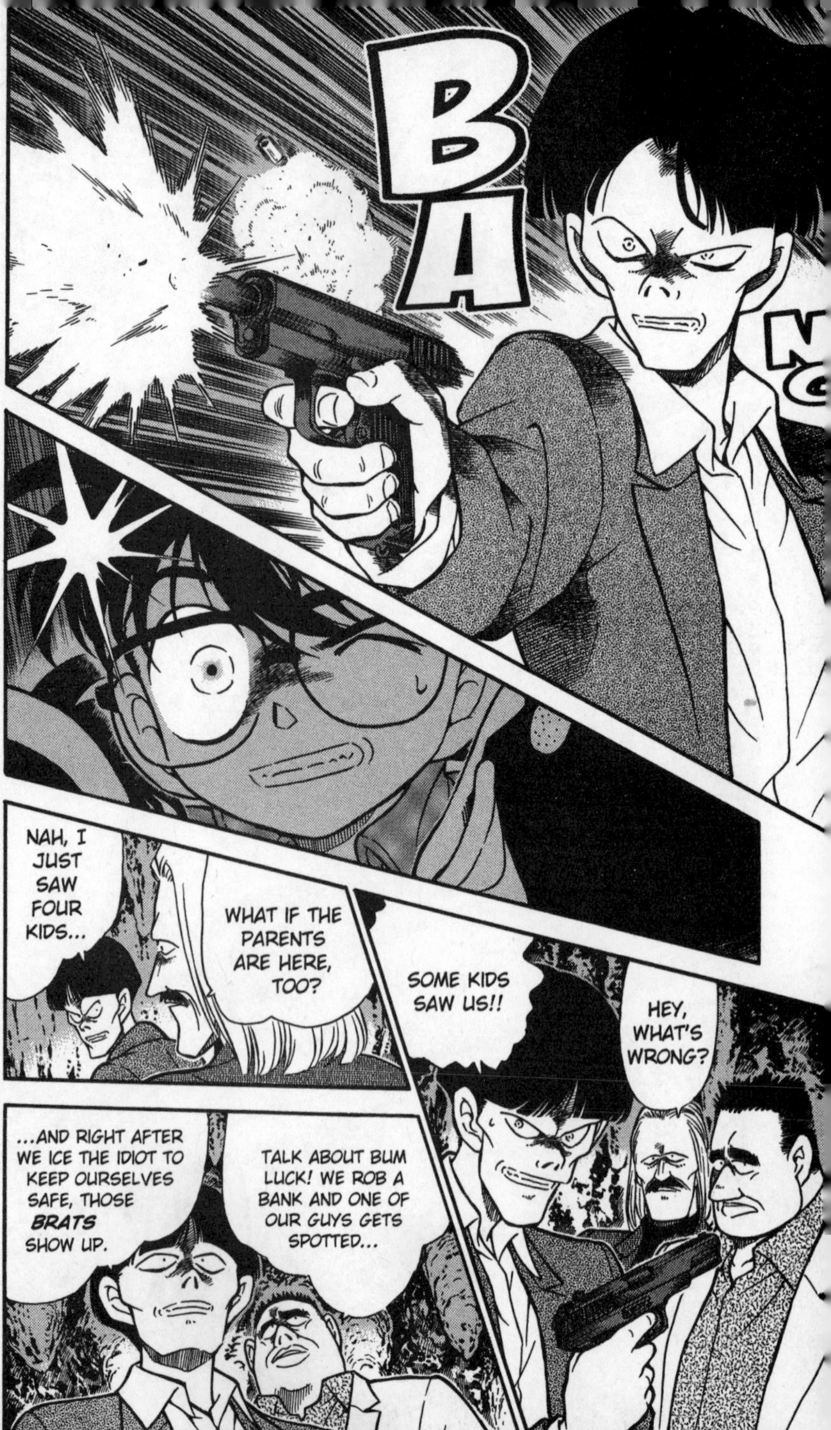
BA
HEY, WHAT'S WRONG?
SOME KIDS SAW US!!
WHAT IF THE PARENTS ARE HERE, TOO?
NAH, I JUST SAW FOUR KIDS...
TALK ABOUT BUM LUCK! WE ROB A BANK AND ONE OF OUR GUYS GETS SPOTTED...
...AND RIGHT AFTER WE ICE THE IDIOT TO KEEP OURSELVES SAFE, THOSE *BRATS* SHOW UP.

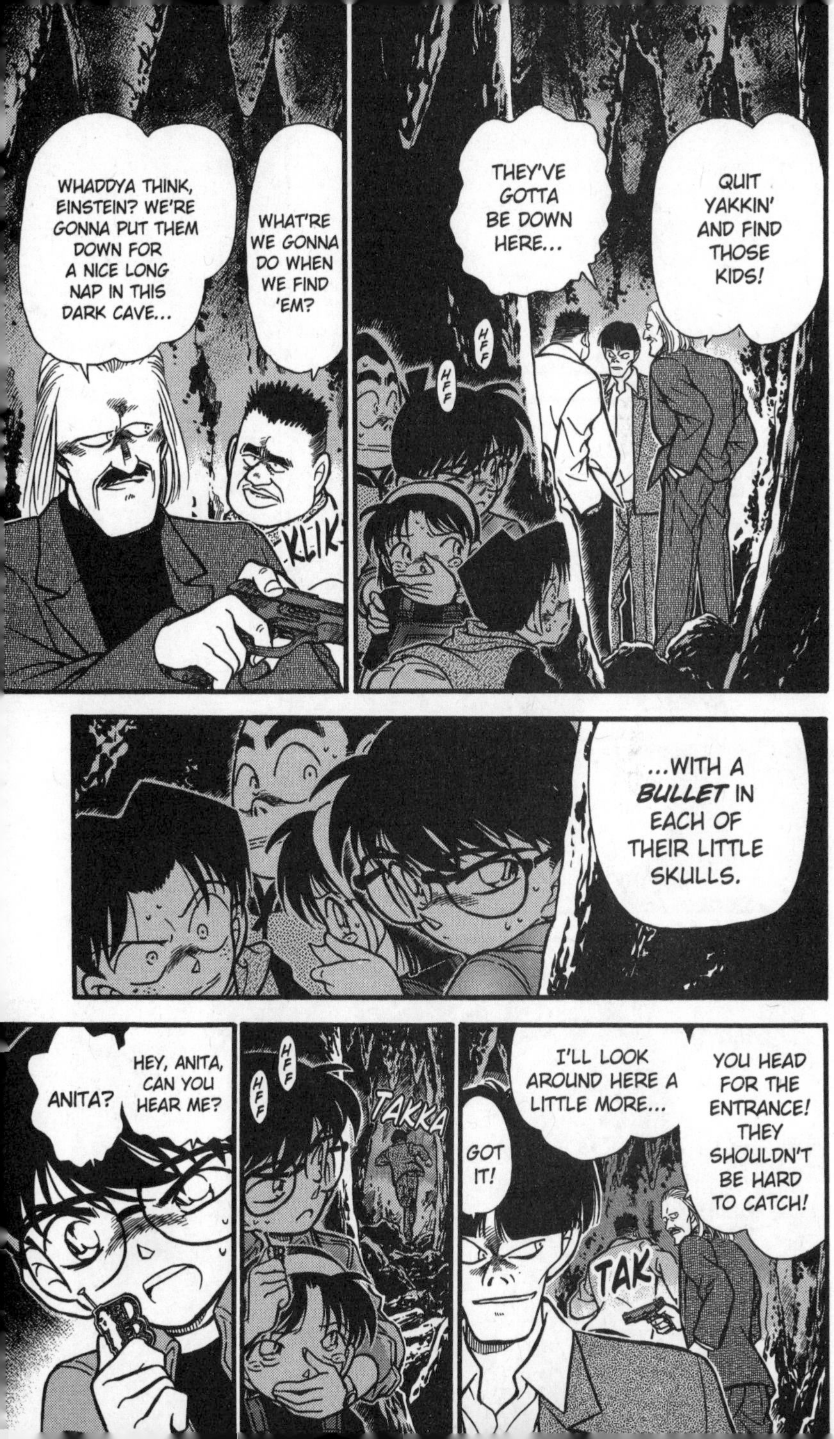
QUIT YAKKIN' AND FIND THOSE KIDS!
THEY'VE GOTTA BE DOWN HERE...
HFF
HFF
WHAT'RE WE GONNA DO WHEN WE FIND 'EM?
WHADDYA THINK, EINSTEIN? WE'RE GONNA PUT THEM DOWN FOR A NICE LONG NAP IN THIS DARK CAVE...
KLIK
...WITH A BULLET IN EACH OF THEIR LITTLE SKULLS.
YOU HEAD FOR THE ENTRANCE! THEY SHOULDN'T BE HARD TO CATCH!
I'LL LOOK AROUND HERE A LITTLE MORE...
GOT IT!
TAK
HFF
HFF
TAKKA
HEY, ANITA, CAN YOU HEAR ME?
ANITA?

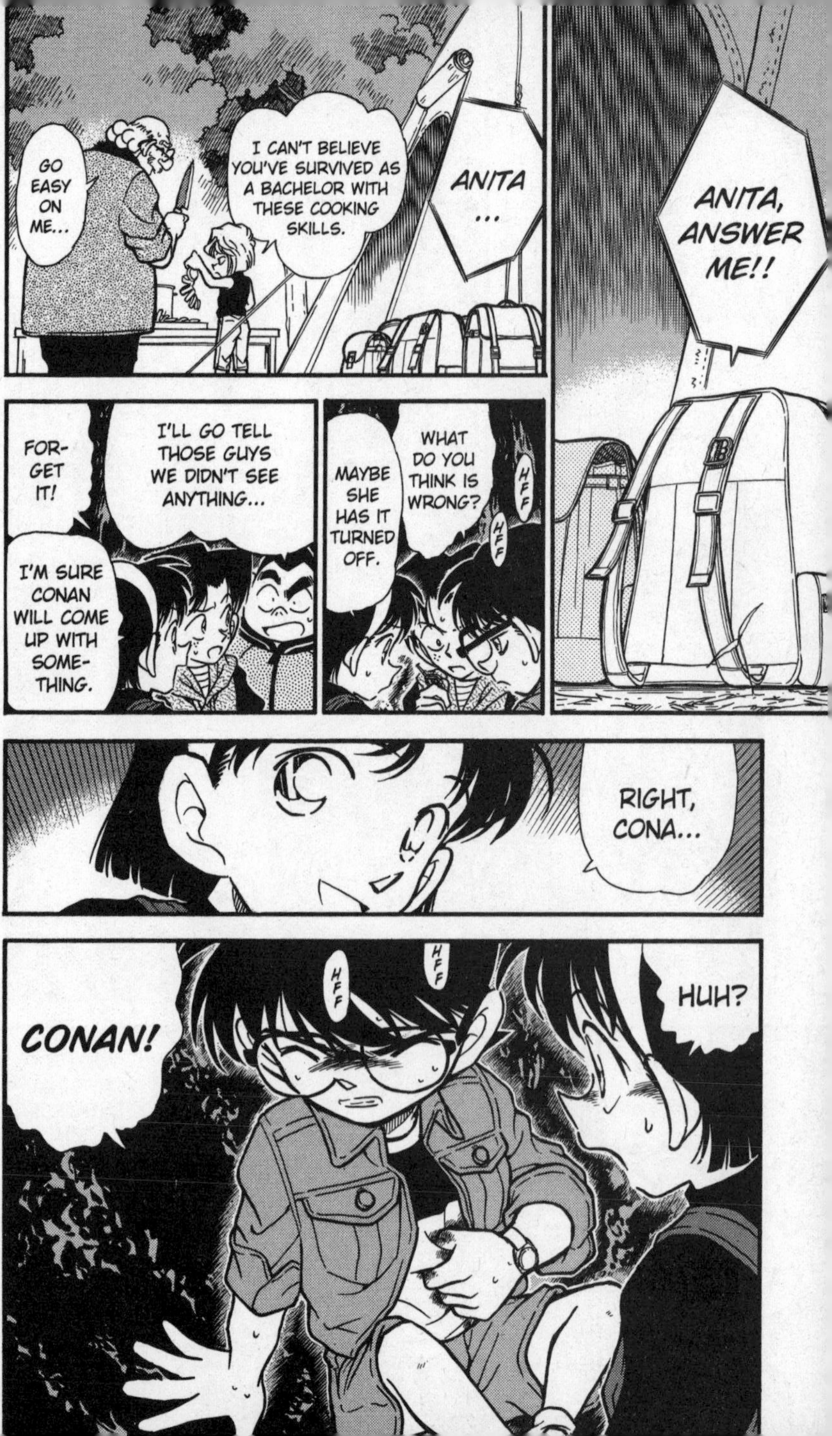
ANITA, ANSWER ME!!
ANITA ...
I CAN'T BELIEVE YOU'VE SURVIVED AS A BACHELOR WITH THESE COOKING SKILLS.
GO EASY ON ME...
WHAT DO YOU THINK IS WRONG?
HFF
HFF
MAYBE SHE HAS IT TURNED OFF.
I'LL GO TELL THOSE GUYS WE DIDN'T SEE ANYTHING...
FOR-GET IT!
I'M SURE CONAN WILL COME UP WITH SOME-THING.
RIGHT, CONA...
HUH?
HFF
HFF
CONAN!

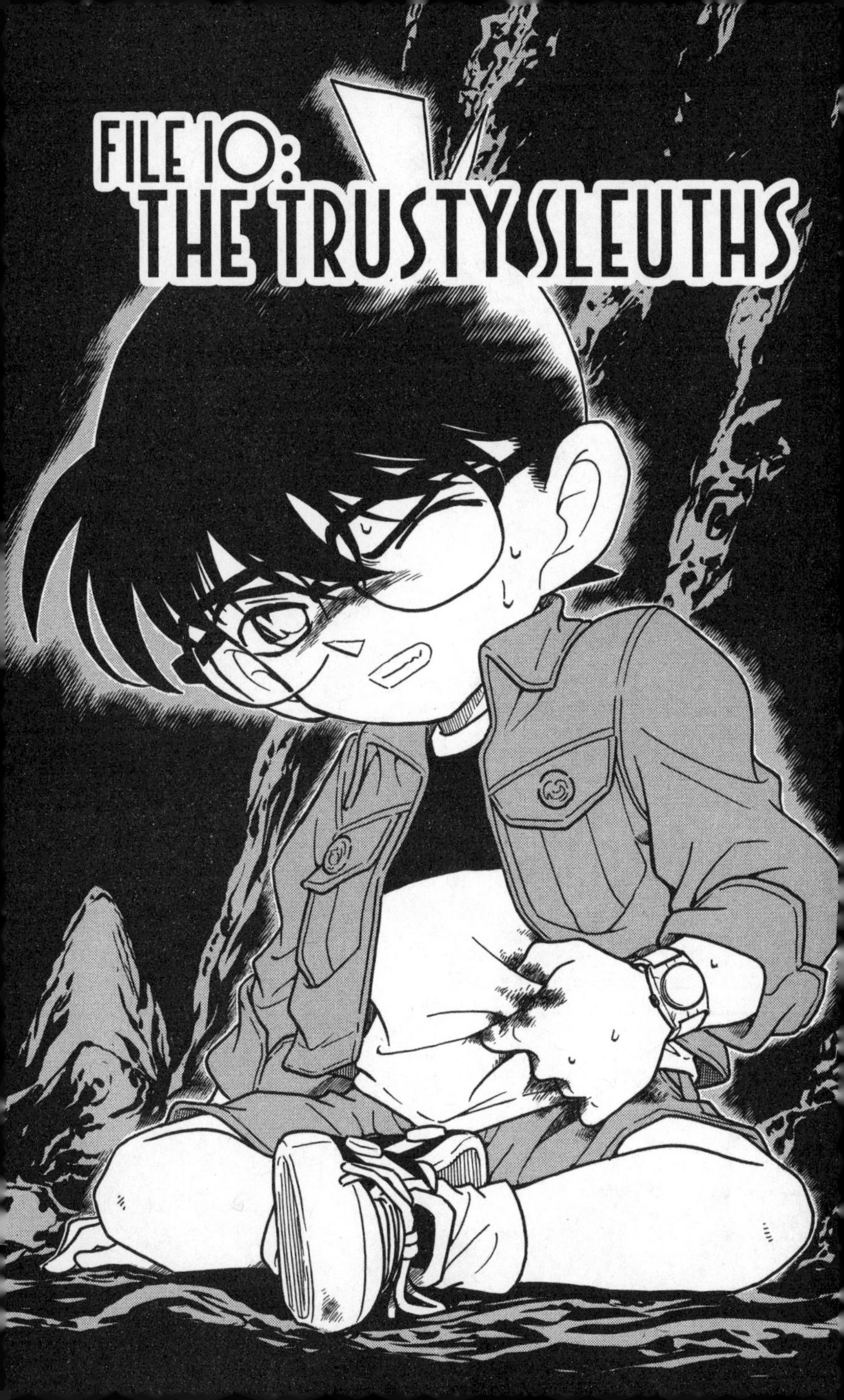
FILE 10:
THE TRUSTY SLEUTHS

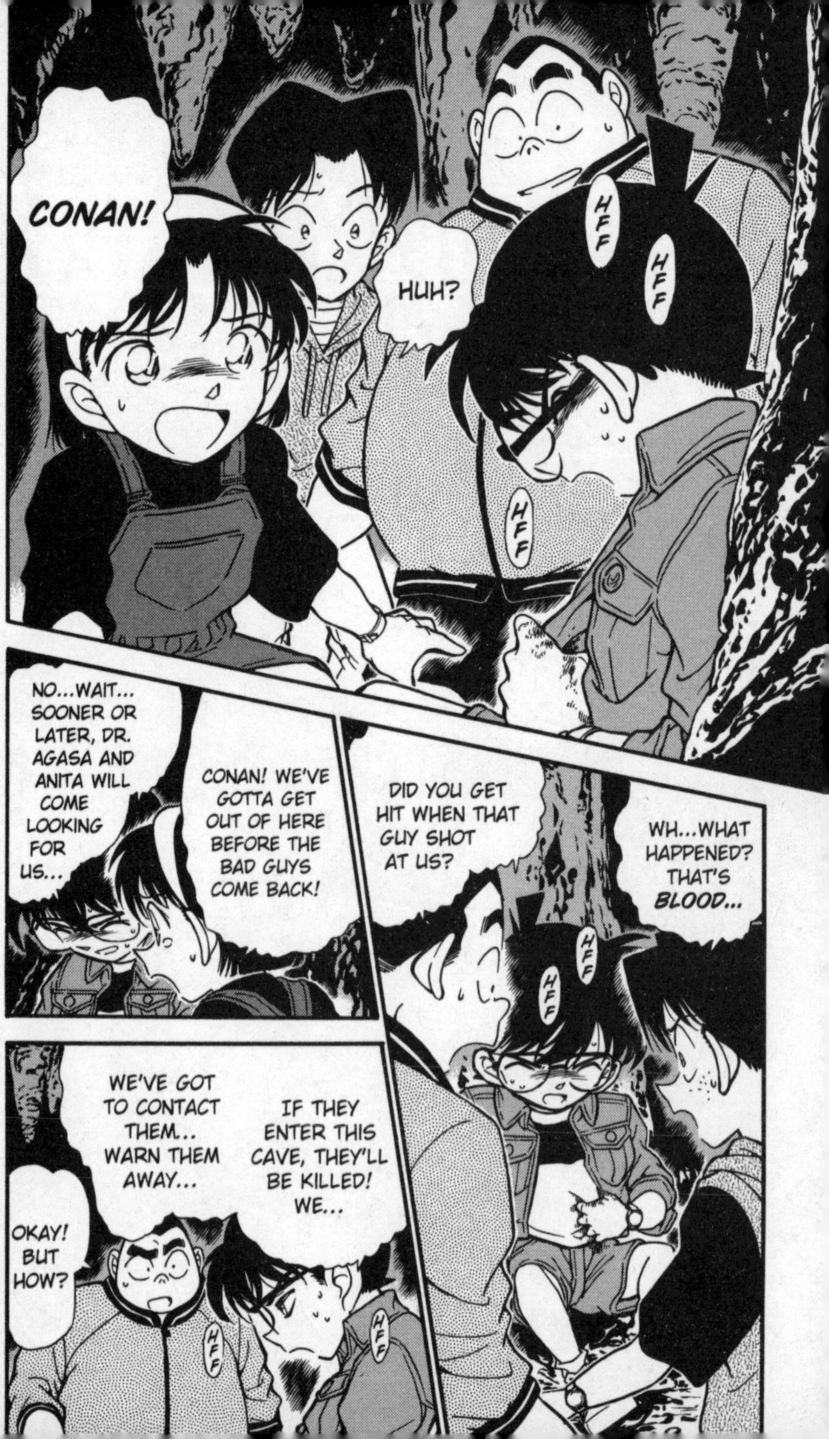
HFF
HFF
HUH?
CONAN!
HFF
WH...WHAT HAPPENED? THAT'S *BLOOD*...
DID YOU GET HIT WHEN THAT GUY SHOT AT US?
HFF
HFF
CONAN! WE'VE GOTTA GET OUT OF HERE BEFORE THE BAD GUYS COME BACK!
NO...WAIT... SOONER OR LATER, DR. AGASA AND ANITA WILL COME LOOKING FOR US...
IF THEY ENTER THIS CAVE, THEY'LL BE KILLED! WE...
WE'VE GOT TO CONTACT THEM... WARN THEM AWAY...
HFF
OKAY! BUT HOW?
HFF

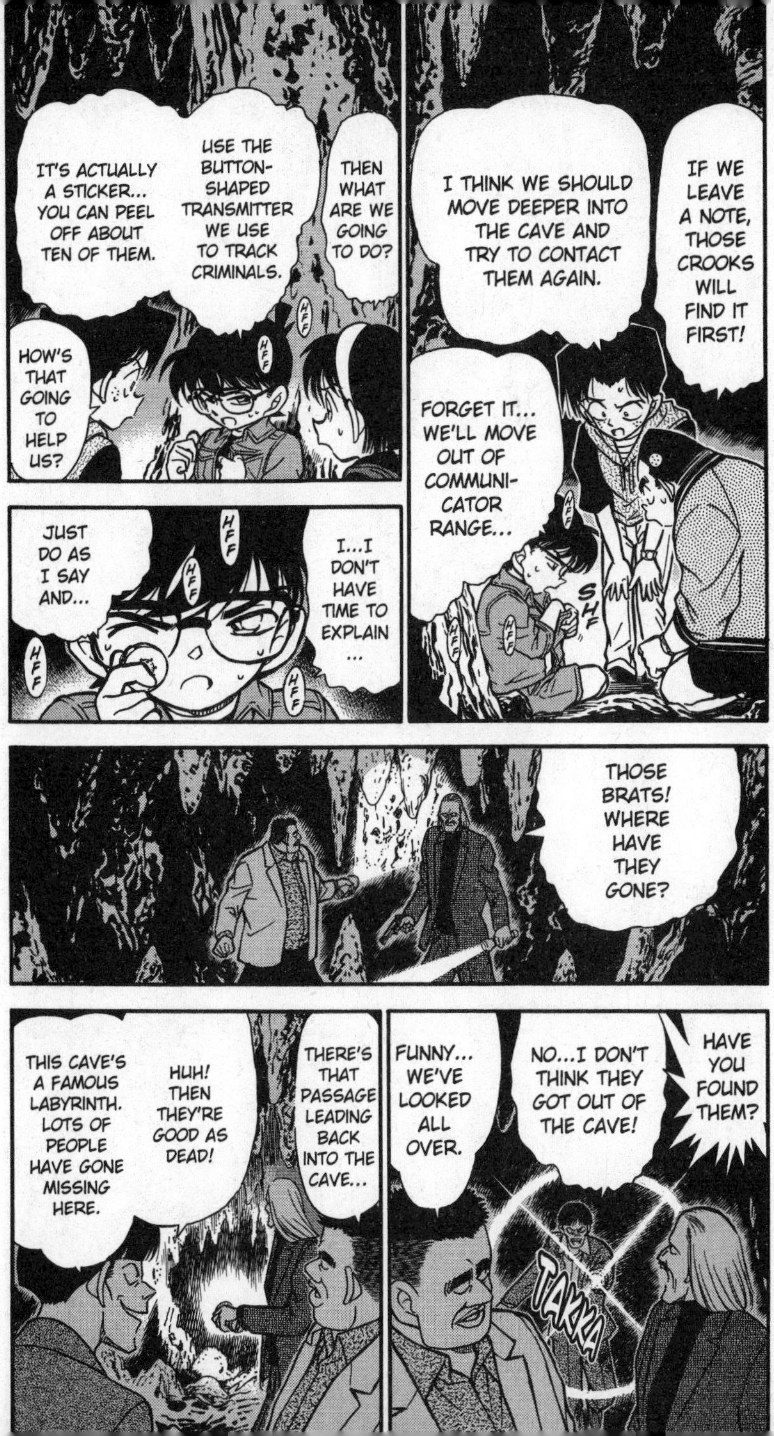
IF WE LEAVE A NOTE, THOSE CROOKS WILL FIND IT FIRST!
I THINK WE SHOULD MOVE DEEPER INTO THE CAVE AND TRY TO CONTACT THEM AGAIN.
FORGET IT... WE'LL MOVE OUT OF COMMUNI-CATOR RANGE...
HFF
SHF
HFF
HFF
THEN WHAT ARE WE GOING TO DO?
USE THE BUTTON-SHAPED TRANSMITTER WE USE TO TRACK CRIMINALS.
IT'S ACTUALLY A STICKER... YOU CAN PEEL OFF ABOUT TEN OF THEM.
HFF
HFF
HOW'S THAT GOING TO HELP US?
I...I DON'T HAVE TIME TO EXPLAIN...
HFF
HFF
JUST DO AS I SAY AND...
HFF
HFF
THOSE BRATS! WHERE HAVE THEY GONE?
HAVE YOU FOUND THEM?
NO...I DON'T THINK THEY GOT OUT OF THE CAVE!
FUNNY... WE'VE LOOKED ALL OVER.
TAKKA
THERE'S THAT PASSAGE LEADING BACK INTO THE CAVE...
HUH! THEN THEY'RE GOOD AS DEAD!
THIS CAVE'S A FAMOUS LABYRINTH. LOTS OF PEOPLE HAVE GONE MISSING HERE.

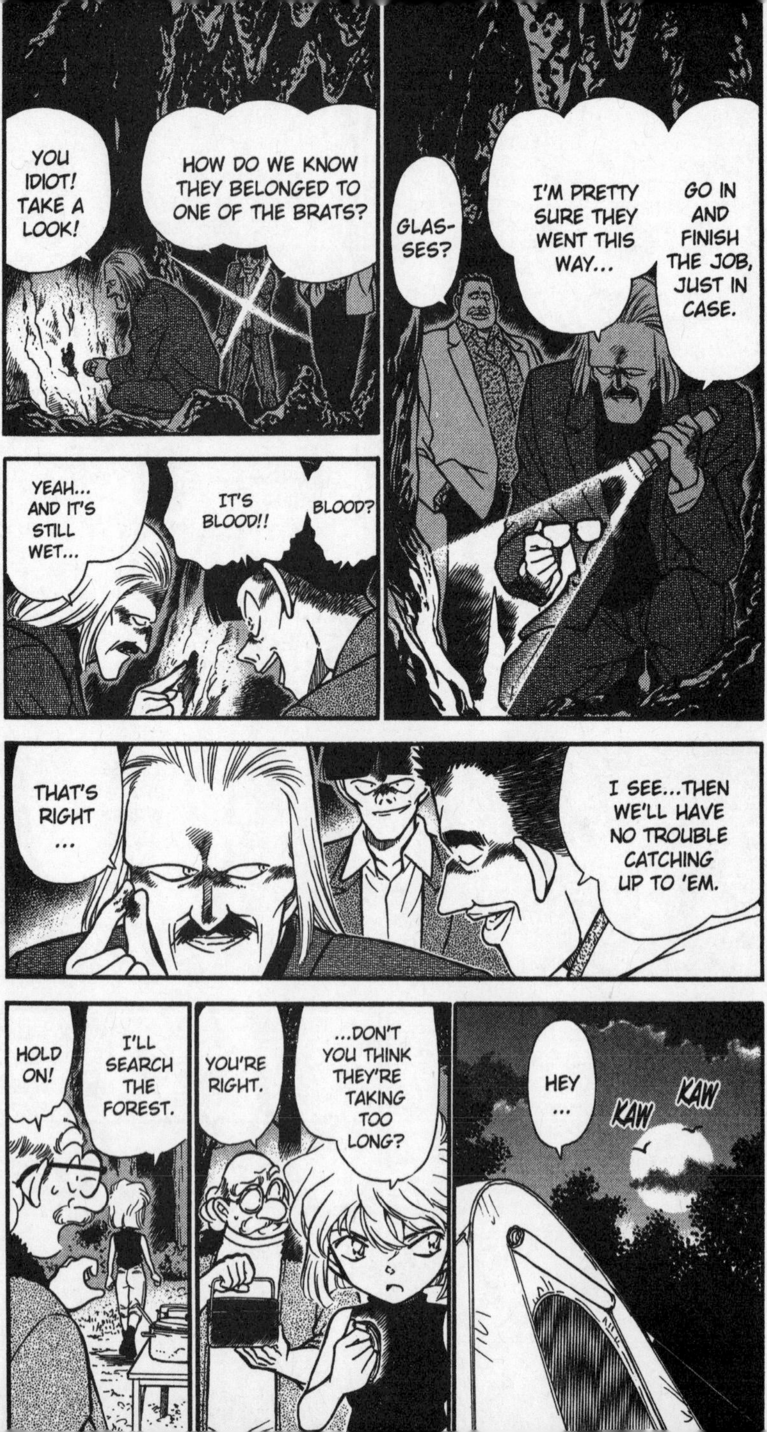
GO IN AND FINISH THE JOB, JUST IN CASE.
I'M PRETTY SURE THEY WENT THIS WAY...
GLAS-SES?
HOW DO WE KNOW THEY BELONGED TO ONE OF THE BRATS?
YOU IDIOT! TAKE A LOOK!
BLOOD?
IT'S BLOOD!!
YEAH... AND IT'S STILL WET...
I SEE...THEN WE'LL HAVE NO TROUBLE CATCHING UP TO 'EM.
THAT'S RIGHT ...
KAW
KAW
HEY ...
...DON'T YOU THINK THEY'RE TAKING TOO LONG?
YOU'RE RIGHT.
I'LL SEARCH THE FOREST.
HOLD ON!

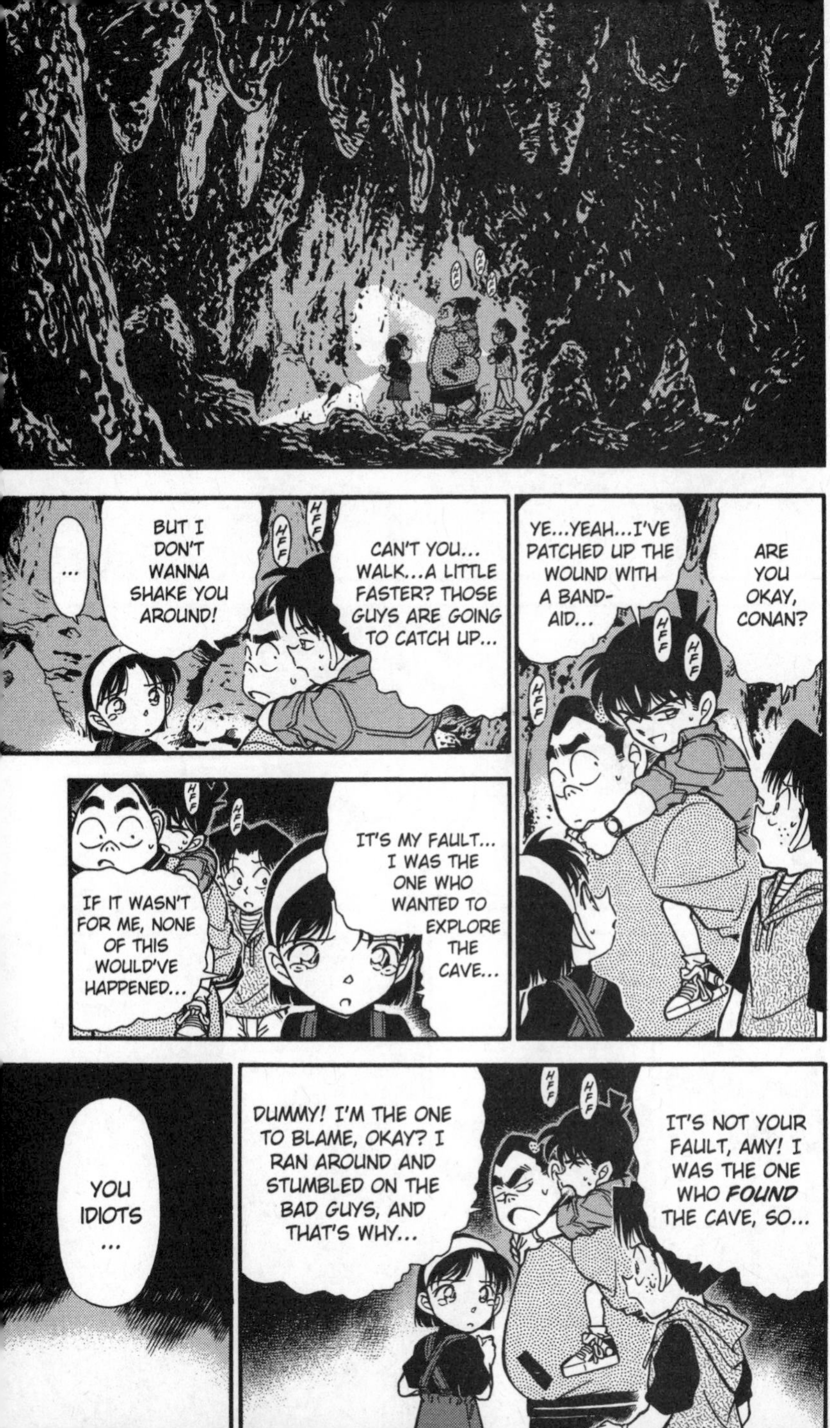
HFF
HFF
HFF
ARE YOU OKAY, CONAN?
YE...YEAH...I'VE PATCHED UP THE WOUND WITH A BAND-AID...
HFF
HFF
HFF
HFF
HFF
CAN'T YOU... WALK...A LITTLE FASTER? THOSE GUYS ARE GOING TO CATCH UP...
BUT I DON'T WANNA SHAKE YOU AROUND!
...
HFF
HFF
IT'S MY FAULT... I WAS THE ONE WHO WANTED TO EXPLORE THE CAVE...
IF IT WASN'T FOR ME, NONE OF THIS WOULD'VE HAPPENED...
HFF
HFF
IT'S NOT YOUR FAULT, AMY! I WAS THE ONE WHO ***FOUND*** THE CAVE, SO...
DUMMY! I'M THE ONE TO BLAME, OKAY? I RAN AROUND AND STUMBLED ON THE BAD GUYS, AND THAT'S WHY...
YOU IDIOTS ...

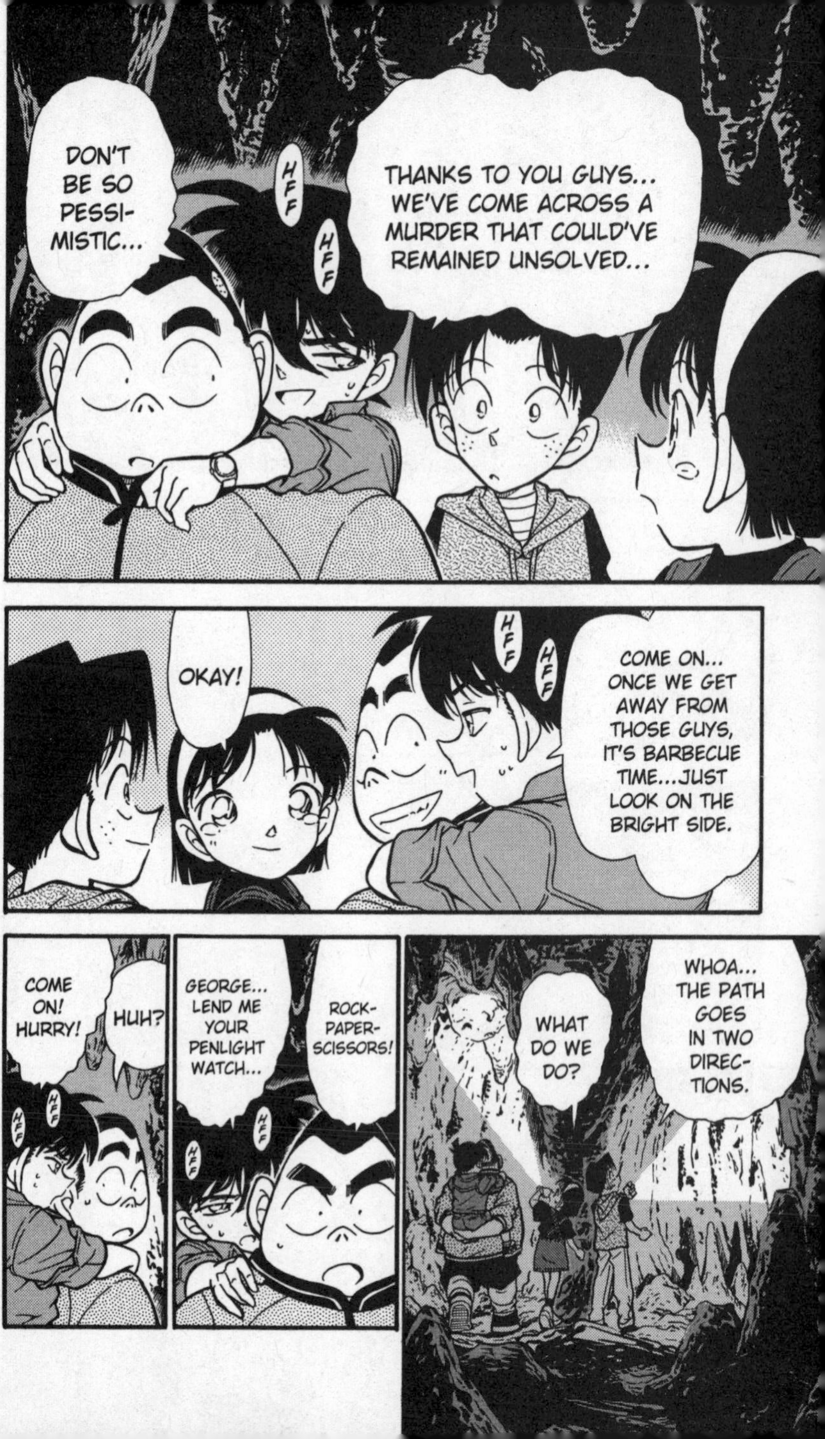
THANKS TO YOU GUYS... WE'VE COME ACROSS A MURDER THAT COULD'VE REMAINED UNSOLVED...
HFF
HFF
DON'T BE SO PESSI-MISTIC...
COME ON... ONCE WE GET AWAY FROM THOSE GUYS, IT'S BARBECUE TIME...JUST LOOK ON THE BRIGHT SIDE.
HFF
HFF
OKAY!
WHOA... THE PATH GOES IN TWO DIREC-TIONS.
WHAT DO WE DO?
ROCK-PAPER-SCISSORS!
GEORGE... LEND ME YOUR PENLIGHT WATCH...
HFF
HFF
HUH?
COME ON! HURRY!
HFF
HFF

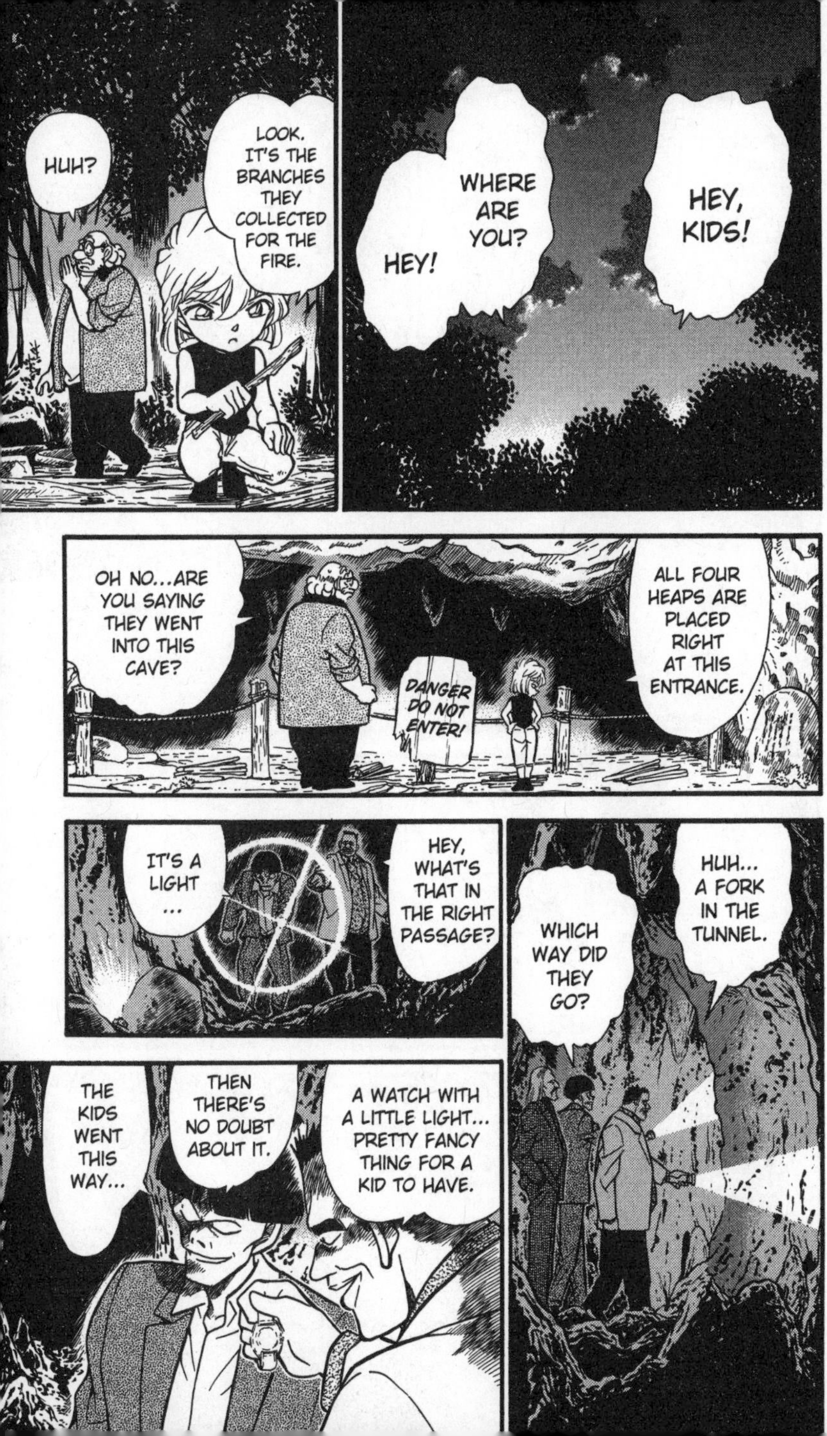
HEY, KIDS!
WHERE ARE YOU?
HEY!
LOOK. IT'S THE BRANCHES THEY COLLECTED FOR THE FIRE.
HUH?
ALL FOUR HEAPS ARE PLACED RIGHT AT THIS ENTRANCE.
DANGER DO NOT ENTER!
OH NO...ARE YOU SAYING THEY WENT INTO THIS CAVE?
HUH... A FORK IN THE TUNNEL.
WHICH WAY DID THEY GO?
HEY, WHAT'S THAT IN THE RIGHT PASSAGE?
IT'S A LIGHT ...
A WATCH WITH A LITTLE LIGHT... PRETTY FANCY THING FOR A KID TO HAVE.
THEN THERE'S NO DOUBT ABOUT IT.
THE KIDS WENT THIS WAY...

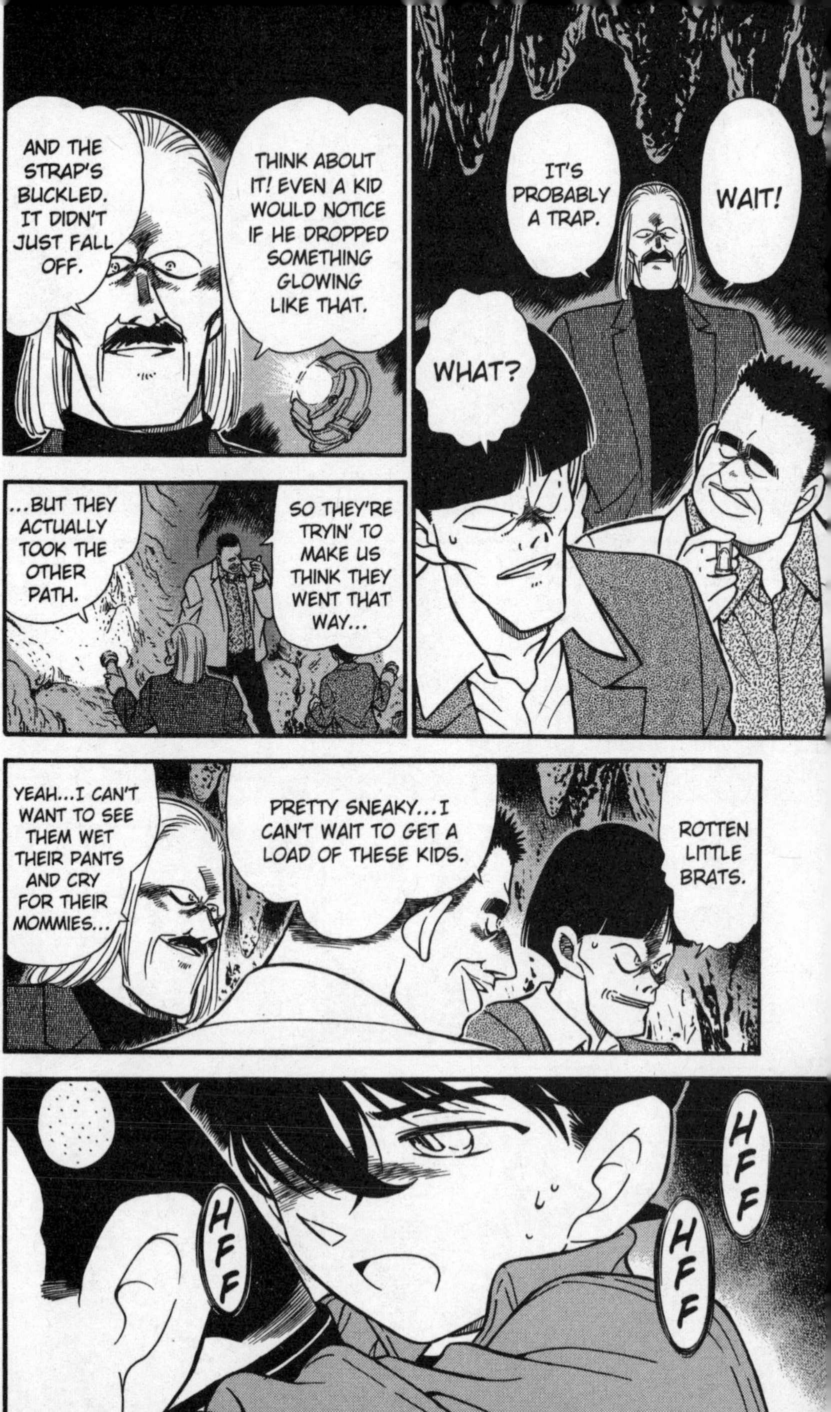
WAIT!
IT'S PROBABLY A TRAP.
WHAT?
THINK ABOUT IT! EVEN A KID WOULD NOTICE IF HE DROPPED SOMETHING GLOWING LIKE THAT.
AND THE STRAP'S BUCKLED. IT DIDN'T JUST FALL OFF.
SO THEY'RE TRYIN' TO MAKE US THINK THEY WENT THAT WAY...
...BUT THEY ACTUALLY TOOK THE OTHER PATH.
ROTTEN LITTLE BRATS.
PRETTY SNEAKY...I CAN'T WAIT TO GET A LOAD OF THESE KIDS.
YEAH...I CAN'T WANT TO SEE THEM WET THEIR PANTS AND CRY FOR THEIR MOMMIES...
HFF
HFF
HFF

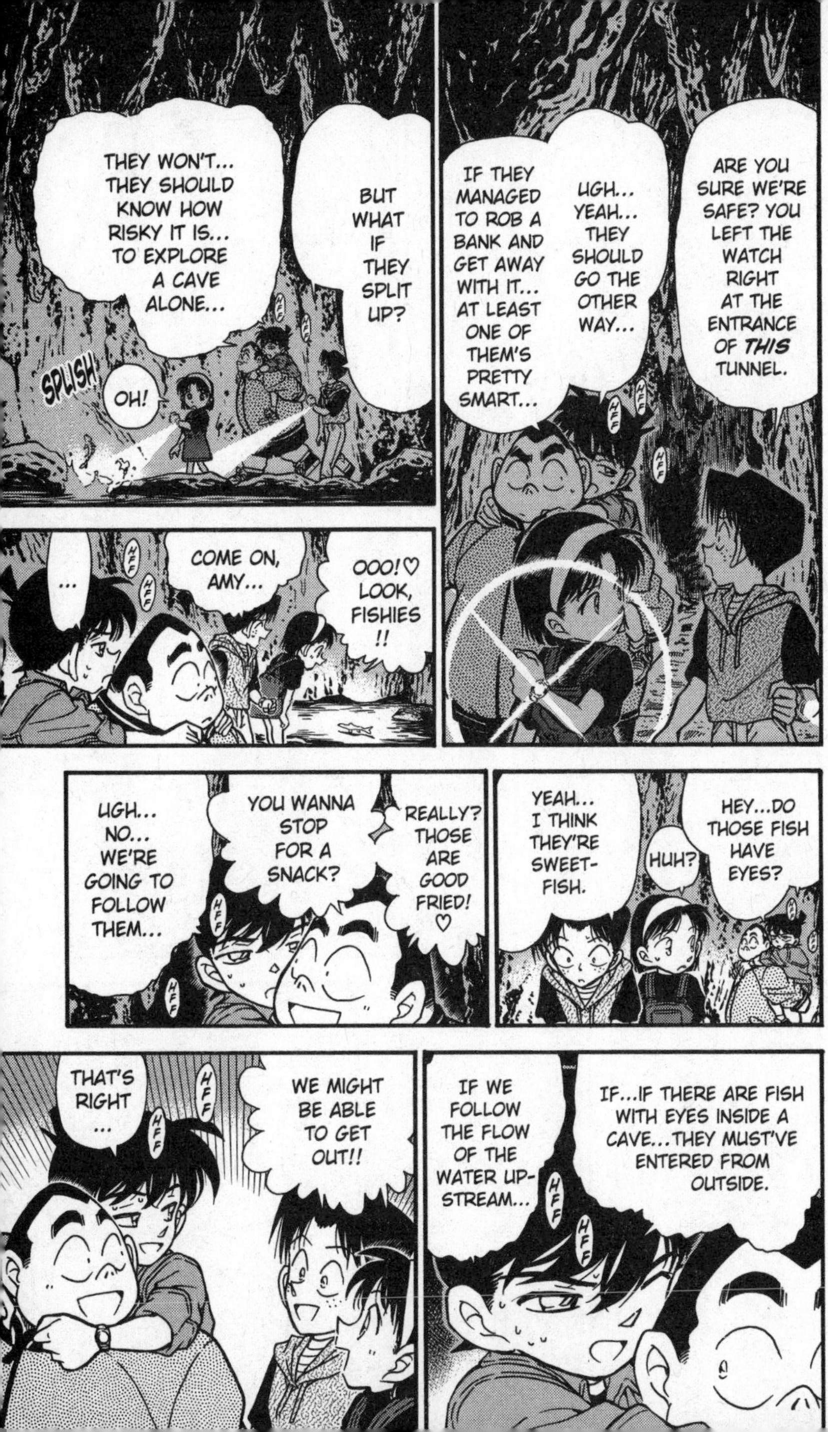

ARE YOU SURE WE'RE SAFE? YOU LEFT THE WATCH RIGHT AT THE ENTRANCE OF *THIS* TUNNEL.
UGH... YEAH... THEY SHOULD GO THE OTHER WAY...
IF THEY MANAGED TO ROB A BANK AND GET AWAY WITH IT... AT LEAST ONE OF THEM'S PRETTY SMART...
BUT WHAT IF THEY SPLIT UP?
THEY WON'T... THEY SHOULD KNOW HOW RISKY IT IS... TO EXPLORE A CAVE ALONE...
OH!
SPLISH
OOO!♡ LOOK, FISHIES!!
COME ON, AMY...
...
HEY...DO THOSE FISH HAVE EYES?
HUH?
YEAH... I THINK THEY'RE SWEET-FISH.
REALLY? THOSE ARE GOOD FRIED! ♡
YOU WANNA STOP FOR A SNACK?
UGH... NO... WE'RE GOING TO FOLLOW THEM...
IF...IF THERE ARE FISH WITH EYES INSIDE A CAVE...THEY MUST'VE ENTERED FROM OUTSIDE.
IF WE FOLLOW THE FLOW OF THE WATER UP-STREAM...
WE MIGHT BE ABLE TO GET OUT!!
THAT'S RIGHT ...

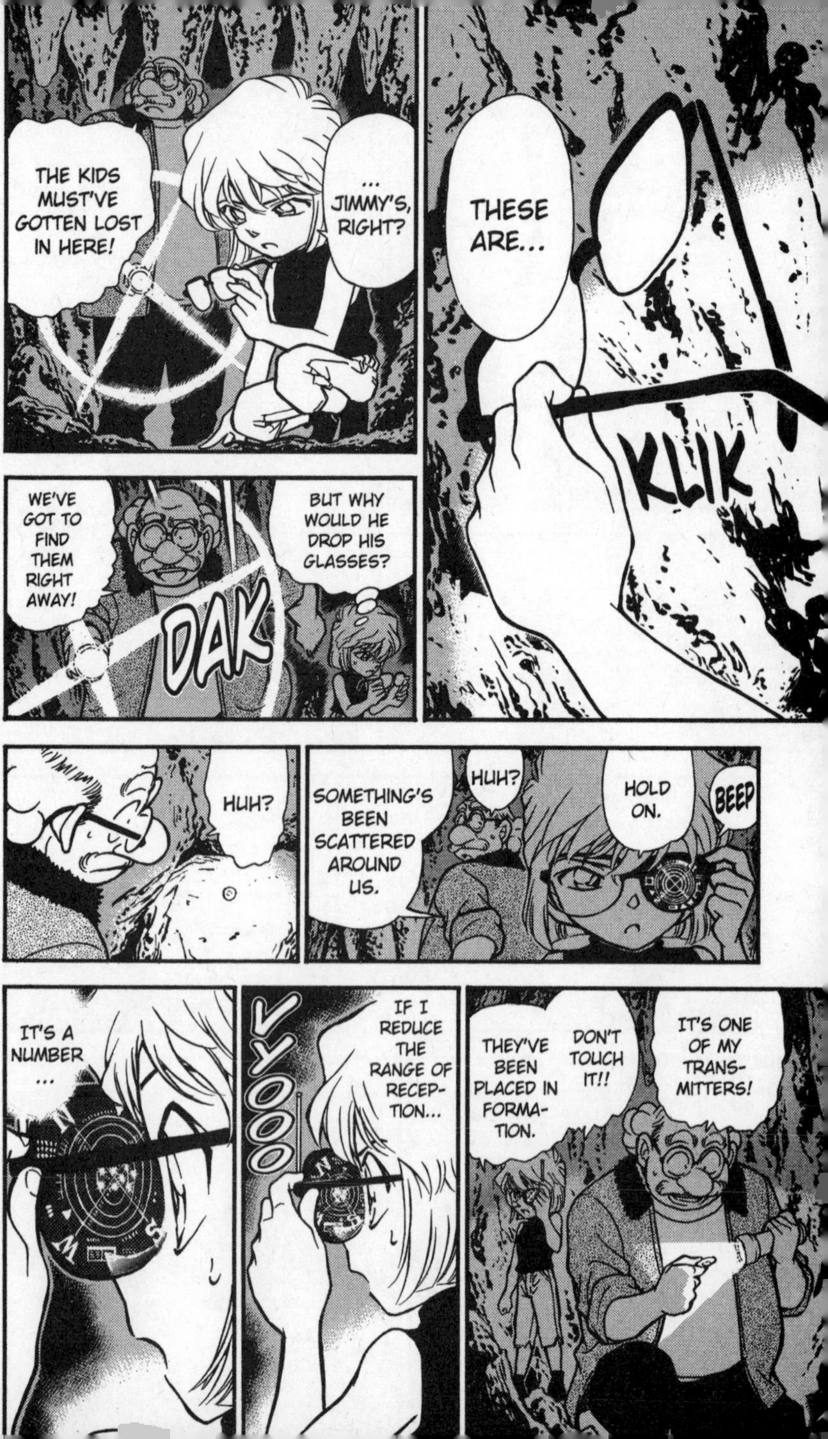
THESE ARE...
KLIK
... JIMMY'S, RIGHT?
THE KIDS MUST'VE GOTTEN LOST IN HERE!
BUT WHY WOULD HE DROP HIS GLASSES?
WE'VE GOT TO FIND THEM RIGHT AWAY!
DAK
BEEP
HOLD ON.
HUH?
SOMETHING'S BEEN SCATTERED AROUND US.
HUH?
IT'S ONE OF MY TRANS-MITTERS!
DON'T TOUCH IT!!
THEY'VE BEEN PLACED IN FORMA-TION.
IF I REDUCE THE RANGE OF RECEP-TION...
VYOOO
IT'S A NUMBER ...

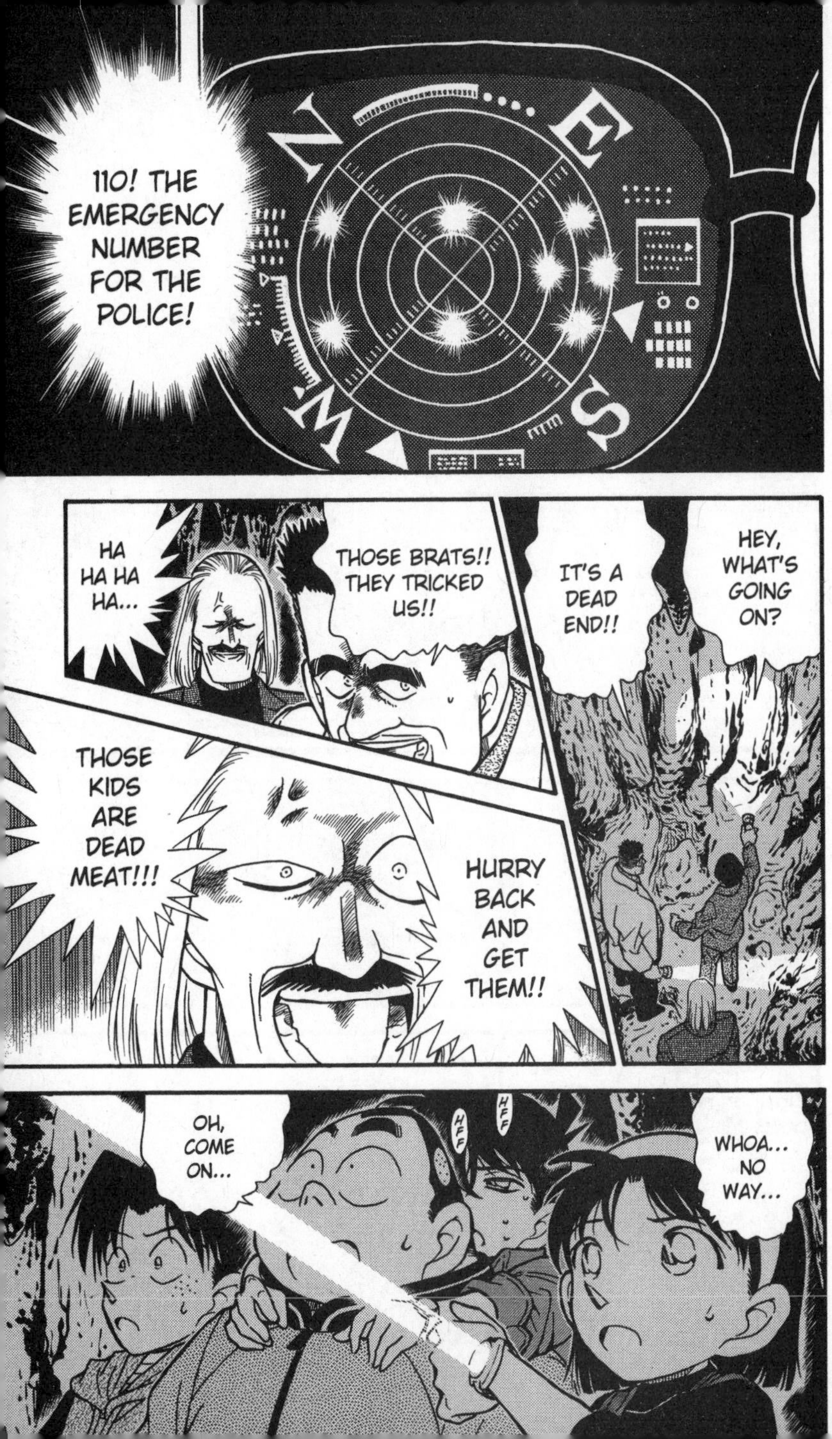
110! THE EMERGENCY NUMBER FOR THE POLICE!
HEY, WHAT'S GOING ON?
IT'S A DEAD END!!
THOSE BRATS!! THEY TRICKED US!!
HA HA HA HA...
HURRY BACK AND GET THEM!!
THOSE KIDS ARE DEAD MEAT!!!
WHOA... NO WAY...
HFF HFF
OH, COME ON...

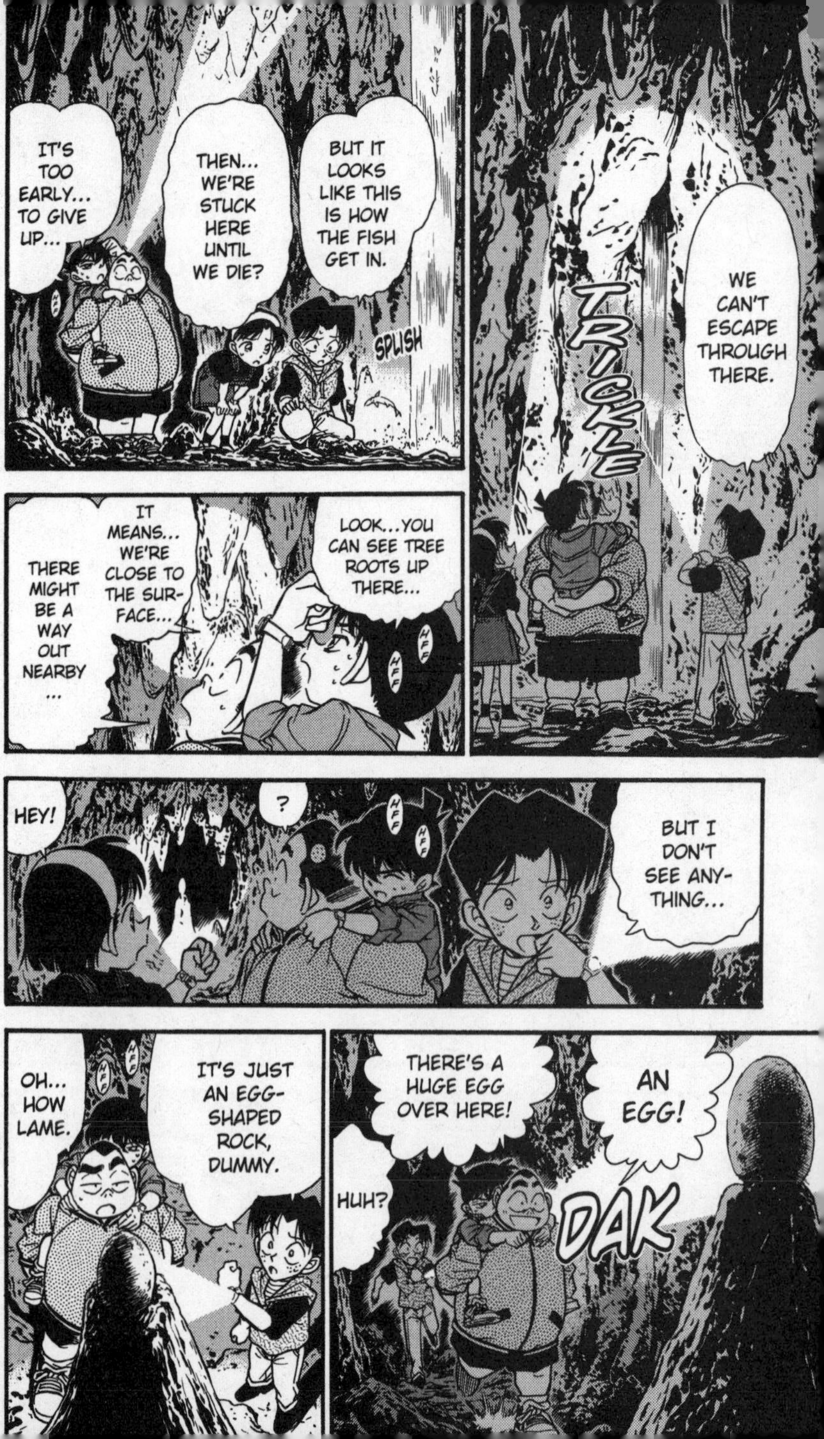
WE CAN'T ESCAPE THROUGH THERE.
TRICKLE
BUT IT LOOKS LIKE THIS IS HOW THE FISH GET IN.
SPLISH
THEN... WE'RE STUCK HERE UNTIL WE DIE?
IT'S TOO EARLY... TO GIVE UP...
HFF
LOOK...YOU CAN SEE TREE ROOTS UP THERE...
HFF
HFF
IT MEANS... WE'RE CLOSE TO THE SUR-FACE...
THERE MIGHT BE A WAY OUT NEARBY...
BUT I DON'T SEE ANY-THING...
HFF
HFF
?
HEY!
AN EGG!
DAK
THERE'S A HUGE EGG OVER HERE!
HUH?
IT'S JUST AN EGG-SHAPED ROCK, DUMMY.
HFF
OH... HOW LAME.

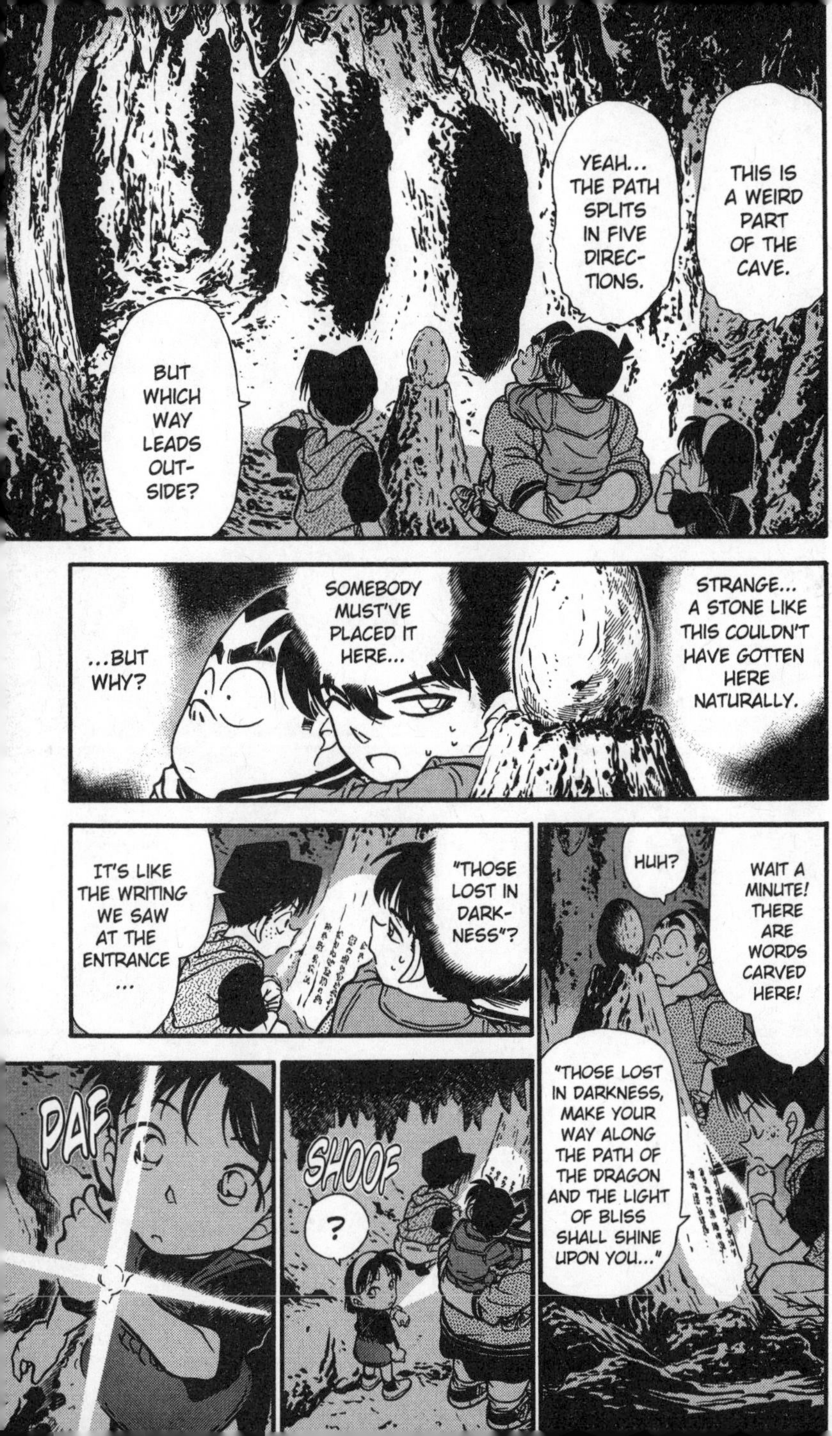
THIS IS A WEIRD PART OF THE CAVE.
YEAH... THE PATH SPLITS IN FIVE DIRECTIONS.
BUT WHICH WAY LEADS OUTSIDE?
STRANGE... A STONE LIKE THIS COULDN'T HAVE GOTTEN HERE NATURALLY.
SOMEBODY MUST'VE PLACED IT HERE...
...BUT WHY?
WAIT A MINUTE! THERE ARE WORDS CARVED HERE!
HUH?
"THOSE LOST IN DARKNESS, MAKE YOUR WAY ALONG THE PATH OF THE DRAGON AND THE LIGHT OF BLISS SHALL SHINE UPON YOU..."
"THOSE LOST IN DARKNESS"?
IT'S LIKE THE WRITING WE SAW AT THE ENTRANCE ...
SHOOF
?
PAF

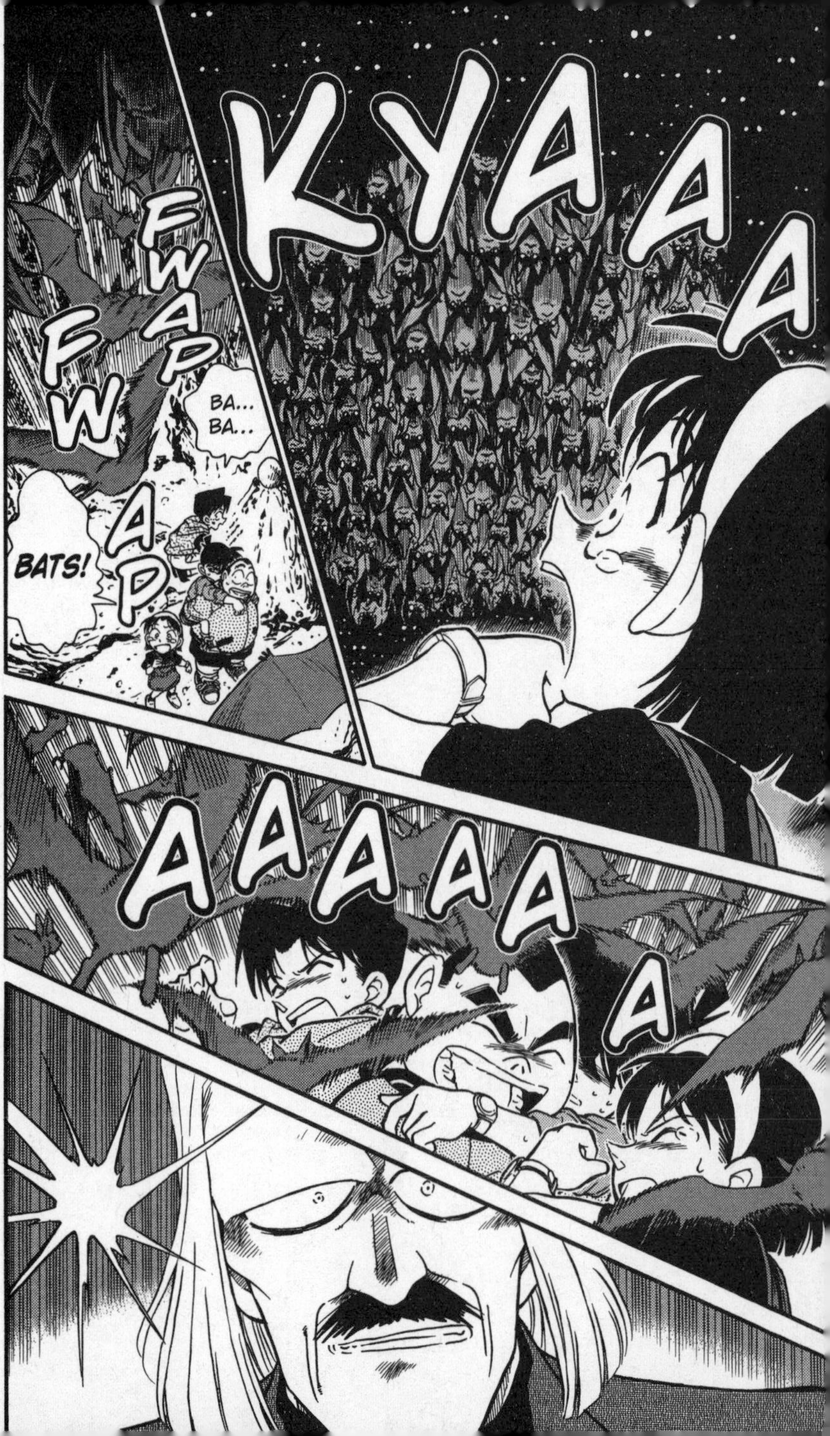
KYAAAA
FWAP
FWAP
BA... BA...
BATS!
AAAAAAA

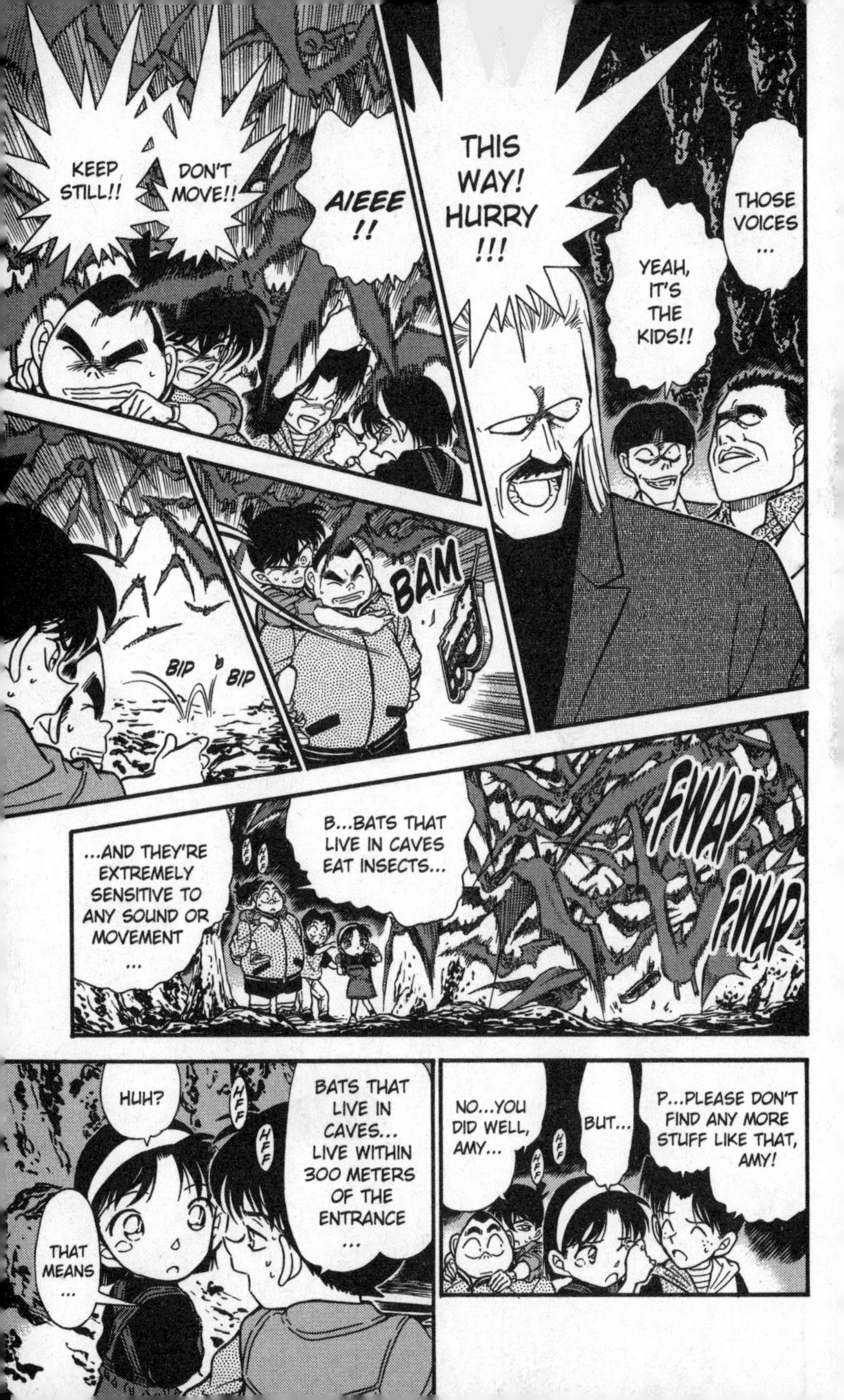
THOSE VOICES ...
YEAH, IT'S THE KIDS!!
THIS WAY! HURRY !!!
AIEEE !!
DON'T MOVE!!
KEEP STILL!!
BAM
BIP BIP
FWAP
FWAP
B...BATS THAT LIVE IN CAVES EAT INSECTS...
...AND THEY'RE EXTREMELY SENSITIVE TO ANY SOUND OR MOVEMENT ...
P...PLEASE DON'T FIND ANY MORE STUFF LIKE THAT, AMY!
BUT...
HFF HFF
NO...YOU DID WELL, AMY...
BATS THAT LIVE IN CAVES... LIVE WITHIN 300 METERS OF THE ENTRANCE ...
HFF HFF
HUH?
THAT MEANS ...

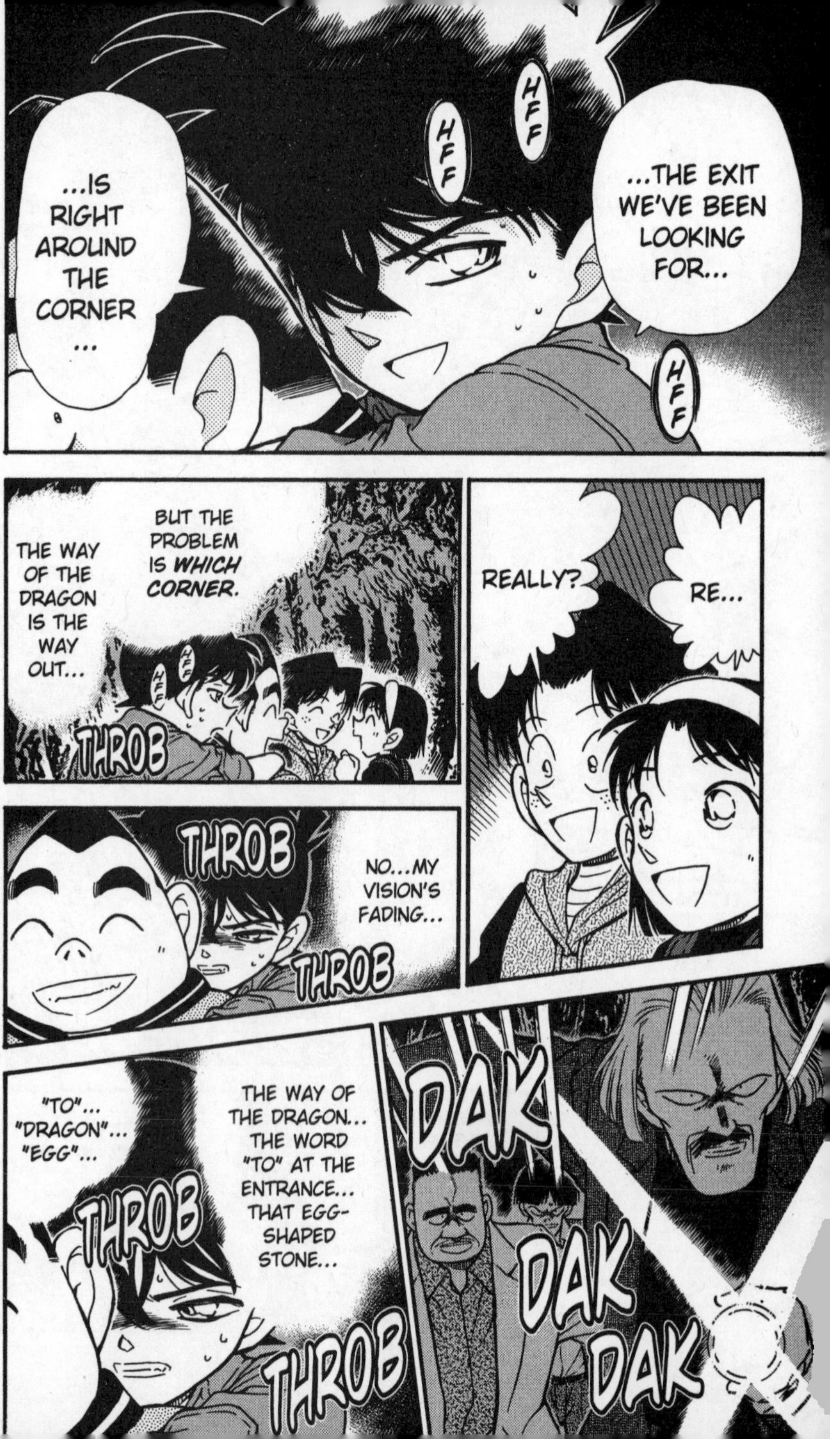
...THE EXIT WE'VE BEEN LOOKING FOR...
HFF
HFF
HFF
...IS RIGHT AROUND THE CORNER...
RE...
REALLY?
BUT THE PROBLEM IS *WHICH* CORNER.
THE WAY OF THE DRAGON IS THE WAY OUT...
HFF
THROB
THROB
NO...MY VISION'S FADING...
THROB
DAK
DAK
DAK
THE WAY OF THE DRAGON... THE WORD "TO" AT THE ENTRANCE... THAT EGG-SHAPED STONE...
"TO"... "DRAGON"... "EGG"...
THROB
THROB

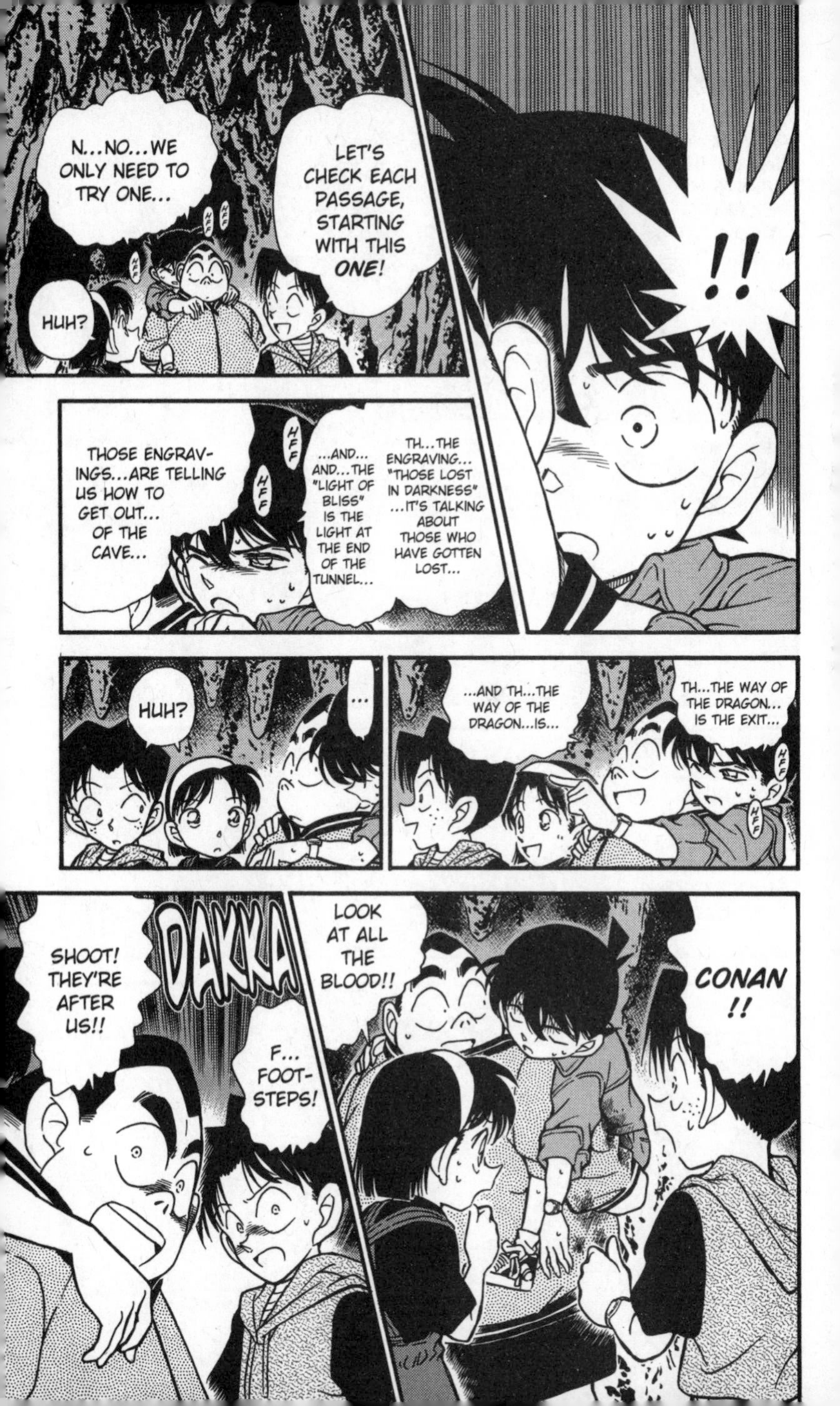
!!
LET'S CHECK EACH PASSAGE, STARTING WITH THIS ONE!
N...NO...WE ONLY NEED TO TRY ONE...
HFF HFF
HFF
HUH?
TH...THE ENGRAVING... "THOSE LOST IN DARKNESS" ...IT'S TALKING ABOUT THOSE WHO HAVE GOTTEN LOST...
...AND... AND...THE "LIGHT OF BLISS" IS THE LIGHT AT THE END OF THE TUNNEL...
HFF
HFF
THOSE ENGRAV-INGS...ARE TELLING US HOW TO GET OUT... OF THE CAVE...
TH...THE WAY OF THE DRAGON... IS THE EXIT...
HFF
HFF
...AND TH...THE WAY OF THE DRAGON...IS...
...
HUH?
CONAN !!
LOOK AT ALL THE BLOOD!!
F... FOOT-STEPS!
DAKKA
SHOOT! THEY'RE AFTER US!!

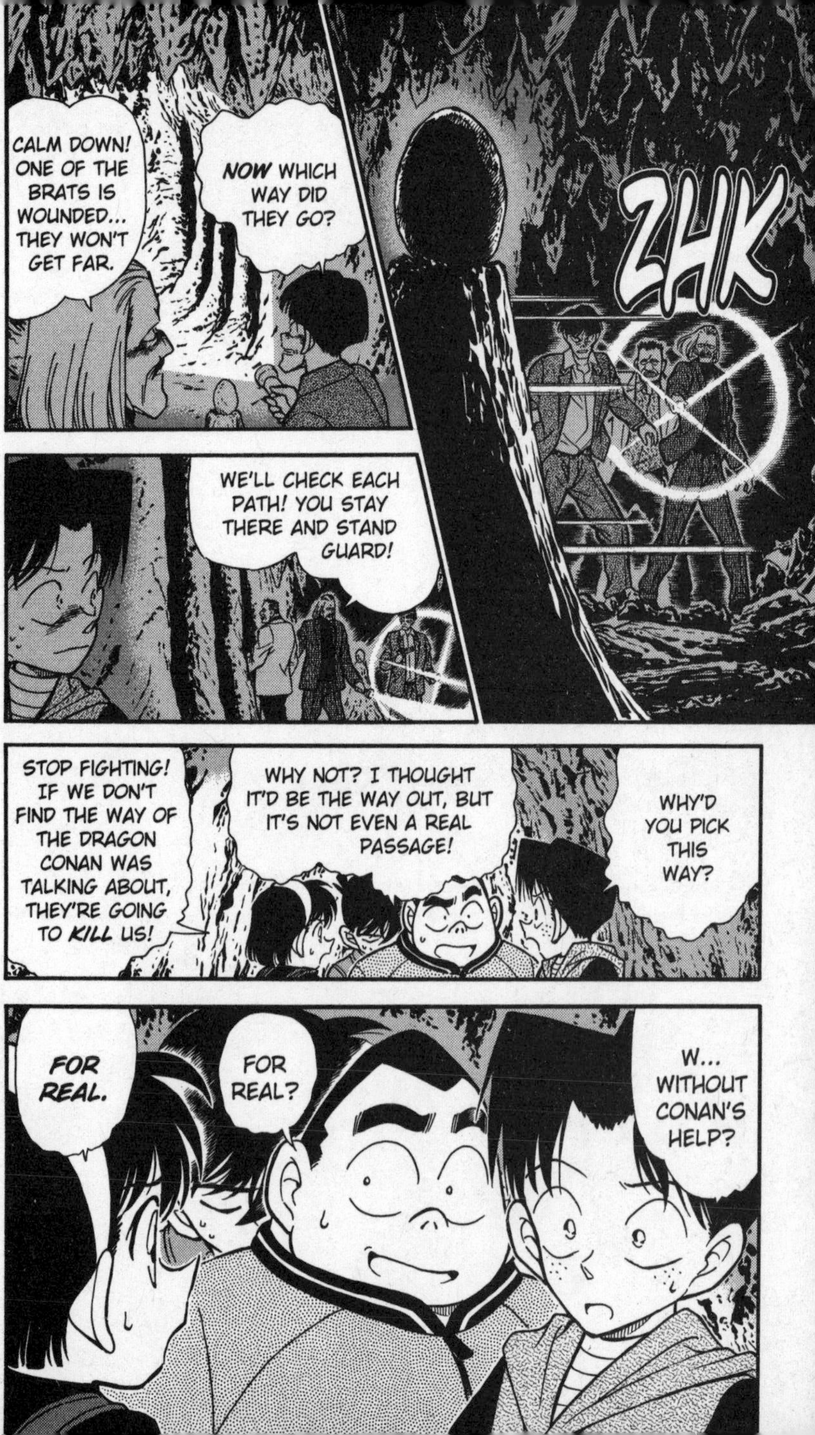
ZHK
NOW WHICH WAY DID THEY GO?
CALM DOWN! ONE OF THE BRATS IS WOUNDED... THEY WON'T GET FAR.
WE'LL CHECK EACH PATH! YOU STAY THERE AND STAND GUARD!
WHY'D YOU PICK THIS WAY?
WHY NOT? I THOUGHT IT'D BE THE WAY OUT, BUT IT'S NOT EVEN A REAL PASSAGE!
STOP FIGHTING! IF WE DON'T FIND THE WAY OF THE DRAGON CONAN WAS TALKING ABOUT, THEY'RE GOING TO KILL US!
W... WITHOUT CONAN'S HELP?
FOR REAL?
FOR REAL.

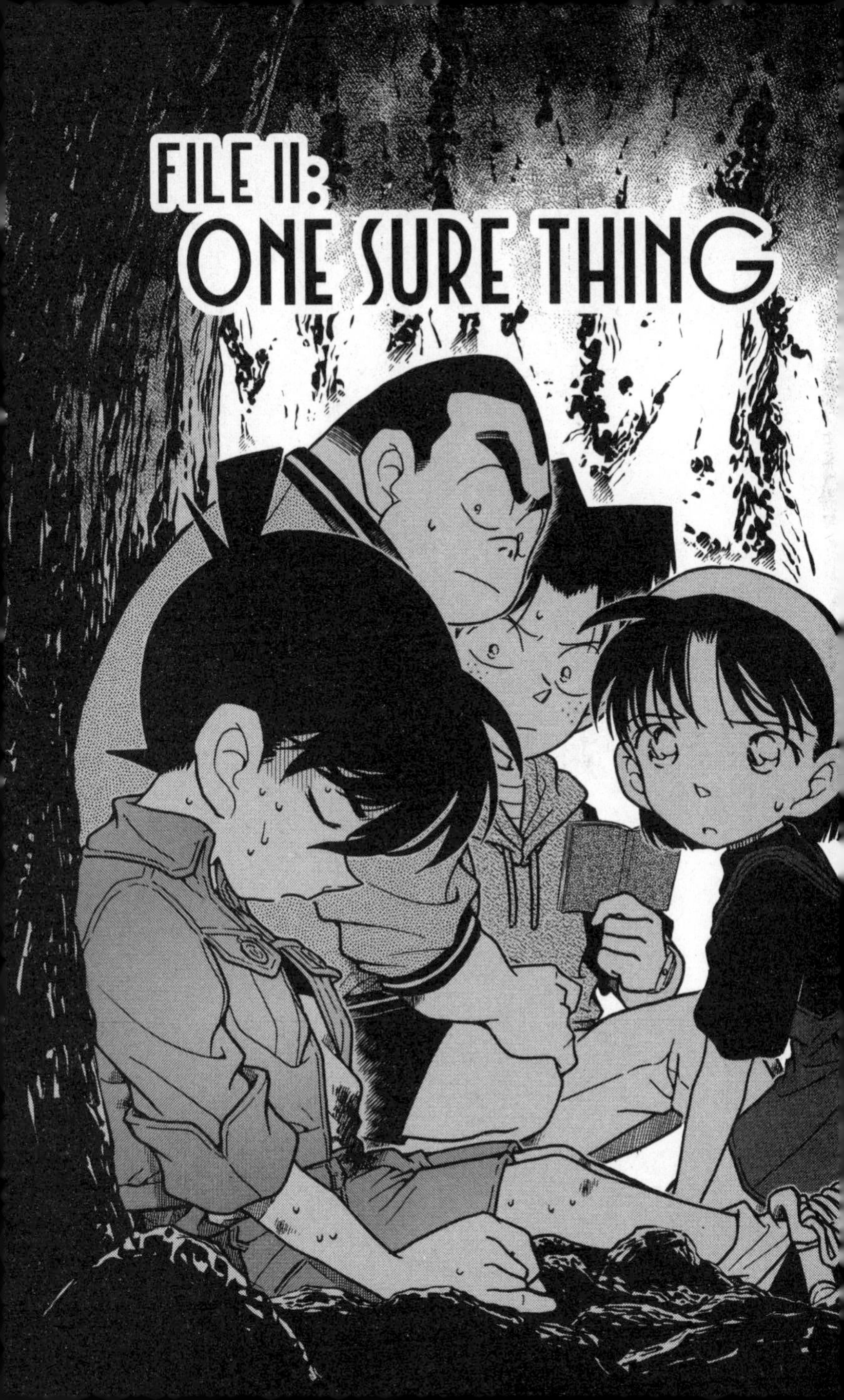
FILE 11:
ONE SURE THING

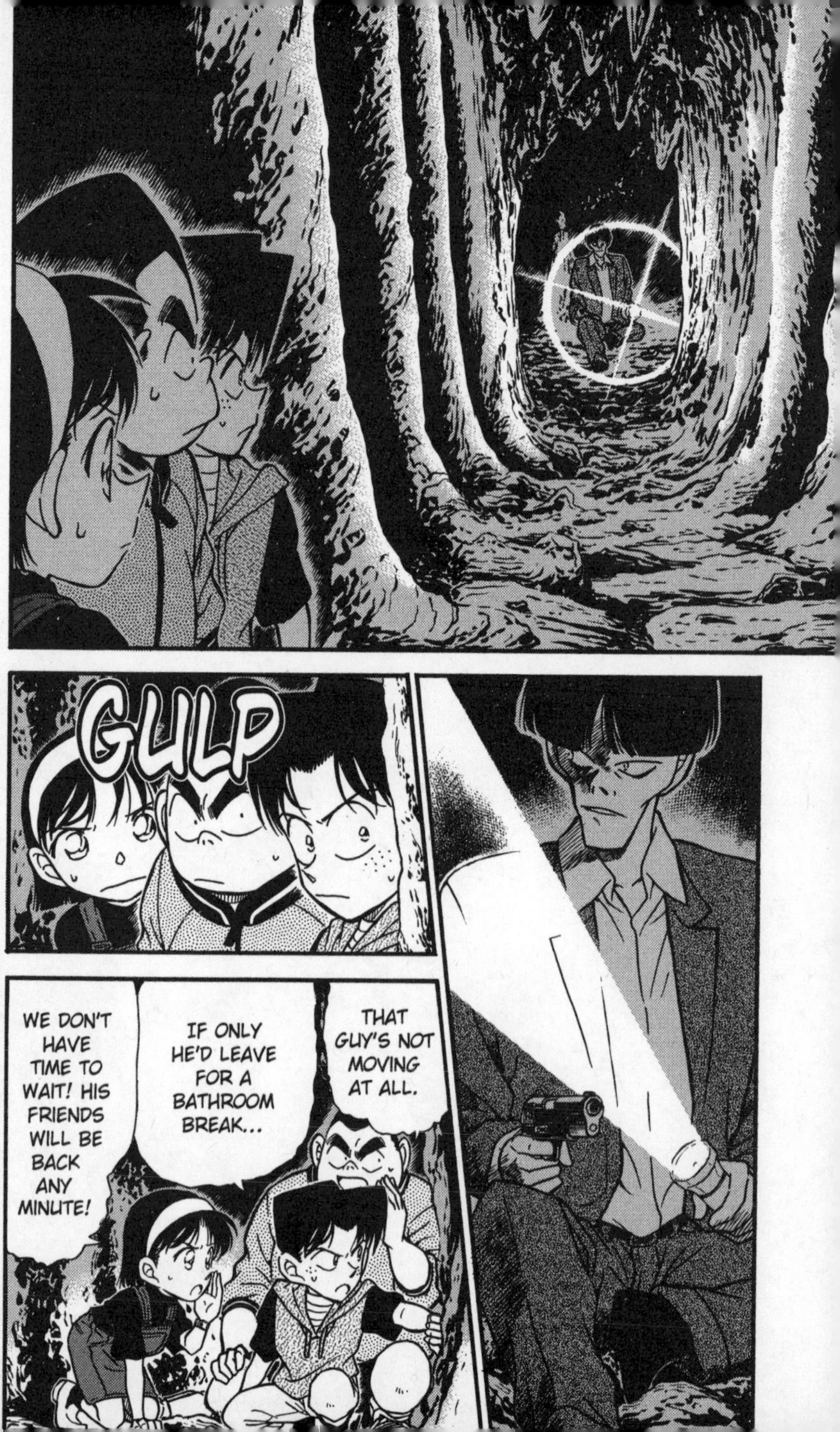
GULP
THAT GUY'S NOT MOVING AT ALL.
IF ONLY HE'D LEAVE FOR A BATHROOM BREAK...
WE DON'T HAVE TIME TO WAIT! HIS FRIENDS WILL BE BACK ANY MINUTE!

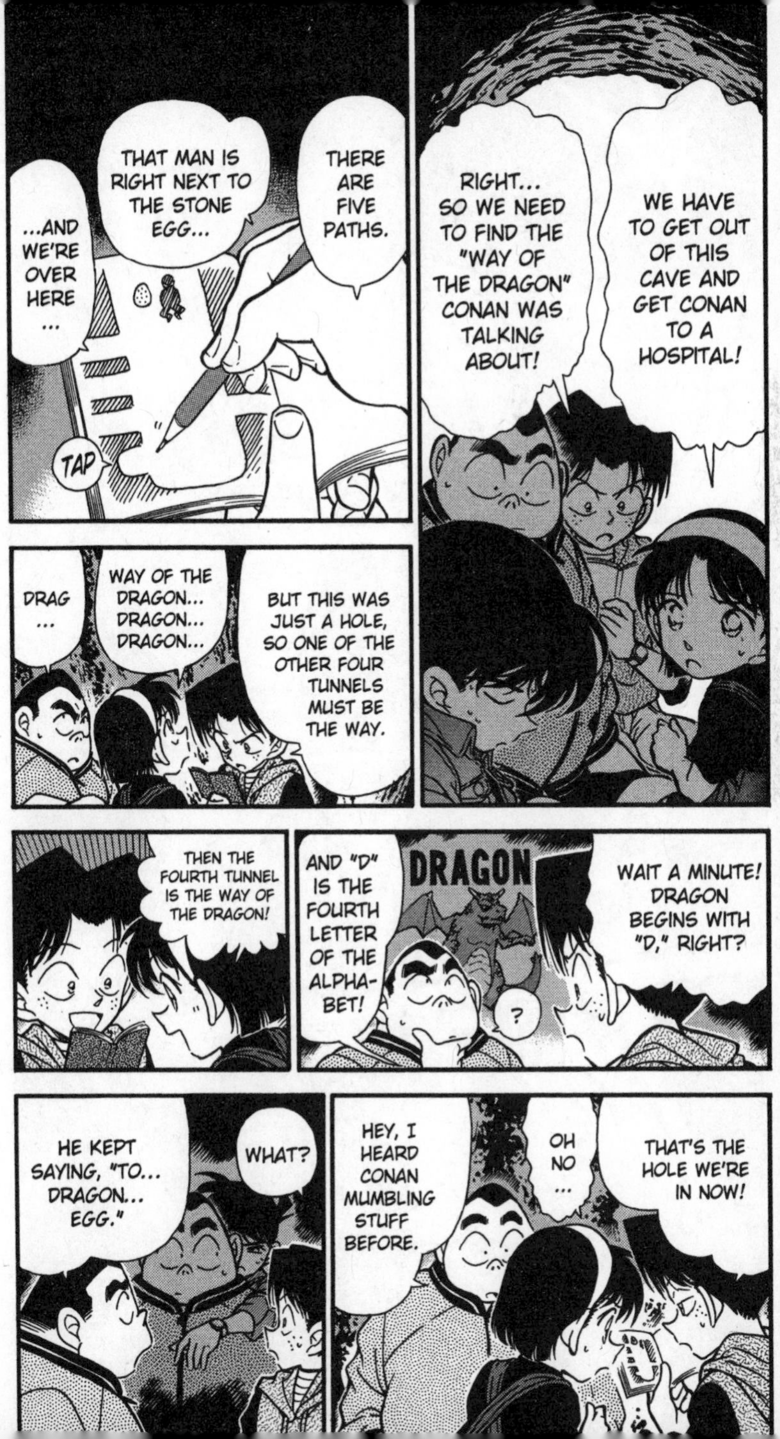
WE HAVE TO GET OUT OF THIS CAVE AND GET CONAN TO A HOSPITAL!
RIGHT... SO WE NEED TO FIND THE "WAY OF THE DRAGON" CONAN WAS TALKING ABOUT!
THERE ARE FIVE PATHS.
THAT MAN IS RIGHT NEXT TO THE STONE EGG...
...AND WE'RE OVER HERE ...
TAP
BUT THIS WAS JUST A HOLE, SO ONE OF THE OTHER FOUR TUNNELS MUST BE THE WAY.
WAY OF THE DRAGON... DRAGON... DRAGON...
DRAG ...
WAIT A MINUTE! DRAGON BEGINS WITH "D," RIGHT?
DRAGON
?
AND "D" IS THE FOURTH LETTER OF THE ALPHA-BET!
THEN THE FOURTH TUNNEL IS THE WAY OF THE DRAGON!
THAT'S THE HOLE WE'RE IN NOW!
OH NO ...
HEY, I HEARD CONAN MUMBLING STUFF BEFORE.
WHAT?
HE KEPT SAYING, "TO... DRAGON... EGG."

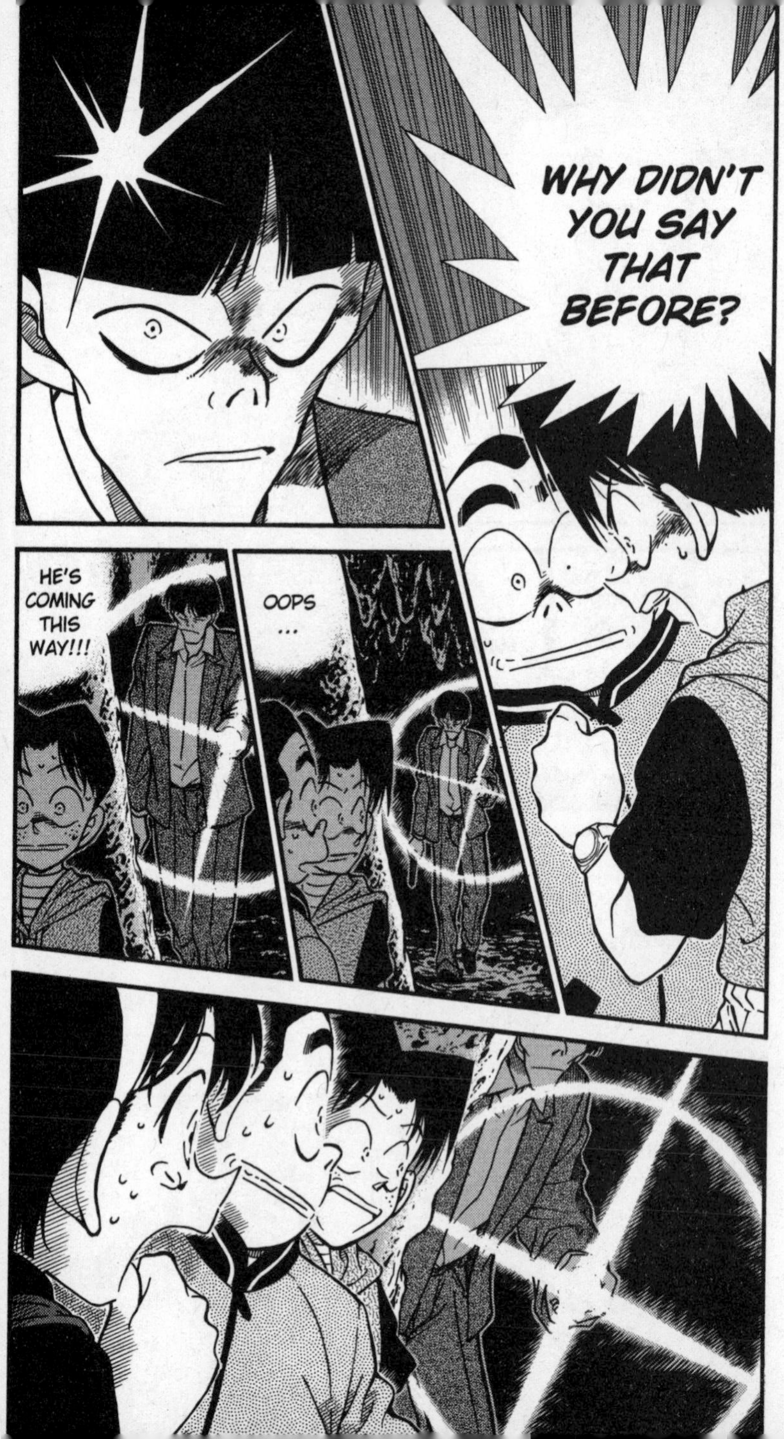
WHY DIDN'T YOU SAY THAT BEFORE?
OOPS ...
HE'S COMING THIS WAY!!!

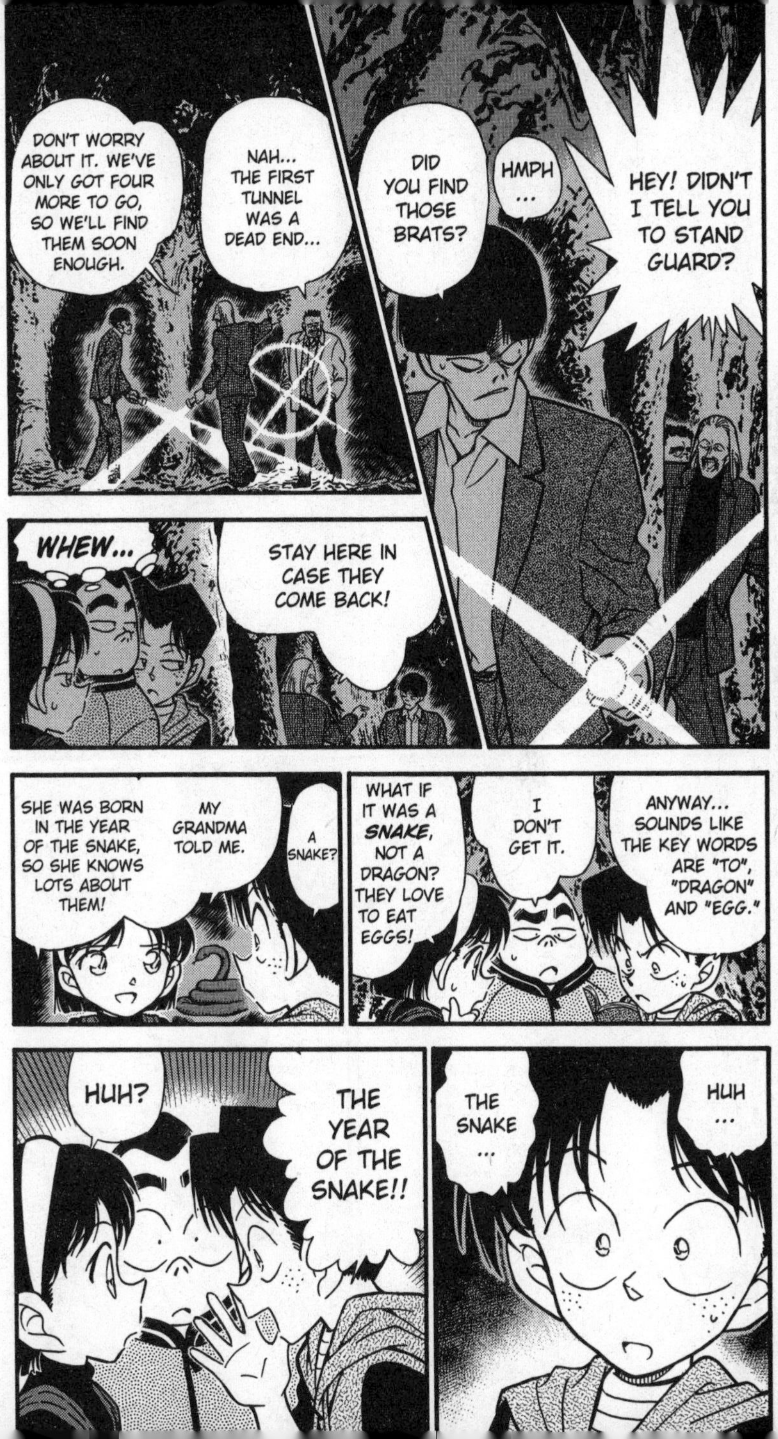
HEY! DIDN'T I TELL YOU TO STAND GUARD?
HMPH ...
DID YOU FIND THOSE BRATS?
NAH... THE FIRST TUNNEL WAS A DEAD END...
DON'T WORRY ABOUT IT. WE'VE ONLY GOT FOUR MORE TO GO, SO WE'LL FIND THEM SOON ENOUGH.
STAY HERE IN CASE THEY COME BACK!
WHEW...
ANYWAY... SOUNDS LIKE THE KEY WORDS ARE "TO", "DRAGON" AND "EGG."
I DON'T GET IT.
WHAT IF IT WAS A SNAKE, NOT A DRAGON? THEY LOVE TO EAT EGGS!
A SNAKE?
MY GRANDMA TOLD ME.
SHE WAS BORN IN THE YEAR OF THE SNAKE, SO SHE KNOWS LOTS ABOUT THEM!
HUH ...
THE SNAKE ...
THE YEAR OF THE SNAKE!!
HUH?

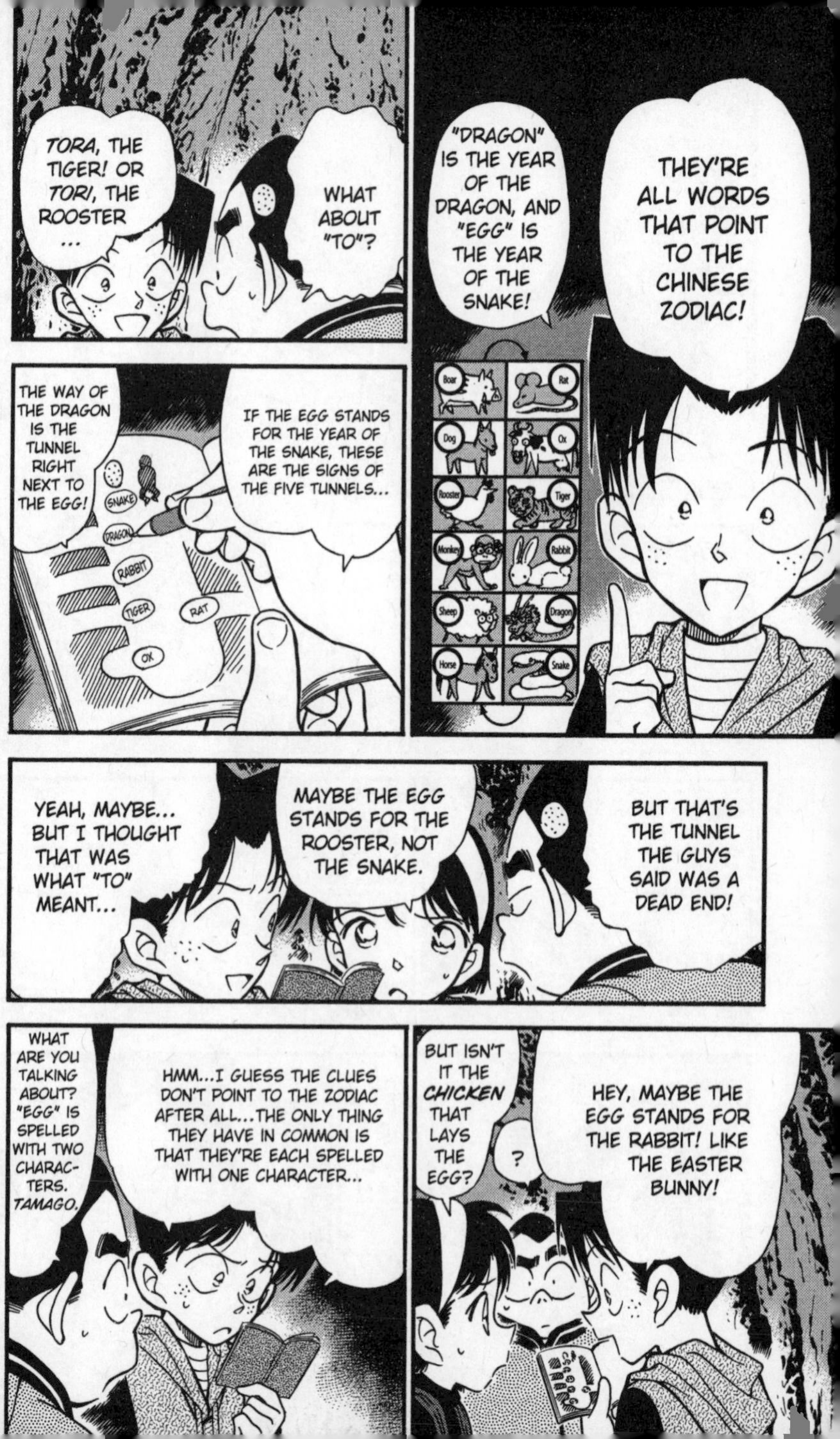
THEY'RE ALL WORDS THAT POINT TO THE CHINESE ZODIAC!
"DRAGON" IS THE YEAR OF THE DRAGON, AND "EGG" IS THE YEAR OF THE SNAKE!
Rat
Boar
Ox
Dog
Tiger
Rooster
Rabbit
Monkey
Dragon
Sheep
Snake
Horse
WHAT ABOUT "TO"?
TORA, THE TIGER! OR *TORI*, THE ROOSTER ...
IF THE EGG STANDS FOR THE YEAR OF THE SNAKE, THESE ARE THE SIGNS OF THE FIVE TUNNELS...
THE WAY OF THE DRAGON IS THE TUNNEL RIGHT NEXT TO THE EGG!
SNAKE
DRAGON
RABBIT
TIGER
RAT
OX
BUT THAT'S THE TUNNEL THE GUYS SAID WAS A DEAD END!
MAYBE THE EGG STANDS FOR THE ROOSTER, NOT THE SNAKE.
YEAH, MAYBE... BUT I THOUGHT THAT WAS WHAT "TO" MEANT...
HEY, MAYBE THE EGG STANDS FOR THE RABBIT! LIKE THE EASTER BUNNY!
?
BUT ISN'T IT THE *CHICKEN* THAT LAYS THE EGG?
HMM...I GUESS THE CLUES DON'T POINT TO THE ZODIAC AFTER ALL...THE ONLY THING THEY HAVE IN COMMON IS THAT THEY'RE EACH SPELLED WITH ONE CHARACTER...
WHAT ARE YOU TALKING ABOUT? "EGG" IS SPELLED WITH TWO CHARAC-TERS. *TAMAGO*.

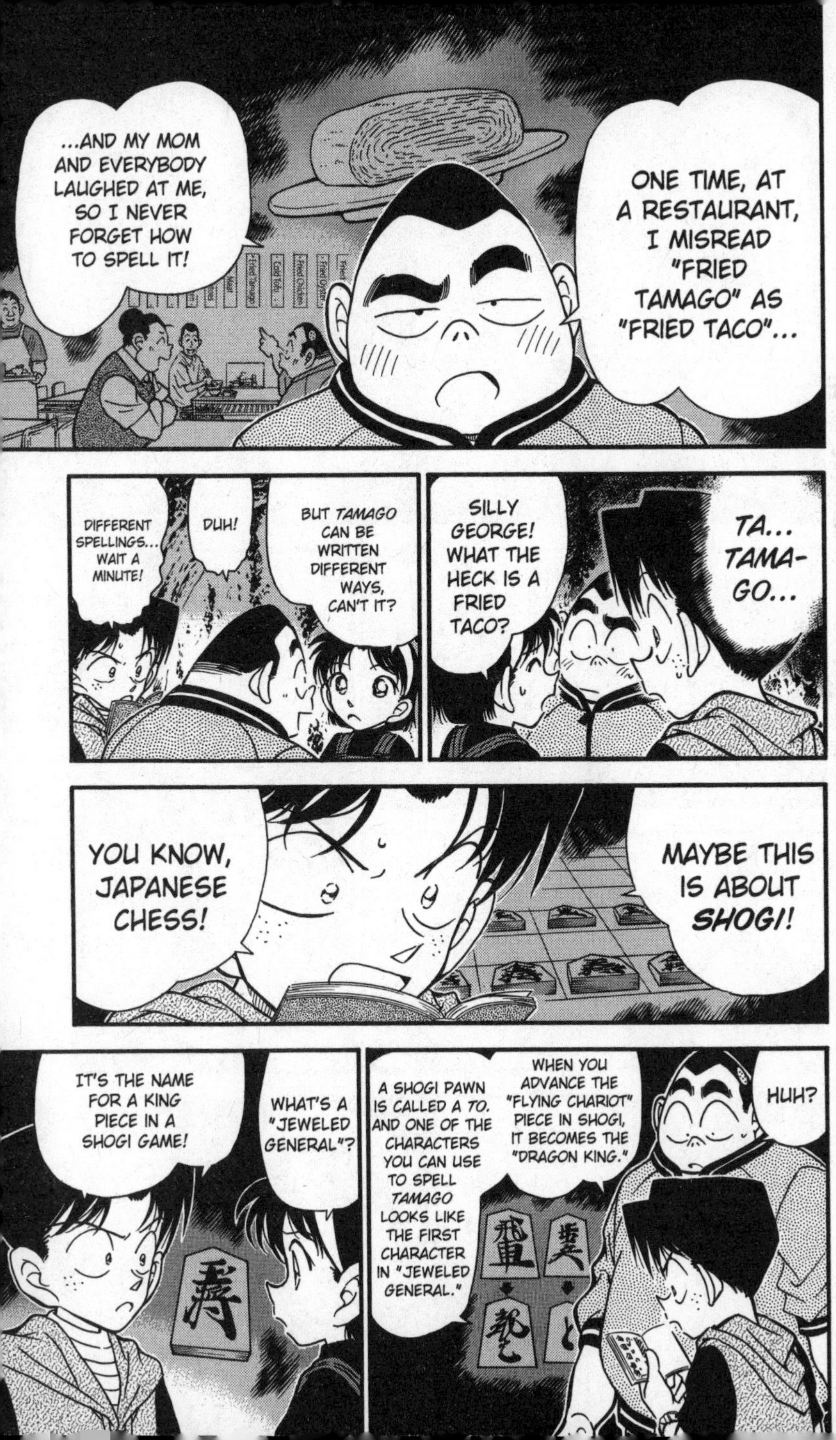
ONE TIME, AT A RESTAURANT, I MISREAD "FRIED TAMAGO" AS "FRIED TACO"...
Fried Oyster
Fried Chicken
Cold Tofu
Fried Tamago
Meat
...AND MY MOM AND EVERYBODY LAUGHED AT ME, SO I NEVER FORGET HOW TO SPELL IT!
TA... TAMA-GO...
SILLY GEORGE! WHAT THE HECK IS A FRIED TACO?
BUT *TAMAGO* CAN BE WRITTEN DIFFERENT WAYS, CAN'T IT?
DUH!
DIFFERENT SPELLINGS... WAIT A MINUTE!
MAYBE THIS IS ABOUT *SHOGI*!
YOU KNOW, JAPANESE CHESS!
HUH?
WHEN YOU ADVANCE THE "FLYING CHARIOT" PIECE IN SHOGI, IT BECOMES THE "DRAGON KING."
A SHOGI PAWN IS CALLED A *TO*. AND ONE OF THE CHARACTERS YOU CAN USE TO SPELL *TAMAGO* LOOKS LIKE THE FIRST CHARACTER IN "JEWELED GENERAL."
WHAT'S A "JEWELED GENERAL"?
IT'S THE NAME FOR A KING PIECE IN A SHOGI GAME!

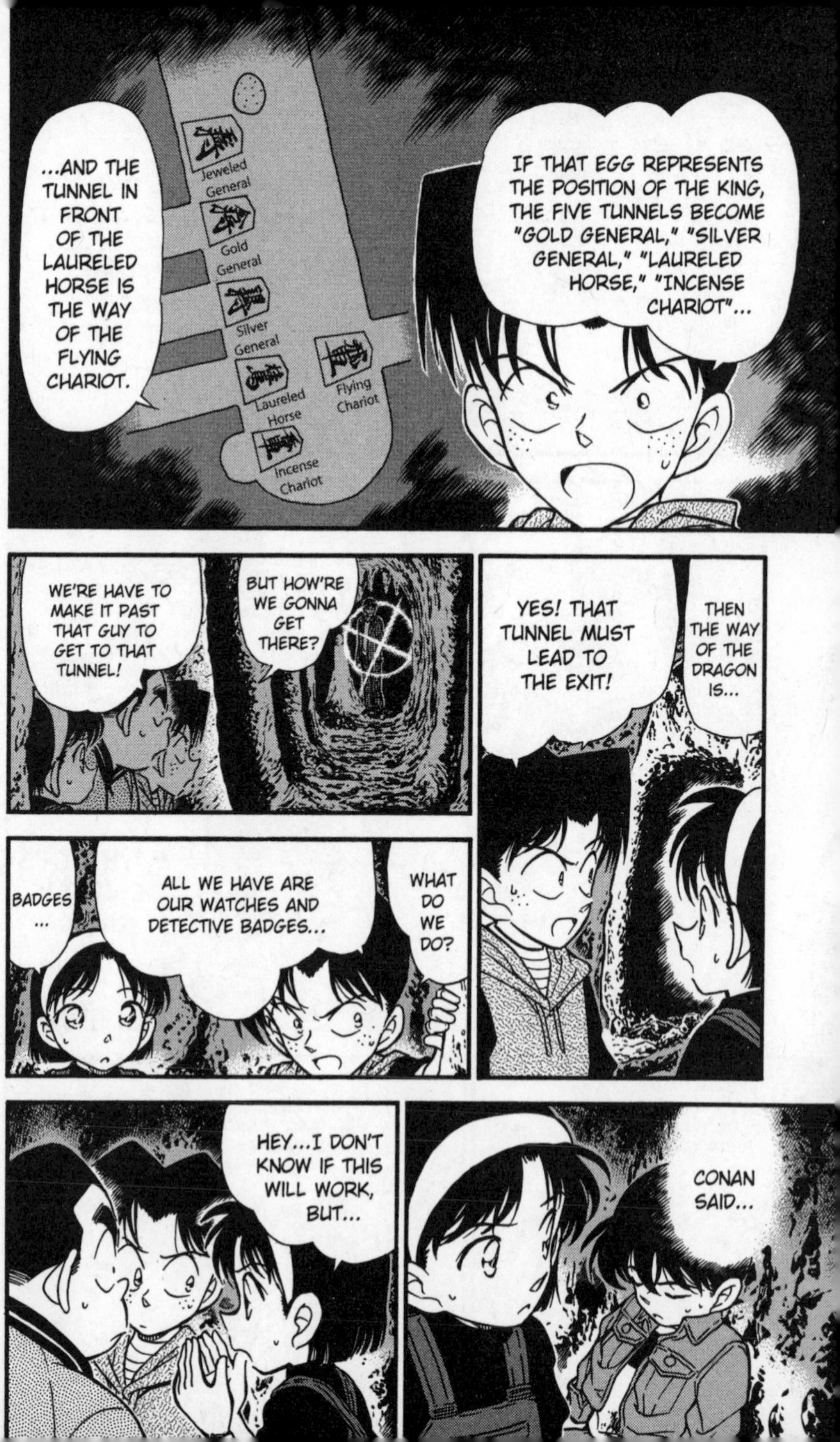
IF THAT EGG REPRESENTS THE POSITION OF THE KING, THE FIVE TUNNELS BECOME "GOLD GENERAL," "SILVER GENERAL," "LAURELED HORSE," "INCENSE CHARIOT"...
Jeweled General
Gold General
Silver General
Laureled Horse
Flying Chariot
Incense Chariot
...AND THE TUNNEL IN FRONT OF THE LAURELED HORSE IS THE WAY OF THE FLYING CHARIOT.
THEN THE WAY OF THE DRAGON IS...
YES! THAT TUNNEL MUST LEAD TO THE EXIT!
BUT HOW'RE WE GONNA GET THERE?
WE'RE HAVE TO MAKE IT PAST THAT GUY TO GET TO THAT TUNNEL!
WHAT DO WE DO?
ALL WE HAVE ARE OUR WATCHES AND DETECTIVE BADGES...
BADGES ...
CONAN SAID...
HEY...I DON'T KNOW IF THIS WILL WORK, BUT...

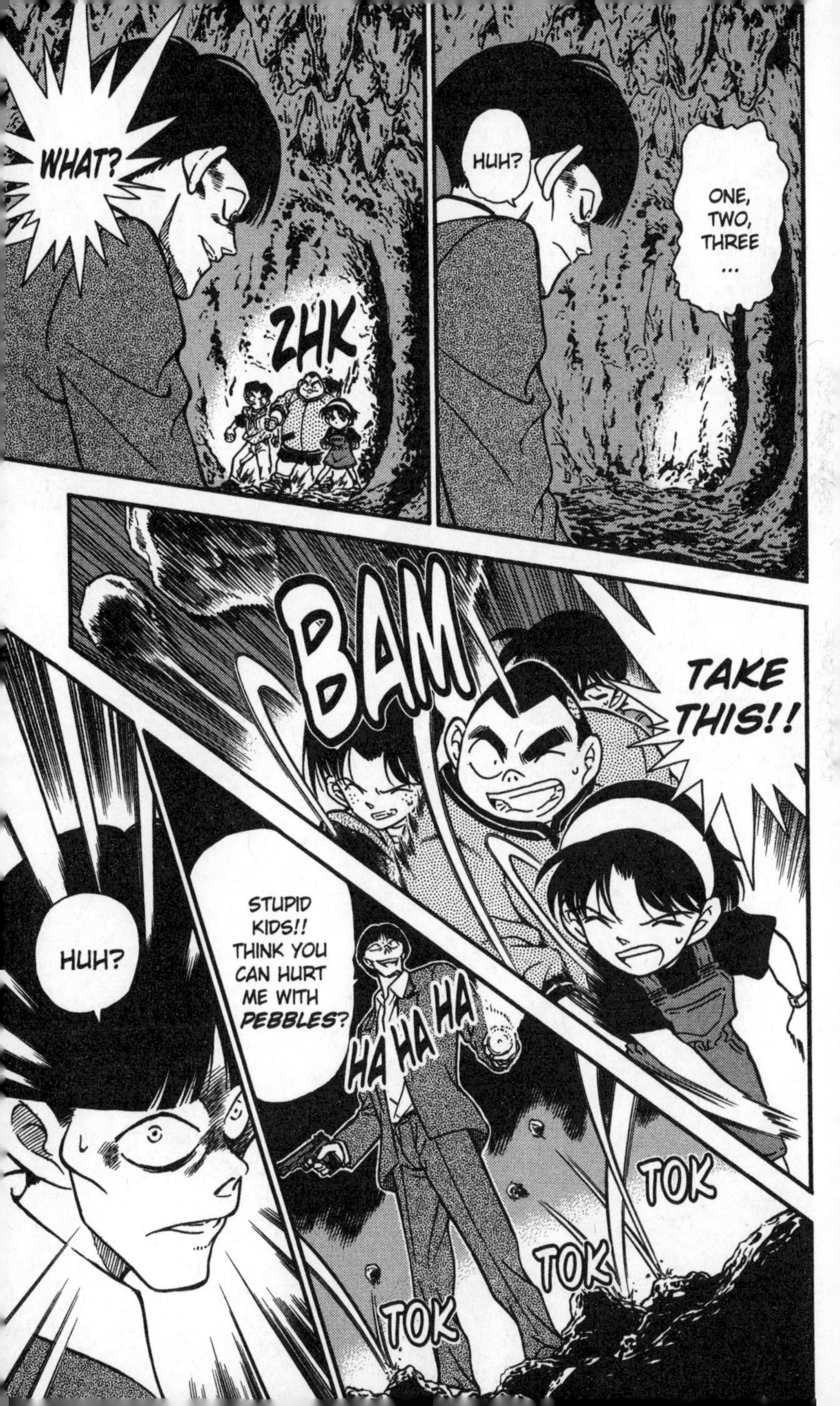
HUH?
ONE, TWO, THREE ...
WHAT?
ZHK
BAM
TAKE THIS!!
STUPID KIDS!! THINK YOU CAN HURT ME WITH *PEBBLES*?
HA HA HA
TOK
TOK
TOK
HUH?

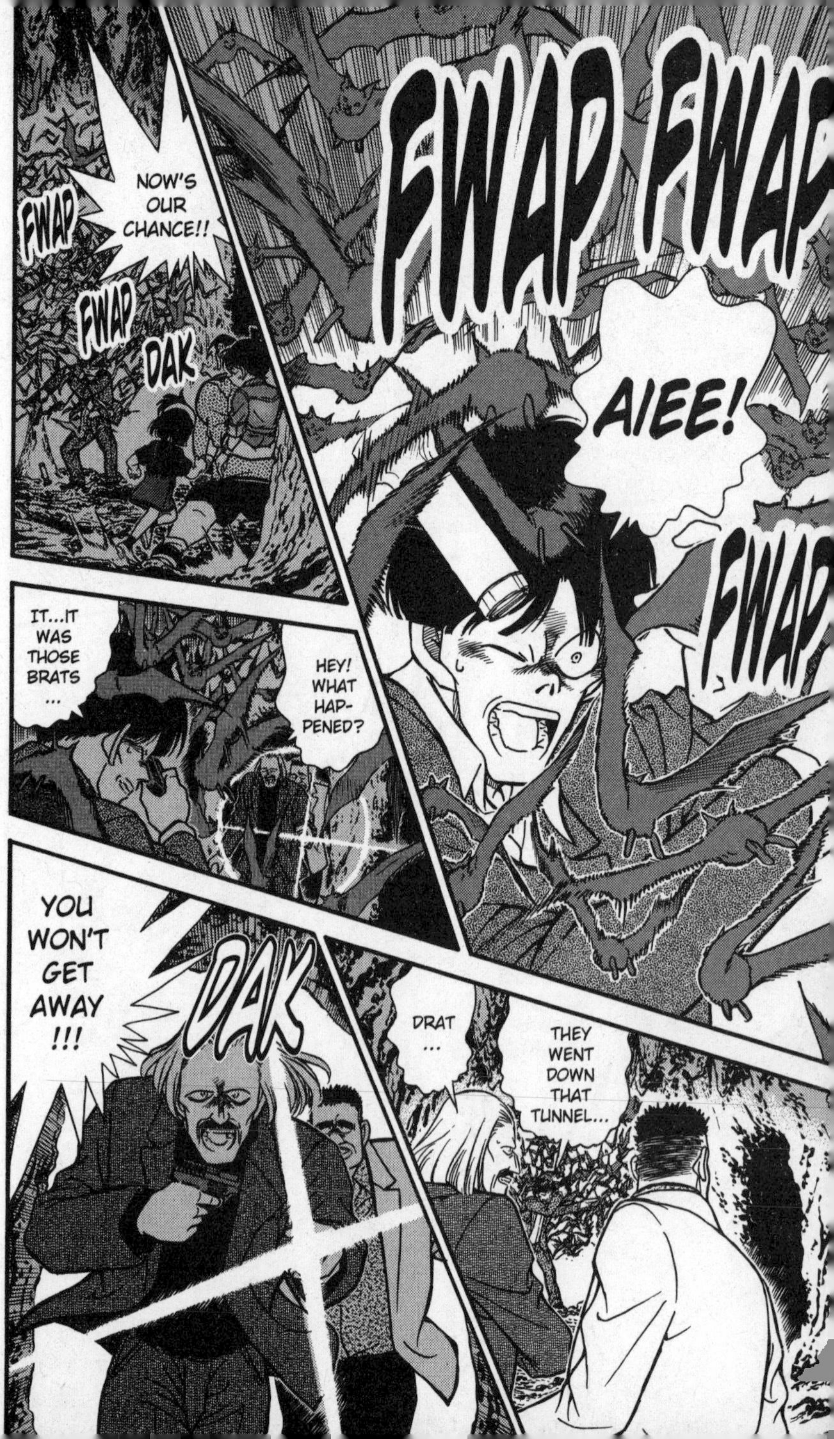
FWAP FWAP
AIEE!
FWAP
NOW'S OUR CHANCE!!
FWAP
FWAP
DAK
HEY! WHAT HAPPENED?
IT...IT WAS THOSE BRATS...
THEY WENT DOWN THAT TUNNEL...
DRAT...
YOU WON'T GET AWAY!!!
DAK

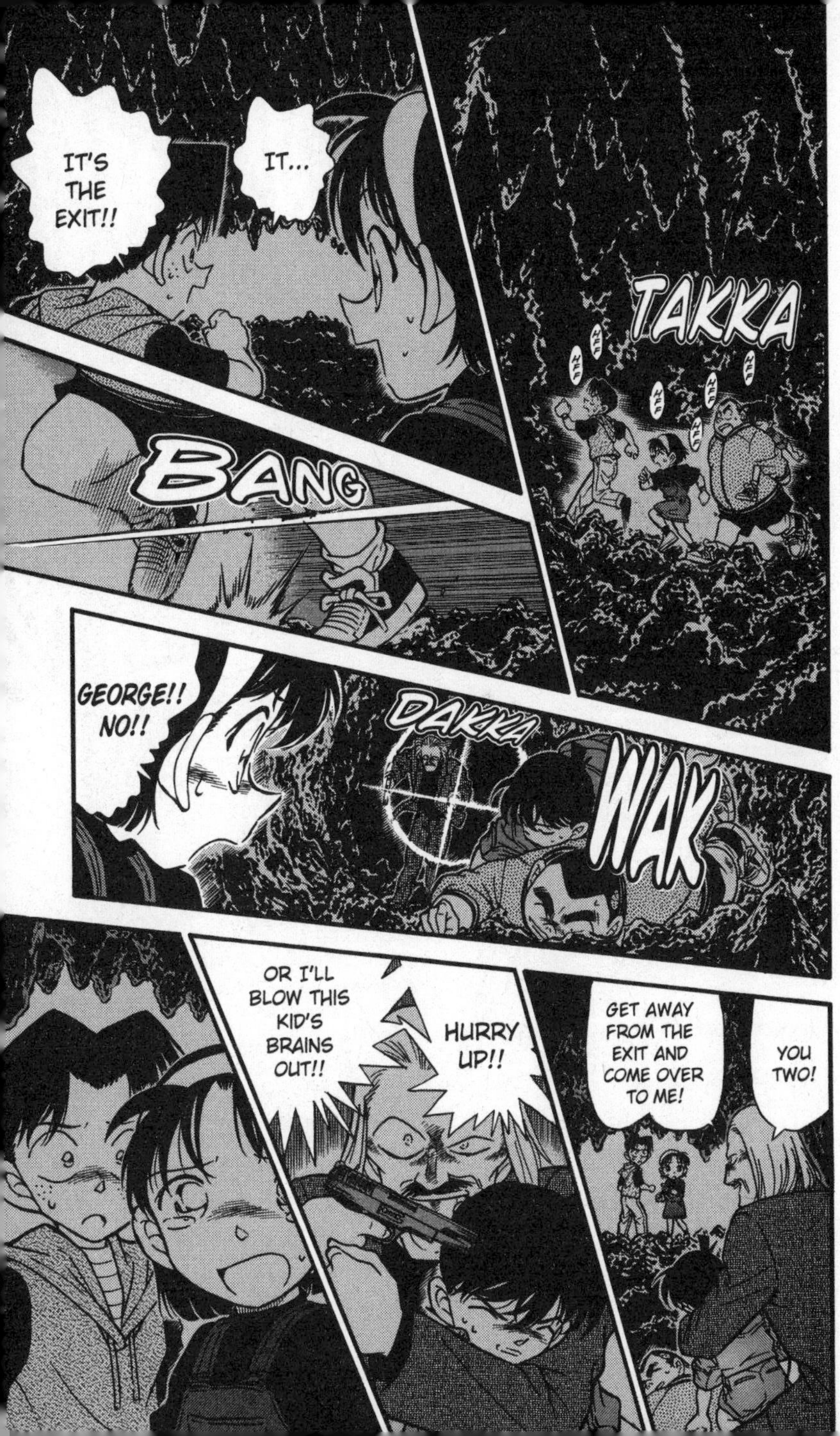

TAKKA
HEFF
HEFF
HEFF
HEFF
HEFF
HEFF
IT...
IT'S THE EXIT!!
BANG
WAK
DAKKA
GEORGE!! NO!!
YOU TWO!
GET AWAY FROM THE EXIT AND COME OVER TO ME!
HURRY UP!!
OR I'LL BLOW THIS KID'S BRAINS OUT!!

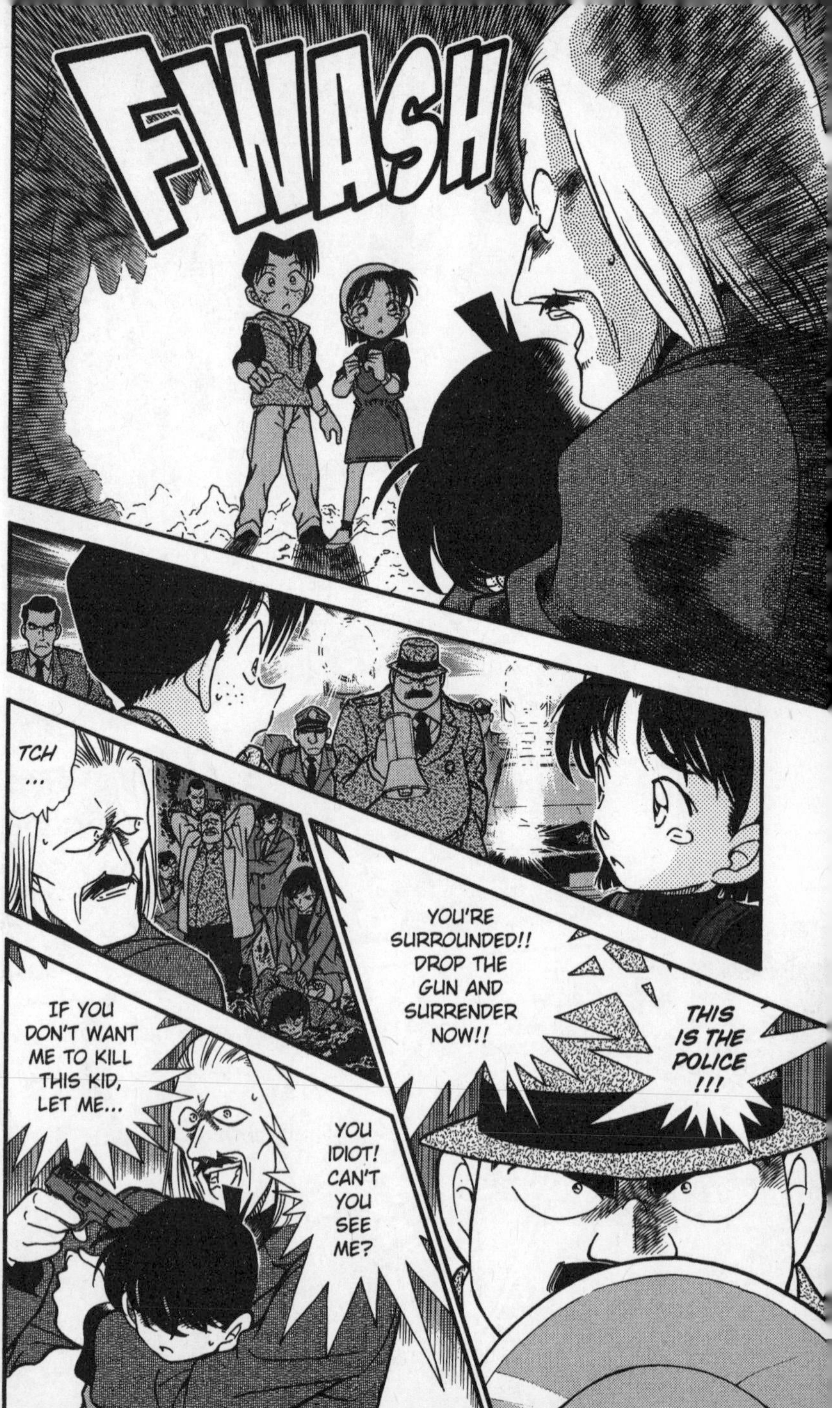
FWASH
THIS IS THE POLICE!!!
YOU'RE SURROUNDED!! DROP THE GUN AND SURRENDER NOW!!
TCH...
IF YOU DON'T WANT ME TO KILL THIS KID, LET ME...
YOU IDIOT! CAN'T YOU SEE ME?

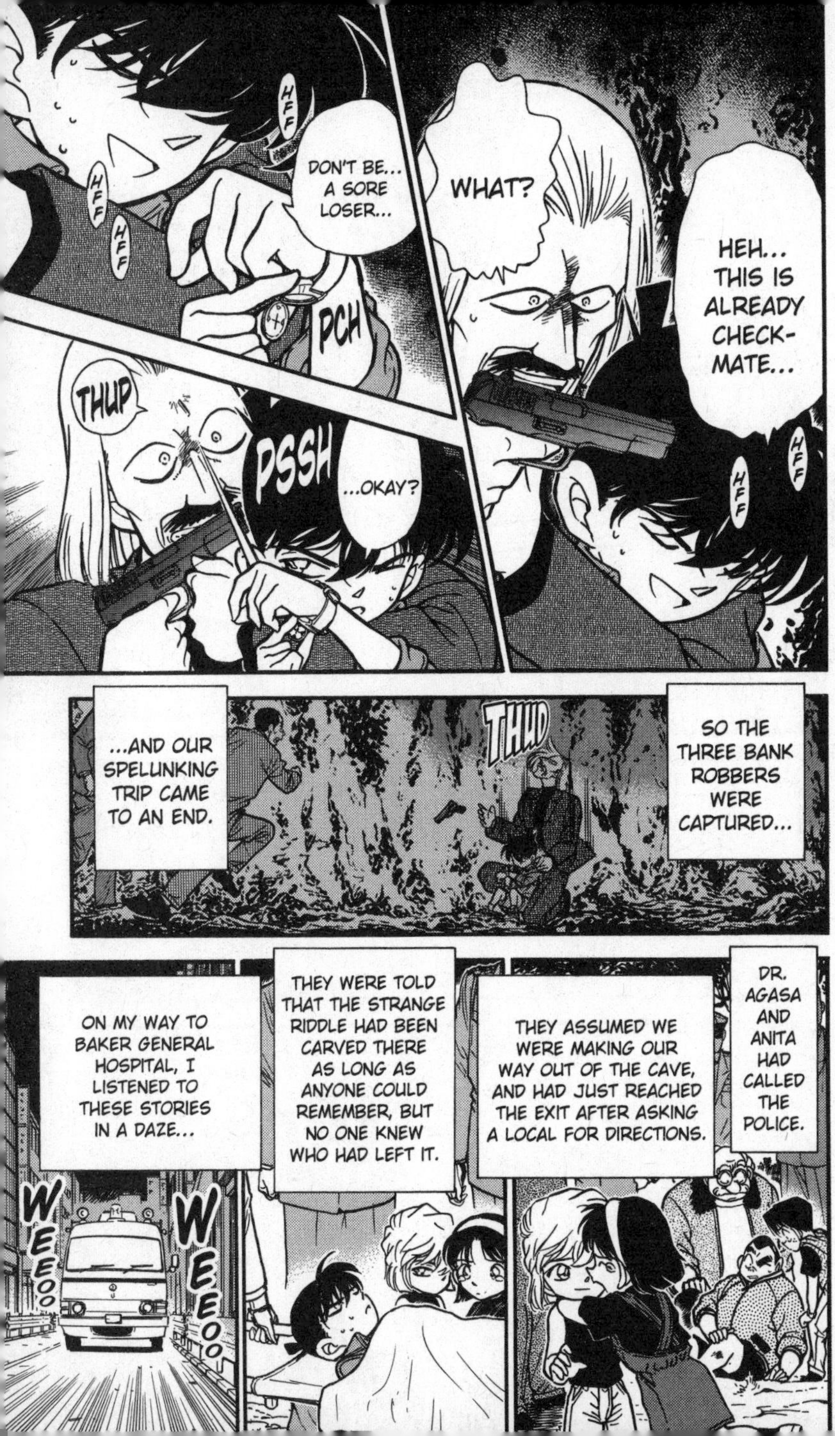
HEH... THIS IS ALREADY CHECK-MATE...
WHAT?
HFF HFF
HFF HFF HFF
DON'T BE... A SORE LOSER...
PCH
THUP
PSSH
...OKAY?
SO THE THREE BANK ROBBERS WERE CAPTURED...
THUD
...AND OUR SPELUNKING TRIP CAME TO AN END.
DR. AGASA AND ANITA HAD CALLED THE POLICE.
THEY ASSUMED WE WERE MAKING OUR WAY OUT OF THE CAVE, AND HAD JUST REACHED THE EXIT AFTER ASKING A LOCAL FOR DIRECTIONS.
THEY WERE TOLD THAT THE STRANGE RIDDLE HAD BEEN CARVED THERE AS LONG AS ANYONE COULD REMEMBER, BUT NO ONE KNEW WHO HAD LEFT IT.
ON MY WAY TO BAKER GENERAL HOSPITAL, I LISTENED TO THESE STORIES IN A DAZE...
WEEOO
WEEOO

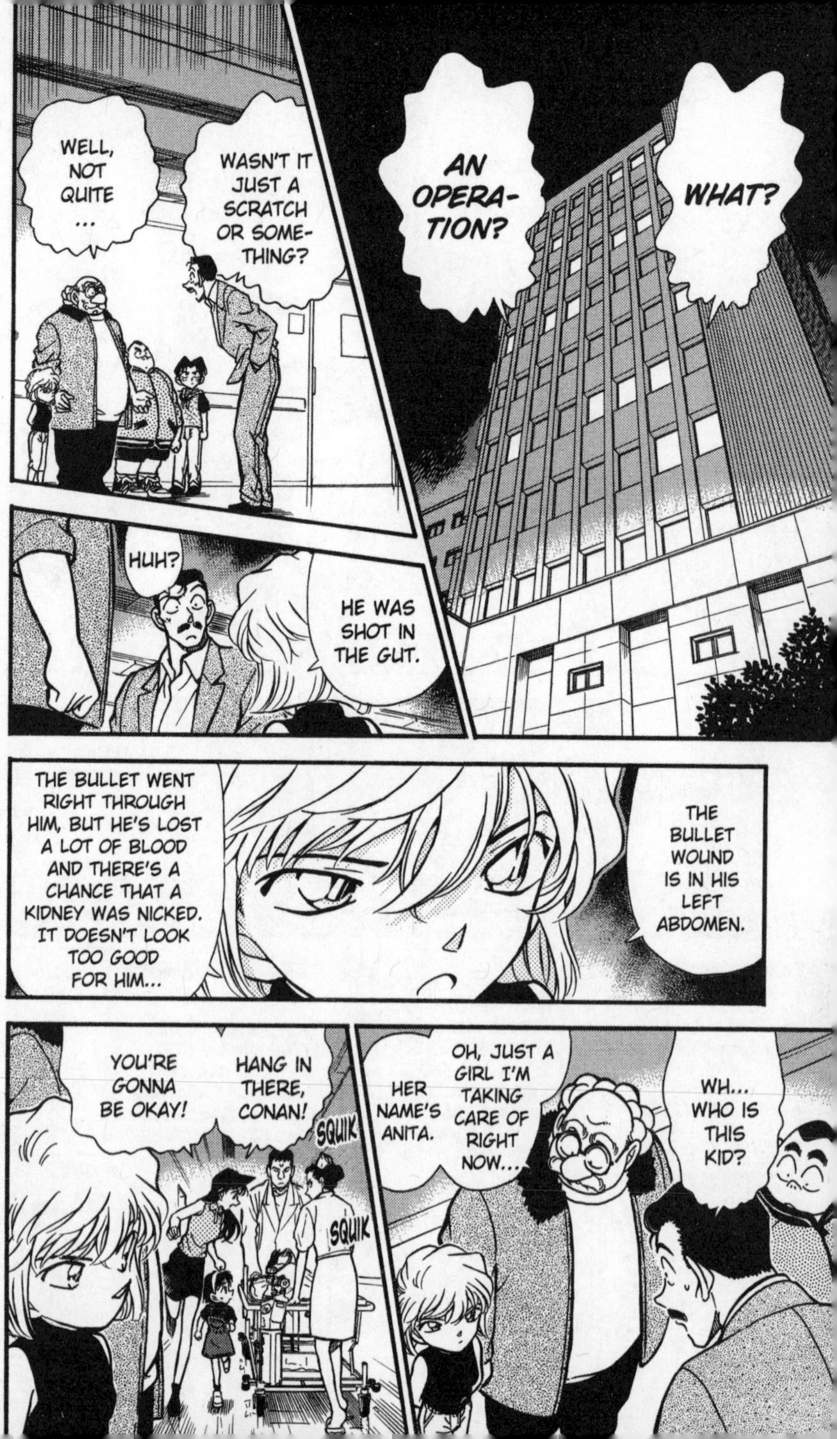
WHAT?
AN OPERATION?
WASN'T IT JUST A SCRATCH OR SOMETHING?
WELL, NOT QUITE ...
HUH?
HE WAS SHOT IN THE GUT.
THE BULLET WOUND IS IN HIS LEFT ABDOMEN.
THE BULLET WENT RIGHT THROUGH HIM, BUT HE'S LOST A LOT OF BLOOD AND THERE'S A CHANCE THAT A KIDNEY WAS NICKED. IT DOESN'T LOOK TOO GOOD FOR HIM...
WH... WHO IS THIS KID?
OH, JUST A GIRL I'M TAKING CARE OF RIGHT NOW...
HER NAME'S ANITA.
HANG IN THERE, CONAN!
YOU'RE GONNA BE OKAY!
SQUIK
SQUIK

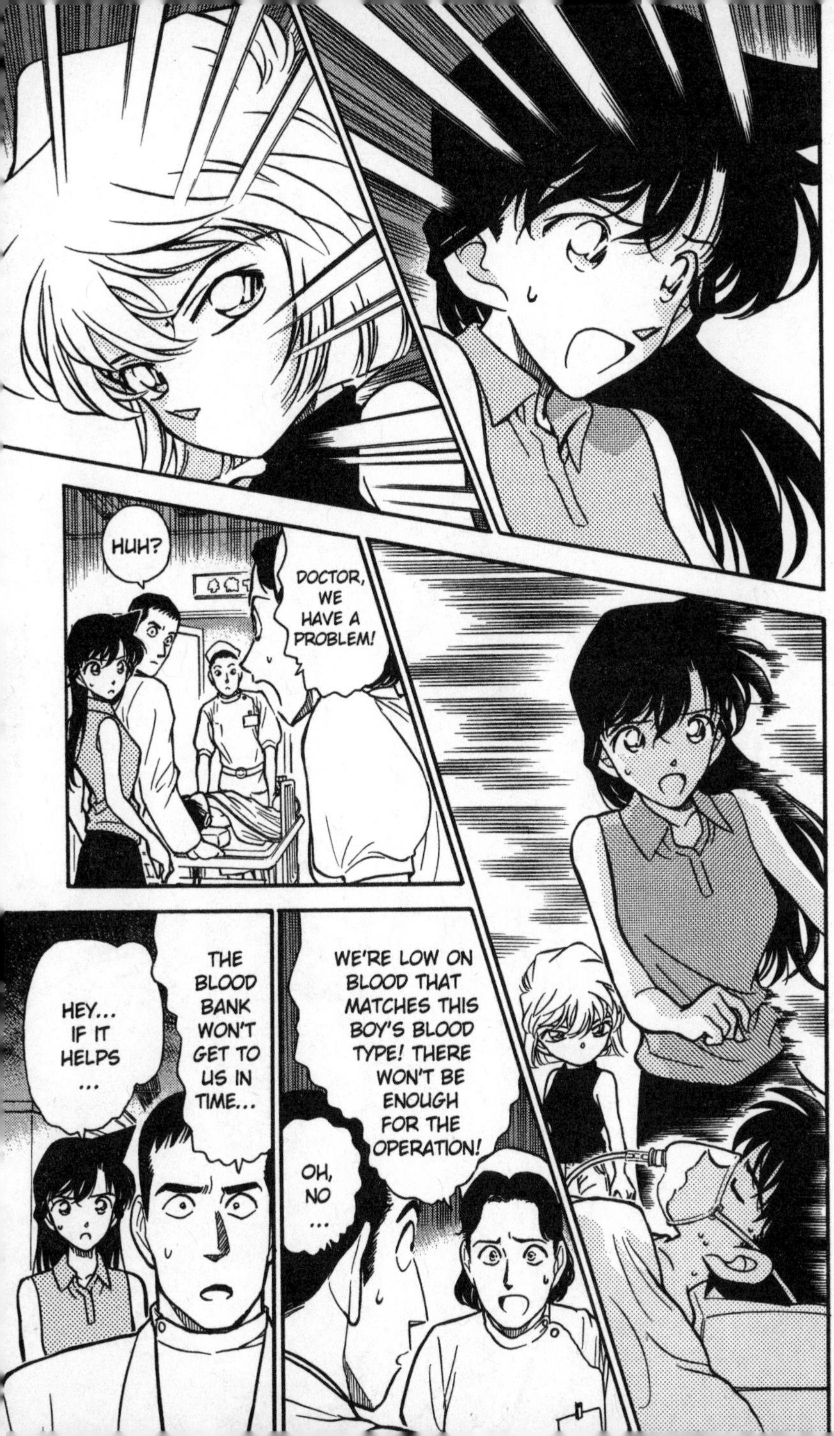
DOCTOR, WE HAVE A PROBLEM!
HUH?
WE'RE LOW ON BLOOD THAT MATCHES THIS BOY'S BLOOD TYPE! THERE WON'T BE ENOUGH FOR THE OPERATION!
OH, NO ...
THE BLOOD BANK WON'T GET TO US IN TIME...
HEY... IF IT HELPS ...

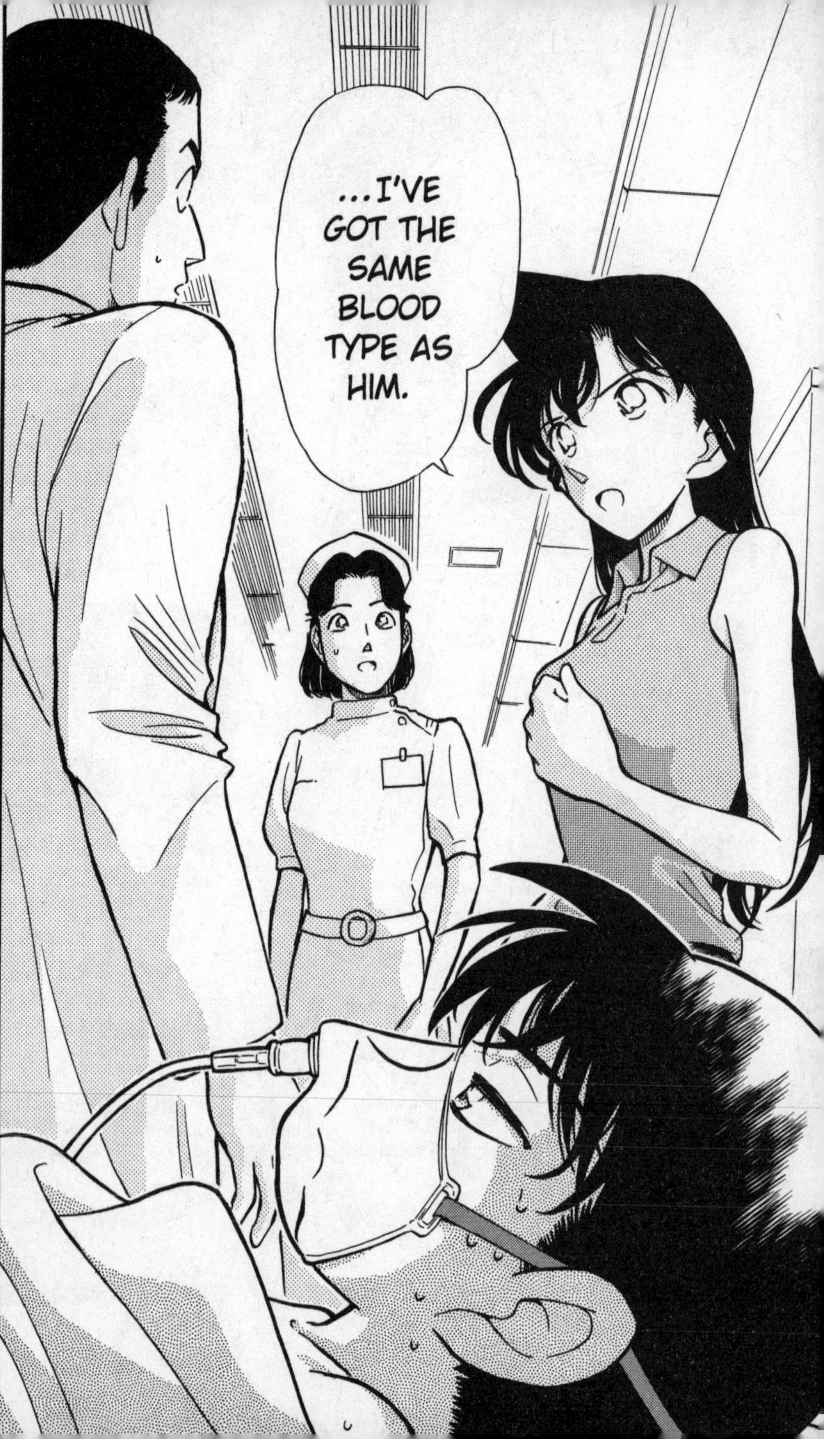
...I'VE GOT THE SAME BLOOD TYPE AS HIM.

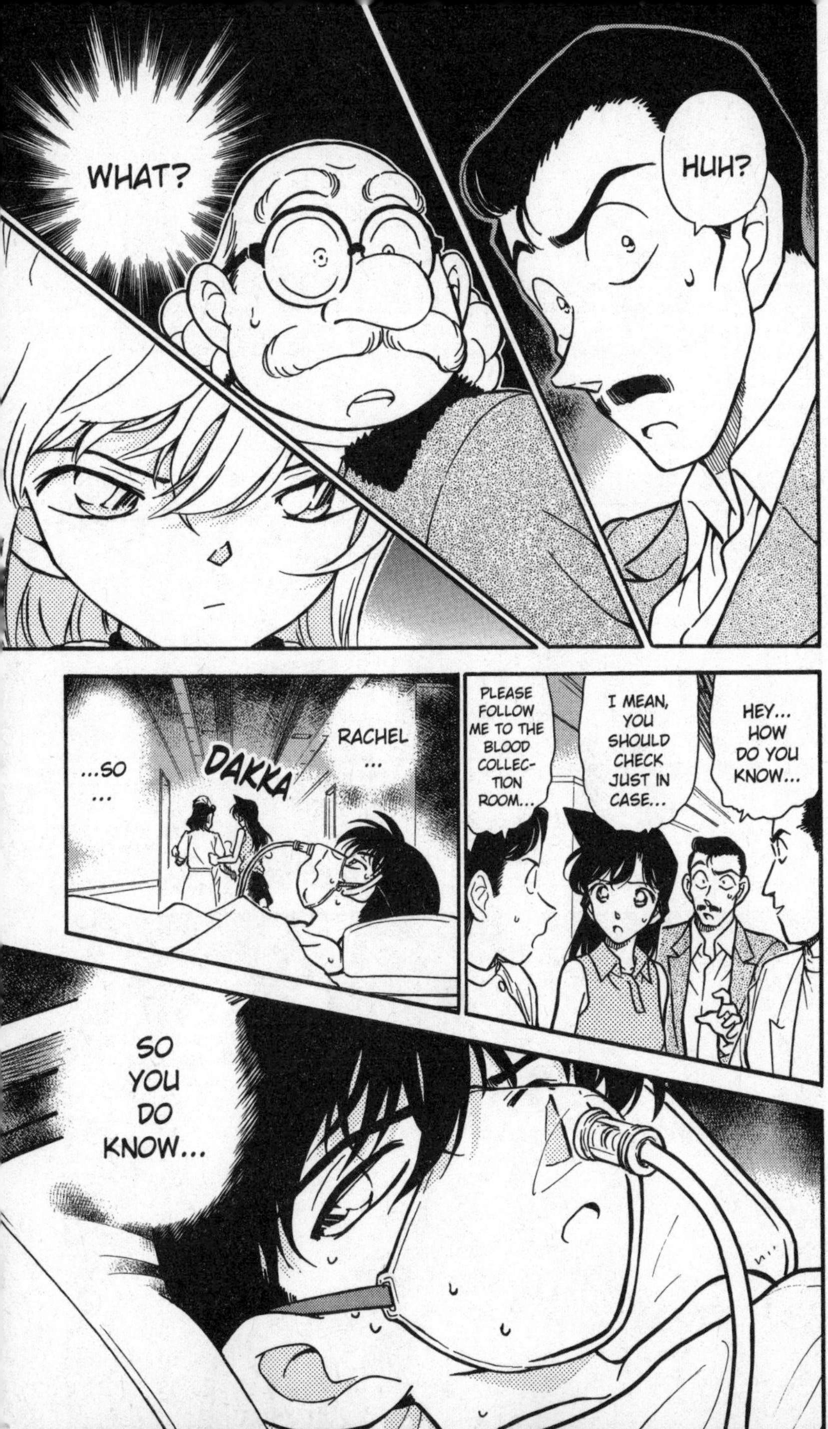
HUH?
WHAT?
HEY... HOW DO YOU KNOW...
I MEAN, YOU SHOULD CHECK JUST IN CASE...
PLEASE FOLLOW ME TO THE BLOOD COLLECTION ROOM...
RACHEL ...
DAKKA
...SO ...
SO YOU DO KNOW...

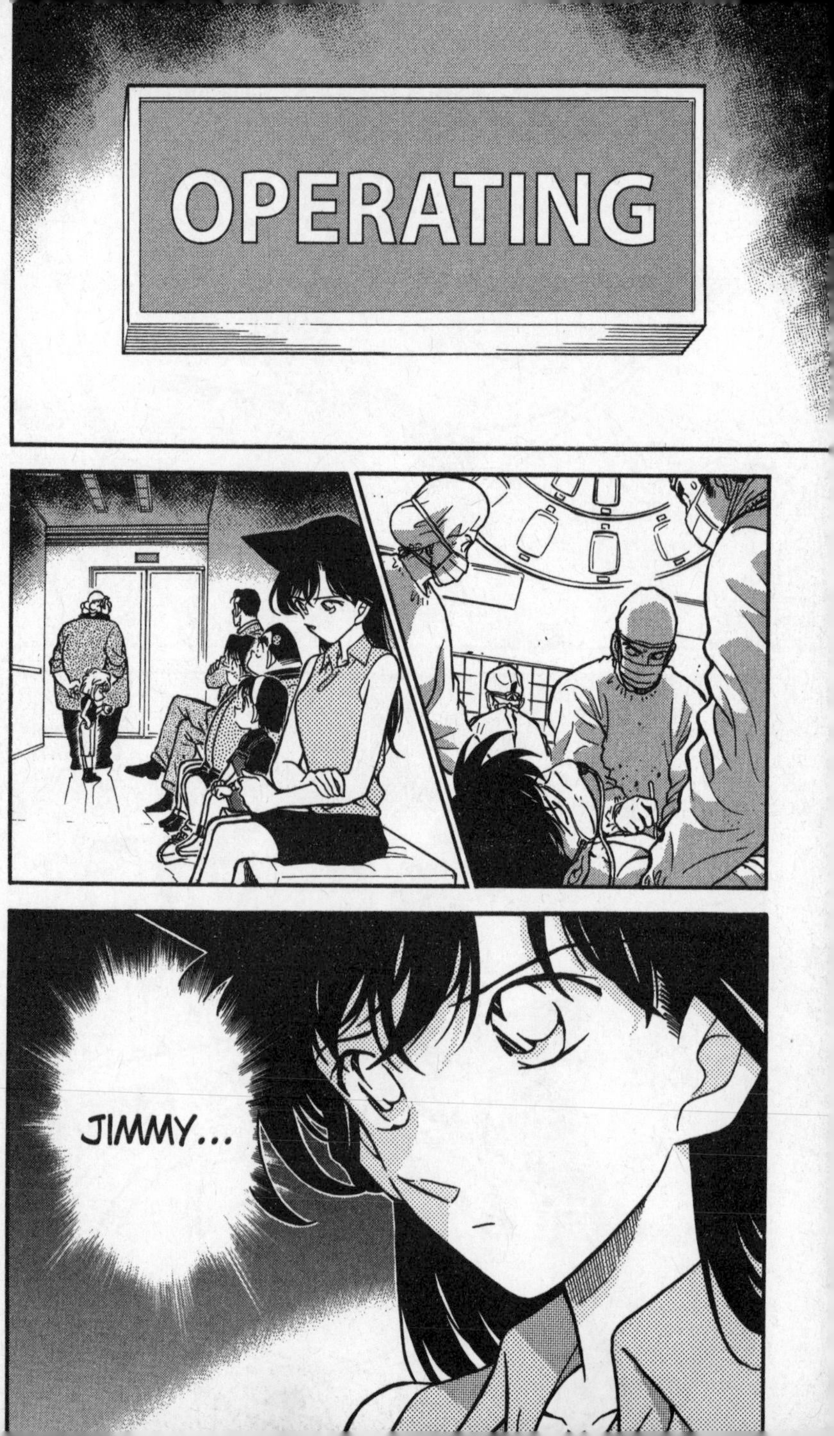
OPERATING
JIMMY...

Hello, Aoyama here.

Eva's pet cat appears on the November/December page of
the 2000 *Conan* calendar! It's a Snowshoe cat, and its name
is Goro. She claims that she named it Goro because it's lazy,
but who knows? Ha ha...

*Editor's note: This is a pun on Detective Moore's Japanese name,
Kogoro Mori, and the Japanese word *gorogoro*, meaning "to loaf around."

TORTOISESHELL HOLMES

So far we've talked about many kinds of detectives, but the one I'm introducing today isn't even human. She's Holmes, a tortoiseshell cat named after the most famous detective in the world! Holmes is a slender female cat with white, black and brown fur. Ever since her uterus was removed due to an illness, she often seems to be "lost in thought" over something...but even though she's a master sleuth, she's still a cat, so she can't explain her deductions or catch criminals on her own. So her owner, Detective Yoshitaro Katayama, cracks the cases for her. Detective Katayama is a tall, baby-faced man who can't hold his liquor, hates the sight of blood...and, to top it all off, is terrified of women. Not your typical heroic detective. Holmes's unusual behavior always gives him the decisive clue he needs to solve a case. Detective Katayama seems to have what it takes to become a great sleuth himself, but he always remains humble, claiming, "It was Holmes who cracked it." If only my Detective Moore were like him...I recommend the movie *Mikeneko Holmes no Suiri* (The Deductions of Tortoiseshell Holmes).

Komi Can't Communicate

Story & Art by Tomohito Oda

The journey to a hundred friends begins with a single conversation.

Socially anxious high school student Shoko Komi's greatest dream is to make some friends, but everyone at school mistakes her crippling social anxiety for cool reserve. With the whole student body keeping its distance and Komi unable to utter a single word, friendship might be forever beyond her reach.

Kidnapped by the Demon King and imprisoned in his castle, Princess Syalis is...bored.

Sleepy Princess in the Demon Castle

Story & Art by
KAGIJI KUMANOMATA

Captured princess Syalis decides to while away her hours in the Demon Castle by sleeping, but getting a good night's rest turns out to be a lot of work! She begins by fashioning a DIY pillow out of the fur of her Teddy Demon guards and an "air mattress" from the magical Shield of the Wind. Things go from bad to worse—for her captors—when some of Princess Syalis's schemes end in her untimely—if temporary—demise and she chooses the Forbidden Grimoire for her bedtime reading...

RATED TEEN

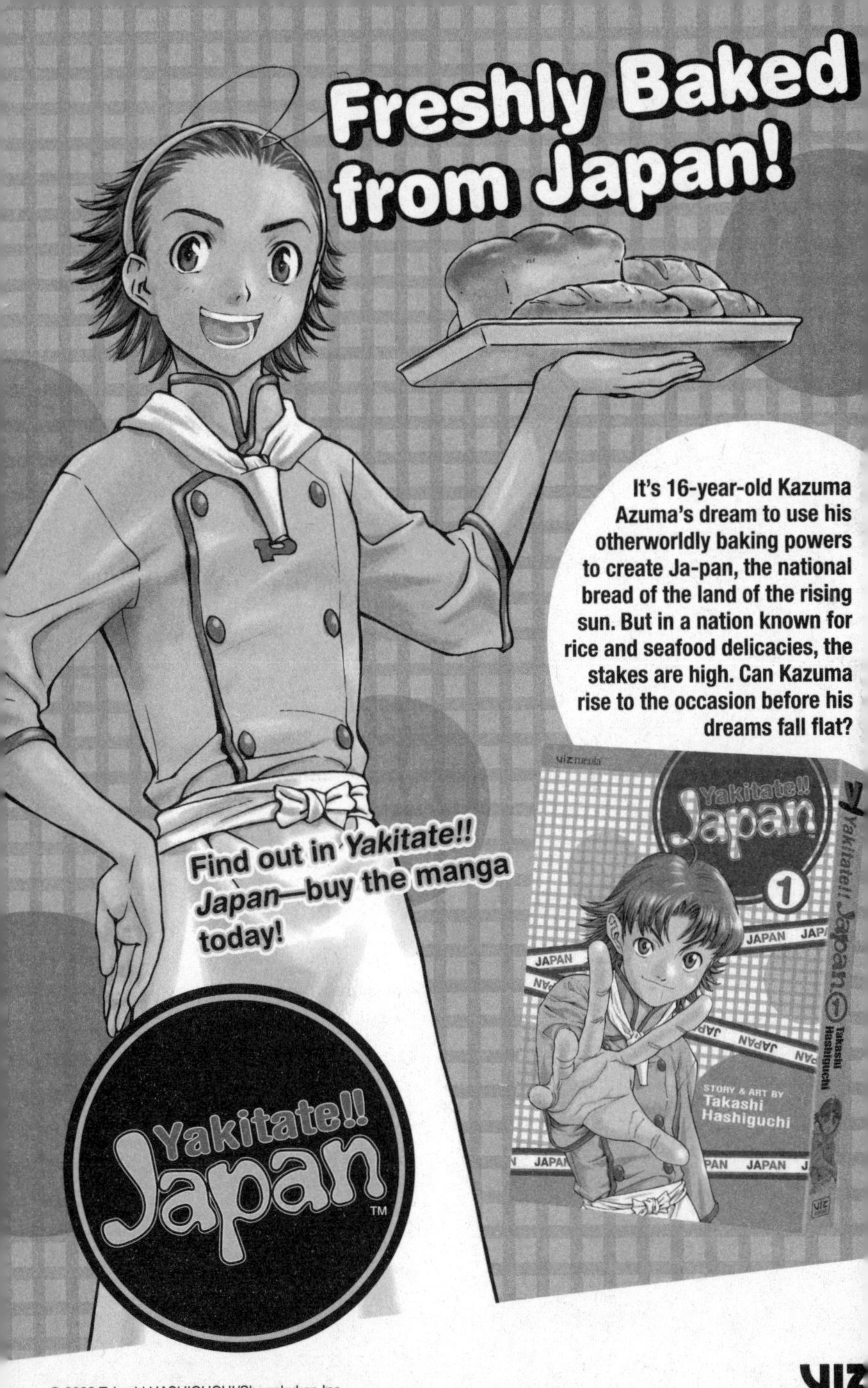
Freshly Baked from Japan!
It's 16-year-old Kazuma Azuma's dream to use his otherworldly baking powers to create Ja-pan, the national bread of the land of the rising sun. But in a nation known for rice and seafood delicacies, the stakes are high. Can Kazuma rise to the occasion before his dreams fall flat?
Find out in Yakitate!! Japan—buy the manga today!
Yakitate!! Japan™
Yakitate!! Japan
1
STORY & ART BY
Takashi Hashiguchi
VIZ

Hey! You're Reading in the Wrong Direction!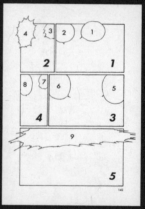

This is the **end** of this graphic novel!

To properly enjoy this VIZ graphic novel, please turn it around and begin reading from **right to left.** Unlike English, Japanese is read right to left, so Japanese comics are read in reverse order from the way English comics are typically read.

Follow the action this way

This book has been printed in the original Japanese format in order to preserve the orientation of the original artwork. Have fun with it!